The Worlds
of Carol Shields

The Worlds
of Carol Shields

Edited by
David Staines

Reappraisals: Canadian Writers
University of Ottawa Press

uOttawa

The University of Ottawa Press acknowledges with gratitude the support it receives from Heritage Canada through the Canada Book Fund and Livres Canada Books, the Canada Council for the Arts, and the Ontario Media Development Corporation (OMDC), the Canadian Federation for the Humanities and Social Sciences through the Awards to Scholarly Publications Program, and especially that of the University of Ottawa.

Copy editing: Trish O'Reilly-Brennan
Proofreading: Barbara Ibronyi
Typesetting: Atelier Typo-Jane and CS
Cover illustration and design: Bartosz Walczak

Library and Archives Canada Cataloguing in Publication

The worlds of Carol Shields / edited by David Staines.

Includes bibliographical references.
Issued in print and electronic formats.
ISBN 978-0-7766-2206-4 (pbk.).--ISBN 978-0-7766-2186-9 (pdf).--
ISBN 978-0-7766-2185-2 (epub)

1. Shields, Carol, 1935-2003--Criticism and interpretation.
I. Staines, David, 1946-, editor

PS8587.H46Z96 2014   C813'.54   C2014-907212-0
                                              C2014-907213-9

To the memory of
Lorraine McMullen 1926–2003

Table of Contents

Table of Contents

Acknowledgements

This book originated in a conference funded by the Social Sciences and Humanities Research Council of Canada. The editor gratefully acknowledges the Council and its financial support. He also acknowledges the support and cooperation of the University of Ottawa Press and its director, Lara Mainville, its acquisitions editor, Dominike Thomas, and its production editor, Elizabeth Schwaiger.

Three individuals deserve special tribute:

Zachary Abram gave exemplary dedication to the planning and execution of the conference, including his superb skills as a computer authority.

Donald Shields gave his blessing to the planning of the original conference and supported its organization.

The late Carol Shields wrote the fiction and non-fiction, the poetry and plays behind these essays. Without her, there would not be this book.

David Staines

Introduction

DAVID STAINES

For Carol Shields, novelist and short story writer, biographer and literary critic, playwright and poet, art offers a means of confronting the joys and dramas of the human condition. As she said in her seminar, "A View from the Edge of the Edge," at Harvard University on February 10, 1997:

> Years ago, in an introduction to a book of short fiction, the American writer Hortense Calisher talked about the short story being mainly a new world form. Reports from the frontier, she called them, a lovely and accurate phrase that caught my attention. Perhaps, I remember thinking, this is what all of literature is: a dispatch from the frontier, news from the edge. Even given that the edges and centres of society are forever shifting, it does seem to me that the view from the edge offers a privileged perspective. Also freedom from cynicism if not from anger. Also a kind of real or willed innocence which is what I believe every writer must keep alive in order to write.

And Shields knew well the problems of "the edge," as she continued, for she stood at the edge, too, by virtue of gender.

> Where I grew up in Oak Park, Illinois, I attended, first, Nathaniel Hawthorne Public School, and when I was a little older, Ralph Waldo Emerson Public School. I knew who these bearded, bespectacled, frockcoated gentlemen were; their portraits hung in a place of honour in our schools. They were writers. They were men. They were dead.

As Margaret Atwood observes, "Possibly feminism was something she worked into," yet Shields was always aware of who she was, of her many readers both male and female, and of the power of art to give her "a privileged perspective" on life. Her unique voice, compassionate and forever human and humane, gave her the power to portray the worlds around her in her own wise manner.

The Worlds of Carol Shields brings together twenty-three people, some of them her friends, some of them scholars who are her readers, to shed fresh light on her many achievements. The author of ten novels, four collections of short fiction, three volumes of poetry, four published plays, one volume of literary criticism, and one biography, she carved out her special place in Canadian letters. Her many honours include the Canadian Authors' Association Award for Fiction for 1976, the Arthur Ellis Award for Best Canadian Mystery, the Governor General's Award, the National Book Critics Circle Award, the Pulitzer Prize, the Orange Prize, and the Charles Taylor Prize for Literary Non-Fiction. She is among the most honoured of all Canadian writers.

The Worlds of Carol Shields opens with four close friends, some of them relatives, of Carol Shields. For many years her admiring friend, Margaret Atwood pens an obituary which is a unique tribute to Shields's life and career. Eleanor Wachtel divulges the history of her strong friendship with Shields, explaining its origin and its effect on her life. Then the novelist Anne Giardini, Carol Shields's daughter, and her son Joseph use their intimate knowledge of the Shields family to stand back and examine Shields's poetry and its thematic relationship to her fiction.

Coral Ann Howells begins the examination of Shields's fiction. Studying her novels and her short stories as well as her biography of Jane Austen, she posits a close connection between Shields's works and the *écriture féminine* espoused by such feminist scholars as Hélène Cixous, uncovering the feminist directions of Shields's writings. Elizabeth Waterston examines *Small Ceremonies*, the first novel of the neophyte Shields, and Wendy Roy furthers this exploration, analyzing *The Box Garden* as the sequel to *Small Ceremonies* and *A Fairly Conventional Woman* as the sequel to *Happenstance*. Exploring *Swann* is a question, according to Cynthia Sugars, of understanding the allure and even the necessity of literary ancestors. Patricia Life seeks the Canadian antecedents to *The Stone Diaries* in Shields's indebtedness to her own literary ancestors, Ethel Wilson and Margaret Laurence. And John Van Rys observes the male-pattern bewilderment of *Larry's Party*.

The only person (thus far) to have written an entire book on Carol Shields, Alex Ramon studies the Canadian and American dimensions of her fiction, beginning with a careful analysis of her volume of literary criticism, *Susanna Moodie: Voice and Vision*; her poetry; and her short fiction, leading into new readings of *The Stone Diaries* and *Larry's Party*. Margaret Steffler and Tim Heath offer their own readings of Shields's final novel, *Unless*. And Shelley Boyd traces the presence of guerrilla gardeners in Shields's writings as a further instance of her rebellious literary cultivations.

The final three essays on Shields's fiction look at her short stories. Marilyn Rose argues for cool empathy in her short fiction, Elizabeth Reimer posits a comparison between Joyce Carol Oates and Shields, and Aritha van Herk provides an overview of *The Republic of Love* and the short stories in emphasizing Shields's love of the preposition in her writings.

Nora Foster Stovel ends the discussion of Shields's writings with a detailed analysis of her plays, in particular *Thirteen Hands*. And Catherine Hobbs brings her archivist eyes to a concluding study of the final resting place of the Carol Shields's fonds.

The Worlds of Carol Shields ends, as it began, with four friends of Carol Shields, who offer their unique perspectives on her, her life, and her career. Joan Clark and Jane Urquhart present reflections on the woman they knew so well. Wayson Choy pays tribute to the teacher who inspired him and his own writing. And Martin Levin recounts his personal and professional dealings with Carol Shields, "whose ardent and consistently expressed feminism need not be inconsistent with domestic happiness."

Shields received her master's degree from the University of Ottawa in 1975 with a thesis, the first in Canada, on the writings of Susanna Moodie. Twenty years later, she returned to the university to receive the first of many honorary degrees for her writings. At the awarding of the degree, she was heralded: "Carol Shields is a wise and articulate chronicler of contemporary men and women as they search for meaning in this life, as they search for meaning in their own lives. Whether her focus is urban marriage or a self-absorbed academic world, she holds up a compassionate mirror to the pains and joys, frustrations and misunderstandings, that characterize and give meaning to the human condition."

The Worlds of Carol Shields sets out to examine her many worlds in new and different ways, inviting the reader to explore the complexity and the delight of her unique vision.

To the Light House

Margaret Atwood

The beloved Canadian author Carol Shields died on July 16, 2003 at her home in Victoria, British Columbia, after a long battle with cancer. She was 68. The enormous media coverage given to her and the sadness expressed by her many readers paid tribute to the high esteem in which she was held in her own country, and her death made the news all around the world.

Conscious as she was of the vagaries of fame and the element of chance in any fortune, she would have viewed that with a certain irony, but she would also have found it deeply pleasing. She knew about the darkness, but—both as an author and as a person—she held on to the light. "She was just a luminous person, and that would be important and persist even if she hadn't written anything," said her friend and fellow author Alice Munro.

Earlier in her writing career, some critics mistook this quality of light in her for lightness, light-mindedness, on the general principle that comedy—a form that turns on misunderstanding and confusion, but ends in reconciliation, of however tenuous a kind—is less serious than tragedy, and that the personal life is of lesser importance than the public one.

Carol Shields knew better. Human life is a mass of statistics only for statisticians: the rest of us live in a world of individuals, and most of them are not prominent. Their joys however are fully joyful, and their griefs are real. It was the extraordinariness of ordinary people that was

This selection, which originally appeared in the *Guardian* on July 26, 2003, is reprinted by permission of the author.

Shields's forte, reaching its fullest expression in her novels *Swann, The Republic of Love*, and especially *The Stone Diaries*. She gave her material the full benefit of her large intelligence, her powers of observation, her humane wit, and her wide reading. Her books are delightful, in the original sense of the word: they are full of delights.

She understood the life of the obscure and the overlooked partly because she had lived it: her study of Jane Austen reveals a deep sympathy with the plight of the woman novelist toiling incognito, appreciated only by an immediate circle but longing for her due.

Born in 1935 in the United States, Shields was at the tail end of the postwar generation of North American college-educated women who were convinced by the mores of their time that their destiny was to get married and have five children. This Carol did; she remained a devoted mother and a constant wife throughout her life.

Her husband Don was a civil engineer; they moved to Canada, beginning with Toronto in the 60s, a time of poetic ferment in that city. Carol, who was already writing then and attended some readings, said of that time, "I knew no writers." Undoubtedly she felt relegated to that nebulous category, "just a housewife," like Daisy in *The Stone Diaries* and like Mary Swann, the eponymous poet who is murdered by her husband when her talent begins to show.

(Canadian readers would understand the allusion, but British ones who might consider this plot far-fetched will be interested to know that there was a Canadian woman poet murdered in this way: Pat Lowther, whose best-known collection is *A Stone Diary*.)

After obtaining an MA at the University of Ottawa, Shields taught for years at the University of Manitoba, in Winnipeg, where she began publishing in the 70s. But this was the decade of rampant feminism, in the arts at least. Her early books, including *Others, Intersect, Small Ceremonies*, and *The Box Garden*, which examined the vagaries of domestic life without torpedoing it, did not make a large stir, although some of their early readers found them both highly accomplished and hilarious. She had her first literary breakthrough—not in terms of quality of writing, but in terms of audience size—in Britain rather than in North America, with her 1992 novel *The Republic of Love*.

Her glory book was *The Stone Diaries*, which was shortlisted for the Booker Prize and won the Canadian Governor General's Award, and then, in 1995, the American Pulitzer Prize, a feat her dual citizenship made possible. Her next novel, *Larry's Party*, won the Orange Prize in 1998.

To say that she was not thrilled by success would be to do her an injustice. She knew what it was worth. She'd waited a long time for it. She wore her new-found prominence with graciousness and used it with largesse. One of the last instances of her enormous generosity of spirit may not be well-known: she supplied a jacket quotation for Valerie Martin's fine but challenging novel, *Property*—a book which went on to win the 2003 Orange Prize. It takes place in the American south during slavery, and none of the characters are "nice," but as Carol remarked in a letter she wrote me, that was the point.

Unless, her last novel, was written in the small space of time she spent in England, after beating cancer the first time and before it came back. It's a hymn to the provisional: the sense of happiness and security as temporary and fragile is stronger than ever.

Unless was published in 2002; although it was shortlisted for just about every major English-language prize, the Munro Doctrine, informally named after Alice Munro, had set in by then—after a certain number of prizes you are shot into the stratosphere, where you circulate in radiant mists, far beyond the ken of juries.

Several months before her death, Carol published—with co-editor Marjorie Anderson—*Dropped Threads 2*, the sequel to the spectacularly successful 2001 anthology *Dropped Threads*. This was a frankly feminist collection, taking "feminist" in its broadest sense: contributors were asked to write about subjects of concern to women that had been excluded from the conversation so far.

Those who had heard Carol Shields interviewed were probably surprised by this strain in her character, and by the angry letters addressed to male pundits dismissive of woman writers in *Unless*, because in conversation she was discreet and allusive. The little frown, the shake of the head, said it all.

Possibly feminism was something she worked into, as she published more widely and came up against more commentators who thought excellent pastry was a facile creation compared with raw meat on skewers, and who in any case could not recognize the thread of blood in her work, though it was always there. The problem of the luminous is that their very luminosity obscures the shadows it depends on for its brilliance.

I last saw Carol Shields at the end of April. Her new house was spacious, filled with light; outside the windows the tulips in her much-loved garden were in bloom. Typically for her, she claimed she couldn't quite believe she deserved to live in such a big and beautiful house. She felt so lucky, she said.

Although she was very ill, she didn't seem it. She was as alert, as interested in books of all kinds, and as curious as ever. She'd recently been reading non-fiction works on biology, she told me: something new for her, a new source of amazement and wonder. We did not speak of her illness. She preferred to be treated as a person who was living, not one who was dying.

And live she did, and live she does; for as John Keats remarked, every writer has two souls, an earthly one and one that lives on in the world of writing as a voice in the writing itself. It's this voice, astute, compassionate, observant, and deeply human, that will continue to speak to her readers everywhere.

Art Is Making: Carol Shields in Conversation and Correspondence

Eleanor Wachtel

I am writing about Carol Shields, about our friendship, and how I came to put together a book about her.[1] But first, Carol:

A few years ago, a journalist writing a profile of Carol, called me up. We met and talked for an hour and then—although he certainly wasn't writing any kind of muckraking piece—he lamented that he couldn't find anything bad about her, that he couldn't find anyone who would say anything bad about her. The article didn't get published. But, I thought, there has to be something.

Ah, I thought, go to the children. *Mommie Dearest*. And that's how I found out about the wooden spoon drawer. Carol has five children. When the kids were naughty, she'd threaten them with the wooden spoon drawer. "I'm going to the wooden spoon drawer," she'd say, and they'd run away, shrieking. Sometimes she rattled the handle. She never actually opened the drawer and certainly didn't brandish a spoon.

One day, John, the eldest (and only boy), said to his sisters, "Don't move when Mum heads for the drawer." So they didn't. Carol threatened again. They didn't move. They saw an anxious look cross her face and then, sensing something wrong, uneasy, they ran off shrieking. Another time, when they were acting up, Carol not only threatened to phone Santa and tell him that they were misbehaving and undeserving but she actually did. There they were in tears, and it was too late, she was already on the phone, talking.

Of course Carol wasn't always a mean mother. There was the time when the children were late getting off to school, and so there she stood beside the stove, shaking the egg timer to make the sand go through quicker, so they could have breakfast in time. And she never told them to "go out and play." She thought that wasn't a very nice thing to say to anyone, and besides, why would you want to go out and play if you could stay in your room and read? And the children didn't have to clean up their toys because Carol thought that would spoil the fun of playing. (22–23)

I've interviewed literally hundreds of writers over the years. *Random Illuminations* was my fourth selection of interviews—there was *Writers & Company, More Writers & Company*, and *Original Minds*—but my most personal.

Carol was a very fine writer and a remarkable human being, a wonderful person whose work I closely followed for more than twenty years. I interviewed her frequently over those years, with virtually every work she produced—novel, radio drama, play, book of stories. So I had a good sense of the span of her work and also her evolution as a stylist.

But the key reason I wanted to make a book focusing on her life and work is that we were friends. That not only offered a whole other side to the relationship, but it also meant that I was deeply affected by her illness and death. In a sense, I wanted to bring together everything I had—those conversations that had been recorded, some of her letters, my recollections, speeches, journalism—and to pay tribute to and, moreover, to evoke a very special person. The book was not an elegy; it was about—what Carol was so attuned to—the shape, the arc of a life.

I first met Carol Shields in 1980 in Vancouver—at the Literary Storefront in Gastown. I'd already reviewed her second novel, *The Box Garden*, for the *Vancouver Sun*. I remember liking her (as well as her work—I subsequently reviewed her other books) but unfortunately, we didn't get to know each other then, and that was the only time we lived in the same city.

But in the fall of 1987, when I'd newly moved to Toronto and started working full time for CBC Radio, Carol (who lived in Winnipeg at this point) published *Swann: A Mystery*. I loved this book—and I was gratified when ten years later, Carol said it was *her* favourite. Here's the conversation where that came up (onstage at Harbourfront in Toronto, October 1999):

EW: You once said that, of all your characters, it was Jack, the historian at the centre of your novel *Happenstance*, who was your favourite character. You've written more books and more characters since then. [Do you have a new favourite now?]

CS: I still like Jack very much, and I identify with him because he's someone who elected the stance of the outsider, looking rather than doing. He's a historian, and that's what historians do, I think. It's a posture that I have felt comfortable in. I'm not really a doer. I'm someone who watches other people do. So, I do identify with him.

My favourite book, I have to say, is *Swann*. When I wrote that book, I was reading a lot of postmodern criticism, which can be very damaging to a writer, but at the same time, it had this effect: it made me realize how accommodating the novel form is. I had written four quite traditional novels, and suddenly it seemed to me that the novel could be much more elastic, and it could contain more. It seemed like a big, baggy thing that I could put anything into, and I did. I worried a little bit about whether this book would be published, of course. You always have to think about that. But, for some reason, I didn't care when I was writing that book. I felt that I could make a structure that was very different from the structure of my other novels, or of any novel that I'd ever read. I could do something quite different. There's a film script at the end of this novel, which a few people had trouble with, and I can remember the publisher saying, "Oh, couldn't you recast that? Isn't there something you could do?" But I was also filled with a lot of courage at that time in my life, and I said, "No, it's going to stay here. This is the way I want it to work." The novel doesn't work perfectly. I had an idea in mind of these two gears going around. One was a big gear, and it was the mystery of how art gets made, how people of ordinary breadth can make works of art, and I've never been able to figure that out. And then there's this little, tiny mystery going around which is the mystery of the book: the disappearing manuscripts and the theft and so on—kind of a Tinkertoy mystery, it seems. And I wanted them to fit perfectly together. They don't quite do it. But I just loved the energy that was flowing through me when I wrote that book, so I remember it as a period of great happiness. (118–19)

To go back to when she wrote *Swann*, I was in Toronto, working as a literary commentator for CBC's *State of the Arts*, so I did a short radio piece about the novel. Then I decided to put together a special issue on Carol for *Room of One's Own*, a feminist literary magazine I'd been associated with for a dozen years in Vancouver. It ended up being a double issue. And I went on to use some of the material for a cover story about Carol for *Books in Canada*. That was my first real conversation with her—and what a luxury it was, spread out over two days on two different occasions, and it covered everything—from birth (and growing up in Oak Park, Illinois) to her latest novel.

But let me share with you a little from that time. We met twice—first in my apartment, the second time, for lunch. I used our lunch as a scene-setter when I wrote about Carol for *Books in Canada*:

> Carol Shields is sitting at a restaurant, looking like a character from one of her early novels. What used to be called sensibly dressed: a soft cream-coloured sweater fastened at the neck with a gold bow pin. Matching skirt, pumps. Simple stud earrings; pearl ring and gold bracelet on one hand; gold wedding band and diamond engagement ring on the other. Shields is thin, with short blonde hair and clear blue eyes behind thick-lensed glasses, which she removes and folds on the table. She has a small, soft, sometimes hesitant voice. She admits to a certain passivity, a reticence. And then disarms by saying, "Okay, ask me something personal." ("Telling It Slant" 9)

I remember a lot of those first conversations—for instance, how Carol's learning to read at four was the central mystical experience of her life. "Just at that moment," she said, "you know Helen Keller's wonderful moment when she put it all together? Realizing that those symbols meant something that I could be part of was like an act of magic" (*Random Illuminations* 14).

And how fond she was of Dick and Jane in the school readers. "I *understood* Jane," she said. "Jane was very sturdy and knew her own mind. And I loved the way that Dick was good to her, protective of her. Everyone was terribly good to everyone else; there were no bad intentions" (15).

Then she told me a little story about her slightly older brother and herself when they were children. "When we walked in the back lane," she said, "he always said the moon followed him and then I said, 'No, it always follows me.' We paced off and we walked, and I suddenly saw it followed everybody. This was a sort of revelation" (15). Carol drew on some of these vivid childhood experiences for her central character Reta Winters in *Unless*.

I thought this was so characteristic of Carol's generosity of spirit. Her particular kind of humanity has always dazzled me. It's the foundation of her commitment to writing as a form of redemption, redeeming the lives of lost or vanished women—whether it's Mary Swann or Daisy Goodwill (in *The Stone Diaries*). Or, for that matter, Larry Weller in *Larry's Party*. She's interested in nothing less than the shape of a human life, the possibilities for self-awareness, and, really, consciousness itself—the hum inside our heads. Indeed, one of the reasons that she switched from biography to fiction was because she felt that ninety percent of what happens to us occurs inside our heads and this is inaccessible to the biographer.

A few days after those first conversations, she had some more thoughts and wrote me a letter:

> I've never for a minute doubted the value of women's experience. Whenever my books met with critical scorn because of their subject matter, I just shrugged. Other critical comments I listened to, but not this one. When I told you living in England made a socialist of me, I meant that was when I became active. The exact moment of enlightenment came years earlier in a high school class when a teacher explained about the division of wealth in terms of need. (This was in the McCarthy era and I was astonished that this was what the fuss was about. Why, this sounded suspiciously like what I had learned in Methodist Sunday School! And it sounded so sensible!) Just one of the many double messages floating around in those days. I think I did recognize the doubleness, but thought it ironic and funny—and couldn't get too worked up about it. (16)

It's funny, radio interviews can create "instant intimacy"—talking about often personal things, just the disembodied voices. But I actually very rarely become friends with people I interview for radio. It used to happen occasionally with print. When I've written profiles of writers, and had more opportunity to spend time with them, follow them around, get to know them, talk to their friends, and so on. But that's what happened with Carol. I think our friendship began when I was editing that special double issue. I became a kind of commissioning editor too, and we discussed some stories that she contributed for the issue. We corresponded.

And from then on, we stayed in touch and would meet whenever she came to Toronto. Later, I spent a little time with Carol and her husband Don in France—I stayed at their place in the Jura and another time, in Burgundy. I think all this laid the ground for a friendship that only intensified after she became ill.

Initially, at least, a lot of our communication was about books. What we were reading, what we thought of it, what we would recommend, literary gossip, and so on. And for someone who was unfailingly nice—too bland a word, unfailingly kind and considerate—she could be fierce. For instance, there were two books I was sure she'd like because of the France connection. First, *Flaubert's Parrot* by Julian Barnes. (Carol was also a big fan of Flaubert and had read his correspondence, and so on.) But she *hated* the book. Then, in a letter, she marvelled at how much *Flaubert's Parrot* irritated her. "I do seem uncommonly vexed," she wrote me, "infuriated" (57). As she quoted from her journal,

> Because [the novel] begins with a dazzling piece of description that makes you think you're in the hands of a great storyteller, and then it's all downhill. Because he insults and belittles and bullies the reader. . . . Because he's aggressively cute. . . . Because he's intellectually shallow but with high pretensions. Because more than half the book is quotations. Because the skinny little story he keeps promising is a bore. . . . Wow, pow—what a dose of vitriol. I wonder why. A headache maybe, or rainy weather. (57–58)

The second France-related author I was wrong about was John Berger, who lives in the Jura and has written *Pig Earth*, among other books, set amongst the peasantry, all of which she found deeply patronizing. But much more common were Carol's enthusiasms, which make these other moments stand out.

Carol could be very funny. In one instance, long before she wrote a small biography of Jane Austen, she gave a talk at a Jane Austen conference in Ottawa. Carol's interest in Austen went back to her own childhood and her search for intelligent female heroines in fiction. The focus of this talk was *Emma* and she spoke about "the image of the body, or rather, the lack of image of body." Her paper was subtitled, "No Fingers, No Toes" because Austen "never in all her books mentions these bodily bits" (18). As Carol wrote to me at the time,

> No hips, no kidneys, wombs, shins, skin, intestines, navels either. Thank heavens someone's done a concordance, and so I'll be able to report accurately that in all of Austen there are 8 necks, 6 knees, 2 eyebrows, 10 ears, and 1 ankle, etc. Actually there are six breasts, but they all belong to men. (18)

Speaking of body parts, when I asked her once if she thought she ever unconsciously revealed things about herself in her writing, she told me about a letter she got from a dental hygienist in northern California who wanted to write a column in their national journal about Carol, because there were so many teeth in her novels. The woman proceeded to quote with page numbers all the places Carol had mentioned teeth. She wanted to know why. Carol said,

> I had really never noticed this drift toward dental hygiene. I wrote back that teeth are a part of life, an important part of life, you have to maintain them and use them and so on, but even to me that sounded inadequate. So now I have to subject myself to severe analysis and find out what it is. (96)

In the fall and winter of 1993–94, Carol and Don were on sabbatical in Berkeley. This was also the season of *The Stone Diaries*, which won the

National Book Critics Circle Award, the Pulitzer, and the Governor-General's Prize for Fiction. One of the first honours was being a finalist for the Booker Prize—ultimately won that year by Roddy Doyle for *Paddy Clarke Ha Ha Ha*. In one of her letters, Carol described going to London for the ceremony (the contenders don't know ahead of time whether they've won):

> Now follows a brief Booker Report. Brief because it seems so faraway, dreamlike, though it was only a few weeks ago. It was both dazzling and awful. Extraordinarily sophisticated and curiously boorish. The Guildhall where the awards dinner was held is utterly beautiful—and people, men in black tie, women sparkling with jewelry, and wearing mostly black too, were also rather beautiful. (I bought new earrings for the event, my only investment in beautiful-peopledom.) We sat at round tables for the dinner, trying to ignore the TV cameras which seemed to be everywhere. Cigars were passed after dinner. Now that's pretty boorish. The speeches had little cynical edges on them, past grievances trotted out, not quite "nice." (The head of Booker Inc.—an immense, red-faced man—informed me that Winnipeg was a very, very dull place, and I was quite lost for a reply. "Is it?" I said. Lamely.) Our table was Fourth Estate people with some *Guardian* people too— they are a major investor in the firm. I thought the head of Fourth Estate, Victoria Barnsley, would burst into tears when Roddy Doyle's name was announced, but I have to admit—ever the pessimist—I'd expected it. By the way, Roddy Doyle and I both forgot to bring our invitations to the dinner and had to go into a little anteroom to be "interviewed" before they'd let us in. Security at the dinner was extremely tight since Salman Rushdie was there—looking, I might say, exactly like Salman Rushdie. Someone whispered into my ear after dinner: "Mr. Rushdie would like to meet you," and then led me through what I thought was a crowd of friends, but was, in fact, a crowd of bodyguards, four men deep. We had a nice chat about the Future of the Novel, and he said he was in the middle of mine. I didn't know whether to believe this or not, but decided I might as well. I also met Stephen Spender, 84, erect and handsome still, and his wife, who looks like an El Greco ghost, very old, very stately—they both told me they were rooting for me, though I think they put it more elegantly. After dinner I met Margaret Drabble; we had a pleasant chat, very polite and friendly, though I don't think we said anything memorable to each other. All quite marvelous, so that I almost forgot I'd lost. I also met all the other nominees briefly, including Caryl Phillips who gave me a stiff hug and whispered something about the tyranny of colonialism in my ear. A sort of rollercoaster night, and, suddenly it was over, and I was on the way to California. Then back to Toronto. Then back to

California. Back to normal, whatever that means. I think it means being able to formulate my own breakfast and knowing where I am when I open my eyes in the morning. (62–63)

The search for a home, the idea that she said went right back to *Ulysses,* that literature was about trying to find your true home—metaphorically, the place where you have always been destined to be—is one of the themes that engaged Carol. Where you're at rest in your body and mind, enabled, at peace with other people, "a sort of longing for belonging," as she put it (117). Where you're free to be creative. But while she was engaged with the idea of finding a "home," I don't think she herself deeply identified as an outsider. And in that she was a rarity, as she was in so many things. Because if I had to find one common thread, to name one characteristic most frequently found amongst writers, it would be their self-proclaimed marginality, their outsider status. It's something that may, or might have been, the source of pain or loneliness, but it is something that most writers prize.

But Carol was unusual in this regard too. She came at it from a different angle. When I asked her if she was searching for a place of belonging—for a home, she said that she thought more and more that she had reached that place of being free to do whatever she wanted to do—which was to write books. She said, "I've been able to write exactly what I've wanted to write, so I suppose that is a way of finding your home" (118).

In Winnipeg, she belonged to a book club, although that reflected her talent for friendship as much as her love of books. Despite many moves, Carol had friends going back to her childhood in Oak Park, Illinois. In her own writing, she was witty, often ironic, always affectionate, with a delicacy and subtlety of language. Sentence for sentence, she was a marvel. I remember she told me about trying to write a *non*-ironical story for that special issue of *Room of One's Own.* With all that irony, she said, she was "beginning to get a case of lockjaw." But then she added, "You may find it a bit sappy" (16).

Carol was a gutsy writer, experimenting with a range of narrative approaches—omniscient, direct, fractured. When she turned fifty, her writing turned a corner. "You get older and braver," she said, "braver about what you can say and what can be understood" (17). She was once quite tickled when someone described her work as "post-epiphanist." She was very conscious of courage—the word came up a lot—I think because to her, courage was a muscle she developed in herself. Deliberately. Heroically.

Carol wasn't just a good writer; she was also a good reader and an attentive reviewer. At the end of her review of Lucy Maud Montgomery's Journals, Carol referred to "the transcendent and healing possibility of art" (97). So I asked her about what writing had meant in her own life. She said,

> I think a lot about this business of art and who makes it and who gets to name the culture in our society. And what it means to make art. Without getting too pretentious about this, I think that the ability to take the words in my head and to put them on paper has again and again rescued me from what I might think of as emotional bankruptcy. The fact that I can actually still do this has given me the sense of making something. The filmmaker Jean Renoir once described art this way, "art is making." It's a very nice definition and it's exactly what I feel. Art isn't looking at something and appreciating; it is actually making. And I feel that this making that I have been privileged to do has given a centre to my life that I might not otherwise have. So healing, yes in the sense that it's a place that I can go to, it's a refuge. It doesn't always work perfectly. And I know that when I have a good day that I'm going to be punished for it the next day. There are bad days, the days when everything you put on paper doesn't match that golden book in your head, but getting it as close as possible gives me a kind of pleasure that very few other things do. (97)

She said this before she became mortally ill, but I don't think that fundamentally changed her relationship to writing. Writing continued to provide a refuge, a space she could inhabit where she wasn't sick or preoccupied with illness.

I want to share with you another bit from the interview I did with Carol onstage (at the International Festival of Authors at Harbourfront in Toronto). This is about a year after her diagnosis:

> EW: You've talked about being concerned about—this is how you put it—"the unsettling self-absorption" that cancer had led you into. How did you escape that?

> CS: I don't know that I have. One of the things that has worried me more than anything else, is self-absorption. Every muscle that twitches, every little pain you feel—you're always listening to your inner music and testing yourself against the healthy people in the world. I worried about this, that it would make me too self-absorbed. Part of the joy of my life has been reaching out and having people around. They say writers aren't sociable, but they are. They are terribly sociable beings.

> EW: And you've talked about your "desperate curiosity," as you once said.

CS: Yes and I didn't want to lose that. I think the worry is diminishing now because I'm feeling a little stronger, and I'm living in a different place this year. I'm having new experiences every day. I'm getting out of this terrible introspection. (112)

Every now and then, Carol and I would go to the movies. Five months before she died, we went to see *The Hours*—which was based on a novel that neither of us liked very much. But she enjoyed the film, especially because it gave her images she could conjure up later and reflect on. There was a line in the film about staying alive for the people you love and I asked if she thought that was true. She said no, you stayed alive for yourself, but that you might have some extra medical treatment for the people you love. And I remembered her having recently asked me about whether she should have more treatment. And how I knew I was giving her the wrong answer when I said yes.

Because Carol thought she might not be well enough, or even alive, for the publication of what was her last novel, *Unless*, she did publicity ahead of time. I recorded an interview at her home in January 2002. One of the things I talked to her about was a new performance piece that she had contributed to, called *Mortality*:

EW: Do you ever think in terms of "something *unless* something" . . .?

CS: Do you mean in terms of something after this life? No, I don't. . . . This is it and this is why we have to use the time we've got to . . . blurt bravely and get some words on paper and have lots of conversations with lots of people. I think that's very important—connecting and having conversations, that's a huge part of my life. Somehow I've been able to remain interested in everything that's happening, and you want to hang onto that as long as you can.

EW: As your character in the performance piece *Mortality* says, she goes "right up to the wall." It's not even a breath away.

CS: Yes. I find that a very comforting thought. If you think of death as a part of life—and, in fact, it is—it just intersects exactly with it, and it's just a breath away. It's not that big a thing. (179–80)

Knowing Carol Shields was such a gift—first through her writing and then as a friend. The whole idea of "random illuminations"—of moments of transcendence that cut through everyday experience in a miraculous sort of way, when some sort of pattern to the universe is glimpsed: clarity, harmony, whimsy—this fits Carol so perfectly; her openness and her enduring sense of engagement and curiosity.

It could be something as simple as sharing an umbrella with a stranger in Tokyo and walking in synchronicity together. She said, "I believe in these moments, when we feel or sense the order of the universe beneath the daily chaos. They're like a great gift of happiness that comes unexpectedly" (17).

Carol was inspiring. I was conscious of that, and I continue to think about her vivid sense of life. But what I miss most in the more than ten years since her death are conversations. She herself mentions how important they are to her. And there are so many things we would have talked about—from every literary prize shortlist and winner to the books we were reading, to the parts of the world we were visiting, and, of course, more personal experiences—there's so much we would have shared. But I can't really conjure it up because I could never predict what or where her imagination would take her, or the originality of her mind. It's that—along with all the obvious aspects of friendship—that I miss so terribly much. That absence that can't be illuminated.

Note

1. That book was *Random Illuminations: Conversations with Carol Shields*. Except where otherwise noted, all quoted material in this chapter is from *Random Illuminations*.

Works Cited

Wachtel, Eleanor. "Telling It Slant: Carol Shields's Fiction Approaches Its Truths Obliquely." *Books in Canada* 18.4 (1989): 9–11. Print.

———. *Random Illuminations: Conversations with Carol Shields*. Fredericton: Goose Lane, 2007. Print.

The Square Root of a Clock Tick: Time and Timing in Carol Shields's Poetry and Prose

ANNE GIARDINI AND JOSEPH GIARDINI

As the eldest daughter and the eldest grandchild of Carol Shields and her husband Don, we have spent many hours in their homes surrounded by the sight and sounds of the antique clocks that Don collected. There were dozens of them, many quite plain and some more elaborate with gilded dials, mother-of-pearl inlays, or detailed gingerbread carving. Don, a retired engineer, has always kept them in good order and so they click and chirp and sound out the hours, not simultaneously—they are antiques after all—but near enough.

Visiting Don and Carol's house as a child, Joseph recalls, I was always interested in how their clocks rendered time as a physical entity with their insistent motion and ticking. In most of the rooms of the house the noise the clocks made kept me aware of the passage of each second, and I frequently followed the movements of the clock hands intently. Often, I would escape to clock-free rooms to play, so that I might be cut loose from a few of those hours; with the clocks around me (I reflect now, and perhaps my memories have a deceptive clarity) I was too aware of each marked moment to focus comfortably on everything else. I wonder now at Carol's writing practice. Was her work affected when each passing moment, productive or not, was so crisply demarked? Or did she find a place away from the clocks for writing, so that she might lose herself to it for a few hours, as I did with my Lego, puzzles, and other toys?

Don and Carol's collection of clocks has always reminded me, Anne recalls, of doves in a dovecote, or hens; they share with birds the making of companionable noises for a while, with the peaceable clucking interrupted by flurries of purposeful noise that soon subsides again into the usual settled, background, harmonious rustling. When I was growing up, from time to time we had a houseful of guests—friends and their children, or aunts and uncles and cousins. I didn't mind being displaced from my bedroom downstairs to the living room couch. The long, green couch was stuffed with down and feathers and it was very comfortable—Don still has it, recovered in tasteful yellow and cream—and there were good lights at each end, perfect for reading into the night. The ticking and chiming of all those clocks, however, could be maddening. One night I got up and stopped them all, only to find, when I lay down again, that the house seemed to be missing its heartbeat. I felt like a murderer. I almost confessed the next morning when my father was going around all of the rooms of the main floor, starting up the clocks again, resetting them to the proper hour, but I could not quite bring myself to do it, unsure of what the penalty for a murder of the minor sort might be.

It cannot be a coincidence that in Carol Shields's poetry we see repeated attention to time and temporality. She was always thoughtful about time, and she was surrounded by reminders of its dual nature—both cyclical and linear. Later in life, she became critical of advice that had been doled out at her graduation address when she graduated from an American liberal arts college in 1957. The talk was given by a popular math professor. Part of his advice was *tempus fugit*—"time flies." He said that, unless the graduands seized the moment—every moment—their lives would get away from them. Their days and years would be eroded, erased, wasted. Thrown away through carelessness . . . lost.

As a result, in the years that immediately followed, Shields commented:

> years in which I might be changing diapers, washing floors, driving children here and there, sewing, shopping, cooking meals, writing thank you notes, weeding the garden, reading a little poetry on the sly . . . those words would occasionally come back to me: "Tempus Fugit." ("Commencement Address")

Time is a recurring motif in Carol Shields's poems as well as in her stories and novels. Her focus is often on its pull on all of us, how time's sheer relentlessness may (seem to) render everything we do ineffective, even meaningless. Against this, Shields strove to give value back to the everyday, the domestic, and the feminine so that our actions large and small are not devalued against time, frittered away in the minutes and seconds and hours, but lived and then remembered without in any sense time wasted, least of all in the way that the professor warned about.

Often Shields showed clocks as strange, almost mystical objects that pull upon the characters in ways that—it seems—must be resisted. Her first book, her 1972 collection of poems, *Others*, opens with a poem titled "A Woman We Know Who Suffers from Occasional Depression":

> Afternoons collapse
> when five o'clock frays
> toward night, and days
> launched in order, lapse
> into riot.
>
>   I housekeep
> in rooms of my making, squares
> of reason stacked against the clock.
> Then darkness leaks like gas to block
> the logic of supper, belief, prayers
> and sleep.
>
> The trick
> is to find the square
> root of a clock tick
> and hide there. (1)

Against the motion of time, the speaker seeks refuge in the everyday activities of housekeeping, trying to conceal herself from what is described as time tipping towards disorder. Rather than lending order to a life, time is shown here to be almost corrosive. Time frays, leaks, blocks the logical order of things. We are reminded of Elizabeth Grosz, who wrote in *The Nick of Time*, "Instead of containing and controlling time, life succumbs to its rhythms, direction, and forces, to the ever pressing forces of development, growth, and decay" (5). Shields's speaker seeks to reverse this dynamic and find or create a space for herself apart from time's actions.

Themes that characterized Shields's writing up right up to her death present themselves in this short poem. Clocks. Time. Domesticity. The stratagems we employ to manage our days and lives. The ways in which we are mysterious to each other. This is, after all, a poem that ends with a decision to seek out active concealment. Reading this poem forty years later, we find it possible to wonder how much of it could be self-referential. Shields spoke often of how she managed her hours as a writer with five young children.

Here is what she told Terry Gross in an interview for his program *Fresh Air* on National Public Radio. When asked, "How did you find the time to write *Small Ceremonies*?" she replied:

> Everyone asks me this, including my own children. What my children forget is that I did not have a job; they are all raising children and having jobs. But I didn't have a job. I didn't write until they went to school, and I didn't write on weekends and I didn't write in the evening. None of this was possible. But I used to try to get that hour just before they came home for lunch, 11 to 12. You know, got all those socks picked up, etc. and then I tried to write a couple of pages. That was all I ever asked myself to do. Then sometimes, in the afternoon, before they came home from school, I would get back to those two pages, and maybe have a chance to do them over again. But I really only had about an hour or an hour and a half a day. This was how I organized my time, that I would give myself one or two pages a day, and if I didn't get to my two pages, I would get into bed at night with one of those thick yellow tablets of lined paper, and I would do two quick pages and then turn off the light. I did this for nine months, and at the end of nine months, I had a novel. I could see how it could be done in little units. I thought of it like boxcars. I had nine boxcars, and each chapter had a title starting with September, and then October, November, December, so it was a very easy structure for someone writing a first novel to follow. ("Interview with Terry Gross")

The opening poem of Shields's second poetry collection, *Intersect*, which was published in 1974, displays similar concerns for the way that time erodes the substance of a life:

Pioneers: Southeast Ontario

They existed.   Butter bowls
and hayrakes testify,
and ruined cabins
their grievous roofs
caved in.

But they're melting to myth,
every year harder to believe
in, and the further we travel away
the more we require
in the form of proofs.

Of course
you still meet those who
are old enough to
claim kinship, but eye

witnesses are scarce
now and unreliable.

We want sealers, cutlery, clods
of earth, flames from their fires,
footsteps, echoes, the breath
they breathed,
a sign, something to
keep faith by
before they go the way
of the older gods. (9)

Here, again, we see the domestic as a means of keeping faith against decay. "They existed" we are told, in reference to the pioneers, but then Shields offers humble "butter bowls" as the first piece of evidence. Household objects like hay rakes, sealers, and cutlery are what we are given to "keep faith by," rather than lists of dates or a record of significant events, the information that would more commonly appear in an account or chronicle of the lives of the pioneers. Shields's poem suggests that, without a grounding knowledge in everyday domestic life, made possible by means of physical evidence, the passage of time causes things to begin "melting to myth," to "go the way / of the older gods." Events deemed historically important are slotted into a (mythical) narrative of progress, and this, Shields claims, is not what we should be seeking.

"Pioneers: Southern Ontario" is not after all about the existence of butter bowls. Rather, the butter bowls are witnesses and the enduring artefacts of—proof—that our ancestors were here. And we crave them. We want these *lares and penates* as "a sign, something to keep faith by." They are temporary gods, Shields suggests; they too will "go the way of the older gods," though they are necessary nonetheless. She used to say that either all of us are extraordinary or none of us is. It is the same with the objects that we craft and use. Gods and sealers and cutlery all pass away, never to be seen again, leaving only fragments and the fading echo of those ringing clods of earth.

Intersect also contains Shields's homage to Emily Dickinson, titled after the poet:

Minutes hide their tiny Tears

And Days weep into Aprons.

A stifled Sorrow from the Years

And Silence from the Eons. (19)

The units of time grow larger—minutes to days to years to eons—and we eventually reach silence, the greatest expanse of time reducing all of experience to nothing. The use of the word "apron," with its gendered connotations of female domesticity, is surely relevant. By placing such a commonplace domestic item in this poem about the silencing effect of time, Shields highlights the fact that women's experiences are much less likely to be remembered than those of men; they are often, instead, unrecorded, trivialized, and forgotten. Excluded from many realms of achievement, women's lives are less likely to be found in the historical myths which linger longest in time's passing. This focus on domesticity is a counterpoint to time's drive toward forgetting, Shields is seeking to imbue with value the lives of women who would otherwise be left off the historical record.

Shields spoke of becoming a writer because there were not enough books that examined women's friendships and women's inner lives. She wrote, as she often said to us, "the kind of book I wanted to read but couldn't find. Their hours and minutes and the achievements of their years were not recorded."

Here is the start of another of the poems in *Others*, "The New Mothers":

> Nearly seven,
> walls loosen, it's already dark. . . . (7)

The "I" in the poem "Insomniac" is still awake at midnight, and

> Hourly I grow more over-defined
> like a figure squared off on a graph,
> advancing by rigid degrees
> toward death (15)

Time brings good things, too. In the poem "Our Artist Friends," after a day's "Old Testament storm":

> At six the clouds
> rolled up like laundry,
> the yellow yoke of sun poked
> out and we cheered
> from the window, astonished
> to find it mattered
> so much. (22)

The *Intersect* poem "Suppertime, 1950" must refer to Shields's birth family. She was born in 1935, and so in 1950 she was Carol Ann Warner, aged 15 or so, at 5 foot two, eyes of blue, the very image of a middle-class

American teenage girl in the middle of the last century. She was a short seven years away from meeting her future husband Don Shields.

Suppertime 1950

Six o'clock. This hour
encircles itself, measured
out in voices and doors,
running water and the graceless scraping
of vegetables and showers
of steps on patterned floors.

We are so easily reassured
by mere clatter
by the sweet pleasing rise
of familiar steam shaping
what we've more or less
come to recognize
as happiness. (16)

So much in this one small poem looks ahead to the themes that recur in Shields's writing—time, domesticity and the nature and texture of happiness. It seems that happiness is set against time, as if it is the one thing that can suspend it. Happiness. Not love. Love is the condition that is most frequently assigned this role in examinations of human life—the role of suspending time. But the word "love" is entirely missing from *Others* and *Intersect*. Instead, Shields focuses on something that is at the same time more complex and more familiar and more evocative—the small, familiar events of the days that taken together make up a life. "[B]y sitting here," she writes in the poem "Rough Riders," "we hold the seasons still" (20). It is the sitting that does it.

In "Couple," it is eleven o'clock and a couple go about their nightly routine, including treading stairs that "exhausted by ritual complain through carpet" (36). One of them sets the alarm to "choose the hour of our waking," the other adjusts the electric blanket, and then the happiness of moving together in sheets that, helpfully, slide back of their own volition to accommodate them.

Intersect ends with a clock poem:

As For Us

Why can't we live like
    this old clock,
    sure of our polished skin,
    set in motion by a careful key,

> all our knowledge coiled in
>   one accomplished spring, its wound-
>   up heart, its slow
>   and calculated
>   letting go,
>
> our accurate hands pulled round and round
>   every day completed
>   every hour a victory. (59)

Shields's next book of poetry came many years later, after she had established herself as a novelist, playwright, and short story writer. *Coming to Canada* includes poems from *Others* and from *Intersect*, and also a number of new poems. In his introduction to *Coming to Canada*, the poet Christopher Levenson observes that the poem "Getting"

> is only one of the many later poems that deal with time and its effect on human happiness. Whereas the concern is obvious in, say, "The Invention of Clocks," "Quartz," or "At the Clock Museum," in "Work," by contrast, where husband and wife are stacking cordwood against the garage for the winter, or in "Cold Storage," which describes fur coats and stoles being put away for the summer, we find a subtler link with two of Carol Shields's favourite and inter-related themes, themselves both aspects of time, rituals and seasons. (xxiii)

The first poem in *Coming to Canada*, "Getting Born,"[1] addresses time's arrival and departure. Shields addresses her own birth, in Chicago in 1935, and also the time that had elapsed since then. The hospital has had a new wing added to it. The doctor who delivered her is "not only dead but erased" (3).

Shields acknowledges time's allure for her head-on in the short poem "Confession," a poem that reminds us a bit of Cole Porter, at least until the last line:

> An anxious twitch of the nerves
>   is all I get
>   from sunsets, meadows, birds
>   and all that
>
> Mountains go flat
>   on me and trees fall
>
> but time's tenanted chronicle
>   fills me full (63)

Shields admits here that she finds her subject matter not in the wonders of the natural world, but in the "tenanted chronicle" of time. Most of the poems after "Confession" return to this theme.

"Quartz," another clock poem, describes how time is measured out by quartz, "accurate, clean and quiet," but, notwithstanding, "cool moonly rituals / oddly persist" (74). "Daylight Saving" is about the hour that is lost and later found again when the year is "cut and spliced" in the way that almost all Canadians are familiar with, since the losing and the finding of that errant hour are an annual rite (81). The theme is picked up again in "Falling Back:"

> It's easily done, spring and fall.
> a dial turned or hands pushed and suddenly all
> our lightly traced routines
>   are differently lit—
>
> Morning lopped
> off, stone-cold and sharp with
> crevasses, cutting harsh
>   corners off yellow kitchens
>
> But evenings yield,
> grow soft, mouse-like, crushed
> with fur, and cars
> ascend greyed air
> wave on wave, rising
> while children test their breath
>   against emboldened light
>
> Seasons expand and shrink
>   minutely
>
> Planets cruise unstopped,
>   their unaccompanied flight (86)

"The Invention of Clocks" is new to *Coming to Canada*. It can be seen to speak directly to the exclusion of women from historical/mythological conceptions of time:

The Invention of Clocks

> First imagine history as a long dull night,
> a drift of unlayered absence,
> impacted, unknowable, profound until
> that moment, a Sunday? (1274 some say,
> guessing of course) when a young man
> (probably) a sword-maker by trade
> (here picture him as he may have been,
> smallish and thoughtful and wearing
> a coarse shirt and suffering—who knows—
> from medieval angst, certainly boredom)

> playing idly with an iron toy newly made
> a thing of teased springs and wheels
> and weights, queer marrying of metal parts
> mathematics and foolishness, all
> this so that whatever it is, that substance
> that stands between the lifting and lowering
> of his wife's hands (she is dropping turnips
> into boiling water) can be measured
> defined, possessed and offered back
> to God who swings his musical old beard
> like a pendulum (71)

The poem imagines what might be called the invention of history. With the ability to measure and weigh time, history stops being "a long dull night," "unlayered," "unknowable" (71). But the question mark after "Sunday," the guessing at the year, and the qualification of the inventor's gender problematize the clarity that the invention of clocks might bring to history. By introducing these uncertainties, and by describing the first clock as a "toy," and a "queer marrying of metal parts / mathematics and foolishness" Shields delicately and deftly detracts from the historical weight that might otherwise be given to this moment, making it seem less of a clean break from previous times of obscurity. In inventing this moment, even as she minimizes it, she focuses on the heavily contextualized nature of history, which is never completely objective, but is continually invented and reinvented based on current fashions, ideas, and ways of perceiving the evidence.

The objective notion of history is heavily gendered in the poem, made possible through the inventiveness of a man, and presided over by a male God. In a characteristic action, Shields places the lone female presence in the poem beside or outside of the action: the inventor's wife off to the side, preparing a meal. Her husband's invention does affect her, however. Time, "that substance that stands between the lifting and lowering" of her hands, is taken away from her, "measured / defined, possessed and offered back to God" (71). The wife's actions are the sort of actions that would typically be excluded from a normal historical account, the kind of narrative made possible by the man-made recording of time. In gendering this "invention of history" so heavily toward the male, and against the female presence in the kitchen, Shields speaks again to the tendency to exclude female voices from the historical record, and to privilege male action. Not only is the wife excluded from the act of invention, but she is about to lose the right to own and allocate the time she spends on tasks. She is not far off from the time efficiency studies that were part of the great sweep of science that turned "domestic" into "domestic science."

"At the Clock Museum" follows "The Invention of Clocks." The first two stanzas detail the surface features of the clocks assembled in the museum, their imposing, "kingly" presence. Shields writes of the "cheerful / oily willingness" of clocks "to "keep" time":

> or at the very least to measure
> and record that insoluble
> other-water in which we float
> or sometimes   but rarely
>   swim (72)

The word "keep" appears in quotation marks, lending a sceptical quality to the claim that clocks might actually be able to capture or hold the actual experience of time's effects on our lives.

The last poem in *Coming to Canada* is "Season's Greetings," which describes the annual arrival of cards. These cards do not bring "good cheer or love":

> but an eye blinked
> backward at other richer
> seasons, something more slender
> than truth and more kind
> or less kind
>   than letting go (91)

In Shields's novels, time is seldom addressed as directly as it is in her poetry, and when it is, it is often the subject of tweaking or subversion. In *Swann*, the disappearance of Mary Swann's days of domestic life and creation occurs in a literal fashion: as the narrative progresses the remainders of the murdered Mary Swann's life disappear, or are stolen, appropriated, or misplaced. Her rhyming dictionary is tossed into the garbage, her books of poems vanish one by one, and the contents of her home are tossed away and replaced with more presentable objects.

Toward the end of the novel, the very authenticity of Swann's published poems is called into question. The original manuscripts are in disarray and Frederic and Hildë Cruzzi help matters along, going so far as to supply "missing lines, and even the greater part of a missing stanza." Swann's absence is the missing centre around which the book revolves, and every character invents a version of her that they are able to work into their own narratives, manufacturing evidence to fit their needs and discarding evidence that displeases them. At the novel's end, however, in a chapter written in the form of a screenplay, there is a converging moment of collective endeavour to remember Swann on what may be closer to (or farther from) her own terms, as the collected academics at the Swann Symposium strive to reconstruct her poems from recollected fragments.

Margaret Atwood has commented on the way that memory in this final scene functions in a punning way, as an un-dis-membering. Swann's corpus, having been pulled apart by conflicting and inflated academic readings, is brought together in time, reassembled, with attention paid to the particularities of word, instead of guessed-at symbolic meanings or over-laboured biographical clues. Despite the ironic distance of the film script form, and the fact that Swann's poems, as published, do not necessarily match her manuscripts or intentions, this ending is transcendent. Memory and genuine fondness and collaborative creativity seem to create alchemy which undoes some of the effects of fleeting time, and insists against its erasures. This collaboration at a specific moment in time feels more likely to be authentic to the lost Mary Swann. Although she remains marginal, she is made extraordinary.

Small Ceremonies, Shields's first novel, has a straightforward structure rooted in time. The story of Judith Gill is told in a year of months, and the books became steadily braver, more mischievous with time.

The tale of Daisy Goodwill Flett in *The Stone Diaries* does not flow in a linear fashion and the markers of life are distorted, further disturbing the sense of how time is marked. This, an unwritten autobiography, is subversive when it comes to the markers of Daisy's life, taking us between and behind and after but never squarely on life's markers. Each chapter in *The Stone Diaries* is separated by roughly ten years. We are given descriptions of events *around* Daisy's birth (but not the birth itself), through to her approaching death (but not her death), including moments she could not possibly have witnessed or remembered. Early in the novel there is this reflection on the effects of time and narrative:

> It has never been easy for me to understand the obliteration of time, to accept, as others seem to do, the swelling and corresponding shrinkage of seasons or the conscious acceptance that one year has ended and another begun. There is something here that speaks of our essential helplessness and how the greater substance of our lives is bound up with waste and opacity. Even the sentence parts seize on the tongue, so that to say "Twelve years passed" is to deny the fact of biographical logic. How can so much time hold so little, how can it be taken from us? Months, weeks, days, hours misplaced—and the most precious time of

life, too, when our bodies are at their greatest strength, and open, as they never will be again, to the onslaught of sensation. (27–28)

Though *The Stone Diaries* may represent Daisy's effort (or an effort on her behalf) to extricate herself from the "obliteration of time," it is evident to any reader of the book that much of her life is not present. Daisy herself rarely appears directly. Although she is not as entirely absent as Mary Swann, her presence is often filtered through the experiences and thoughts of others. For instance, we are presented with the (imagined) theories of Daisy's friends about what has happened to her, as opposed to Daisy's self-reflection, in chapter seven, "Sorrow, 1965." In chapter six, "Work, 1955–1964" we are given letters written to Daisy, but none that she has written herself. The final chapter includes a long—and heartbreaking—list of experiences that Daisy has never had and ends with her final (unspoken) words, "I am not at peace" (361). The absences and voids are as much the story as the text. The erasures tell us more about Daisy than she can tell herself. And Daisy's final dissatisfaction calls us to recognize that there is not only something wrong with the story, which is so out of joint, there is something wrong with the life. On reflection, the reader is also led to question traditional representations of life stories, which usually have clear linear progressions and give the most importance to the events that *The Stone Diaries* elides. But the gaps in time in Carol Shields's work, though unmarked or unemphasized or even erased, have a weight, a heft of their own. They are as important as what is written, and they fascinate, dazzle, because they are left open to our interpretation. In this way, Shields engages us and keeps engaging us. The creative act *includes* us. Time and the experience of time is an act of creation that underlies Shields's work, a story behind the story, a doubling of the act of reading and understanding.

What of the commencement speaker who warned that unless the young men and women seized the moment—every moment—their lives would get away from them? Remember, he said that their days and years would be eroded, erased, wasted. Thrown away through carelessness . . . lost.

In her *own* commencement address to a graduating class at the University of British Columbia, in 1996, Shields reflected on this advice:

Time was hurrying by. Brushing past me. I could almost hear the flapping of the winged chariot. My little life was left behind in the dust. I was standing still or so I thought. The words "Tempus Fugit" whenever I paused to recollect my graduation day spooked me, scared me. I was persuaded that I had failed, because I was not filling every day with accomplishment. I was not pushing forward and making the most of my allotted time on earth.

And so today, fully conscious of the presumption of graduation speakers' smugness, I would like to revise that dictum:

"Tempus does not Fugit."

Time is not cruel. Given the good luck of a long healthy life, as most of us are, we have plenty—plenty of time. We have time to try our new selves. Time to experiment. Time to dream and drift. Time even to waste.

Fallow time. Shallow time.

We'll have good years and bad years. And we can afford both. Every hour will not be filled with meaning and accomplishment as the world measures such things but there will be compensating hours so rich, so full, so humanly satisfying that we will become partners with time and not victims of it.

Most of us end up seeing our lives not as an ascending line of achievement but as a series of highly interesting chapters. ("Commencement Address")

NOTE

1.   "Getting Born," with its echo of begetting, is again echoed in the poem "Getting," which is about "getting / older."

WORKS CITED

Grosz, Elizabeth. *The Nick of Time*. Durham: Duke University Press, 2004. Print.

———. Levenson, Christopher. "Introduction." In *Coming to Canada*. By Carol Shields. Ottawa: Carleton University Press, 1992: xi–xxiv. Print.

Shields, Carol. *Coming to Canada*. Ottawa: Carleton University Press, 1992. Print.

———. "Commencement Address." University of British Columbia Commencement. War Memorial Gym, Vancouver. 28 November 1996. Lecture.

———. *Intersect*. Ottawa: Borealis Press, 1974. Print.

———. "Interview with Terry Gross." *Fresh Air*. NPR. 1 May 2002. Radio.

———. *Others*. Ottawa: Borealis Press, 1972. Print.

———. *The Stone Diaries*. Toronto: Random House Canada, 1993. Print.

All That "Below-the-Surface Stuff": Carol Shields's Conversational Modes

CORAL ANN HOWELLS

In her last interview with Eleanor Wachtel in 2002 Carol Shields spoke about the double dynamic of her life, about how "we have to use the time we've got to . . . get some words on paper and have lots of conversations with lots of people. I think that's very important—connecting and having conversations, that's a huge part of my life. Being interested" (Wachtel 179). Carol talks about language, speech, and writing in the same breath: as a writer she's interested "in the way the language comes out and goes onto the page, how you can give it voice" (Wachtel 117), and as a reader she's interested in the way that "the novel keeps us in contact with voices other than our own" (Wachtel 170). For her, the "intimacy of voice" was a major part of the appeal of women's writing, and she presents the image of "women writers sitting at their desks . . . speaking . . . to individual readers, as though those readers were in the same room, and what they are speaking of is the texture of their own lives" ("A View from the Edge" 27). I was reminded here of similarities with and differences from Laurence Sterne's *Tristram Shandy*, for Tristram writes: "Writing , when properly managed (as you may be sure I think mine is) is but a different name for conversation" (Sterne 127). Carol shared those sentiments but expressed them more modestly: "I suppose that's something that I would like to learn to do" (Wachtel 169). It is with the mystery of Carol's translation of spoken language into written discourse that I am concerned here in my analysis of conversational modes in her writing which, I shall suggest, constitute her version of *écriture féminine*. How does she construct the illusion of conversation, establishing relationships and interaction between fictional characters in her novels and short stories, and between text and readers in her non-fictional essays and her Jane Austen biography? How does she manage to position her readers in a dialogic framework as if taking part in a conversation? Likewise, how does she represent the nuances of spoken conversation, so many of which are unspoken—all that "below-the-surface stuff" as Blanche Howard phrased it when congratulating Carol on *Larry's Party* (Howard and Howard 340). Conversation for Carol represents another dimension of her narrative artifice.

In discussing the layering of written and spoken language in Carol's work I draw on a variety of approaches. For spoken conversation, the obvious place to start is sociolinguistics with its research into women's gossip and gender differences in conversational strategies. These differences have been quite brilliantly codified by the linguist John D. Locke as "duels" and "duets," "duetting" referring to women's collaborative harmonious verbal interaction, in contrast to men's more agonistic disputatious style of "duelling" (Locke 4). I suspect, however, that Locke is much happier with duelling than duetting, and he is overly committed to his hunter-gatherer, dominant-submissive biological and evolutionary theories to explain differences. I prefer the more diversified approach to language and gender research adopted by the female sociolinguists Jennifer Coates and Pia Pichler, editors of a 600-page book of essays which offers a critical overview of the development of the discipline from the 1970s to the present day. In a section on theoretical debates in this area, they note a shift from a "dominance" approach to one based on "difference," which allows for the discussion of women's talk within a more egalitarian framework outside traditional binary structures (483–528). This seems to me a more congenial context for an analysis of conversational practices in Carol's work. Some of the insights of affect theory in recent feminist studies are also useful, with their emphasis on embodied female subjects and the communication and sharing of feelings, a process referred to as an "affective economics," which is social in its circulation (Ahmed 45). With its emphasis on relationality and responsiveness to signs of emotion which remain unsaid, affect provides a way of reading what is unspoken in conversation.

Perhaps controversially, given their very different cultural contexts, I refer to Carol's writing as a version of *écriture féminine*, suggesting her affinity with Hélène Cixous's rhetorical strategy of metaphorical thinking as a way of inscribing an alternative mode of feminine understanding. This is best exemplified in "The Laugh of the Medusa" and best explained as a style of writing which unites ideas and feelings via images in a lived continuum. As a French critic has speculated, "This continuity may be one of the striking features of women's writing, whether it is fiction or theory" (Defromont 119). I also call on Mikhail Bakhtin, who describes novel discourse as a "social heteroglossia" (Bakhtin 292) with its diversity of voices and speech types orchestrated on a dynamic principle of social and verbal interchange. Bakhtin's insight gives us a way of thinking about how Carol keeps the sociological function of the novel alive through her conversational modes.

So, what is conversation? Quite simply, it is a mutual exchange—usually verbal—a social and cultural practice which is essentially relational. A linguist's definition would be "Conversation is an intersubjective construction of meaning and social order" (Schegloff 542), or, as one of Carol's male protagonists remarks, "Talking isn't just words" ("Milk," *Collected Stories* 392). And how right he is. Words are only the signals for a whole network of relations—intellectual, affective, but essentially *social*. The closer we look into Carol's work, the more dazzling examples we find of different conversational modes. In the fictions we might consider two women speaking confidentially, or women's group conversation (perfect examples of women's "duetting" with their collaborative harmonious interaction, as opposed to male "duelling"). There is the animated conversation between women and men in the bravura performance at Larry's dinner party, which contrasts with those weary conversations between older married couples after years of "too much sorrowful sharing" (*Collected Stories* 386). Then there's the "intimacy of voice" when a narrator like Reta Winters in *Unless* speaks out of the fiction to the reader, and perhaps most fascinatingly when in her non-fiction Carol speaks directly to an audience (as in "Narrative Hunger," which was first delivered as a lecture and later published) or when she invites her readers to engage with her in speculation about Jane Austen's life. Carol mimes a wide variety of conversational modes, mainly but not exclusively women's, always alert to transformations in the shift from speech to writing. She is a virtuoso interpreter of spoken language and what lies beneath in those half-articulated revelations which would be indicated in speech by a sideward glance or a smile. Her "conversations" are complex constructions which oscillate between authenticity and artifice, a quality that Ellen Levy catches exactly in her description of Shieldsian discourse "with its occasionally transparent indicativeness and its more often inflected figurative indetermination" (Levy 198).

As readers we do not necessarily notice how often Carol uses metaphors to effect that shift of emphasis from realism into the spaces of the imagination. And my first example is perhaps the most startling: it is the silent conversation between the party of deaf-mutes in the restaurant at the end of *Small Ceremonies*, where Judith Gill has gone with her husband Martin for a celebratory meal. The setting is realistic enough, but it is the unreality of the visual spectacle of their animated body language that enthralls Judith. She watches their silent conversation reaching a crescendo over a fillet of sole in "a mad flurry of wrists and flying fingers" which she transforms through poetic imagery into a lyric display of "the shapes of birds, flowers, and butterflies," then resolves that "mad flurry" into order as "the shape of a private alphabet of air"(*Small Ceremonies* 178). Not only does Judith *use* metaphor but the scene itself is a metaphor for what conversation is: an animated mutual exchange. It is via that imaginative metaphorical thinking that Judith apprehends the lives of those others: "I am expanded by the surreal and passionate language of their speechlessness. We revolve together" (179). Glancing at her husband who is watching Judith instead of the deaf-mutes, she recognizes the difference between them, which may be a male/female difference: "He has no need of the bizarre," but what he does need is Judith as "translator" of that silent language, "a reporter of visions he can't see for himself" (179). The language glides easily between everyday social context of the meal and Judith's insights into the deaf-mutes' conversation together with her own role as translator and creator, which is surely an image of the writer. The literal and the figurative mesh together, for Judith knows that soon Martin will pay the bill and say, "Ready, Judith?" and she "of course, will smile back and say: 'Yes'" (179). The novel ends with a reassuring return to a familiar domestic framework and ordinary conversation. This mode of metaphorical thinking, which Françoise Defromont has explored in the writings of Virginia Woolf and Hélène Cixous, is also a striking feature of Carol's writing, "as if writing, thinking and living were just one continuous whole" (Defromont 119). As Reta Winters says, "Those human mysteries—cleaning my house, fantasizing about the lives of other people—keep me company, keep me alert" (*Unless* 109).

I have looked at this passage in detail because metaphorical thinking allows Shields to introduce dimensions of the unspoken into conversation, and it is also an important element in what I have called her *écriture féminine*. Carol Shields and Hélène Cixous? This might look like an unlikely pairing between Carol and that polemical French feminist whose most famous text "The Laugh of the Medusa" was published in French and translated into English in the mid-1970s. At least it is unlikely until we consider how they both use metaphorical language to explore the affective dimensions of women's difference and how they share the same aspirations for women's writing. Shields does not write *like* Cixous, and Cixous herself says, "It is impossible to define a feminine practice of writing . . . which doesn't mean that it doesn't exist" (253). We cannot be certain that Carol even read Cixous though she was reading a lot of postmodern theory in the 1980s,[1] but what I am saying is that they both view women's writing through the same prism, and that they both write versions of *écriture féminine*. Cixous begins "Medusa" with a clarion call: "I shall speak about women's writing: *about what it will do*. Woman must write her self: must write about women and bring women to writing, from which they have been driven away as violently as from their bodies" (245). Carol says: "As a woman who has elected a writing life, I am interested in writing away the invisibility of women's lives, looking at writing as an act of redemption" ("A View" 27–28). She and Cixous share the same sense of rebelliousness against masculine writing and what Carol calls its "phantom set of rules" ("Arriving Late" 246), and they both talk about the "privileged relationship with the voice" (Cixous 251) that women writers share. They are also angry at the structural subordination of women—for Cixous, women are the "repressed of culture" (248) and Carol's Reta Winters protests at how "women are dismissed and excluded from the most primary of entitlements" (*Unless* 99). Carol, however, does not share Cixous's incendiary politics nor her utopianism; even Danielle Westerman, that elderly French feminist in *Unless* whose memoirs Reta is translating, is disappointed that women's "big step forward" (*Unless* 251) will not occur in her lifetime. Writing about North American white middle class women, Carol's view is rather more grounded in the everyday, for her ardent feminism coexists alongside her domesticity. Yet, despite her realistic recognition of constraints, Carol herself remained determinedly optimistic about women's writing and *what it will do*: "We have wonderful women writers here in Canada, England, the United States, India. . . . And their work is an oeuvre; it has a different shape to it, and it's not going to fit with the old formula of novels. Women's writing is going to remake our literature and make it whole, I think" (Wachtel 175).

As for "writing the female body" as Cixous had urged, sometimes Carol does that explicitly as with the childbirth scene in *The Stone Diaries*, but she also does it metaphorically in the conversation scene between Reta Winters and Gwen Reidman in *Unless*.[2] Meeting for lunch in Baltimore when Reta is on a book promotion tour, she is alarmed to see her old friend dressed in "what looked like large folds of unstitched, unstructured cloth" (*Unless* 94) and she wonders for one awful moment if Gwen has been ill or undergoing chemotherapy. In this salmon-coloured shroud, Gwen looks a bit like Cixous's "uncanny stranger on display" (Cixous 250) whose body has been confiscated from her, and it functions as a metaphor for Gwen's malaise: her erasure as a woman and her condition of abjection. That unspoken affective dimension runs as undercurrent to the two women's conversation, amplified by Reta's anecdote about Gwen's grief and anger at having had her navel closed by a plastic surgeon many years ago, and her noticing now how sad Gwen looks and how she does not congratulate Reta on winning the Offenden Prize. Elizabeth Reimer has brilliantly analyzed the "Scarf" conversation as "an economy of femininity" in this book, focusing on the risky project of gift giving and on the women's broken empathetic dialogue. All I shall add is that this looks to me like "an affective economics of pain" (Ahmed 62), which voices the theme of female neediness and feminist protest. It might seem as if we are overhearing women duetting as they both admire the beautiful silk scarf (which Reta has actually bought for her daughter), but then comes the shock as Gwen appropriates the scarf and slips it into her plastic bag, saying "Thank you, darling Reta, thank you. You don't know what you've given me today" (97). With Reta's unspoken reply, "But I did, I did," the focus suddenly shifts from the conversation with Gwen to Reta's direct address to the reader with the question, "But what does it amount to?" If it makes someone happy, does it really matter who receives the gift? She launches into a brief analysis of sexual power politics, referring to the silenced voices of her mother, her mother-in-law, and her three daughters as their inheritors, summing up as "None of us was going to get what we wanted." The next chapter engages in an imaginary debate with the reader: *But we've come so far*; that's the thinking. So far, compared with fifty or a hundred years ago. Well, no, we've arrived at the new millennium and we haven't 'arrived' at all" (99).[3] The scarf episode provides a specific painful example, and it's within that wider perspective of women's needy condition, "reaching out blindly with a grasping hand but not knowing how to ask for what we don't even know we want" (98) that Reta is able to adopt a compassionate view which converts Gwen's theft into a gift. That topic of women's wanting (not "lack" in a Freudian sense) is one to which Carol returns repeatedly. As she commented in 2002, "Women in the twenty-first century haven't had much practice at expressing our wants. I think we can hardly do it as women . . . I suppose it's the not being able to complete that sentence, ['I want'] not knowing what we want or deserve. It always comes down to that, of course, for women: What we deserve and what's good enough for us" (Wachtel 161–62).

By contrast, Carol often presents women speaking *à deux* in mutually supportive ways, as in the brief conversation over coffee on the back porch between Judith Gill and her friend Nancy Krantz in *Small Ceremonies* (169–70), which provides an exemplary instance of the redemptive power of female friendships. Again, Carol is dealing with an affective economics of pain, but as she traces this conversational arc, it moves from the impersonal dimensions of aphorism and anecdote to the revelation of these women's painful family memories, to end with a moment of intimacy and mutual deliverance from private demons. Beginning with Nancy's pronouncement—needlessly harsh, it might appear—"Living meanly is the greatest sin. . . . It thins the blood. Cuts out the heart," the two women swap "frugality stories," taking turns to tell about a prosperous Montreal lawyer who used to buy all his clothes at the Salvation Army outlet, and then about a woman who travelled home on the subway after her mastectomy operation, "With a great white bandage where her left breast had been." This is another classic duet structure, with one woman speaking the main part and the other making supportive noises: "Terrible, terrible," breathes Judith, and "'That's awful,' Nancy says in a shocked whisper." Pursuing what we might call a thematic development, the narrative kernel below the surface begins to emerge with Judith's cautious confession that the woman on the subway was her own mother, to which Nancy responds with her matching revelation that the man with the second-hand suits was her own father. Through this sharing of secrets, the women have "for a moment, transcended abstractions," focusing instead on the particularities of their own and each other's experiences. Their intimate sharing has enabled them to take a distance from their secret pain as if they have made "a sort of pledge," united in their "refusal to be stunned by the accidents of genes or the stopped-up world of others." Locke sums up what Carol has represented so delicately in this feminine version of dialogue: "Duets are inherently interactive, almost as interactive as dancing. What they do involve, at their deepest level, is two beings working together to locate, hence to share and express, some sort of personal enjoyment or meaning" (Locke 106).

Collectively Carol's women also enjoy gossip. In *Unless* Reta and her three friends meet for their Tuesday morning coffee get-together at the Orange Blossom Tea Room, where incidentally women's bodies feature again: "We talk about our bodies, our vanities, our deepest desires" (120). The socio-linguist Jenifer Coates describes all-women conversation as having "as its chief goal the maintenance of good social relationships" (Coates 202). She outlines the formal structure of such conversations, using a musical analogy with the exposition of theme, followed by its development and recapitulation, possibly ending with a coda; she also analyzes the conversational strategies women frequently use like questions, supportive minimal responses, personal anecdotes, all signifying a collaborative negotiation and shared feelings. Reta's friends' conversation can be analyzed according to that model. Someone introduces the topic of "trust": "How do I know my bicycle [parked outside the window] won't be stolen?" and the three others try in turn to reassure her: "Because this is Orangetown;" "Because school's in session;" or (with a touch of irony) "Because it's a twenty-year-old bike . . . Not that it isn't a terrific model." The topic develops incrementally, as they all contribute examples of scary possibilities from road rage attacks to planes crashing into houses to a madman coming into the café "right this minute brandishing a sword" (77). "Trust" gradually shifts to "distrust," which is underlined by Reta's final comment that we are disabused of trust "one second after birth. I'm sure of it" (77). There are clearly two levels here: the general and the personal. The theoretical situations these women rehearse find their focus in Reta's worries about her daughter Norah living on the street in Toronto, and though nobody actually mentions it, this conversation provides a space where "the speakers work together to sort out what they feel" (Ahmed 206).

Carol also introduces a metacritical dimension on conversational modes via Reta's comments on that little connective word "So," which is the chapter title. This word can be spelled in a variety of ways ("So" or "So-oo-oo" or even "Soo-ooo-oo") indicating the inflection of a voice and the context in which "so" is being used, highlighting the different aspects of a word's "socio-verbal intelligibility" (Bakhtin 277). "So" is "what people say when they are about to introduce a narrative into the conversation or when they are clearing a little space so that you can begin a story yourself. It can be sung to different tunes, depending on the circumstances" (74). Reta likens "so" to "the oboe, signalling the A pitch to the strings. So, where do we go from here?" Bakhtin refers to a similar phenomenon when he talks about "the dialogic orientation of a word among other words which creates new and significant artistic potential in discourse," arguing that words are the "living dialogic threads" through which any utterance derives its "stylistic profile" (Bakhtin 276). Shields's chapter is full of phrases beginning with "So," such as "So, is there anything new?" or "So what!" and ending with "So it goes" (78). We are reminded again of the sophisticated playfulness of her writing—"an inquiry into language held in an envelope of language" ("Arriving" 251)—but there is no break between the conversational and the theoretical: "We never think about the aboutness of talk; we just talk" (78).

A different metacritical meditation on conversation, this time between a man and a woman alone, is introduced in the short story "Milk Bread Beer Ice" (*Collected Stories* 382–94), where instead of that freely flowing interchange between women, here the two characters are caught in a mesh of silence, broken only by occasional "idle questions and observations" (387). Carol once commented (in relation to *Happenstance*) that she was very interested in "the silences between people, the acceptable silences between people. I wanted to write about two people who were more or less happily married, but who were in fact strangers to each other and always would be, and about the value of the strangeness" (Wachtel 44). That is the territory which she is exploring in her short story about a middle-aged couple, Barbara and Peter Cormin from Toronto, who are on their fifth day of driving through a rocky desert landscape in Texas on their way to an estate auction in Houston. This story belongs to the genre of domestic fiction in the realist tradition, but just as its title is both banal and mysterious, so the narrative towards the end slips away from realism into an unexpected moment of redemption and reconciliation which illuminates all that "below-the-surface stuff" which is embedded in a long married relationship.

Focused almost entirely through Barbara's perspective and rendered through her indirect discourse, the story opens unpromisingly enough with her question to Peter, "What's the difference between a gully and a gulch?" This seemingly innocuous question, referring ostensibly to the geological features of the landscape they are passing through, is quickly shadowed by the omniscient narrator's remark that "These are the first words to pass between them in over an hour, this laconic, idle, unhopefully offered, trivia-contoured question" (382). Indeed, as she expects, Peter with his mind concentrated on driving through the drizzle, does not answer: "Two minutes pass. Five minutes," and the woman is left sitting beside her husband in silence, filling the wordless space with her busy interior monologue, speculating alternately on words like "drizzle" and "bruine" and "Chateau d'eau" as they drive past a water tower, for "Almost all her conversations are with herself." In a story which is structured on the oppositions between speech and silence, mobility and stasis, togetherness and isolation, it would seem that gullies and gulches are not so very different from each other, both being ravines cut by rivers into rock; in this context, Barbara's question reads like her sly insinuation of the gap between herself and her husband. What she does not hope for is any response from Peter, yet surprisingly after a long silence (five pages later in the story) Peter does answer her question, "Not unkindly, not even impatiently: 'A gully's deeper, I think'" (386). Ironically he is wrong, but far more significantly, his response is the sign of a hidden dialogic connection between them, though he is not interested as Barbara is in "the little fates and accidents a conversation can provide" (387). This reminds me of Locke's account of the distinction which the linguist Deborah Tannen made between "men's tendency to use language as a vehicle for the transmission of information in factual, newslike bulletins" which she called "report talk" and women's more affiliative mode which she labelled "rapport talk." As he commented, "Tannen helped readers appreciate some *linguistic* reasons why men and women, particularly married couples, might fail to communicate" (Locke 7).

But are Barbara and Peter failing to communicate? In her more subtle analysis, Carol takes the topic of conversation a stage further, as Barbara silently ponders the different conversational roles that she and Peter have taken up during their thirty-three years of marriage: "There was breakfast talk and dinner talk and lively hurried telephone chatter in between," sometime with her in the role of ingénue and sometimes as trickster exerting subversive strategies of control. That train of thought is prompted by her memory of a kind elderly aunt's comment: "Marriage can be defined as a lifelong conversation" (388), which is given an ironical twist when Barbara also recalls that she and Peter had their longest conversation in a marriage counsellor's office when they were contemplating a separation: "The histories they separately recounted were as detailed as the thick soft novels people carry with them to the beach in the summer. Every story elicited a counter-story" (390). From that outpouring of words they emerged with an awareness that marriage was "at best, a flawed and gappy narrative," but still together. We are presented here with an alternative version of the popular *True Romance* cliché: "*Just the two of us, this paradise*," translated into a particular private narrative as Barbara remembers something that Peter had said about their trip which she had forgotten: "We can break in the car and have a few days together, just the two of us" (392). There is no mention of paradise, yet what remains unstated but powerful is a life narrative of emotions intertwined.

At the end of the day they drive off the interstate highway on to quiet narrow roads in search of a motel, passing through little towns which "have seen better days" with their crumbling sidewalks, lovely old houses neglected and deteriorating, boarded-up shops, a world where everything is shrunken, reduced, and diminished. Only then do they see the homemade advertisement signs inscribed with the four words "MILK ICE BREAD BEER," repeated with variations in every town they pass through: "BEER ICE BREAD MILK," "BREAD BEER MILK ICE" and later still, "BEER MILK ICE BREAD" (393). Though these printed words are signs drawn from a widely understood cultural code of homely products, their referential function is suspended as Barbara and Peter take it in turn to read the words aloud, chanting them like "a rhythmic spell and counter-spell." Their word game could not feasibly be called a dialogue, but we might see it as an alternative cross-gendered form of duetting, a patterned interaction between the two protagonists.[4] As the words become defamiliarized, so their function is transformed: "Cryptic messages, they seem designed to comfort and confuse Peter and Barbara Cormin with loops of flawed recognition and to deliver them to a congenial late-evening punchiness" (393). The promise made here is fulfilled in the final paragraph, where "surprisingly, the short unadorned sounds . . . take on expanded meaning," opening up "space for strangeness to enter" ("Segue," *Collected Stories* 17)—or in this case, for the deeply familiar to emerge from the edges of consciousness. In silence, Barbara contemplates the enchanted landscape of a "lesser world," the features of which she realizes that she loves, "its weather and depth, its exact chambers, its lost circuits, its covered pleasures, its submerged pattern of communication" (394). Through the strategy of metaphorical thinking (for this "lesser world" is a mirror image of their marriage) the silences between husband and wife are redeemed to become the "acceptable silences" within a long relationship where an ongoing affective dialogue below the verbal surface reaffirms and gives fresh meaning to the old-fashioned adage, "Marriage can be defined as a lifelong conversation."

Turning now to the full-dress performance of male–female conversation with Larry's dinner party, we see how Carol interweaves rituals of sociability with the idiosyncrasies of guests' individual voices, and Larry's interior monologues. As she once commented: "I love the *idea* of parties. I love the idea of people gathering under a roof, strangers or friends or both, where there's a flow of food, a flow of talk, movement, human movement, where certain possibilities are produced that don't occur in our non-party lives" (Wachtel 85). The conversation proceeds realistically via multiple topics, interruptions, and digressions, but actually moving towards the unstated goal of Larry and Dorrie's reconciliation after fourteen years which is embedded within this conversational maze. Mindful of Carol's "Woolfian bias" ("A View" 27), I was reminded of Virginia Woolf's *boeuf en daube* dinner party in *To the*

Lighthouse, but actually there's very little spoken conversation there, for Woolf's emphasis is on what is unspoken. Certainly there are Woolfian echoes here, but really it is the voices which dominate. (Alex Ramon has traced similarities with Iris Murdoch's party conversations [Ramon 141–43], adding yet another layer to the intertextual densities of Carol's writing, but I cannot pursue that fascinating intertextual insight here.) A microanalysis would show the complexity of the sequence development with its changes of direction and narrative perspective, but I shall concentrate on what I think is the central conversational thematic, the topic of masculinity in crisis at the end of the twentieth century. The subject of changing gender roles is introduced by jokes made by his female guests about Larry's cooking, and someone (probably Beth, the feminist academic) is prompted to ask, "What's it like being a man these days?" (*Larry's Party* 316). Interestingly, as the conversation shifts between male and female voices, it is the men who sound diffident and the women who sound assertive, collaborating with each other as Shields tries to deconstruct traditional binaries between the sexes. The discussion opens out into a consideration of the changing cultural meanings of gender identities, as the four women—his sister, his two ex-wives, and his present partner—all take turns telling intimate stories of their mothers' advice on how to treat a husband. So they carry the topic forward, transforming social history into lived experience, gliding quite smoothly beyond the question of masculinity into far more dangerous personal territory when the heavily pregnant Beth ("Sperm bank. I've wanted a baby for years" 326) announces that she is planning to take an academic job in Toronto where, as a single mother, she would have Larry to help her to look after the baby. To this Larry responds with a surprisingly loud "Oh." It is that conversation stopper, likened to the progress of "a small marble rolling slowly across the sudden silence at the table" (327), which prepares for the dramatic shift beyond realism into what Carol has called "the subjunctive mode" ("Arriving" 247) with the silent moment of mutual recognition between Larry and Dorrie as they exchange smiles across the candlelit dinner table. Enclosed in that shimmering mirage, with everyone else on the outside arrayed "as though in a holographic image," realism gives way to romance as Larry and Dorrie find themselves "in this alternative vision of reality, partners in a long marriage, survivors of old quarrels long since mended" (328). It is a difficult manoeuvre to modulate back into a realistic mode, but Shields manages it via the conversation over the chocolate cake, sustained by the women who refloat the evening with their trivial anecdotes, doing what Woolf would call their feminine duty of "being nice." During coffee, the narrative focus shifts from group to group, creating a realistically polyphonic effect, but the most significant conversation is between Larry and Dorrie, in what Bakhtin would call "double voicing," where "another dialogue is embedded . . . one as yet unfolded" (Bakhtin 325), and where the key words are "lost" and "found."

The dinner party scene ends there, and the novel finishes with a wittily multivoiced ending, detailing all the guests' thank yous the next day. They have to communicate by note, email, fax, and voicemail, for Larry (and we have to assume Dorrie with him) is not answering the phone—just like Fay MacLeod and Tom Avery in *The Republic of Love*, who spend their honeymoon in Tom's apartment with the phone off the hook, deaf to the voices of others.

Moving from fiction to her non-fictional prose, I shall glance at Carol's conversational modes when speaking in her own voice in her public address "Narrative Hunger and the Overflowing Cupboard" and her Jane Austen biography.[5] Christl Verduyn has done an excellent analysis of both these texts, showing how she "take[s] empirical facts and transform[s] them through speculation into wide-reaching conclusions" (73). Taking a different approach, I am going to focus on "intimacy of voice" to show how, within what is essentially a solo performance, Carol invents a mode which contains the potential for dialogue, inviting a responsive understanding from her listeners/readers. Again, we hear the inimitable Shields voice—unassuming, endlessly surprised by oddity, combining serious thinking with feminine playfulness, at the same time rescuing femininity from stereotypical "charm"—always remembering Reta's dismissive description of "charm" as "nothing but crumpled tissue paper" (*Unless* 29). Carol turns the "feminine" into a positive attribute, where Locke's concept of the "duet" can be extended to her attitude to her listeners/readers as she positions them within a framework of relationality and empathy.

Cixous commented that in public speaking, for a woman, "Her speech, even when 'theoretical' or political, is never simple or linear or objectified" (251), and Carol's lecture exemplifies this in the rhetorical strategies which she uses. These include metaphor, as in the title of the lecture, where "Narrative Hunger" is evidently a metaphor for her key thematic of storytelling as a basic human need, and the "Overflowing Cupboard" for the vast variety of raw story material in the world which is always tumbling out at us in a disordered mass. Early in her discussion, Carol explains the need for metaphor rather than abstract discourse: "Language, which is useful in the province of the intellect, is a relatively clumsy vehicle in the expression of emotion and of narrative movement" ("Narrative Hunger" 23). As an interesting parallel with the first passage from *Small Ceremonies* which I discussed, here a metaphorical approach allows her to situate theoretical thinking in the context of everyday experience. Carol also copies the surface features of spoken conversation, for there are lots of personal anecdotes, domestic images, phrases like "I hope you'll agree with me," and her favourite device—the question and answer, indicating her acute awareness of interaction with her audience:

> Do we accept the fact that fiction is not strictly mimetic? . . . Yes, you will say, or perhaps no, and your response will depend on the culture you live in, the era into which you were born, and the width or narrowness of your aesthetic or moral responses. (26)

From there she moves into more formal theoretical discourse about realism and postmodernism, women's writing, political correctness, and the need to reassess the proper territory of fiction: "Our narrative cupboard is far from being bare, but it seems it needs restocking" (34). Interestingly, in the latter part of the lecture when she knows she has her audience with her, there are fewer questions and more direct statements. The lecture ends in a manner which combines the personal, the relational, and the explicitly literary as she appeals to "what many of us value most in narrative: the interior voice. Reflecting, thinking, connecting, ticking, bringing forward a view of a previously locked room, and, to paraphrase John Donne, making that little room an everywhere" (35–36)—which is also a final comment on her own art as a novelist.

In her Jane Austen biography, Carol sometimes adopts a mode which is closer to gossip, as she persuades her readers to engage with her in speculation about enigmas in the narrative of Jane Austen's life. I am thinking about the relationship with her mother, mothers and daughters being a very important topic for Carol: "Jane Austen chose to focus her writing on daughters rather than mothers . . . but nevertheless mothers are essential in her fiction" (*Jane Austen* 15). And motherhood was an essential component of Carol's own identity: "I couldn't have been a novelist without being a mother" (Giardini R1). Indeed, she introduces her biography by affectionate reference to the joint paper that she and Anne Giardini gave at a Jane Austen conference in Richmond, Virginia, in 1996: "Our talk centered on what Anne and I called the 'politics of the glance'" (*Jane Austen* 2). It is that feminine glance—"even a half glance able to shame or empower or redirect the sensibilities of others"—that Carol translates into words in her discussion of Jane Austen's mother. How does she do it? Perhaps the first question to ask is one behind the narration which challenges the very project of biography. What kind of a woman was Mrs. Austen? We know very little about her, though Carol is struck by Jane's account of how when she was very ill, she would sometimes rest "on three sitting-room chairs lined up together, leaving the sofa for her mother." Scenting a mystery here, Carol seizes our attention too: "What can we make of this improbable scene?" (16). In a series of questions all focused on the sofa, she tries to peel away layers of domesticity to uncover "all that below-the-surface stuff" which would reveal the secret of this seemingly inexplicable behaviour. Did her mother not notice? Was Jane indulging in some strange kind of martyrdom? Did her mother have a prior claim to that sofa? Or was it that Mrs. Austen was selfish and insensitive? Our interest is stimulated by these unfinished story fragments, but the adverse judgment that Mrs. Austen was "a demanding and self-absorbed woman" is the one which seems to have prevailed historically.

In true gossipy style, Carol then slides sideways into a discussion of Mrs. Bennet in *Pride and Prejudice* and her attitude to daughters, wondering if "we as readers [have] been completely fair to Mrs. Bennet" (17), before turning back to Jane Austen's mother, "who may or may not have had a spirit similar to Mrs. Bennet's" (18). In the absence of facts, digression via a fictional mother casts doubt on the popular negative view of Mrs. Austen. As a biographer Carol is neither forgiving nor judgmental, insisting that Mrs. Austen's character and the meaning of the "improbable" sofa scene can never be determined. As she said elsewhere in reference to this particular incident, "We don't know. It's funny about families, which is what she writes about, and a family is ultimately covered by curtains. We don't know how they operate or what goes on inside families" (Wachtel 129). All this is very like gossip in which Carol's voice persuades the reader to participate, for like Alice Munro, she challenges "what people want to know. Or expect to know. Or anticipate knowing. And as profoundly, what I think I know" (Boyce and Smith 227).

To conclude, as a woman and as a writer, Carol was very much engaged with telling and listening, trying to make sense of what is only half-heard or seemingly incomprehensible, trusting always in "the connections that make our lives worth living, that series of conversations tipping one way and then the other" as she wrote in an email to Blanche Howard in 2002 (Howard and Howard 521). Through it all runs the energizing narrative self-consciousness of a woman writer who believed that we need "to place our own stories beside those of others: to compare, weigh, judge, forgive, and to find an angle of vision that renews our image of where we are in the world" ("Narrative" 21).

NOTES

1. Carol's scepticism about theory is evident in a letter to Blanche Howard in 1988: "I have tried reading critical theory, but it leaks out of my head as fast as I pour it in, and besides, I distrust a good deal of it" (*Howard and Howard* 180).

2. This episode appeared first as a short story, "A Scarf" in *Dressing Up for the Carnival*, and was then resituated in a slightly altered version as a chapter in the novel, within a quite explicitly feminist context; the chapter is called "Otherwise."

3. Reta goes on to speak about how women's writing has been sidelined by male critics, and disturbingly, a recent article in the *New York Times Book Review* could have been written by Reta. Entitled "The Second Shelf," it asks the question, "Are there different rules for men and women in the world of literary fiction?" (Wolitzer 6). Meg Wolitzer, the writer of the article, concludes that there are; in other words, to quote Shields, "we haven't 'arrived' at all."

4. In my analysis I have been influenced by Roland Barthes's essay "The Rhetoric of the Image", though Barthes's Panzani spaghetti advertisement is composed of visual image and linguistic message, where the verbal text anchors the image; the opposite happens here where, in the absence of a visual image, the words become floating signifiers. Marta Dvořák analyzes similar instances of Shields's defamiliarization of the building blocks of language in her essay "Disappearance and 'the Vision Multiplied': Writing as Performance" in *Carol Shields and the Extra-Ordinary*.

5. "Narrative Hunger" was first given as an address by Carol Shields at her alma mater, Hanover College, Indiana, in September 1996 and then revised as the first essay in *Carol Shields, Narrative Hunger, and the Possibilities of Fiction*.

WORKS CITED

Ahmed, Sara. *The Cultural Politics of Emotion*. Edinburgh: Edinburgh University Press, 2004. Print.

Bakhtin, Mikhail. *The Dialogic Imagination: Four Essays by M. M. Bakhtin*, ed. Michael Holquist, trans. Caryl Emerson and Michael Holquist. Austin: University of Texas Press, 1983. Print.

Barthes, Roland. "The Rhetoric of the Image." In *Image–Music–Text*, trans. Stephen Heath. New York: Hill and Wang, 1977: 142–48. Print.

Boyce, Pleuke, and Ron Smith. "A National Treasure: Interview with Alice Munro." *Meanjin* 54.2 (1995): 222–32. Print.

Cixous, Hélène. "The Laugh of the Medusa." In *New French Feminisms*, ed. Elaine Marks and Isabelle de Courtivron. Brighton: Harvester Wheatsheaf, 1981: 245–64. Print.

Coates, Jennifer. "Gossip Revisited: Language in All-Female Groups." In *Language and Gender: A Reader*, 2nd ed. Oxford: Wiley-Blackwell, 2011: 199–223. Print.

Coates, Jennifer, and Pia Pichler. Language and Gender: A Reader. 2nd ed. Oxford: Wiley-Blackwell, 2011. Print.

Defromont, Françoise. "Metaphorical Thinking and Poetic Writing in Virginia Woolf and Hélène Cixous." In *The Body and the Text: Hélène Cixous, Reading and Teaching*, ed. Helen Wilcox, Keith McWatters, Ann Thompson, and Linda R. Williams. Brighton: Harvester Wheatsheaf, 1990: 114–25. Print.

Dvořák, Marta. "Disappearance and 'the Vision Multiplied': Writing as Performance." In *Carol Shields and the Extra-Ordinary*, ed. Marta Dvořák and Manina Jones. Montreal and Kingston: McGill-Queen's University Press, 2007: 223–37.

Giardini, Anne. "My Mother's Steady Gaze." *Globe and Mail Weekend Review* 19 July 2003: R1. Print.

Howard, Blanche, and Allison Howard, eds. *A Memoir of Friendship: The Letters between Carol Shields and Blanche Howard*. Toronto: Penguin Canada, 2007. Print.

Levy, Ellen. "'Artefact Out of Absence': Reflection and Convergence in the Fiction of Carol Shields." In *Carol Shields and the Extra-Ordinary*, ed. Marta Dvořák and Manina Jones. Montreal and Kingston: McGill-Queen's University Press, 2007: 191–204. Print.

Locke, John D. *Duels and Duets: Why Men and Women Talk So Differently*. Cambridge: Cambridge University Press, 2011. Print.

Ramon, Alex. "A Literary Foremother: Iris Murdoch and Carol Shields." In *Iris Murdoch: A Reassessment*, ed. Anne Rowe. Houndmills, Basingstoke, UK: Palgrave Macmillan, 2006: 136–47. Print.

Schegloff, Emmanuel A. "Whose Text? Whose Context?" In *Language and Gender: A Reader*, 2nd ed. Oxford: Wiley-Blackwell, 2011: 533–47. Print.

Shields, Carol. "Arriving Late: Starting Over." In *How Stories Mean*, ed. John Metcalf and J. R. (Tim) Struthers. Erin, ON: Porcupine's Quill, 1993: 244–51. Print.

———. *Carol Shields: The Collected Stories*. Toronto: Random House Canada, 2003. Print.

———. *Jane Austen*. New York and Toronto: Viking Penguin, 2001. Print.

———. *Larry's Party*. 1997. London: Fourth Estate, 1998. Print.

———. "Narrative Hunger and the Overflowing Cupboard." In *Carol Shields, Narrative Hunger, and the Possibilities of Fiction*, ed. Edward Eden and Dee Goertz. Toronto: University of Toronto Press, 2003: 19–36. Print.

———. *Small Ceremonies*. 1976. London: Fourth Estate, 1995. Print.

———. *Unless.* Toronto: Random House Canada, 2002. Print.

———. "A View from the Edge of the Edge." In *Carol Shields and the Extra-Ordinary*, ed. Marta Dvořák and Manina Jones. Montreal and Kingston: McGill-Queen's University Press, 2007: 17–29. Print.

Sterne, Laurence. *The Life and Opinions of Tristram Shandy.* 1759–67. London: Penguin English Library, 1967. Print.

Verduyn, Christl. "(Es)Saying It Her Way: Carol Shields as Essayist." In *Carol Shields and the Extra-Ordinary*, ed. Marta Dvořák and Manina Jones. Montreal and Kingston: McGill-Queen's University Press, 2007: 59–79. Print.

Wachtel, Eleanor. *Random Illuminations: Conversations with Carol Shields.* Fredericton: Goose Lane, 2007. Print.

Wolitzer, Meg. "The Second Shelf." *New York Times Book Review* 1 April 2012: 6–7. Print.

Guilt, Guile, and Ginger in *Small Ceremonies*

Elizabeth Waterston

Last winter in Florida I unceremoniously bombarded my friends with *Small Ceremonies*. I wanted to see how readers not familiar with Carol Shields's work would respond to this book, her first published novel. They ritually responded, "What's with this character Furlong? So he is an American draft dodger—Why should that seem so hilarious to a Canadian author?"

Oh, but—"Carol Shields was not strictly a Canadian author when she published this book in 1976. She had spent the better part of her life as an American citizen . . . . "

"The better part—yeah, I'll go for that!"

So we brewed a little American tea (warm water and a tea bag), and they began again. "Anyway, what kind of a book is this? Right at the central point, this woman Judith spends the month of January in bed with the flu?"

"It's Canadian," I reply. "And it's dated. In the 1970s, before flu shots were common, we all spent most of January in bed with the flu."

So I have garnered at least two questions about *Small Ceremonies*: "What kind of book is it?" and "Is it Canadian?" The question of "kind" is easy. It is a wry, comic novel set in a small university community, like Robertson Davies's Salterton novels. It is a satiric novel about a group of academic people who are all writing novels. Prepare for a shock: each of them is plagiarizing another writer's work.

Judith Gill, in England with her husband Martin on an exchange year, discovers and reads the dusty manuscripts hidden by her British host in a dark cupboard. Back home in Canada, in a creative writing seminar, experiencing writer's block, she remembers the plot of one of those manuscripts and fleshes it out into a novel of her own. Well—her settings, her characters—but definitely the Englishman's plot.

Furlong Eberhardt, the professor who runs the creative writing seminar, is himself a novelist; he too at this point is experiencing a block. Judith has told him to shred her submission; instead he reads it, adapts her plot—and turns it into a wildly successful novel. Radio interviews! Offers of a movie rights contract! Judith, belatedly reading his work, attacks Furlong furiously for his theft—of the work she has based on a stolen plot.

Finally, the Englishman who originated the story comes to Ottawa, en route to New York to see his publisher. He also has now written a much heralded novel, but has come to confess that he based its plot on letters about the Gill family written by Judith's son to his daughter. "You stole our lives!" Judith's husband cries.

"Oh no, no, no, no, no!" the British professor protests—but he has indeed done so. To complete the circle, Judith asks him whether he has read Furlong's now-popular work. She worries that he may recognize the embers of his own discarded failure of a book. "Cracking good story!" he replies, obliviously, and swings away to New York and fame.

Furlong, the teacher of creative writing, says, "Do you know there are only seven distinct plots in all of literature?" to evade Judith's accusation of theft. But it is hard to think of other stories with the same configuration as *Small Ceremonies*. Maybe the archetypal romance plot of circular linkage: A is in love with B, B loves C, who hankers after A? But the links among this circle of thieving writers have nothing to do with love. Each of the academic writers is contemptuous of the others.

This is a comedy of transgressions, not biblical but academic, small sins without retribution. Two of the plagiarists achieve success, and Judith, the initial thief, adjusts sociably to both the man whose plot she stole and the man who stole her plot. In the end, she even forgives herself: "I didn't actually go through with it. And I didn't profit from it the way Furlong has profited." The story of transgression ends with acceptance and sociability.

What, I may ask, is the connection between this plot and characters and the life story and nature of the author? I may indeed raise this question because it is raised conspicuously in the novel. Judith Gill, the narrator, is a biographer of Susanna Moodie, a British novelist who emigrated to Canada in 1832. Judith studies the themes of Moodie's flimsy romances in relation to her later life choices, before turning to Moodie's major work, *Roughing It in the Bush*. Judith stoutly insists, "an author's work should be read in the context of her life."

Furthermore, in *Small Ceremonies*, Judith objects scornfully to the critical position of a young colleague who airily ignores the life of an author when assessing his work. Roger Ramsay's doctoral dissertation "Furlong Eberhardt and Canadian Consciousness" proposes "to eschew the personality and beliefs of the author and concentrate instead on close textual analysis." Judith huffs, "Why would anyone set out to purify prose by obliterating the personality that had shaped it?" and scoffs, "How did this nonsense get past an examiner?" In contrast, Judith herself pries into the connections between Furlong Eberhardt's popular modern Canadian novels and his private life.

So I feel justified in similar prying and in taking a biographical approach. I watch, with some awe, Carol Shields, at the threshold of a fine career, concocting this odd plot about theft and creating this curious Judith character in 1975. She had already published two thin books of poetry, thanks to Frank Tierney and Glenn Clever, members of the English Department at the University of Ottawa who had established the admirable Borealis Press. She had sold three short stories, and she had written an unsuccessful mystery novel, sent to three publishers who rejected it but offered praise and encouragement. She had also taken graduate courses at the University of Ottawa, encouraged to do so by her husband, a professor in the Faculty of Engineering there. She had begun work on her MA in 1969 after the birth of her fifth child.

Yes, five children in ten years, 1958 to 1968. This scholar/writer was also a multi-mum. She had spent ten years of counting the nine months of gestation, waiting for the first cry of the new babe, "a hairpin scratching the sky" (to quote one of her poems). Then for another five years she had waited till all the children were off to school, while she worked sporadically on her master's thesis, "Susanna Moodie: Voice and Vision." She completed it in 1975: time for a little voice and vision of her own.

Now, every morning at eleven o'clock, in the hour before the five children came home demanding peanut butter sandwiches, she settled into writing *Small Ceremonies*. In those stolen moments before lunch, Shields created Judith Gill—a secret thief—and Furlong, another committer of theft.

My guess is that the *Small Ceremonies'* focus on small crime slipped into the book because Carol Shields was herself filled at the time with a typical contemporary female sense of guilt. Even when she was absorbed in her writing, she always harboured a twinge of worry that she should be doing the washing or reading books about parenting or planning the next birthday party: "Too small a crime to punish, but at the same time . . . too large to let go unacknowledged" (112). She was "shirking her responsibilities" in the watchword of the time. Shields displaced her sense of guilt and created a character that really was guilty—of small but real transgressions. She could have named her anti-hero Judith Guilt instead of Judith Gill.

As she told Eleanor Wachtel and other interviewers years later, "I wrote two pages a day and at the end of nine months I had a novel" (Wachtel 41; Terry Gross in 2002 on NPR, drawing on an 1984 interview, also on NPR). Another gestation, and the end this time was the birth of a good novel by a writer who was also a mother. The sense of the significance of a nine-months' block of time never leaves a graduate from motherdom, so the three neatly interlocked thefts of intellectual property are neatly packaged into a nine-month time frame, September to May, set up in three trimesters.

In the first chapters, titled "September," "October," and "November," as in any first trimester, the action is hidden, dimmed into Judith's flash-backs to the sabbatical in England, discovery of the hidden manuscript, and dreams of writing a novel.

Second trimester is usually a time of discomfort and disturbance and perhaps resentment. In December Judith begins and then abandons her novel and jealously watches Furlong on TV, serenely successful. January brings a descent into a limbo of illness. February finds fury at Furlong when Judith reads his book and recognizes her own plot. She survives the trimester, "doing my balancing act between humour and desperation" (123). She knows she "will get through it"—a six-month feeling!

The third trimester inevitably moves to emergence and happiness. In March Judith's husband Martin is publicly glorified as a creator. Spring bursts out in April, Furlong is granted forgiveness—"Poor Furlong. Dear Furlong!"—and Judith's young friend Ruthie St. Pierre goes into labour. Yes—the climax of this third trimester comes in a natural wonder-ful ending, and in May the baby joins in his parents' wedding party.

Having set up a nine-month structure, Shields has built in a subplot involving a literal pregnancy and birth. This adds a new theme: secrecy.

Not theft and guilt, but secrecy and guile. Ruthie St. Pierre, flower-child librarian, keeps her pregnancy secret from her partner, a leftover hippie, because he is opposed to commitment. Her secret swells to include others: Furlong furtively hides her in the apartment he shares with his mother; Judith's daughter Meredith stumbles on the secret and hides it from her mother. Furlong is also hiding his real name and his American origins. More secrets: Richard, Judith's son, has hidden the contents of his letters to the Sparlings' daughter in England; Judith hides from her husband Martin not only the memory of her secret prying into Sparling's manuscripts, but also the fact that she has found a mysterious stash in the drawer of Martin's desk. She deserves yet another name: not Judith Gill but Judith Guile.

More significantly, Martin Gill, professor of Renaissance literature, instead of preparing proper lectures on Milton, has been secretly weaving coloured wool into a tapestry representing the interwoven themes in Milton's *Paradise Lost*. I believe that this part of the story relates to Carol Shields's experience at the time, not as a mother, but as a writer. Martin, shielding his secret artwork, reflects Shields's situation as she wrote in those pre-lunch hours in her secret, obsessive creativity. Like Martin, weaving his tapestry, like every creator of fiction, she was living in a universe unavailable to the people surrounding her in the real world—even to her ever-supportive husband. Living her daily communal and familial life, she was also weaving something in the darkness of her subconscious, threading together themes and scenes in ways that must have surprised even herself, yet controlling the process by the shuttling synapses of a calculating artistry.

Carol Shields, beginning novelist, no doubt developed a necessary guile in tucking away the excitement—sometimes the frenzy—of creativity. Sometimes the mystery of creative work is hidden even from the writer; writers cannot discuss, let alone fully understand, the secrets of their writing experience. Shields must hide the progress of her work even from her husband—a stance presented in reverse in the little rift that threatens marital paradise in her novel.

So there really are two stories in *Small Ceremonies*. First is the literary plot about thieving writers and writings, a mystery story with small wiles and little red herrings, a gentle mystery with no blood on the carpet. Second is a story about secrecies and separateness at the hearth of close family and friends, again a story of aloneness moderated by warmth and humour. This is a double novel, into which Shields poured the essence of her two lives, as wife and mother, and as writer and solitary.

But wait—there is a third strand in Carol Shields's c.v. She was a mother, a writer—and, most recently, officially a Canadian. Born in Illinois, happily at college in Indiana, she had met western Canadian Donald Shields in Scotland while on an overseas term in the United Kingdom. She came back to Indiana to finish her undergraduate studies and to earn a bachelor of arts degree. Then she returned to her home in Illinois to wait for her reunion and marriage to Don, now on the threshold of his fine academic career. With him, Carol entered Canada in 1957 as a landed immigrant. She maintained that status for fourteen years. After a brief period in Vancouver, Don accepted a position in Ottawa. There, fourteen years later, in 1971, after adding five Canadian-born babies to the world, she went through the citizenship ceremony.

She became officially Canadian as a crucial era in Canadian literary history opened. She was experiencing a unique Canadian spring, like so many of us. In 1972 Margaret Atwood published both *Survival* and *Surfacing*. The next year my own *Survey: A Short History of Canadian Literature* was accepted as a text across the country in the new high school CanLit courses suddenly popping up on the curriculum. Schools were declaring Canada Day and all kinds of Canadian writers—not Furlong, of course, but Farley and others equally astonishing—came to high schools to discuss the need of "thinking Canadian." "What is Canada? What is Canadian literature?" were *the* hot topics in Canadian educational circles.

How did new-Canadian Carol Shields respond as a writer to all this Canadianness? First, she focused on Furlong, the phoney Canadian. As Furlong says, and Judith repeats, "Every writer uses the material that is at hand." At hand was the silly side of the new Canadianness, the world of people studying Furlong (Rudyard) Eberhardt. In many ways *Small Ceremonies* is an uproarious send-up of the hectic Canadian fever—raging like flu in academic circles in the mid-1970s.

Shields's ironic narrator Judith mocks Furlong's novels with their "Canadian theme" of pitiless storms and brave, simple sheltering homes: a redo of "roughing it in the bush." Furlong himself lives a precious apartment life with his doting American mother. Shields marks Furlong's focus on "Canadian consciousness" as false idolatry: she gives his popular book the title *Graven Images*. Though she mocks the pretentiousness of contemporary Canadian consciousness, Shields's tone is affectionate rather than acid: more the tone of the amused observer of Mariposa than the sharpness of a Sinclair Lewis or a Sherwood Anderson.

A more serious kind of nationalism appears in the focus on Susanna Moodie. Throughout the novel, Shields traces the intricate interlacing of

Judith Gill's life with that of the earlier Canadian woman. Mid-novel, when Judith lies in bed levelled by flu and fatigue, she recalls Susanna's moment of fierce, fate-resisting action and rises to resume control of her life and to attack Furlong and his deviousness. The details of Susanna Moodie's life as chronicled in *Roughing It in the Bush* include a rickety house, the perils of child-bearing, the tensions of marriage to the man she always refers to as "Moodie," the impinging of a wilderness world inhabited by bears, "Yankee" neighbours, and a frightening pitiable "Solitary." Awareness of these elements sharply accents Judith's own detailing of contemporary suburban life on "Beaver Place" (with never a beaver in sight, let alone a bear) and on the essential coziness of her family life and her interactions with friends and colleagues. Hers is a life of loving relations between the generations, and an assumption of fidelity in marriage. The balance of *Small Ceremonies* swings toward emphasis on optimism and warmth. Yet Judith echoes Moodie in self-mockery, insecurity, and in the shrewd wry tone of her acceptance of reality.

Susanna Moodie's manner and method also ratifies Shields's own tone and style. In her fierce commitment to writing, Moodie was a "fore-mother" (to use Lorraine McMullen's term) of modern Canadian women writers. Moodie's fierce resolve to chronicle specifically Canadian life rises from her conviction of the importance of writing, as well as from the sharpness of her perception of real experience. Canadian women writers in the 1970s lifted their own lives into similar sharp focus. Moodie's biting fidelity to her life as woman and writer had begun to reappear in the late 1960s work of Margaret Laurence and Alice Munro. Later writers including Jane Urquhart, Elizabeth Hay, and many others, maintaining Moodie's wry female perspective and creating their own versions of magic realism, would be buoyed by Shields's special variant of the Moodie manner.

Shields's life was in some ways more like Moodie's than were the lives of those other major writers. Shields, like Moodie, was a mid-life immigrant, though neither would have dreamt of thinking of herself that way. Both were locked into a life they were not born to, coping with an unfamiliar physical environment simultaneously with the predominant demands of marriage and motherhood. Both trailed with them a memory of a less-constricted, more elegant and privileged life.

Unlike Moodie, however, in the newly affluent life of twentieth-century Canada, Shields could experience and relish the small ceremonies surfacing in suburban academic life. Against the formlessness of Moodie's life in the "bush," leading eventually to madness, Shields pictures a modern Canadian woman bound to her community by seasonal rituals. These are wittily represented by the meals shared by Judith and her friends and family as the story progresses.

Some of these meals are borrowed from other cultures, like the British high tea that opens the story, some are American, like the elegant, rather pretentious lunch that Furlong offers (with a punch concocted from vodka, cranberry juice, and—his secret ingredient gleefully disclosed—ginger). The menu for each meal serves as a metaphor for the special rung of social living. There is a confessional lunch at a panelled men's club, shared with Judith's feisty feminist friend Nancy: two dry sherries and a curry. The English Department enjoys a buffet at the country home of the gentle chairman and his bossy wife (chunks of meat in wine sauce). A rigidly formal end-of-term party at the Faculty Club (roast beef, sliced very thin) is followed by two parties at the Gills': first an evening of lasagna and salad, organized to show the visiting professor from England what Canada is really like; and then a backyard wedding party, with homemade wine brought by the surprised new father, and a wedding cake decorated by romantic seventeen-year-old Meredith, with shells (for fertility).

I imagine Shields chuckling as she worked out these metaphorical menus. I remember her at an early Ottawa "Reappraisals" conference saying, "Writing fiction is like making soup"—and explaining the process, starting with "a nice meaty bone" and adding some spice. (Someday, I prophecy, someone will write a master's thesis on "Shields on Meals.")

The small Canadian ceremonies end with an elegant international meal. Mushrooms à la grèque lead to a Black Forest cake for dessert—with Thousand Island dressing on salad in between. Judith and Martin eat this dinner in amiable celebration of the success of his creative foray into theme-weaving. They consume the small glories of the newly global cuisine in a chic surreal revolving restaurant sky-high above their small city. A wide panorama spreads beneath them, but closer at hand is a group of people conferring in the silent mystery of hand signals. Judith explains their silent hilarity to her husband, saying of her own vantage point, "I am translator, reporter . . . a watcher, an outsider, whether I like it or not."

Carol Shields too is a translator, a watcher. A mature student at the fringes of academic life, she emerges in her first novel as a crafty comic chronicler of that life. We are left with her voice: wry, shrewd, ironic, yet loving and amused, translating, reporting. It will be part of the Canadian voice—though it will take Shields many years before she can write, in 1992, the poem "Coming to Canada – Age Twenty-Two":

> It took years to happen: . . .
> and years before COME
> BACK SOON changed to
> here and now and home
> the place I came to
> the place I was from (27)

Yet "My own life will never be enough for me," says Judith. And so said neophyte novelist Carol Shields as she moved on to the next phase of her work—always with her secret touch of ginger.

WORKS CITED

Gross, Terry. "Interview with Carol Shields." *Fresh Air.* NPR. 1 May 2002. Radio.

Shields, Carol. *Coming to Canada.* Ottawa: Carleton University Press, 1992. Print.

———. *Small Ceremonies.* Toronto: McGraw-Hill Ryerson, 1976. Print.

Wachtel, Eleanor. *More Writers and Company.* Toronto: Knopf, 1996. Print.

Revisiting the Sequel:
Carol Shields's Companion Novels

WENDY ROY

The current proliferation of sequels in both literary and cinematic venues suggests an abiding interest in stories that follow up on and expand previously circulated stories. Sequel novels are written, published, and read for many different reasons, the most commonly expressed being a desire by the reader for repetition, but with difference; a wish by the author to explore in more detail a character or situation from a previous book; and a need expressed by the author or publisher, or both, to continue an economically successful venture. One of the most oft-quoted commentaries on sequels is Terry Castle's 1986 study of Samuel Richardson's sequel to *Pamela* (1740); in it, she calls originating novels "charismatic texts, those with an unusually powerful effect on a reading public" (133) and argues that "So powerful is the charismatic story that it creates in readers a desire for 'more of the same'" through "a deep unconscious nostalgia for a past reading pleasure" (134).[1] As Paul Budra and Betty Schellenberg point out in the introduction to their 1998 collection *Part Two: Reflections on the Sequel*, however, this focus on the reaction of the audience to the originary text obscures the complexity of the interactions among writers, readers, and publishers around novels and their sequels (5–6). In particular, I would argue, the emphasis on reception downplays the author's motivations and choices in the production of the sequel.

Sequels do present challenges for authors, editors, and audiences. Perhaps the most obvious is that the reader's desire for repetition is often in conflict with a competing desire for novelty. Castle states categorically that it is "commonplace" that sequels are "disappointing" (133). The difficulty, she argues, is that the sequel "cannot literally reconstitute its charismatic original," but that readers "persist in demanding the impossible: that the sequel be different, but also *exactly the same*" (134; italics in original). A second, related challenge for writers and publishers of sequels is that literary critics (although not always ordinary readers) almost invariably judge the sequel more harshly than the originating book. Erica Brown and Mary Grover discuss this twentieth-century critical disdain for the sequel in their introduction to the 2012 collection *Middlebrow Literary Cultures*, arguing that sequels are often interpreted by critics simply as "repetition motivated by profit" (8). A third problem with sequels, again primarily for writers and publishers, is that because of these critiques, the precursor work, even if initially a well-received, stand-alone novel, is often retroactively devalued by critics simply because of the appearance of a sequel.

Carol Shields negotiated both motivational factors and challenges related to sequels during the composition and publication of two of her relatively early novels: *The Box Garden* (1977) and *A Fairly Conventional Woman* (1982). While the generic categorization of sequels continues to be debated, a sequel is normally defined, in reference to literature, as a work of fiction that continues the story of a previously stand-alone work by the same author, using the same narrative style and featuring the same characters.[2] Following this definition, *The Box Garden* could be considered a sequel to *Small Ceremonies*, published in 1976, while *A Fairly Conventional Woman* could be defined as a sequel to *Happenstance*, which appeared in 1980. Indeed, many reviewers responded to the second book in each of Shields's pairings as though it were a sequel. The pairs of books were also remarketed in such a way as to emphasize their connections: while the original titles had not linked the novels to their precursors, the books were definitively linked when each set was republished together in one volume, *Small Ceremonies* and *The Box Garden* in 2003 as *Duet*, and *Happenstance* and *A Fairly Conventional Woman* in 1991 as, simply, *Happenstance*.

Examined in more detail, however, the second in each of these two pairs of books is not a sequel in the conventional sense of the word. *The Box Garden* does not continue the story of a major or even secondary character of *Small Ceremonies*; instead, while its events are chronologically subsequent, it is focalized through a character who is only briefly mentioned in the precursor book. *A Fairly Conventional Woman*, in contrast, is not chronologically subsequent to *Happenstance*; instead it is set at exactly the same period of time. Because of these important differences, the books cannot be defined simply as sequels. Indeed, while interviewing Shields in 1988, Harvey De Roo called the pairs of novels instead "sets of twins" and "companion pieces," while in that interview and in the Introduction to *Duet* Shields herself named them "countertext[s]" and "companion" novels (De Roo 45, 47; Shields, "Introduction to *Duet*" n.p.).

The factors that influenced Shields to rework elements of the precursor novels into countertextual narratives can be traced through reviews of the various incarnations of the books, interviews in which Shields discusses her writing decisions, and archived letters between Shields and her writer friend Blanche Howard, which have since been published as *A Memoir of Friendship*. These sources show that Shields's reworking was sparked by similar motives to those of writers of sequels: she wanted to engage with already defined characters and situations, and in doing so she was responding to encouragement and criticism by readers, editors, and critics. In producing these second novels, however, Shields constructed not sequels, but works that fall into another, distinctive generic category that can best be named using Shields's own terminology: the *companion novel*. This naming is significant, since the principal meanings of *companion*, "One who associates with or accompanies another," "a colleague, partner, etc." (*OED* online), suggest both mutual support and equality of status.[3] Because of these characteristics, the genre avoids at least some of the pitfalls of conventional sequels and at the same time allows Shields to explore significant postmodernist questions related to the instability of the individual perspective in fiction. By focusing on companionship in both subject matter and form, Shields explores duality in fictive narrative voice, presenting what she calls a "mirror commentary" that highlights what she also explicitly labels "Otherness" (De Roo 47, 43).

Sequels have been produced for centuries and have been criticized whenever and wherever they appear. In her 1753 *The Adventures of David Simple, Volume the Last,* Sarah Fielding points out that sequels are "generally decried" as an "endeavour to put off a second-rate insipid Piece, void of the Spirit of the first" by exploiting "public Approbation" (iii, v), while in the preface to his 1719 *Farther Adventures of Robinson Crusoe*, Daniel Defoe maintains that this second book is "every Way as entertaining" as the first, "contrary to the Usage of Second Parts" (Preface 3). In the Canadian context, Lucy Maud Montgomery found herself so pressed by her publisher to write sequels to her 1908 *Anne of Green Gables* that she worried about being "dragged at Anne's chariot wheels the rest of my life" (74). In contrast, Mazo de la Roche's publisher was concerned that the expanding number of sequels to her 1927 critical success *Jalna* would undermine its acclaim (Panofsky 177), and, indeed, that devaluation occurred; a 1960 reviewer of de la Roche's sixteenth *Jalna* book judged that "[t]he Jalna marathon has, indeed, moved outside the range of literary criteria" ("Such Darling Dodos" 477). Despite these criticisms, however, sequels such as these have been devoured avidly by generations of readers who, according to Carole Gerson in her discussion of Montgomery's novels, like the way that they "prolong the pleasure of inhabiting" an "alternative world" (145). This long history of the advantages and challenges of sequels, both outside and inside Canada, faced Carol Shields in 1976 when she considered whether to write and publish a second related novel after *Small Ceremonies*.

In *Liminal Spaces: The Double Art of Carol Shields*, Alex Ramon argues that "while not precisely a sequel" to *Small Ceremonies*, *The Box Garden* contests that first novel's apparent "completeness" and "closure" (37). Despite Shields's contention that she invented the term *companion novel* to describe books such as *The Box Garden* (Shields, "Introduction" to *Duet* n.p.), other such novels were published long before her venture into the genre. Examples in the Canadian context are Robertson Davies's Salterton Trilogy (1952 to 1958), Deptford Trilogy (1970 to 1975), and Cornish Trilogy (1982 to 1988). In the second and third novels of the Deptford trilogy, Davies takes minor characters from the originating text, *Fifth Business*, and reconfigures them as the subsequent books' focalizers; the novels complement one another and refer to incidents that overlap chronologically without providing a continuous narrative. Shields follows in the footsteps of Davies through her experiments with divergent perspective in *The Box Garden* and, later, unconventional chronology in *A Fairly Conventional Woman*, to make evident other distinctions between sequels and companion novels.

Small Ceremonies is narrated through the first-person, mostly present-tense voice of fictive Canadian biographer Judith Gill (who, readers discover only in the subsequent book, lives in Kingston, Ontario) and details her experiences with work, friends, and family over a nine-month period. In an interview with Eleanor Wachtel in 1989, Shields said that her next novel, *The Box Garden*, came out of "a kind of post-partum feeling" and a feeling of "missing the people" in *Small Ceremonies* (Wachtel 31): "I remembered that there was a sister that I'd just alluded to a couple of times. I thought maybe I'd start with her. It seemed so easy to flow into it because I already knew the family, I knew the set-up" (31). To emphasize the parallels between the two novels, Shields chose a narrative style similar to that of *Small Ceremonies*. In *The Box Garden*, Judith's sister, Charleen Forrest, a Vancouver poet, narrates her life during the time of their mother's remarriage, which takes place chronologically a year after the conclusion of *Small Ceremonies*. Thus, in choosing to write the second novel, Shields was responding to her own desire for familiarity with already conceived characters and situations. The book itself, however, is distinctive from *Small Ceremonies*, especially in terms of incident and plot, because of Shields's response to criticism of that first book by both reviewers and her publisher.

Small Ceremonies received mostly positive evaluations, although a few reviewers damned it with faint praise; most of these commented on the ordinariness and domesticity of character and incident, a judgment on her writing that would plague Shields until toward the end of her literary career. Robert Lecker's "All Plot Little Thought" in *Essays on Canadian Writing*, for example, calls the book "a reasonably entertaining story about the significant trivialities of everyday suburban existence" (80). DuBarry Campau's "Diary of a Mod Housewife" in *Books in Canada* begins with the line, "Unhappily, this is the sort of book that will have housewives all over Canada darting to their typewriters," then calls the novel a "pleasant, unpretentious book" (22). Reviews such as these led Shields toward a less domestic and, in her opinion, less successful plot for *The Box Garden*. Shields said in a letter to Blanche Howard that she considered *The Box Garden* "a badly flawed book" in part because she "listened to the critics last time around—all that talk about nothing happening" (25 Oct. 1977; Shields and Howard 16). She told Wachtel that an editor with McGraw-Hill Ryerson had also commented that "there was not much happening" in *Small Ceremonies*. As a result of these criticisms, she introduced a "pseudo-kidnapping" of Charleen's son near the end of *The Box Garden* (Wachtel 32), as well as a number of other plot complications.

The critical reviews of *The Box Garden* focused, again, on the supposedly ordinariness of the novel's characters, but some reviews also paradoxically criticized plot excesses such as the kidnapping. A review by Barbara Amiel in *Maclean's,* scathingly titled "Look Back in Stupor," begins with the line, "Ordinary people will be the undoing of contemporary literature" and goes on to argue that Charleen is an example of a deplorable trend in Canadian literature, "the smaller-than-life hero" (54). Laura Lippert in *Room of One's Own* took the opportunity to review both novels together, exemplifying that, as often happens with sequels, the publication of *The Box Garden* provoked a reconsideration and devaluation of *Small Ceremonies*. Lippert dismissed the earlier work as well as the later with the sentence, "While both novels are nice, easy 'reads,' they both lack scope, breadth of vision and significance" (52). Sandra Martin, in contrast, wrote in her review in *Books in Canada* that she was determined *not* to read *The Box Garden* as a second novel (and thus that she was attempting to avoid the inherent critique of secondariness). Her review was more positive than Lippert's and Amiel's, but she did lament that toward the end of the novel "Shields goes berserk," referring of course to the kidnapping of Charleen's son (15), which Michael Taylor also later criticized as "gothic excess" (107).

Although Shields said she found reviews such as Amiel's "devastating" (Wachtel 33), they did not prevent her, several years later at the beginning of the 1980s, from publishing a second set of companion novels that also focused on characters who could be considered, if one focused only on surface manifestations, "smaller-than-life." Shields told Harvey De Roo in an interview that while *Small Ceremonies* and *The Box Garden* "touch only tangentially," *Happenstance* and *A Fairly Conventional Woman* fit together "like a puzzle" (De Roo 45). Using third-person, mostly past-tense narration, *Happenstance* offers the perspective of historian Jack Bowman of Elm Park, Illinois, while *A Fairly Conventional Woman* is from the viewpoint of his spouse, quilter Brenda Bowman. Each novel is set during the same week that the married couple is geographically separated because Brenda travels to a crafts convention in Philadelphia, and each novel relates its main character's experiences with and perspectives on vocation, marriage, family, and acquaintances. The overlapping chronology, paired with shifts in setting, character, and perspective, allows for *Happenstance* and *A Fairly Conventional Woman* to present a more complex pairing than *Small Ceremonies* and *The Box Garden*.

Shields said in an interview that she started writing *A Fairly Conventional Woman* because she was feeling stuck on the novel she had started after *Happenstance*—the novel that was eventually published, a half-dozen years later, as *Swann*. She decided to focus on Brenda's story, she told Eleanor Wachtel, "because people had asked me whatever happened to Brenda . . . when she went away. I thought, 'I can do that'" (Wachtel 35). Shields had chosen third-person limited narration for *Happenstance*, she revealed to another interviewer, because "it felt too risky using the first person 'I' with a male character" (De Roo 52). But even though the narrative was not presented through his voice, the limitation to Jack's perspective permitted detailed insight into his motivation and character, as well as his responses to others around him. Again to emphasize the continuity between that book and *A Fairly Conventional Woman*, Shields employed that same restricted third-person narrative style to tell Brenda's story.

Shields thus embarked on *A Fairly Conventional Woman* both to address a kind of personal writer's block and in response to requests from readers. In 1989 Shields said that she considered *A Fairly Conventional Woman* her best book to that point, although "hardly anyone agrees" (Wachtel 35). She also said that she loved the complexity of writing two books about one couple developing a relationship in the 1950s: "Marking off their comprehended territory, teasing it through their separate voices, was the happiest writing I've ever done," she said (De Roo 45–46), and "I loved fitting those two novels together. It was like a game" (Wachtel 35). For example, she had to make sure that the cheese sandwich that appeared during the Bowmans' inaugural courtship lunch in the first book also made an appearance in the second. Other details, however, are deliberately discrepant from book to book, raising the intriguing possibility that these inconsistencies are not errors on Shields's part, but an attempt to explore individuals' unique interpretations of life events.

Happenstance had received mostly positive reviews, with several critics, such as Joy Parks in *Quarry*, lauding its introduction of "a new type of male character": "A vulnerable man who doesn't fear his vulnerability, nor force himself to hide it away" (78; see also French, "Narrow" 18). However, as with the earlier books, many critics also used the words "average" and "ordinary" in their reviews. While *A Fairly Conventional Woman*, like its precursor novel, received some encouraging reviews, other reviewers found the return to the same territory as *Happenstance* unnecessary. Anne Collins argues in "Can This Marriage Be Saved— Again?" (published, like Amiel's critical review of *The Box Garden,* in *Maclean's*) that *Happenstance* "yielded all a reader would want to know about a happy marriage suffering a mid-life crisis" and concludes that *A Fairly Conventional Woman* is "as exciting as an oversized issue of *Family Circle* magazine" (78). Even one of the book's editors, Shields wrote in a letter to Howard, criticized *A Fairly Conventional Woman* as "too housewifey" (a comment to which Shields responded, "Who does he think reads novels, I wonder"? [21 April 1985; Shields and Howard 96]). Other reviewers, however, approved of the double-voicing; William French, who had reviewed all three earlier books, referred in the *Globe and Mail* to *A Fairly Conventional Woman* and its predecessor as a "double feature" whose "cross-references . . . expand both novels" ("Exploring" 23).

Both *The Box Garden* and *A Fairly Conventional Woman* thus garnered some of the same critical responses as sequels often do, and the earlier books were in some reviewers' eyes retroactively devalued because of that perceived sequelization. Lippert and Collins, for example, seem to be arguing that Shields was cheating by not writing something completely new or original. What these reviewers fail to acknowledge was that Shields was doing something uncommon, in several important ways. While *The Box Garden* and *A Fairly Conventional Woman* exploit some of the techniques of sequels, they are successful precisely because they are not sequels and thus do not lull or annoy readers with a false sense of sameness. Like sequels, the second of each of Shields's companion novels or countertexts is patterned on the first in structural ways and through corresponding incident: as well as their parallel narrative styles, both *Small Ceremonies* and *The Box Garden* begin with meals and conclude with weddings, for example, while both *Happenstance* and *A Fairly Conventional Woman* also begin with meals and end with references to the future reunion of the couple at the airport. In *Small Ceremonies* and *The Box Garden*, however, Shields focuses on very different main characters and separates the two stories chronologically by a full year; these differences are emphasized in the combined volume, *Duet*, which puts Judith's story first and drops the original titles, calling the two parts simply "Judith" and "Charleen." And in her second set of companion novels, *Happenstance* and *A Fairly Conventional Woman*, Shields rejects the sequel convention of presenting incidents that occur later (or earlier, as with so-called prequels); instead, the second book covers the same period in the characters' lives as its precursor, but with a change in point of view and setting. Because the two protagonists are separated geographically, most of the incidents of the "present" of each novel are distinctive. This shift in incident and perspective but overlapping chronology is emphasized by the design of the dual volume, which is titled *Happenstance* and subtitled "The Husband's Story" and "The Wife's Story." In many editions the volume has two front covers (in the 1993 Vintage edition, featuring a blue quilt for Jack's story and a pink flipside for Brenda's), with the narratives progressing so that the chronologically simultaneous endings of each book converge toward the middle of the volume.[4] There is no sense that one novel comes first and the other second, and in fact when my sister read the volume, she began with Brenda's story, not Jack's. This reading order, which contradicts the publication order of the novels, may be encouraged by the fact that the ISBN code and price, normally on the back cover of a book, can be found at the bottom of the cover that introduces "The Husband's Story." Indeed, some later criticisms, such as by Sarah Gamble in 2003 and Ellen Levy in 2007, treat the two novels as though they are in fact one artistic work and make no critical distinctions based on publication order; while Gamble briefly acknowledges that the two novels were originally published separately (48), Levy calls the combined volume simply "this novel" (193).

Perhaps the most striking feature of each of Shields's companion books, one that distinguishes it further from a sequel, is that the second enters the consciousness of a different character than its predecessor, in an attempt to understand what that "other" person is thinking and feeling. As Shields said of her decision to follow *Happenstance* with *A Fairly Conventional Woman*, "I wanted to write about two people who were more or less happily married, but who were in fact strangers to each other and always would be, and the value of the strangeness" (Wachtel 35). Her companion novels explore otherness in family situations, examining how people who are intimately related can approach life events, can think about the world around them, in radically different ways. And those of us who have siblings or spouses—in other words, most of us—will recognize that sense of familial estrangement or difference within intimate relationships that Shields articulates.

Shields discussed her fascination with otherness in her 1988 interview with De Roo, when she said that one of the main subjects of her fiction is "the unknowability of others. Otherness" and the "state of ignorance" about others' lives (De Roo 43).[5] Shields's first two companion novels address the concept of *otherness* explicitly. On the last page of *Small Ceremonies,* Judith as narrator reflects on the need to "embrac[e] others along with their mysteries. Distance. Otherness" (179). In *The Box Garden*, Charleen muses that she "can never quite believe in the otherness of people's lives. That is, I cannot conceive of their functioning out of my sight" (117). She recognizes, though, that on her son's first day at school, "he had entered into that otherness, that unseeable space which he must occupy forever and where not even my imagination could follow" (117). In addition to these overt references, both novels also implicitly address and indeed celebrate the unknowability of others, in numerous ways. In *Small Ceremonies*, Judith is mystified by her professor-husband's actions, especially when she discovers that he is creating a visual representation of John Milton's *Paradise Lost* by weaving the poem's themes into a tapestry. She understands neither her son, who writes secretive letters to a pen pal in England; nor her daughter, who seems obsessed with a writer friend of the family; nor her mother, who takes the subway home after mastectomy surgery. The novel does not close with the idea that others should in fact be knowable, however. Instead, it ends with Judith choosing to conceal what she has learned about an author friend; confident that a character based on her in a novel will be unrecognizable; and certain that she will never completely pin down her current biographical subject, nineteenth-century Canadian writer Susanna Moodie. In *The Box Garden*, Charleen knows so little about her ex-husband, Watson Forrest, that it is not until late in the book that she recognizes that he is also Brother Adam, the man with whom she has been carrying on a long correspondence. Similarly, their mother remains as much a mystery to Charleen as she has been to Judith, especially as Mrs. McNinn prepares for remarriage to an enigmatic fiancé. Reading the two novels together emphasizes this focus on otherness, since the two sisters are represented, especially in the second book, as both intimately acquainted with one another and their mother (whom they characterize very similarly, although in varying detail) and at the same time uncomprehending of their familial others' desires and motivations.

In *Happenstance* and *A Fairly Conventional Woman*, the irreconcilable otherness of the spouses is also evident in each novel individually, but underscored when the two novels are read as a pair. On the second-last page of each book, the narrator muses on the way that each member of the reuniting couple is ultimately a stranger to the other, made even more strange by their brief geographical separation (*Happenstance* 196; *Fairly* 192). Brenda, we are told, knows that there are parts of Jack's life "that will remain unknown to her, areas as large as football fields" (*Fairly* 157). In less overt but no less evocative representations of difference, the novels' narrators tell us that Jack "could never reconcile" the fact that Brenda's "finely channeled sensitivity was spent on the creation of *things*" (*Happenstance* 30), while Brenda thinks, but does not say, that she finds the book that Jack is writing "bewildering in its purposelessness" (*Fairly* 164). Like Shields's earlier companion books, these two later novels present other members of the protagonists' joint family as also unknowable to them: in *Happenstance* Jack is baffled when their son, apparently inexplicably, embarks on a week-long fast, while the narrator of *A Fairly Conventional Woman* notes that Brenda recognizes both of their children as "secretive and ultimately mysterious" (157).

Shields's companion novels address otherness not just through juxtaposition of character and situation but also through emphasis on multiple narrative perspectives, in a style that in Shields's later novels has been labelled postmodernist. A number of those later books present various perspectives within one volume: think of the four focalizers of

Swann (1987), or the alternating narrative perspectives of *The Republic of Love* (1992), or the multiplicity of voices that overtake Daisy Goodwill Flett's story in *The Stone Diaries* (1993).[6] In her still-relevant 1988 study *The Canadian Postmodern*, Linda Hutcheon describes postmodernist literature of the 1970s and 1980s in Canada in ways that are relevant to Shields's first four companion novels, as well as her later works. While she does not consider Shields's fiction in detail, Hutcheon discusses other Canadian works of fiction that unsettle the notion that it is possible to have one definitive and objective representation of a past event. She uses the term "historiographic metafiction" to refer to works that address this unsettling of historical records (13–14), but she also considers how fiction that has multiple narrative perspectives can provoke a questioning of the possibility of verifying the truth of personal events and encounters.

Multiple possible interpretations are celebrated in Shields's companion novels. Even when the books are read on their own, some multiplicity of perspective is evident. In *Small Ceremonies*, for example, Judith's straightforward first-person narration is interspersed with passages from another writer's diary (38–39), short biographies of her husband and a friend (96–97, 154–55), a newspaper article (143), letters to and from other characters (144–47), and a party invitation (148). *The Box Garden* also steps outside its apparently conventional narrative format by including letters (179), several lengthy monologues by Charleen's mother (102–03, 112–13), and three pages of dialogue in which the speakers, who keep changing, are never explicitly identified (210–12). Similarly, *Happenstance* and *A Fairly Conventional Woman* present a multiplicity of voices through such things as a note from Jack's son (*Happenstance* 105), passages from the book Jack is writing (*Happenstance* 140, 145), a business card (*Fairly* 31), overheard conversations (again with the speakers unidentified, *Fairly* 76–80), and a newspaper article (*Fairly* 145). Additionally, *Happenstance* and *A Fairly Conventional Woman* focus on the variability of interpretations of past events through reflections on Jack's work as a historian (*Happenstance* 1–9) and on the kind of folk history represented by quilts (*Fairly* 102, 126–28). One of Brenda's fellow quilters even concedes that quilts presenting a simplified "story" are misleading because "most stories have three or four endings, maybe even more" (143). Multiple narratives about a supposedly singular past are therefore represented as not only possible but also inevitable.

The companion-book format allows for intriguing alternation of perspective even when the narration of each book, taken on its own, is mostly from one point of view. Shields's term "countertext" may be especially relevant in this context, since one perspective seems to counter the other. Judith, who in *Small Ceremonies* presents herself as not as happy as she would like to be (1) and who is critical of the way she negotiates complex relationships with her children, husband, and friends, is reinterpreted in *The Box Garden* through her sister's outside, and thus more superficial, perspective as being simply serene (13), "embalmed in a stately, enviable, suburban calm" and with a "seeming immunity to the shared, sour river of our girlhood" (68). Similarly, the broad-strokes portrait of Charleen that Judith has rendered in *Small Ceremonies* is overturned by Charleen's more detailed self-narration in *The Box Garden*; instead of the sour, bitter person that Judith briefly describes (*Small Ceremonies* 124), Charleen shows herself open to learning bravery and kindness (*Box Garden* 13, 206–07). More minor characters and events are also reinterpreted in ways that demonstrate contrasting viewpoints and point to possible variations in the way historical events are perceived and reported; for example, Judith recounts their father's "quiet death, a heart attack in his sleep" (*Small Ceremonies* 99) while Charlene describes it as a "massive heart attack . . . darkness crushing him" (*Box Garden* 23).

A similar broadening and thus unsettling of the fixity of perspective is evident when *Happenstance* and *A Fairly Conventional Woman* are read together, in part because of the complementary and contradictory ways that the personal histories of Jack and Brenda are narrated in the two books. At one point, the narrator of *Happenstance* likens these differing perspectives to another medium, the medium of film: "It was as though he [Jack] carried a film strip around with him, a whole history of Brenda Pulaski Bowman that was altogether separate and different from her history of herself. No doubt she had a film strip on him, too— he could not imagine what it would consist of, but its details would be puzzling and foreign" (161). Indeed, the companion-novel format emphasizes those differing outlooks, sometimes self-consciously. For example, in Jack's narrative the focus in the description of their first lunch together is on the sexual spark between them, although we are also told that he was attracted to the way she said "Wine for lunch isn't my cup of tea" (*Happenstance* 132). Brenda's narrative emphasizes, instead, Jack's place in her desire to fulfill 1950s expectations of domesticity, and while *A Fairly Conventional Woman* repeats the comment about wine and tea, it is presented as only something Jack claims Brenda said, with the additional commentary, "*She* cannot imagine saying anything as witless as this" (112). As Ramon argues, "these novels suggest that different recollections of the *same* past event always problematise any simple definition of where the 'truth' of the past might lie" (50). Jack and

Brenda's marital past is presented in *Happenstance* and *A Fairly Conventional Woman* as a joint construction necessarily made up of inconsistencies and contradictions.

Twenty years after the publication of these last two companion novels, Carol Shields explored the pitfalls of fictional sequels in *Unless* (2002) through narrator Reta Winter, who is engaged in writing a sequel to a popular first novel. Reta is familiar with sequel conventions: she has chosen a title that echoes the first book, and she has a third title in mind "in the event I decide to go for a trilogy" (140). She understands that she must focus on the same characters, setting, and problems as in the first book (243), and that she must use first-person narration because the precursor novel "employed the first person, and a sequel must be consistent in such matters" (205). Reta's editor tries to bully her into abandoning the sequel because, he says, he wants "quality fiction" rather than "popular fiction" (280); he also tells her that "a sequel, on average, only makes two-thirds the money that the original has earned" (281). But his underlying reason, Reta eventually realizes, is that he does not want her to write a second novel centred on what he considers an overly domestic and thus trivial female character. Shields's comically serious exploration, in her last novel published before her death, of the struggles of a writer who wants to publish a sequel with a woman as continuing protagonist indicates that Shields had not forgotten her experiences with her first four novels. When she launched into the writing and publication of *The Box Garden* and *A Fairly Conventional Woman,* she was motivated similarly to creators of sequels: like her fictional protagonist, Reta, she wanted to work with already defined characters and situations, and as the writing progressed, she responded not just to her own desires but also to those of readers, editors, and critics of the precursor books. But unlike Reta, who insists on writing a conventional sequel, Shields herself chose to make deliberate transgressions of generic boundaries to ensure that *The Box Garden* and *A Fairly Conventional Woman* are not in fact sequels. Instead, they are what Shields calls mirror commentaries (De Roo 47) that allow her to examine the wavering image of human otherness not just through the books' subject matter but also through chronological divergence or concurrence and through presentation of alternative and thus unsettling points of view. The juxtaposition of differing narrative voices in Shields's companion novels provides a fascinating implicit commentary on the instability of individual perspective in fiction, implying that the definitiveness of any narrative focalized through one character can be called into question. This questioning identifies Shields's first four published novels, from the late 1970s and the early 1980s, as the beginning of her postmodernist experimentation with multiple perspectives that is even more evident in later works such as *Swann* and *The Stone Diaries*.

NOTES

1. In her 2006 study *A Theory of Adaptation*, Linda Hutcheon supports this idea while phrasing it somewhat differently; she argues that sequels evoke in readers the wish that the story might never end, in contrast to adaptations, which she defines as attempts "to retell the same story over and over in different ways" (9).

2. See, for example, the definition in Budra and Schellenberg (7) and their use of the term "repetition-with-variation" to characterize sequels (9). In my analysis, I distinguish between 1) *serials*: longer works published in installments in a newspaper or magazine; 2) books written as part of a pre-designed *series*, sometimes, as with the Nancy Drew books, with individual volumes composed by different authors but published under the same pseudonym; and 3) the *sequel*: a book written to follow up and complement what was initially a stand-alone publication by the same author. Brown and Grover use the term "serial" to refer to what I would call sequels, while in *Sequels: An Annotated Guide to Novels in Series* (1982; revised edition 1990), Janet Husband and Jonathan F. Husband do not distinguish between sequels and series; they define both as works that show "development of plot or character from book to book" and have some progression of chronology (vii). Other theorists, such as Laurie Langbauer in *Novels of Everyday Life: The Series in English Fiction*, argue that a blurring of the distinctions between the three types of literary works can be productive (8). I contend that a more narrow definition allows me to consider more productively whether or not Shields's books can be labelled sequels.

3. My thanks to Marilyn Rose for suggesting that I investigate the meaning of the word *companion*. In some phrases such as "hired companion" and "companion star" (which, like "companion novel," turns the noun into an adjective) the companion is subordinated to the primary person or thing; Shields, however, appears to intend no such subordination when she employs the term.

4. The 2003 edition of *Happenstance* published by the Fourth Estate (HarperCollins) places Jack's narrative before Brenda's, instead of having the two converge; in this way the book is similar to the same publisher's edition of *Duet*.

5. In his study of her fiction, Ramon connects Shields's exploration of otherness to concepts of intersection. Levy's essay, meanwhile, includes a brief discussion of the sense of estrangement between couples in *Happenstance* and *Small Ceremonies* (193–94).

6. See my essay "Autobiography as Critical Practice in *The Stone Diaries*" for a discussion of multiple perspectives in that later novel.

WORKS CITED

Amiel, Barbara. "Look Back in Stupor." Rev. of *The Box Garden*, by Carol Shields. *Maclean's* 5 Sept. 1977: 54–56. Print.

Brown, Erica, and Mary Grover, eds. *Middlebrow Literary Cultures: The Battle of the Brows, 1920–1960*. Basingstoke, UK: Palgrave Macmillan, 2012. Print.

Budra, Paul, and Betty Schellenberg, intro. and eds. *Part Two: Reflections on the Sequel*. Toronto: University of Toronto Press, 1998. Print.

Campau, DuBarry. "Diary of a Mod Housewife." Rev. of *Small Ceremonies*, by Carol Shields. *Books in Canada* 5.6 (June 1976): 22. Print.

Castle, Terry. *Masquerade and Civilization: The Carnivalesque in Eighteenth-Century English Culture and Fiction*. Stanford: Stanford University Press, 1986. Print.

Collins, Anne. "Can This Marriage Be Saved—Again?" Rev. of *A Fairly Conventional Woman*, by Carol Shields. *Maclean's* 18 Oct. 1982: 78. Print.

Davies, Robertson. *Fifth Business*. Toronto: Penguin, 1970. Print.

Defoe, Daniel. *The Farther Adventures of Robinson Crusoe*. London: Taylor, 1719. E-book.

De Roo, Harvey. "A Little Like Flying: An Interview with Carol Shields." *West Coast Review* 23.3 (1988): 38–56. Print.

Fielding, Sarah. *The Adventures of David Simple, Volume the Last*. London: Millar, 1753. E-book.

French, William. "Exploring the Angst of a Married Woman." Rev. of *A Fairly Conventional Woman*, by Carol Shields. *Globe and Mail* 7 Oct. 1982: 23. Print.

———. "A Narrow, Ironic Slice of Life." Rev. of *Happenstance*, by Carol Shields. *Globe and Mail* 18 Sept. 1980: 18. Print.

Gamble, Sarah. "Filling the Creative Void: Narrative Dilemmas in *Small Ceremonies*, the *Happenstance* Novels, and *Swann*." In *Carol Shields, Narrative Hunger, and the Possibilities of Fiction*, ed. Edward Eden and Dee Goertz. Toronto: University of Toronto Press, 2003: 39–60. Print.

Gerson, Carole. "'Dragged at Anne's Chariot Wheels': L. M. Montgomery and the Sequels to *Anne of Green Gables*." In *Part Two: Reflections on the Sequel*, ed. Paul Budra and Betty Schellenberg Toronto: University of Toronto Press, 1998: 144–59. Print.

Husband, Janet, and Jonathan S. Husband. *Sequels: An Annotated Guide to Novels in Series*, 2nd ed. Chicago: American Library Association, 1990. Print.

Hutcheon, Linda. *The Canadian Postmodern*. Toronto: Oxford University Press, 1998. Print.

———. *A Theory of Adaptation*. New York: Routledge, 2006. Print.

Langbauer, Laurie. *Novels of Everyday Life: The Series in English Fiction, 1850–1930*. Ithaca, NY: Cornell University Press, 1999. Print.

Lecker, Robert A. "All Plot Little Thought." Rev of *Small Ceremonies*, by Carol Shields. *Essays on Canadian Writing* 5 (Fall 1976): 80–82. Print.

Levy, Ellen. "'Artefact Out of Absence': Reflection and Convergence in the Fiction of Carol Shields." In *Carol Shields and the Extra-Ordinary*, ed. Marta Dvořák and Manina Jones. Montreal: McGill-Queen's University Press, 2007: 191–204. Print.

Lippert, Laura. Rev. of *Small Ceremonies* and *The Box Garden*, by Carol Shields. *Room of One's Own* 3.4 (1978): 52. Print.

Martin, Sandra. "The Perils of Charleen." Rev. of *The Box Garden*, by Carol Shields. *Books in Canada* 6.10 (December 1977): 15–16. Print.

Montgomery, L. M. *The Green Gables Letters: From L. M. Montgomery to Ephraim Weber, 1905–1909*, ed. Wilfrid Eggleston. Toronto: Ryerson, 1960. E-book.

Panofsky, Ruth. "'Don't Let Me Do It!': Mazo de la Roche and Her Publishers." *International Journal of Canadian Studies* 11 (1995): 171–84. Print.

Parks, Joy. Rev. of *Happenstance*, by Carol Shields. *Quarry* (Spring 1982): 77–78. Print.

Ramon, Alex. *Liminal Spaces: The Double Art of Carol Shields*. Newcastle: Cambridge Scholars, 2008. Print.

Roy, Wendy. "Autobiography as Critical Practice in *The Stone Diaries*." In *Carol Shields, Narrative Hunger, and the Possibilities of Fiction*, ed. Edward Eden and Dee Goertz. Toronto: University of Toronto Press, 2003: 113–46. Print.

Shields, Carol. *The Box Garden*. 1977. Toronto: Vintage, 1994. Print.

———. *Duet*. Rpt. of *Small Ceremonies* and *The Box Garden*. London: Fourth Estate (HarperCollins), 2003. Print.

———. *A Fairly Conventional Woman*. 1982. Rpt. as *Happenstance: The Wife's Story* in combined volume, 1991. Toronto: Vintage, 1993. Print.

———. *Happenstance*. 1980. Rpt. as *Happenstance: The Husband's Story* in combined volume, 1991. Toronto: Vintage, 1993. Print.

———. Letters to Blanche Howard. Blanche Howard fonds. RBSC-ARC 1256. University of British Columbia Rare Books and Special Collections, Vancouver.

———. *Small Ceremonies*. 1976. Toronto: Vintage, 1995. Print.

———. *Unless*. Toronto: Random House, 2002. Print.

Shields, Carol, and Blanche Howard. *A Memoir of Friendship: The Letters between Carol Shields and Blanche Howard*, ed. Blanche Howard and Allison Howard. Toronto: Penguin, 2007. Print.

"Such Darling Dodos." Rev. of *Jalna*, by Mazo de la Roche. *Times Literary Supplement* 29 July 1960: 477. Print.

Taylor, Michael. Rev. of *Happenstance*, by Carol Shields. *Fiddlehead* (Spring 1981): 106–07. Print.

Wachtel, Eleanor. "Interview with Carol Shields." *Room of One's Own* 13.1–2 (1989): 5–45. Print.

Bio-Critical Afterlives: Sarah Binks, Pat Lowther, and the Satirical Gothic Turn in Carol Shields's *Swann*

CYNTHIA SUGARS

[T]he birth of the reader must be at the cost of the death of the Author.
—Roland Barthes, "The Death of the Author" (148)

What if the body of work is still alive and breathing?
—Carol Shields, *Swann* (82)

Some time in the early 1970s, Carol Shields, then a master of arts student at the University of Ottawa, sat in the audience at one of the university's Canadian Literature symposia, the very same symposium series that hosted a conference dedicated to the work of Carol Shields in 2012. Given the strange reflexivity of this coincidence, it is worth noting that Shields directly commented on the symposia and the debates about literary tradition and influence that they helped to foster. Registered as a master's student in the university's English Department from 1969 to 1975, and working under the supervision of Lorraine McMullen, Shields was struck by the intensity of the emotional investments of academics and authors who took part in the annual colloquia. She recalls, in particular, the "emotional final session [of the Klein symposium] in which Irving Layton castigated the ghost of Klein for abdicating his role as a poet and selling out to commerce" (qtd. in McMullen 133). The experience of these conferences, Shields said, planted in her mind a "certain scepticism about literary scholarship" which would inform her work thereafter (133).

And so it did. The famous "Swann Symposium" that concludes Shields's 1987 novel *Swann* is surely a parodic nod to some of the University of Ottawa symposia that contributed to Shields's emergent literary critical aesthetic. Faye Hammill hastily dismisses the Swann Symposium and its real-life antecedents for "their over-valorizing of Canadian authors and their elaborate quests for traces of national and regional identity in the texts" (128). I think, however, that this should give us some pause, for there is another impetus in the novel that invites a more complicated perspective on national identity and literature than a mere dismissal of it. Indeed, in *Swann*, Shields grapples with questions of literary influence and geographical determinism, particularly as she conjures the ghosts of Canadian literary predecessors through her presentation of the uncanny bio-critical afterlife of Mary Swann.

In her novel, Shields is interested in the allure, even the *necessity*, of literary ancestors, not only as sites of individual projection but also as forms of communal emplacement and connection. Although she satirizes the ways literary critics engage in this quest, this concern self-reflexively evokes her own compulsion for literary precursors in her bio-critical studies of Susanna Moodie and Jane Austen. Literature creates an imagined community—between authors, between authors and readers. As one character in the novel perceives it, literature "binds one human being to the next and shortens the distance we must travel to discover that our most private perceptions are universally felt" (179). Stephen Greenblatt memorably described this as "a desire to speak with the dead" (1)—much as we see in Layton's appeal to the ghost of Klein at the University of Ottawa symposium. As Margaret Atwood puts it in *Negotiating with the Dead*, "dead bodies can talk if you know how to lis- ten to them, and they *want* to talk" (163). We *want* to speak with ghosts, and it is through literature that this communing becomes possible, since writing, in "chart[ing] a process of thought," survives as the "voice" of the dead (Atwood 158). Shields's parody of the colloquia in *Swann*, I would argue, is not in the interests of wholly debunking them, nor in the name of a cynical rejection of literary scholarship. Rather, it emerges from an awareness of the importance literary authors continue to have for personal and communal needs. Shields questions the projections and blindnesses that inform these needs, to be sure, particularly in the reconstruction of female precursors, but she does not place herself outside of this dynamic. Indeed, the narrative of *Swann* itself is presided over by the ghosts of two significant Canadian literary predecessors: the legendary Saskatchewan lyricist Sarah Binks (from the 1940s) and British Columbia poet Pat Lowther (from the 1970s). Shields's metaperspective on her novel's own

parodic stance finds its clearest expression in these two Canadian literary intertexts that go into the construction of Mary Swann, particularly
since what binds together the various critics in the novel is their search
for literary precursors.

Swann, in one sense, is Shields's tribute to her fellow (though not
contemporaneous) University of Manitoba professor Paul Hiebert, who
retired from the university in 1953; indeed, *Swann* was published in the
same year that Hiebert died. Hiebert was the author of the 1947 Governor-
General Award–winning satirical novel, *Sarah Binks*, a novel that poses
as a biography of a Saskatchewan poet named Sarah Binks. In its portrayal
of the academics, biographers, and groupies who grapple over the reputation of the poet Mary Swann, Shields's novel offers a satirical reworking,
exactly forty years later, of *Sarah Binks*, the fictional and dubiously
talented "Songstress of Saskatchewan" (vii). In both texts, the biography
and literary legacy of the absent poet are fabricated through scraps of
poetry, sentimental pronouncements, and scattered biographical details,
evoking the often willed distortion of academic sleuthing and celebrity
boosterism. More insistently, it is the humble and rural origins of Binks,
like Swann, that make the "miracle" of her supposed talent all the more
exceptional. Binks's fictional biographer "takes exception" to the theory
that Binks was "an isolated genius" who "sprang spontaneously" from
the soil (x). Instead, he insists that she has been integrally shaped by the
fabric and historical legacy of her Saskatchewan environment; "her roots
go deep," he maintains (x). As he puts it, Binks was "the product of her
friends, of her books, and of the little incidents which shaped her life"
(viii). This is echoed in Mary Swann's meagre and mysterious origins: a
farm wife who has left no identifiable legacy; an overworked and tired
woman who lived in squalor, had few refined tastes, no literary influences,
and had not been farther than Belleville in her entire life. How *could* an
individual of so restricted experience write the heartfelt and probing
verses that she did? Well might the critics ask this question. At the
Swann Symposium, critics debate whether or not Mary Swann did produce
the works that are attributed to her (ironic, of course, given that we discover
that she, in fact, did not write most of them). In the life of Sarah Binks,
a similar question arises through a controversy about the authorship of
her poetry: Professor Marrowfat speculates that "Sarah could not have
written these poems . . . because she lacked the profound philosophical
background which characterizes the poems" (78). This is further complicated when we later learn that the foremost "Binksian," Miss Rosalind
Drool, who is credited with the discovery of Sarah Binks (much like Sarah
Maloney in *Swann*), "permitted her sweeping admiration" of Binks's

work "to carry her beyond the reading of it into the actual addition of several verses of her own," a fact that "has made it difficult, according to Professor Marrowfat, 'to decide which is Binks and which is Drool'" (150).

That Sarah Binks is a fictional invention, the subject of a mock literary biography, offers a further reflection on Shields's novel in which the theme of biographical invention is overtly explored. Not only is Swann, in a sense, a fabrication of the scholars who promote her work, but her inventedness becomes highlighted the further the novel proceeds, since the "evidence" of Swann's existence is slowly disappearing (the photograph of her; the pen she used to write with; her notebook; the last remaining copies of her book *Swann's Songs*; the original manuscripts; and the reminiscences themselves). Both texts reveal Swann and Binks to be ciphers, textual constructs, both as fictional creations of their authors, but also in the sense that the "author" position is itself a construction fabricated by a community of readers. In both texts, a seminal literary manuscript is destroyed by the keepers of the poet's reputation: Cruzzi's wife Hildë in Swann uses the manuscript to dispose of fish scraps, while in *Sarah Binks* an original manuscript is "used for kindling by the curator" of "Binksiana" (51).[1] In both texts, the critical blindnesses of literary academics are mocked. The parallel extends to the verses themselves, of course. Sarah Binks, according to her biographer, is the poet of the unabashedly "trivial" (xiv), as is Mary Swann; they both attempt to link the trivial with the profound (as does Carol Shields throughout her work). At the same time, however, the parodic effect of both novels is expressly that the poetry does not merit the kind of literary-critical attention that it receives—at least, this is true of Sarah Binks . . . in Mary Swann's case it is a little more ambiguous.

What establishes the parodic effect in *Sarah Binks* is the gap between the sentiment and the quality of the verse. In short, Binks's poetry is no good. Gerald Noonan explores the parodic workings in Sarah Binks in his 1978 article in *Studies in Canadian Literature*. According to Noonan, there is a split effect in the reading experience of *Sarah Binks*, for on the one hand her writing has the mark of "trivia" upon it, but on the other hand, the reader experiences a sense of nostalgia for a time when it may have been possible to have believed in the profundity of such a confined world. Sarah's life is significant expressly because it is of a time that is no more. Noonan describes this effect as one of both "incongruity and nostalgia," which is in turn dependent upon the reader's "unconscious awareness of the discrepancy between Hiebert's and Sarah's under-standing" (3). As Noonan writes, "We both recognize the incongruous reality and feel a nostalgia for a lost possibility" (4). This element of nostalgia, I would argue, is entirely absent in Shields's text. But there is something else at work here, for it is through the figure of Pat Lowther that Shields enables us to effect this crossover. By superimposing Lowther's tale atop Binks's, the story becomes a feminist commentary about the invisibility (from literature, if not elsewhere) of women's lives. The sweet songstress of Saskatchewan, in other words, points to the sallow spectre of misogyny.

Shields's Mary Swann evokes numerous parallels with the real-life Canadian poet Pat Lowther, who, like Swann, was violently murdered by her husband in 1975.[2] Indeed, the title of Shields's 1992 novel, *The Stone Diaries*, echoes Lowther's posthumous poetry collection *A Stone Diary* (1977; Lowther 183–252), the text of which, like *Swann's Songs*, Lowther had submitted to a publisher shortly before her disappearance and which, in turn, clinched her literary reputation. Shields, in fact, had met Pat Lowther during her student days at the University of Ottawa when Lowther was a visiting reader on the campus in 1974 (Wiesenthal 301); the two established a passing friendship, both publishing poetry collections in 1974 that were reviewed together in the *Canadian Forum*. The parallels between Lowther and Swann in the novel are substantial. Both women were bludgeoned to death with a hammer by their husbands; both submitted a major poetry manuscript to a publisher shortly before their deaths which was published posthumously; both are authors of posthumous poetry collections whose composition and "authenticity" are uncertain (in Swann's case because the poems were inadvertently destroyed by Hildë Cruzzi; in Lowther's case because her husband had plundered her manuscripts to amass "evidence" from her poems that she was having an extra-marital affair, and subsequently Lowther's personal papers were rifled through by others as they became material for a criminal investigation); both achieved notoriety, in part through the fact of their untimely ends; both had their names linked to a public institution: in Lowther's case to the "Pat Lowther Memorial Award" given by the League of Canadian Poets, in Swann's case to the "Mary Swann Memorial Room" in the local Nadeau museum.

More interestingly in terms of the storyline of *Swann*, an obvious parallel exists in the posthumous deification—indeed gothicization—of the two poets. The celebration of Mary Swann as a martyr/victim (and, indeed, as a kind of ghost who haunts her readers) echoes the propagation of the "poet as victim" myth which circulated in the wake of Lowther's death. In her biography of Lowther, Christine Wiesenthal outlines the posthumous construction of Lowther as "the proverbial sacrificial lamb" (83). The myth (and subsequent controversy that followed) began with a 1975 tribute to Lowther that was aired on Peter Gzowski's CBC radio program shortly after her death. As Wiesenthal describes it, the "'special report' opened with a recorded reading by Pat Lowther of a short poem entitled 'Nightmare'" (75). The poem is a quirky piece of black humour, very much in the vein of Margaret Atwood, and at the end of the reading Lowther chuckled in response to the humorous concluding line: "I try to cry out: / *I'm harmless!* / but the words can't / get through my fangs" (76). Wiesenthal explores the ways Lowther's "mordantly clever little 'Nightmare'"—and Lowther's work overall—was "re-recorded as 'a true nightmare' for the living, [a slippage that] requires no explanation or apology" (76). The Gzowski tribute inspired a subsequent feature article in the 1976 *Canadian Magazine* written by Paul Grescoe. Entitled "Eulogy of a Poet" and subtitled "Poet as Victim," Grescoe's article traced what he termed "the soul-scarring experience of Lowther's life," which he felt formed the impetus of her uncannily evocative verse. The tributes initiated a series of controversies and debates about who could legitimately claim insight into the poet's life (poet Andy Wainwright, who took issue with the maudlin tone that had entered into discussions of Lowther's life at the expense of her work, was castigated as "an East Coast stranger") and the extent to which one could read the life (and death) into the poems. Critics' insistence on reading Lowther's death into her work is echoed in the ways Shields's biographer-critics seek fleeting glimpses of the "real" traumatized Mary Swann in her writing, simplistically reducing her work to a biographical reflection of her suffering (the very literary approach that is so steadfastly mocked in the reductive poems written by Sarah Binks!). It is not surprising, therefore, that Sarah Maloney in the novel compares Mary Swann's legacy to that of Sylvia Plath (82), a comparison that was made about Lowther as well.[3] In the case of Swann, the profundity that is attributed to the poems is applied in hindsight; the death, in other words, renders the poetry significant, but primarily because of the death.

It would seem that Shields in a sense updated Sarah Binks as a literary foremother through the overlay of Pat Lowther. But by superimposing a gothic prototype atop a satirical one, and a "real" dead author atop a "fake" dead author, the satirical effect of the portrayal of Mary Swann is altered. But why? This is where I want to argue that Shields's novel takes us beyond satire through its very play on the poststructuralist motif of the "death of the author." Shields told Eleanor Wachtel in an interview that when she wrote Swann she was "reading a lot of postmodern criticism"

(Wachtel 118). The desire to pin down the *real* Mary Swann in the novel becomes parodied as a delusion, since Swann (and indeed her works) exist only as simulacra. But is Shields parodying the earnestness with which critics inflate the reputation and intentionality of their literary icons; or is she making fun of the murdering of the author function itself, which, echoing Roland Barthes, leaves behind a text that is—literally—no more than "a tissue of quotations" (146)?

In the novel, the death of the author is literalized and Mary Swann would seem to evaporate in its wake, an outcome that echoes the standard criticism raised by many feminist and postcolonial theorists to the effect that the author was declared dead just as many authors from marginalized constituencies were finding a voice. As Shields said of the novel in her interview with Wachtel, "How can you ever know anything about a person who's been so effectively erased from the world?" (41). Interestingly, Morton Jimroy, Swann's biographer, feels he is committing literary-critical homicide in the very act of constructing a false public face for Mary Swann. He accuses himself "of burying Swann's grainy likeness, keeping her out of sight and shutting her up, a miniature act of murder" (110). There is something particularly troubling about this since, as Jimroy observes, Swann lived a life that was beneath the radar, "a life lived . . . in the avoidance of biography" (110). To represent Swann accurately is to bury her even further, thereby compounding the social and historical erasure of wives and working-class women that has dominated genera-tions of western patriarchal society. Swann is thus the paradigmatic "dead" female author—dead, and erased, as a result of misogynistic male violence. She is also the paradigmatic poststructuralist author—dead in the sense that the work (and, indeed, the written biography) exists outside of the author function—a function that overwrites the historical silencing and oppression of women within which Mary Swann is deeply embedded. Given this context, if all that is left of Swann is a series of trace fragments (and a series of false traces), what are we to make of the real-life "authors"— Sarah Binks and Pat Lowther—who hover, metadiscursively, in the back-ground of Mary Swann? In other words, Shields's invocation of two seminal iconic Canadian literary intertexts in her portrayal of Mary Swann needs to be considered before we can sum up her approach in this book, which has been widely described as a literary-critical and anti-national satire.

Shields's satirical gothic turn adds an important twist to the novel. As *Swann* playfully calls attention to the quest for the suffusing presence of literary precursors, it is itself presided over (haunted?) by the presence of very prominent literary precursors. In so doing, Shields's novel plays out the very "ghost-of-a-ghost" (38) function that Jonathan Kertzer identifies as being at the heart of Canadian literary culture: the sense that poetic ancestors are neither *sui generis* nor posthumous but rather a kind of unresolvable "empty set" which persists in haunting the Canadian literary establishment. This is what Kertzer identifies as the absent *genius loci* in Canadian culture, the emblem that should unite spirit and place (40). Kertzer argues that Canadian authors and scholars will remain haunted "as long as they conceive of literature as the voice of a *genius loci*" (47), that the urgency to link spirit with place is precisely the romantic move that Canadian history disallows. In Kertzer's sense, it is not the Barthesian death of the author that is at issue but rather the cultural-historical legacy of Canada, in which national cultural discourse was built upon a foundation of ambivalence, displacement, and instability. A claim to indigenous authorship, in the sense of a localized emergence from place (which is what critics seek in Mary Swann), is absent. "The ghost cannot be captured," Kertzer writes, "since it is a spectre of thought, banished by the same reflex that seeks it" (38). Mary Swann is just such a ghost: a ghost who refuses to haunt. And *that*, expressly, is the problem. Her readers, all of them, desire evidence of an authenticating haunting— a local woman who has achieved apotheosis—and in so doing they are partially responsible for bludgeoning the author beyond recognition. Swann, in this role, becomes the gothic victim or ghost who is hounded and pursued by scholars who want her to take up residence in them.

For the critics within the novel, it is the origins of genius that pose the greatest conundrum. Yet Shields's novel would seem to inhabit a curious position with respect to this process, since it engages with the question of cultural inheritance and legacy in seemingly contradictory ways. On the one hand, the critics in the novel are obsessed with the question of literary precursors. Sarah Maloney, for example, is perturbed by Swann's apparent lack of literary influences: "There's a gap that needs explaining . . . . How did Mary Swann, untaught country woman, know how to make that kind of murky metaphorical connection. Who taught her what was possible?" (55). Sarah grapples with this conundrum: not so much a Bloomian anxiety of influence as an anxiety of non-influence. "Back to the same old problem," she says to herself, "Mary Swann hadn't read any modern poetry. She didn't *have* any influences" (55). Morton Jimroy, Swann's biographer, is similarly obsessed with identifying Swann's poetic precursors. When he asks her daughter what poetry she remembers her mother reading, the daughter is unequivocal: "'[None] that I can remember. Unless you count Mother Goose as poetry'" (93).

At the conference itself, critic Syd Buswell appalls the crowd by dispelling the question of literary influence head on: there is no modernist poetry contained in the Nadeau public library, he pronounces with satisfaction (259–60). The "mystery" of Mary Swann is thus not the one that is ostensibly posed by the novel—that is, the burglar who is removing the last traces of Swann's existence from the historical record—but rather how genius managed to arise in such lowly Canadian origins (or, to invoke Kertzer's language, how a *genius loci* might be imagined to have arisen there). As Sarah Maloney puzzles, "therein . . . hangs the central mystery: . . . Where in those bleak Ontario acres . . . did she find the sparks that converted emblematic substance into rolling poetry?" (31). The critics in the novel are flummoxed by this idea, and troubled by it. In their view, just as there is no "death" of the author in the sense that Barthes meant it, so is there no "origin" of the author without a genealogical tradition to precede it. In a moment of striking self-perception, Sarah notes that "the fact that art could be created in such a void was, for some reason, deeply disturbing" (44), which, I think, takes us to the heart of Shields's novel. The disturbing element might be the possibility of literature arising in a vacuum, for what does that say about cultural inheritance and continuity? Does that render all of us as alone as Mary Swann, exiled to a metaphorical boneyard of cultural isolationism? Buswell, who suspects Swann of being a fraud, is only voicing what all of the other critics already know: that they are pursuing a spectre of their own desires. Critics want to implant Swann as a *genius loci*, a spirit who both emerges from the land and speaks its authentic "voice" in poetry, yet they are anxious about the notion of a *sui generis* (or self-generated) author because it undermines any sense of literary, cultural, and communal continuity. In both instances they are propelled by a yearning for cultural inheritance, a desire for literary genealogy alongside a subconscious awareness that genealogy may need to be invented.

The novel, then, performs the death of the author in tandem with its characters' fruitless resuscitation of the signifying author (since they obsessively engage in outmoded biographical and intentionalist forms of literary analysis). As Barthes states, the writer "is born simultaneously with the text, [and] is in no way equipped with a being preceding or exceeding the writing" (145). And yet, overlaid atop the absent Mary Swann hover the spectres of Binks and Lowther, both of whom, in different ways, have been integrally identified with their biographies. On a metatextual level, then, Shields performs the very quest for literary precursors that her text appears to be satirizing. If she fills in for the absence of ghosts by making the very absence itself a figure of influence, she also takes her satire one step further by gothicizing the haunting poet Mary Swann. As a literary intertext, *Sarah Binks* on its own might bolster the satirical portrait of the dubiously talented Mary Swann. If it were left here, Shields's satire would seem to be unrelenting in its commentary on Canadian colonial culture (in the spirit of Stephen Leacock's Mariposa). But when Binks is merged with Pat Lowther, a touch of *gravitas* is lent to the portrayal of Swann and the satire becomes gothicized in becoming haunted by its own subject: the *return* of the dead Author. This process charts the enabling construction of a willed haunting that transforms the "ghost of a ghost" (that is, Swann and Binks, who are both fictions) into the "ghost of a (once living) poet."

Shields appears to be saying something about the need for literary haunting as a source of spiritual-cultural sustenance. Does the quest for precursors falsify the endeavour, or is the need authentic as a need? The novel circles around this unresolvable tension. Swann, in effect, is a communal—and, indeed, a textual—creation. Her mythology has been generated by the literary establishment; her poems are partially written by her publisher; her biography is invented by the local Nadeau librarian; and, in the end, the symposium participants have to rewrite, from memory, everything she is thought to have written. If on the one hand this can be read as a puncturing of the insistence on national labels and literary traditions, it also testifies to the important function that art serves for communal identity. In the end, are we to think that Swann's legacy has been subject to distortion, as Hammill asserts (130), or are we to think that it is the haunting effect, finally, which constitutes the power and pleasure of all literary—and literary critical—artifice? As Morton Jimroy says of the miracle of the literary effect: "When he thought of the revolution of planets, the emergence of species, the balance of mathematics, he could not see that any of these was more amazing than the impertinent human wish to reach into the sea of common language and extract from it the rich dark beautiful words that could be arranged in such a way that the unsayable might be said. Poetry was the prism that refracted all of life" (86). By channelling Pat Lowther through Sarah Binks, Shields is able to parody the compromised celebration of literary ancestors while conjuring the human need to connect with a lived past through literature. The tragedy of Swann, then, is the source of its parody: the more the author is dead, the more one wishes to commune with her. In part a send-up of the literary establishment's inexorable and fatuous reinvention of its authors, the novel also provides a self-conscious meditation on the urgent compulsion for literary ancestors in the construction of cultural tradition and collective identity.

Given *Swann*'s apparent deconstruction of national and authorial identity markers, it is ironic that the novel sets itself firmly within an identifiable Canadian literary trajectory, not only lending a touch of poignancy to its portrayal of Mary Swann but also suggesting that localized, even national, culture is not entirely superfluous in an apparently postmodern, post-national era. Moreover, by transposing the Saskatchewan and British Columbia origins of Binks and Lowther into rural Ontario, Shields places her mystery firmly within Canada's celebrated Southern Ontario Gothic tradition, which in many instances (as in the case of Alice Munro) figures the gothic as a function of the quotidian and the local. Shields's novel thus charts and enacts both the making and unmaking of a national poet—a commemorative fusion of Binks and Lowther—through her fictional creation of a haunting literary legend whose authority and origins are evocative, yet spectral. *Swann* adopts a metatextual reflection on its satirical narrative through its real-life poetic gothic intertext, exploring the ways a community embraces literary ghosts in the urge to secure a form of collective memory that may—or may not—be a will-o'-the-wisp, but which is no less necessary for all that. It may be appropriate, then, that the novel concludes with a poem that laments the void that comes with the loss of cultural memory. As Mary Swann says in the poem "Lost Things," it is

> As though the lost things have withdrawn
>
> Into themselves [...]
>
> Lustreless and without history [...]
>
> [...] becoming part of a larger loss
>
> Without a name [...]   (313)

Notes

1. This "manuscript," the author tells us, was a board from one of the buildings of the Binks's farm upon which was written a poem (51).

2. The connection between the two has been noted by a few critics, including Catherine Addison in her review of *Swann* in *Canadian Literature* when the novel was first published. Addison notes Swann's "resemblance to Pat Lowther" in that each is a "female poet murdered by her husband" but asserts that the resemblance ends there (159). I am proposing that the parallel is more extensive, and indeed more suggestive, than this.

3. In their reviews of *A Stone Diary*, both Gary Geddes and Christopher Levenson sought to distance themselves from any comparison of Lowther's legacy with that of Sylvia Plath. Levenson warned against the propagation of "a Canadian Plath cult" (352).

WORKS CITED

Addison, Catherine. "Lost Things." Rev. of *Swann: A Mystery*, by Carol Shields. *Canadian Literature* 121 (Summer 1989): 158–60. Print.

Atwood, Margaret. *Negotiating with the Dead: A Writer on Writing*. Cambridge: Cambridge University Press, 2002. Print.

Barthes, Roland. "The Death of the Author." In *Image–Music–Text*, trans. Stephen Heath. New York: Hill and Wang, 1977: 142–48. Print.

Geddes, Gary. Rev. of *A Stone Diary*. *Globe and Mail* 9 Apr. 1977: E27. Print.

Gzowski, Peter. "Pat Lowther Tribute." *Gzowski on FM*. CBC Radio. 2 Nov. 1975. Radio.

Greenblatt, Stephen. *Shakespearean Negotiations: The Circulation of Social Energy in Renaissance England*. Berkeley: University of California Press, 1988. Print.

Grescoe, Paul. "Eulogy for a Poet: Poet as Victim." *Canadian Magazine* 5 June 1976: 13, 16–19. Print

Hammill, Faye. "Influential Circles: Carol Shields and the Canadian Literature Canon." In *Literary Culture and Female Authorship in Canada, 1760–2000*. Amsterdam: Rodopi, 2003: 115–33. Print.

Hiebert, Paul. *Sarah Binks*. London: Oxford University Press, 1947. Print.

Kertzer, Jonathan. *Worrying the Nation: Imagining a National Literature in English Canada*. Toronto: University of Toronto Press, 1998. Print.

Levenson, Christopher. Rev. of *A Stone Diary*. *Queen's Quarterly* 85 (1978): 352–54. Print.

Lowther, Pat. *The Collected Works of Pat Lowther*, ed. Christine Wiesenthal. Edmonton: NeWest, 2010. Print.

McMullen, Lorraine. "Carol Shields and the University of Ottawa: Some Reminiscences." *Prairie Fire* 16.1 (Spring 1995): 132–37. Print.

Noonan, Gerald. "Incongruity and Nostalgia in *Sarah Binks*." *Studies in Canadian Literature* 3.2 (1978). Print.

Shields, Carol. *Swann: A Mystery*. New York: Viking, 1987. Print.

Wachtel, Eleanor. *Random Illuminations: Conversations with Carol Shields*. Fredericton: Goose Lane, 2007. Print.

Wiesenthal, Christine. *The Half-Lives of Pat Lowther*. Toronto: University of Toronto Press, 2005. Print.

Assembling Identity: Late-Life Agency in *The Stone Angel* and *The Stone Diaries*

PATRICIA LIFE

Two Canadian novels, published twenty-nine years apart, facilitate an examination of identity and agency in relation to aging. Carol Shields's 1993 novel *The Stone Diaries* gestures towards Margaret Laurence's 1964 novel *The Stone Angel* in its recording of the life of an aged central female character, its stone imagery, its depiction of aging as decline and loss, and its enquiry into the themes of late-life recollection and search for selfhood and meaning. Both texts focus on the protagonist's interior life and on the construction of personal identities more than on the action of an external plot. Both present the protagonist as central yet influencing and influenced by other characters and events, that is, as a hub where multiple stories intersect yet are reconfigured into a story or stories focused on the protagonist. The angst of the protagonists provides the energy in their respective texts. Both authors show their aged protagonists addressing their identities as individuals and as women within communities dominated by men.

While Laurence's modernist text presents a fictitious autobiography from the first-person perspective of the elderly protagonist, Shields's more postmodern text portrays the protagonist's fictitious life by means of discontinuous first- and third-person narrative strands, eschewing linearity and embracing ambiguity and multiplicity in order to represent a life. Both texts depict elements of aging-as-decline, a narrative that denotes the belief that a person progresses to the peak of adulthood after which they are "over the hill" and descending towards death. Shields's text also incorporates aspects of aging-as-progress[1] narrative. Taken together, Laurence's and Shields's protagonists provide an intriguing illustration of opposing definitions of late-life identity.

Age studies theorist Margaret Morganroth Gullette argues against those who limit the definition of a person's identity to an unchanging central core essence. She believes instead that people incorporate into themselves over the life course various ongoing experiences, character developments, and interactions with others, ultimately resulting over time in progression towards fuller, more complete selves. She sees identity as being comprised of all that a person has been and has done up until the current point in time: "I think that identity over time can be seen as a sense of an achieved portmanteau 'me'—made up, for each subject, of all its changeable and continuing selves together" (125). While *The Stone Angel* provides an illustration of a protagonist who defines identity as fixed and stable and who strenuously resists all tendencies towards progress narrative, *The Stone Diaries* provides an illustration of a protagonist who appears to accept an identity defined as progress across the life course, as an accumulation of diverse and changing identity elements.

Laurence and Shields depict aging as a dismaying descent into physical ugliness and weakness, yet Shields's depiction is tempered with aspects suggestive of positive-aging ideologies. A comparison between the two texts demonstrates that, unlike Hagar Shipley, Laurence's protagonist, Shields's character Daisy Goodwill bends according to her circumstances, thus serving as an illustration of Gullette's broader definition of identity. Daisy differs from Hagar in that she enables complementary relationships with others, drifts complacently from one living situation to another, and adjusts compliantly to the developments in her identity as she ages. She enjoys periods of positive progress, such as when she finds fulfillment in the art of gardening and in her related work as a journalist. She suffers psychological decline following the loss of her husband and job and physiological decline following her heart attack. Yet, positive progress repeatedly reasserts itself, even during her residency at Canary Palms. Throughout the text, she continually adjusts her internal autobiography as a way to cope with change and re-establish her ever-evolving identities. However, her ruminating attempts to justify the actions of others in order to construct an acceptable social history for herself could be said to verge on denial or even cognitive malfunction.

In 1894, Laurence's and Shields's early literary ancestor, Catharine Parr Traill, wrote *Pearls and Pebbles*, a series of sketches drawn from the previous nine decades of her own life. In it, the protagonist, Catharine, demonstrates a cheerful faith in God as she approaches the end of her life, confidently expecting an afterlife to follow her death. In the 1949 text, *The Innocent Traveller*, Ethel Wilson depicts her protagonist, Topaz, trustingly anticipating eternal adventure as she waits for death. Religious beliefs allow both of these early Canadian protagonists to find purpose in their lives and to face aging and the approach of death without apparent anxiety. Although their approaches to self-definition differ during the course of the texts, both Hagar and Daisy face aging and death with marked disquiet. Neither exhibits the acceptance of aging demonstrated by the earlier characters, Catharine and Topaz. Hagar resists, runs away, and eventually capitulates, perhaps in the end finding some grace. Daisy by comparison repeatedly yields and adapts, seemingly progressing towards old age without resisting. Yet the final pages of the text reveal that "Daisy Goodwill's final (unspoken) words are 'I am not at peace,'" suggesting that she has been compliant but not approving of the channels her life has followed (361). Although Daisy has thus joined Hagar in voicing her dissatisfaction, neither text provides closure regarding its protagonist's eventual state of being.

Both novels illustrate the aging-as-decline narrative that became pervasive following the middle of the twentieth century, and in its presentation of an alternative definition of identity, Shields's text mixes the influence of the decline narrative with some aspects of a more contemporary, aging-as-progress narrative.

Laurence's novel is an early example of a now relatively substantial set of Canadian life-review literature employing a late-life frame narrative to weave a tale of the protagonist's earlier adventures, and, in so doing, to depict the process by which he or she acquires a full late-life identity.[2] Age studies scholars today afford *The Stone Angel* iconic status as an early Canadian work on aging, yet a full consideration of its age-related narrative has yet to be carried out. Sally Chivers argues that, in earlier years, critics ignored, underplayed, or denigrated Hagar's age: "many studies find coherence in the novel because of its biblical or literary imagery, because of its status as a confessional novel, or because of its impact as a feminist novel." Yet she points out that "because many critics avoid the troubling present-tense narrative featuring the indomitable Hagar daunted by age, few refer to the Silverthreads nursing home visit even though it is the central conflict of the novel's frame" (22–23).

As all long-lived literature does, this text provides ample scope for simultaneous interpretations. Many critics disagree with Chivers, seeing different aspects of the novel as the central conflict. Nora Foster Stovel portrays Hagar's visit to the Silverthreads home as the impetus leading to Hagar's symbolic descent into "Hell" at Shadow Point (195), and chooses to focus her analysis on the climactic confession and pseudo-Christian communion she partakes of there in the form of shared wine and soda crackers (Laurence 223). Stovel argues that Hagar finally apologizes to her long-dead son John (as represented by the vagrant Lees) with the words "I didn't really mean it," and that she takes a first step there towards spiritual redemption by relinquishing her Lucifer-like pride (Laurence 247). Religious interpretations of the novel are undoubtedly significant and they help to place it within the rest of the Manawaka series, yet considering that the protagonist's primary obsession in the frame narrative is to align her current distasteful old-aged identity with the image she holds of a preferred youthful self, it seems surprising that age ideology has not been a more central topic of enquiry regarding this novel. Many people today are more immediately concerned with aging and its ramifications than they are capable of or interested in following biblical and Miltonic allusions, so perhaps the age-related aspects of Laurence's work will maintain interest in the text amongst present and future readers.

Like Chivers, Amelia DeFalco primarily addresses the protagonist in her old age and within the frame narrative, discussing the "narrator's appeal to recollection as a means toward self-recognition and the summa-tion of a life" (30). According to DeFalco, Hagar is attempting to reconcile her true free identity with the current, shockingly old version. She argues that "*The Stone Angel* depicts a character struggling to reconcile past and present, and offers a binaristic model of selfhood that corresponds to Hagar's persistent frustration and anger at what she perceives as a delinquent old self that distorts her true, young self" (30). The primary conflict occurs in Hagar's mind as she tries to reconcile the two images of herself.

Laurence's portrayal of Hagar's alienation is, in part, a stark delineation of her acceptance of her society's ageism. In the 1942 text, "Three Score and Ten—The Business of Growing Old," Stephen Leacock famously compares aging to stumbling through the frontline of a war towards oblivion (1). Laurence joins with Leacock and many other authors of the twentieth century in her depiction of one of the most common of aging tropes: the decline narrative.

The Stone Angel predates the pro-agency age ideology instigated by the boomer cohort, yet the central character can be seen to be facing the same type of crisis that third-agers[3] today are attempting to avoid. Hagar is rejecting the arrival of what we would today call the fourth age or *true* old age, the onset of dependency and feebleness; she yearns for the power of her former self, now hidden inside her current bulky, uncooperative hulk. The text explores the fear of the long-term-care institution known as the home, or the gothic home-as-horror narrative that was prevalent at the time Laurence wrote. Hagar sees her helplessness reflected in her aging body and in the aging bodies of others at Silverthreads, and she senses that removal to the home would force her to face her fears about aging.

For Hagar, aging is defined by loss—lost ability, lost possessions, lost privacy, lost autonomy, and lost true identity. Despite her desire to avoid it, she has succumbed to change. Yet she vainly clings to the ideal she held for herself in her early adulthood. In the present-time frame narrative, Hagar is ninety years old, suffers memory confusion, and sometimes falls when attempting to walk, yet she fiercely refuses to relinquish her independence. She has raged and resisted all her life in an attempt to defend herself. Her first antagonist was her judgmental father, whose fiery will she herself has inherited, yet who forced her to "memorize weights and measures" and to submit to being beaten on the hands with a "foot ruler"—metaphorically requiring her to accept his rule over her life and his version of achievement (7).

After her marriage, Hagar had continued to define her power in relation to the restraints imposed by her husband and her sons, until finally she is "rampant with memory" and fighting against her aging body (5). For one moment in time, she had become what she considered to be her true and independent self when she announced to her father that, despite his disapproval, she planned to marry Bram. Once disillusioned by the reality of her married life, she began to forever look backward to this ideal yet lost selfhood.

When forced by circumstances in middle age to go door-to-door selling eggs, Hagar encounters Lottie, a childhood acquaintance who has risen in life while she has fallen. Humiliated by the encounter, she escapes into a public rest room, focusing on her image in the mirror as a way of addressing the perceived discrepancy between her core identity and the ravaged exterior moulded by time:

> I found what I needed, a mirror. I stood for a long time, looking, wondering how a person could change so much and never see it. So gradually it happens . . . . My hair was gray and straight. I always cut it myself. The face—a brown and leathery face that wasn't mine. Only the eyes were mine, staring as though to pierce the lying glass and get beneath to some truer image, infinitely distant. (133)

Hagar refuses to accept the changes time has wrought in her appearance, believing that her true self remains evident only in her eyes.

In the frame narrative's present-time period, right after Doris asks the minister to coax her mother-in-law to accept admission to a home, Hagar looks into another mirror: "when I look in my mirror and beyond the changing shell that houses me, I see the same dark eyes as when I first began to remember and to notice myself. I have never worn glasses. My eyes are still quite strong. The eyes change least of all" (38). Now well into old age, Hagar once again notes that only her eyes match the self she perceives as her true identity. After meeting with the minister, Hagar muses that, even at ninety years of age, she should be able to "look into the mirror softly, take it by surprise [and] see there again that Hagar with the shining hair, the dark-maned colt off to the training ring" (42). As Sally Chivers comments, Laurence "presents a strict division between the interiority and the exteriority of aging," noting that she chooses to accept the veracity of the interior self and to ignore the reflection of the exterior self (14).

Fiercely clinging to her own core selfhood as she perceives it, Hagar is threatened by any behaviour that might compromise it. Since *The Stone Angel* was published in the same decade that saw the birth control pill become available to women, and that saw many women begin to question their traditional roles, her strong will and determination to recapture her moment of absolute freedom suggest a parallel with all the women who rebelled in the 1960s against restrictive roles.[4] When her brother Dan lay dying, she refused to assume the identity of her own mother in order to comfort him because she was not and could not bear to be "a bit like her," that is, to be perceived as a submissive weak woman (25). Throughout her lifetime, she has been determined to fight against any step forcing her to accept a position of submission, weakness, or dependency.

When her son and daughter-in-law claim that she must move to Silverthreads, Hagar becomes desperate at the thought of having her familiar home torn from her:

> my shreds and remnants of years are scattered through it visibly in lamps and vases, the needle-point fire bench, the heavy oak chair from the Shipley place, the china cabinet and walnut sideboard from my father's house . . . . If I am not somehow contained in them and in this house, something of all change caught and fixed here, eternal enough for my purposes, then I do not know where I am to be found at all. (36)

Hagar sees her home as an extension of her own selfhood. The house and its familiar objects, each carrying a piece of the past, anchor her to a preferred version of reality and give her at least a limited sense of permanence. To be torn out of this exoskeleton and exposed to the world resembles a type of death in that it would require her to relinquish her trust that a safe pseudo-eternity can be lived within its walls.

While Hagar sees her home of many years as a comforting shelter and a keeper of her past identities, she sees the nursing home as a new and unwanted shell that will force her to accept a changed identity. Silverthreads and her aged body both resemble encompassing cages that threaten to further restrict and disfigure her true identity. Laurence depicts Hagar looking down at a body she does not recognize as her own: "I . . . see with surprise and unfamiliarity the great swathed hips. My waist was twenty inches when I wed" (56). She no longer recognizes her alien body and feels as if it is betraying her: "as I lower myself to the chesterfield, the windy prison of my bowels belches air, sulphurous and groaning. I am to be spared nothing, it appears. I cannot speak, for anger" (58).

The long-term-care institution, known to her as the "home," repulses her, as the Silverthreads scene makes apparent. She fearfully asks a female resident whether "you ever get used to such a place" and later comments on the unintended path her life has taken, saying, "I never got used to a blessed thing" (104). She has just raged hopelessly, refusing to accept her evolving identities.

Some critics figure Hagar as a fallen-angel Lucifer, an unredeemed sinner of the western Judeo-Christian tradition as seen in the Bible, Milton, and Dante. Laurence clearly intended religious interpretations of her story since she linked her protagonist to the biblical story of Hagar through the name she assigned to her (Stovel 175). According to Christian doctrine, only by an act of confession and a request for forgiveness from God could Hagar be forgiven and reborn. Interpreters who analyze the novel's religious underpinnings disagree as to whether or not Hagar achieves this redemption by the text's conclusion. Paul Comeau argues that, while religious redemption seems a possibility, the text provides no closure to that effect (64). Laurence herself comments:

> In what happens to Hagar at the very end of the novel there is to me some sense of redemption. Close to the end of her life she . . . really can admit to herself, when she says "Pride is my wilderness," that the tragedy of her life has been that, because of her spiritual pride she has been unable to give and receive the kind of love she is capable of . . . she always wondered what the neighbours thought. So I would say that the main theme is survival with the ability to give and receive love. But fitting into that theme and perhaps more important is the sense of a possibility of a kind of redemption. (qtd. in Fabre 193)

As Comeau points out, the qualifiers in Laurence's final sentence cast doubt as to her firm belief in her character's redemption. Although the text suggests the possibility of redemption, as Comeau says, Hagar may not achieve it by "virtue of her inability to bend enough" (64).

It can be interpreted that Hagar willingly changes and acquires a more altruistic identity at the end of the story when she seems to bless her son Marvin (45). Stovel states that in the final scene, "Hagar gives birth to herself as a woman" and dies a "woman and a mother, repeating . . . in her own hands, what she terms 'the mother words'— 'There, There'" (202). Yet Hagar prevaricates, saying that, although she speaks with a "kind of love," she tells "a lie—yet not a lie" to her son when she says he has been a better son than John (304–07). While it remains debatable whether she has fully embraced motherhood, it is clear that she is finally at least willing to play that role in order to give comfort to her son Marvin. This marks a significant change from her refusal to assume the role of mother for her brother Dan. By including these parallel scenes, the authorial voice suggests that Hagar does indeed make a conciliatory gesture.

Stovel interprets the glass of water received from the nurse as a "sacramental symbol," a representation of absolution or baptism (202). No closure, however, can be asserted here because Hagar's rude eagerness to seize the glass could be interpreted as her ongoing attempt to fight off her own helplessness (Laurence 202). It could also be argued that she extends a supposedly redeeming act of charity by getting out of bed and obtaining the needed bedpan for her fellow hospital patient. Yet this could be explained away too by arguing that she is merely refusing to give in to the limitations of her aging body and must therefore prove her continued strength and independence. And although the text's final words "and then" suggest death, Laurence does not make Hagar's achievement of a religious afterlife obvious.

Laurence provides no definitive closure, and so opens the door to multiple interpretations. It is clear that Hagar repeatedly resists patriarchal authority and rejects the restrictions of a changing body, and that she strives until the absolute end of the text to assert her ideal youthful and independent identity. I acknowledge that she has achieved some self-knowledge by the conclusion and that she has become willing to extend a type of kindness towards Marvin. I would also agree that it is *possible* to interpret that she has exerted a type of agency in relinquishing her pride and accepting a religious redemption. Yet the only agency she *definitively* exerts is resistance against patriarchal authority, against her own aging body, and against submission to institutional care. In the last scene, severe discomfort forces her to request pain medication, yet in her final act—grasping the water glass in her own hands—she can be interpreted to have rejected further assistance and to have again attempted to seize the independence that has eluded her throughout her life. Despite Hagar's Lucifer-like qualities and her sheer orneriness, readers admire her plucky fighting spirit and identify with her fight against indignity, helplessness, and debility.

In Western culture, moving to institutional care has long been construed as a loss of independence and autonomy and as one of the most wrenching identity changes of late life. Admission to a nursing home has been equated with loss of youthfulness, with decline towards death. When Laurence published *The Stone Angel* in 1964, nursing homes had come a long way, yet people had not forgotten their ghastly prototypes—the workhouses of the nineteenth century. Laurence reflects the cultural beliefs of her time, presenting a powerful portrait of the fear and loathing such non-homes inspired.

Since roughly 1990, though, some contemporary authors have been reimagining the nursing home as a potential site of personal agency and of ongoing and meaningful identity development. *The Stone Diaries* sits on the cusp of this change, representing a time period when decline narratives were fully entrenched but "positive aging" narratives, "progress" narratives, and new approaches to building long-term care facilities were beginning to alter age ideologies. When Daisy moves into Canary Palms Convalescent Home, she at first says, "I'm not myself here" (324), a sentiment that echoes Hagar's question to a Silverthreads resident about whether "you ever get used to such a place" (Laurence 104). Both comments are compatible with a decline narrative. Yet later, after exerting little resistance, Daisy adjusts to her new situation (324). While Hagar clings to a prescribed and inflexible view of her own identity, Daisy bends and allows herself to move into her new identity as a resident at Canary Palms. She even comes to enjoy small accomplishments and pleasures (324). This character's adaptation implies that she is positioned within a progress narrative—and, in this case, a happier narrative than Hagar's. This difference, perhaps, can be explained partially by the disparities between the personalities of the two protagonists (and/or two authors); possibly, Hagar's innate stubbornness limits her ability to accept changes, whereas Daisy's affable nature allows her to accommodate the forces of circumstance. I would argue, however, that at least in part, these differences reflect the fact that *The Stone Diaries* was published twenty-nine years later than *The Stone Angel*, therefore reflecting changing attitudes towards religion, aging, selfhood, and late-life living accommodations. I am not arguing that Shields is denying the decline narrative in favour of a progress narrative, but that aspects of the progress narrative—such as the idea that identity is multiple and develops over time—are interacting with aspects of the decline narrative within the text.

The Stone Angel is probably Canada's most well-known expression of the decline narrative tradition of the twentieth century. Although Daisy's own experience at Canary Palms suggests progress, Shields's account of Daisy's visit to a nursing home to see a man who might be her father-in-law is as extreme as Laurence's in its expression of horror at old age. Significantly, Daisy's visit concludes with what could be considered to be a positive-aging motif (including the negative connotation often attached to positive aging).

Grandpa Magnus Flett, whom Daisy finds living in a nursing home called Sycamore Manor in the Orkney Islands, is incontinent, blind, bedridden, and 115 years of age. The text's description of the man illustrates the type of gothic horror typically associated with decline narratives: "And now, here was this barely breathing cadaver, all his old age depletions registered and paid for. A tissue of skin. A scaffold of bone; well, more like china than bone" (305). Shields adds Daisy's reactions:

> A few seconds passed—she let them pass—and then he opened his mouth, which was not a mouth at all but a puckered hole without lips or teeth . . . . She felt moved to grope under the sheet and reach for his hand, but feared what she might find, some unimaginable decay. Instead she pressed lightly on the coverlet, perceiving the substantiality of tethered bones and withered flesh. A faint shuddering. The rising scent of decomposition. (305–06)

Clearly Daisy finds the aged state of his body repulsive, and she is eager to leave Sycamore Manor.

Shields couples this clichéd gothic depiction, though, with the upbeat comment that "great old age is heartening to observe" (295). She depicts Daisy leaving the nursing home feeling newly young after comparing herself to Magnus: "Oh, she is young and strong again. Look at the way she walks freely out the door and down the narrow stone street of Stromness, tossing her hair in the fine light" (307). Daisy is shocked by his appearance, yet she successfully recovers by psychologically and physically distancing herself from this very old age, leaving Magnus and the horrible home behind. Although she would be considered to be relatively old by this point, she differentiates between her own level of oldness and her father-in-law's extreme level of oldness. Thus Shields, perhaps unintentionally, provides readers with an early example of the twenty-first-century positive-aging trend that shows relatively old, third-age people such as Daisy happily distancing themselves from those whom they consider to be truly old and frail—those now labelled as being in the fourth age.

In the following chapter, "Illness and Decline," Daisy rapidly drops into her own decline narrative when she suffers a heart attack, which also causes her to fall and break her knees. During the associated hospitalization, she suffers kidney failure, prompting her doctor to diagnose and consequently surgically remove a cancerous kidney. The extent of Daisy's descent into a physiological decline narrative is made apparent in the comments of Daisy's daughter Alice: "She can't possibly go home, the doctor says it's impossible. How would she manage? She's helpless" (316). Daisy also senses her own lost agency: "Suddenly her body is all that matters. How it's let her down" (309).

In this chapter, Daisy is very like the aged Hagar in that she is widowed, feels alone and helpless in her old age, and is "trying to remember a time when her body had been sealed and private" (310). Like Hagar, she has been extracted from the homes that helped to provide her self-definition and has been forced into a new shell following her surgeries: Canary Palms Convalescent Home. Her daughter Alice muses on "life's diminution," looks at her "mother's bedside table at Canary Palms and s[ees], jumbled there, a toothbrush, toothpaste, a comb etc." She thinks, "That three-story house in Ottawa has been emptied out, and so has the commodious Florida condo. How is it possible, so much shrinkage?" (323). Here the text clearly states: aging is loss, not gain.

Daisy presents further aspects of aging-as-decline narrative when the text echoes Hagar's despondent mirror scenes: "She looks into her bedside mirror, so cunningly hidden on the reverse side of the bed tray, and says, 'There she is, my life's companion. Once I sat in her heart. Now I crouch in a corner of her eye'" (336). Like Hagar, she differentiates between the outward self so clearly ravaged by age and an ongoing interior self that has now been relegated to "crouching" in the corner of her life, remaining physically evident only in her eye. Shields hints here that, despite Daisy's tendency to accept alterations to her identity, she remains aware of the point from which she began.

Although there are parallels between the two novels in terms of their protagonists' sense of an interior ongoing selfhood and in terms of their expression of twentieth-century decline narratives, there are further significant differences too—differences that reflect developments in ideology that are characteristic of the late twentieth and early twenty-first century.

Hagar in part rages because she reflects the culture of modernity, a time when most people embraced the concept of free will and the central importance of humankind, but also believed that there was a good chance that God was ultimately in control of all life. By contrast, Shields's postmodern text presents a world in which Daisy drifts forward in time from random event to random event, with no belief in her own or anyone else's ability—and certainly not an omnipotent God's—to provide meaningful direction. Daisy expects a progress narrative, but not necessarily a progression towards happy outcomes.

Hagar tends towards impotent fury when faced with unfavourable changes, whereas Daisy accepts the alterations time brings and does not cling to her previous circumstances. For example, after she is widowed, Daisy travels to Canada and "to Barker Flett as to a refuge," not asking herself "what is possible, but rather what possibilities remain" (146). She complacently marries her much older pseudo-uncle because that is the only opportunity that her haphazardly evolving life seems to hold out to her. The text says that she is "accustomed to crowding her concerns into a shadowy corner" (147).

This pattern is in evidence late in her life as well when she fails to rage against the loss of her health:

> Since her heart attack everything takes her by surprise, but nothing more so than her willingness to let it, as though a new sense of her own hollowness has made her a volunteer for replacement. Her body's dead planet with its atoms and molecules and lumps of matter is blooming all of a sudden with headlines, nightmares, greeting cards, medicinal bitterness, crashes in the night, footsteps in the corridor, the odors of her own breath and blood, someone near her door. . . . (331)

Late in the text, one of her family members comments that "she just let her life happen to her" (356). Not all changes make Daisy happy, as evidenced by the depression she experiences following the loss of her journalism job, but she consistently appears to accept all progressions in identity (229). Such acceptance reflects the influence of a narrative of aging-as-progress.

Cultural shifts in age ideologies are also reflected in the difference between the texts' depictions of Daisy's and Hagar's late-life living arrangements. Although Victoria's move into Daisy's home mirrors Marvin's and Doris's move into Hagar's home, the precipitating causes are exactly opposite. In her middle age, Daisy takes Victoria into her home because Victoria needs care, not because she wants Victoria to care for her.

Daisy later moves out of the Ottawa house and into a Florida condominium in Bayside Towers where she becomes a part of the "Flowers" social group and shares bridge and conversation with Lily, Myrtle, and Glad. Today such a building might be designated as "senior housing." This type of transitional home can act to buffer the shock that occurs when seniors leave a home in which they have lived most of their adult lives to move directly into an institution such as Canary Palms (or Hagar's Silverthreads), where "home" becomes limited to a bed and a dresser.

Shields's depiction of the supportive bond enjoyed by the Flowers would fit what Chivers calls "seriatim relationships" or peer-care arrangements. She recommends "peer care as a possible strategy to redistribute power and to avoid the representation of burdensome old age. Even outside of care situations, the possibilities inherent within late-life friendship allow for a mutuality that might be lacking in inter- and cross-generational relationships" (80). Today, downsizing by stages and arranging for the benefits of a mutually supportive peer network are common in late-life arrangements, yet they were not typically available options in Hagar's time. Thus, Hagar's pride suffers when she lives with her son during late life, whereas Daisy, at least for a time, enjoys the support of peers after she is widowed.

Following Daisy's departure from her condominium as a result of her emergency admission to Sarasota Memorial Hospital, Shields includes a pastoral visit scene that is reminiscent of the one in Laurence's text. In this case, the power relationship favours the protagonist instead of the pastor, perhaps representing Shields's desire to afford lessened respect to the ministry and increased agency to older women. In Laurence's 1964 text, Clergyman Troy meets Hagar's needs by singing an affecting hymn (291), whereas in the 1993 text it is Daisy who meets the needs of Reverend Rick. Daisy is irritated yet also flattered when he seeks her advice as to whether or not to tell his mother that he is gay. Instead of becoming teary like Hagar, Daisy provides instruction and then sends the "room-to-room peddler of guilt-wrapped wares" away weeping out his angst (332–35).

While Laurence clearly intends readers to find religious meaning in Hagar's story of potential redemption, Shields, who is on record as a non-believer, suggests that Daisy experiences little religious meaning in her life. Eleanor Wachtel records that "[n]ot only did Carol not believe in any sort of afterlife, she felt strongly that she didn't want any sort of monuments to her death—no gravestone, not even an urn" (26). Since the time of Laurence's text, the influence of religion in Western life had significantly diminished. Thus the secular emphasis in the novel reflects both Shields's status as a non-believer and her culture's shift away from the church.

While Hagar runs away rather than accept residency in Silver-threads, Daisy moves into Canary Palms and with time adjusts her sense of self and finds sufficient cause to settle in. Despite her original desire to avoid him, she eventually does have an intimate exchange with Reverend Rick. She also shares a joke with Alice (335), and when she applies a little makeup, she comments on her sense of acceptance:

> It surprises Grandma Flett that there is so much humor hidden in the earth's crevasses; it's everywhere, like a thousand species of moss. . . . something amusing will happen on the floor, the nurses kidding back and forth, some ongoing joke. Who would have thought that comedy could stretch all the way to infirm old age?
>
> And vanity too. Vanity refuses to die, pushing the blandness of everyday life into little pleats, pockets, knobs of electric candy. (336)

Looking at her new manicure—"her ten buffed beauties"—she thinks, "[h]ow . . . such a little thing should give her so much pleasure" (337). While it can be interpreted that Hagar never accepts her aging identities and thus remains fiercely dissatisfied with her life, Daisy on many levels appears to adjust and adapt as her life progresses along. She finds ways to be, if not happy, at least complacent or content.

While it is true that the two protagonists' personalities differ, there is enough evidence to assert that contemporary positive-aging ideologies and new age-related customs have permeated Shields's representation of aging. Yet layers of ambiguity in Laurence's and Shields's narrations complicate critical interpretations of both texts. Hagar's harsh public voice hides a more vulnerable interior self, a self *potentially* capable of growth despite her own best attempts to armour herself with prickliness and pride, and Laurence's authorial voice underlies the character's voice to offer a slightly different identity for her protagonist. Searching for the definitive identities of *The Stone Diaries*' narrator, however, may result in the reader becoming lost amongst the multiple strands that constitute the text's narrations. As the title *The Stone Diaries* suggests, no one single voice or identity can be isolated easily as narrator, problematizing attempts to characterize the protagonist.

Although critics disagree widely as to how Shields's narrative is constituted, most would agree that the text suggests that the protagonist has multiple changing identities. Thus Shields could be said to be rejecting the image of aging as erosion of an initial selfhood in favour of aging as progress towards a more complete and complex identity. As David Williams concludes, "each of her narrative choices illuminates what it means to be a series of multiple selves that has come in the postmodern era to supplant a Cartesian model of unified, autonomous identity" (17).

In an interview, Shields herself places Daisy as the narrator, saying that "'diaries' is problematic because it's much more of an autobiography than a diary, and of course it's an unwritten autobiography—she never sits down and writes. This is the autobiography, or diary, that she carries in her head, this construct of one's self that we all carry around with us" (qtd. in Wachtel 49). At least for Shields, Daisy herself speaks, even if only in an internal, unwritten sense.

It is of note, however, that not only does the narration portray Daisy's identity as evolving over time and in relation to others, it also includes fictitious identities for Daisy. Thus it could be argued that the text speculates about the role of memory and imagination in reconstructing identity in late life.

In one narrative account, for example, her son Warren finds her essays in the attic, while in another account the children say that she left them to him in her will (251, 347). Readers might assume that the first account in Warren's voice is in fact Daisy's late-life voice ruminating about what his reaction might have been if he were to have read her essays and discovered evidence of her intelligence. In the second account, Daisy more pessimistically surmises that the children are surprised and stymied as to why he has been willed the essays, having little knowledge of their mother beyond her services to them. The narrator ponders to herself, thinking that

> words are more and more required. And the question arises: what is the story of a life? A chronicle of fact or a skilfully wrought impression? The bringing together of what she fears? Or the adding up of what has been off-handedly revealed, those tiny allotted increments of knowledge? She needs a quiet place in which to think about this immensity. (340)

Daisy imagines various contrasting scenarios and then weighs them to determine her preferred options. In her old age, Hagar irrationally attempts to cling to an outdated vision of herself. Daisy, on the other hand, seems to irrationally create identities for herself that apparently fail to reconcile all historical facts.

Shields's intention may have been for Daisy to act primarily as a composite character representing powerless female literary characters of the past such as Hagar and others. While Hagar is as willful as a mule, Daisy resembles a ship coasting along the canal of life, as if Shields has brought Ethel Wilson's character Topaz forward in time to inhabit *The Stone Diaries*. This apparent weakness in Daisy's personality and the text's tendency to view a character simultaneously from within and without may be present in the text because Shields is tipping her hat to Ethel Wilson's collection of connected short stories, and by so doing allowing Daisy to represent a host of oppressed women from the past. Wachtel records Shields's opinion on this subject: "In many ways, [Daisy] is like so many women of this century who became, in fact, nothing, their lives did not hold many choices, they were this huge army of women, they were mainly voiceless, they were defined by the people around them" (50).

The ghost of Topaz (and women like her) could be said to be another narrative thread or identity within the *Diaries*. Intertextuality is suggested by the fact that Ethel Wilson's portrayal of the pliable Topaz in *The Innocent Traveller* could equally well apply to Daisy: "the private life of Topaz, if life must be compared to a journey, had been like travelling on a canal" or "a water spider gliding across a pond's surface" (Wilson 65, 93). Another inter-text between *The Stone Diaries* and *The Innocent Traveller* is evident in Shields's treatment of narrative point of view. Wilson's narrator Rose assumes a first-person point of view when describing her female ancestor Topaz just as Shields's narrator Daisy does when describing her mother Mercy giving birth—even though neither narrator had been born at the time of the depicted scenes. Rose says, "I was never at a Book Meeting, because I was not alive and had not then been thought of, but I have heard so much about them that I am there with Topaz. There we sat" (57). Like Topaz, Daisy is helpless in the face of male authority, although unlike Hagar, Topaz and Daisy seem to accept their lot in life.

Although appearances throughout the text may suggest Daisy's malleability and outward acceptance of societal pressure, the text's final unspoken words of resistance, "I am not at peace," dramatically impact possible interpretations of *The Stone Diaries* because they acknowledge that, at the text's end, she possibly shares Hagar's resentment of societal powers and may finally feel prepared to take a stand against them. The inclusion of Daisy's final words indicates that, although she has outwardly accepted the random shifts her identity has followed, she may have held other opinions inside. Alternatively, she may have reached a new point of growth where she now holds such opinions.

The aged protagonists of *The Stone Angel* and *The Stone Diaries* both appear to find new meaning or knowledge at the conclusion of the texts—although both texts withhold closure on this point. Despite her reluctance, Hagar acquires improved self-knowledge and assumes the role of nurturing mother—albeit minimally. Daisy adjusts to changes that occur with aging, forgives the other players in her life, and accepts the past—although all of this possibly comes about through her rather questionable reimagining of the past. When she comforts her son Marvin, Hagar tenuously links herself to her mother and the larger community of women, and when Daisy feels herself merging with and becoming "finally the still body of her dead mother," she strongly links herself to her mother and to the entire community of women (359).

At least to some extent, both texts show their protagonists to be representative of all women. Although *The Stone Angel* is not self-reflexive in style and is less pointedly inclusive of other women, few would doubt that this text speaks a feminist position for women of the twentieth century. Both authors show protagonists who struggle against powerlessness and lack of meaning in their male-dominated lives.

Hagar possibly finds redemption through the relinquishment of her pride, through the acceptance of her connection to her mother and son, and/or through the grace of the Christian God. Daisy remains outwardly submissive, inwardly restless, and somewhat inscrutable to the reader.

The Stone Angel epitomizes the twentieth-century's aging-as-decline and home-as-horror narratives. Hagar clings to her youthful identity, thus indicating her internalized ageism and providing an illustration of the definition of identity as core, fixed, and unchangeable. *The Stone Diaries* illustrates aspects of aging-as-decline narrative alongside an aging-as-growth narrative, while its protagonist Daisy illustrates a definition of identity as fluid, multiple, and expanding. Shields may have intended that Daisy's malleability and tendency to outwardly accept the changes in her life course should represent the generally weak position of women in a patriarchal society. The text is opaque and difficult to interpret because of its multiple narrative threads. The gradually evolving and enlarging identity that Daisy illustrates may also be interpreted to reflect the late twentieth-century's internalization of positive-aging and progress narratives and society's changing attitudes towards late-life care and the meaning of aging.

Notes

1.   The "progress narrative" counters the "decline narrative," suggesting that this image of a single rise and fall is overly simplistic. Most people would be considered to experience intermittent and possibly concurrent periods of progress and decline over their entire life course if all measures of psychological, social, physical, and financial states were to be taken into account. When I use the term "progress narrative," therefore, I do not mean to imply necessarily that progress moves towards goodness or happiness or that it completely displaces decline, but merely that it moves towards something further or larger. By contrast, the term "positive aging" (or "successful aging" or "anti-aging") connotes beneficial aging outcomes (such as maintained physical fitness), although in some usages "positive aging" connotes contentious or faux beneficial outcomes (such as can be achieved through consumerist spending on such things as age-defying plastic surgery). This sense of "positive aging" is often construed in opposition to a term such as "healthy aging," which connotes more general public approval.

2.   Think of Sara Gruen's *Water for Elephants,* Mordecai Richler's *Barney's Version,* Lawrence Hill's *The Book of Negroes,* Frances Itani's *Remembering the Bones,* Jane Urquhart's *Away.*

3.   The third age is a new stage of aging carved out by the boomer cohort and inserted between the second age, middle age, and the fourth age, very old age.

4.   Is it a coincidence that Margaret and her husband split up over his dismissal of the novel? In *Dance on the Earth: A Memoir* Laurence writes, "Strange reason for breaking up a marriage: a novel. I had to go with the old lady, I really did, but at the same time I felt terrible about hurting him" (158).

Works Cited

Chivers, Sally. *From Old Woman to Older Women: Contemporary Culture and Women's Narratives.* Columbus: Ohio State University Press, 2003. Print.

Comeau, Paul. *Margaret Laurence's Epic Imagination.* Edmonton: University of Alberta Press, 2005. Print.

DeFalco, Amelia. *Uncanny Subjects: Aging in Contemporary Narrative.* Columbus: Ohio State University Press, 2010. Print.

Fabre, Michel. "From *The Stone Angel* to *The Diviners*: An Interview with Margaret Laurence." In *Margaret Laurence: Critical Reflections,* ed. David Staines. Ottawa: University of Ottawa Press, 2001: 193–209. Web. 03 Aug. 2012.

Gullette, Margaret Morganroth. *Aged by Culture.* Chicago: University of Chicago Press, 2004. Print.

Laurence, Margaret. *Dance on the Earth: A Memoir.* Toronto: McClelland and Stewart, 1989. Print.

———. *The Stone Angel.* Toronto: McClelland & Stewart, 1988. Print.

Leacock, Stephen. "Three Score and Ten—The Business of Growing Old." In *My Remarkable Uncle and Other Sketches.* Toronto: McClelland and Stewart, 1965: 1–5. Print.

Shields, Carol. *The Stone Diaries.* Toronto: Random House, 1993. Print.

Stovel, Nora Foster. *Divining Margaret Laurence: A Study of Her Complete Writings.* Montreal: McGill-Queen's University Press, 2008. Print.

Traill, Catherine Parr. *Pearls and Pebbles*, ed. Elizabeth Thompson. Toronto: Natural Heritage Books, 1999. Print.

Wachtel, Eleanor. *Random Illuminations: Conversations with Carol Shields.* Fredericton: Goose Lane Editions, 2007. Web. 02 Aug. 2012.

Williams, D. "Making Stories, Making Selves: 'Alternate Versions' in *The Stone Diaries.*" *Canadian Literature* 186 (2005): 10–28, 200. Web. 02 Aug. 2012.

Wilson, Ethel. *The Innocent Traveller.* Toronto: McClelland & Stewart, 1990. Print.

Male-Pattern Bewilderment in *Larry's Party*

JOHN VAN RYS

In the winter and spring of 1997, in a June 2 meeting, and through a January 1998 email exchange, Donna Krolik Hollenberg conducted an extended interview with Carol Shields. That timeframe coincides with Shields's finishing, publishing, and promoting her novel *Larry's Party*. In the interview, Shields confides, "I've always been interested in history— what it is, who gets to write it, and what it's for" (341). In other words, one force that lies behind her fiction is the complexity of history—the various understandings of history, its authoring, and its uses. "I know," she goes on to explain, "as everyone knows now, that history is a branch of fiction, a series of selections and personal commentary. This history I learned as a child—what we now call the Maps and Chaps version—had a pronounced and not so secret agenda." By way of contrasting this Maps and Chaps historical education, Shields shares, "I think I always knew that history lives in small domestic moments" (341). Shields's body of work gives ample evidence to the idea that official cartographies and male-centred historical narratives often ignore the depth and vitality of such domestic moments, her best-known example being that of Daisy Goodwill in *The Stone Diaries* (1993), a character Shields describes in the same interview as a "baffled, seeking, third-person character, ever wandering through the construct that she calls her life story" (347).[1]

Such bafflement, it turns out, is not restricted to Shields's female characters. Male-pattern bewilderment is equally evident in the life of Larry Weller of *Larry's Party* (1997), a novel often thought of as a narrative of male experience that functions as a companion and follow-up to

The Stone Diaries. In Shields's thinking, Larry represents something of the struggle of men in the second half of the twentieth century, a time during which, as Shields puts it, "thoughtful, reflective men are feeling themselves in rather a provisional universe" (Hollenberg 355). In *Larry's Party*, Shields offers her response to the "Maps and Chaps" version of history that characterized her education. She relocates historical meaning from the public work of traditional male success and power to the domestic sphere of Larry's story, of his story as a family story. Paradoxically, in this move Shields restores meaning to the larger history in which Larry's history is located. In this reciprocation and re-education, the novel traces Larry's attempts to make peace with time and with history, personal and otherwise. To make sense of this bewildering history, I explore the traces of history in this biographical novel, consider the narrative method by which Shields approaches history, seek to make sense of Larry's male-patterned bewilderment in the face of time, and relate his bewilderment to his maze craze.

However, we first need to explore a bit further Shields's sense of history and her concern for it.[2] Despite her comments in the Hollenberg interview, it is tempting to view Shields as a fiction writer uninterested in history writ large, if not as a writer who actually turns her back on history. Well known, of course, are her early years in the bubble world of Oak Park, Illinois, as well as her awakening to socialism and to feminism in the early years of her marriage, particularly in those years she lived in England. At first glance, it is difficult to see how this bubble bursting impacts her fiction and her sense of history, which seems restricted to biography. After all, Shields chooses for her fictional sphere the domestic world, a choice that at times she defends and other times questions. In her essay "About Writing," she admits, "I continue to worry about my chosen subject of home and family, always imagining it might be read as a retreat from real issues. Nevertheless, over a lifetime I have convinced myself—on good days, at least—that we all possess a domestic space, and that it is mainly within this domestic arc that we express the greater part of our consciousness" (262). Elsewhere, she admits, "The little piece of territory I can cover seems enough, more than enough" (Hollenberg 350). Such a claim links Shields with Jane Austen and the small but fertile piece of ground she revisited in her novels. Early in her biography of Austen, Shields writes that "[b]y indirection, by assumption, by reading what is implicit, we can find behind Austen's novels a steady, intelligent witness to a world that was rapidly reinventing itself" (*Jane Austen* 4). Rapidly reinventing England at the beginning of the nineteenth century stands parallel to the shifting ground of the second half of the twentieth century, just as Shields seems to stand beside Austen in working indirectly to allude to those profound changes informing and shaping domestic life. While the parallels eventually break down, they hold true long enough to see that both authors illuminate familial relations as constitutive of history.

Shields's particular inflection of this issue is coloured, of course, by her late-twentieth-century concerns and her personal vision of life. Hints of this vision are shared in her afterword to *Dropped Threads*, where Shields recounts the story of how the speaker at her 1957 graduation encouraged students to remember *tempus fugit*, "time flies," a phrase that haunted Shields for many years. Eventually, however, she came to a different understanding of time:

> Tempus did not fugit. In a long and healthy life, which is what most of us have, there is plenty of time. . . . Every moment will not be filled with accomplishment; we would explode if we tied ourselves to such a regimen. Time was not our enemy if we kept it on a loose string, allowing for rest, emptiness, reassessment, art and love. This was not a mountain we were climbing; it was closer to being a novel with a series of chapters. (344–45)

In this vision of time (and I would argue of history), there is plenty of time, time understood more fully and fluidly as the gift of living, a blessed unfolding of a personal story. Later in this afterword, Shields conveys that, as a writer, her essential lesson was "the apprehension of a structure that gave fluidity and ease to a long life, the gradually (or suddenly) shifting scenes, each furnished with its own noise and movement, its particular rewards and postures" (347). In "Narrative Hunger and the Overflowing Cupboard," Shields elaborates this vision of time in terms of her own sense of how fiction treats time. "Our stories distort and tease the past" (31), she says at one point; later, she speaks of her own rejection of realism by claiming that "[t]he realistic tradition stressed the divisiveness of human society and shrugged at the rich, potent, endlessly replenished cement that binds us together" (34). Toward the end of this address, Shields conveys her own valuing of the interior voice in fiction: "Reflecting, thinking, connecting, ticking, bringing forward a view of a previously locked room, and, to paraphrase John Donne, making that little room an everywhere" (35–36). That little room of individual consciousness becomes an everywhere; the personal becomes universal; private experience becomes history. As Coral Ann Howells says of Shields's fiction, "Her novels are symptomatic of a particular moment in Western cultural history, with its widespread

skepticism about the metanarratives of history and nation, its questioning of the terms on which identities are formulated, together with an
intense interest in gender construction and the revised dynamics of sexual relationships" (*Contemporary Canadian* 80).

One is tempted to follow up Shields's reference to Donne with his
"No man is an island." Which brings us to Shields's particular attention to
maleness and history, to Chaps and time. As the character Jack Bowman
in her earlier novel *Happenstance* (1980) testifies, Shields has a longstanding interest in this conjunction.[3] It is an interest, however, derived from a
desire to find an alternative to the traditional Chaps narrative club. In "A
View from the Edge of the Edge," Shields relates her trouble reading some
canonical texts: "I found that some of these so-called classics—Hemingway, to a certain extent Conrad—refused to open up to me because they
projected a world in which I did not hold citizenship, the world of men,
action, power, ideas, politics and war" (22). As writers, Hemingway and
Conrad are clearly a chap's chaps, a man's men, and the world of their
fictions is traditional male territory; to a degree, their fiction engages
head-on the dominant historical narratives of Western culture: war, violence, colonialism, culture in conflict with nature, and so on. By contrast,
Shields, especially in *Larry's Party*, is curious about the private, domestic
(though not domesticated) male. Given the historical changes in gender
roles over the last half century, Shields seeks to change the traditional
patterns in fiction, to trace "a life that's full of change and development, a
search for and a finding of the elusive self" (Hollenberg 342). Her position
in relation to Larry is indeed one of sympathy, indeed of love. "I wrote the
book," she says, "because I was curious how men's lives have changed in
response to the new gender thinking. It seemed to me that it was hard to
be a man these days, new comportments to learn, new definitions of masculinity to be absorbed, compromises to reflect upon" (342). This sympathetic stance grows out of both difference and identity. In her interview
with Eleanor Wachtel, "The Arc of a Life," Shields confesses that "[m]en
have always been a mystery, the great mystery to me, the unknown. I don't
understand men. I don't know how they think, what their bodies feel like
to them. So why not spend some time considering this mystery?" (71).
Larry's Party is, in light of these comments, an effort to bridge the difference. In an earlier interview with Marjorie Anderson, Shields expressed
her sense of what is shared by men and women: "men are as damaged as
women are by power, by powerlessness, by loss, by loneliness, by their
need for the other" (Anderson 62). It is both mystery and insight, then,
that guides Shields's exploration of the male in relation to time and history in *Larry's Party*.

At first glance, *Larry's Party* is a novel that appears to turn its back on the history before it. Where, for example, are explicit explorations of the cultural upheavals of the 1960s, race relations, the politics and atomic fear of the Cold War, the oil crisis, economic recessions and rising inflation, the fall of the Berlin Wall? It seems that such historical references are bypassed in favour of attention to Larry's haircut—hardly historical material. But while historical references are not numerous, they are significant, significant as an interrogation of that Maps and Chaps history. It is the history that goes into the making of Larry Weller: the England of his parents after the Second World War, living on rations supplemented by home canning with deadly consequences. It is the feminist history of Beth Prior, Larry's second wife, with her study of female saints, a study both taken seriously and satirized as their marriage moves towards dissolution. It is the England of their Guggenheim studies, along with the European continent, where they explore the history of mazes and where Beth studies images of the Annunciation, "that moment," says the narrator, "historical or mythical, when the angel Gabriel announced to the Holy Virgin that she was chosen to be the Mother of the Messiah. 'The greatest imposition ever perpetrated on a woman,' declared Beth Prior, aged thirty-five, beloved and baffling second wife of Larry Weller" (212). It, too, is Larry's first visit to England, on his honeymoon with Dorrie, including historical tours of castles, churches, stately homes, barns, medieval walls, and museums: "History, it seemed to Larry, left strange details behind, mostly meaningless: odd and foolish gadgets, tools that had become separated from their purpose, whimsical notions, curious turnings, a surprising number of dead ends" (27). Here, Larry finds history disconnected from his life, a collection of artifacts with no meaning for the present. Interestingly, it is "outdoor England," its greenness under cultivation that brings for Larry a "welling up of happiness" (27). In the end, history becomes inflected with gender. Within the narrative's meditation on penises, we read the following: "Was a penis an event? Was it history? Was it sacred or profane? As a boy, Larry didn't know. And at age thirty-six, he still doesn't know" (137). In what ways, asks the novel, does the male body participate in history? In what ways is it constitutive of history? The conversation at Larry's Party repeats, of course, different versions of this question, what is it to be a man at the end of the twentieth century? In one iteration, Beth, now pregnant through reproductive technology, asks, "We want to know what it's like being *you*, at this time in *our* history" (317). The pronouns *you* and *our*, italicized in the text, open up interesting possibilities: is *you* directed specifically to Larry, or does it encompass all men, making the question impossible to answer; is the *our* referencing a history shared by all humanity, or is it one restricted to Western culture, or is Beth speaking for females? The complexities involved in answering multiply.

The difficulty of anyone, let alone Larry, answering such questions about men and their penises in relation to history suggests something about Larry in relation to traditional history, that history of Chaps. Essentially, he lives alongside that history, but invisible to it. In the chapter on "Larry's Words," we learn that Larry's life contrasts the lives of those who live with big, noble words, such as nation, honour, achievement, integrity, righteousness, glory, and learning. As the narrator then relates, "These are the words of those anointed beings who take the long view. Whereas he lives in the short view, his close-up, textured, parochial world, the little valley of intimacy he was born into, always thinking, without knowing he's thinking. Living next door to the great words, but not with them. His share of the truth—what truth?—is going to come (when it comes) modestly packaged and tied with string, he knows that" (90–91). Interestingly, this passage aligns history with truth while questioning truth itself, nevertheless pointing forward to a share of truth granted to Larry, presumably through his study and making of mazes but perhaps through his reconciliation with Dorrie. Larry's sense of standing outside great words and the great history that accompanies such words is echoed in the chapter "Larry So Far," where at the age of forty Larry expresses a wish to wrestle with giants, to be the kind of admirable man kept awake by "[w]ars, plagues, racial injustice, third world poverty, the oppression of women," but he finds himself experiencing an anxiety that "seems merely to vibrate in tune with a saddened world" (169). In the self-analysis that unfolds, he takes stock of his family, his education, his homes, his health, his hobbies, his religion—and finds himself lacking. This lack in relation to self and society, one dimension of Larry's relation to history, characterizes that relationship as deficit.

In his sadness and anxiety, Larry displays the nature of a creature who remembers. In other words, people are characterized by memory, that mental faculty that recovers, reconstitutes, and imagines the past, that makes history and stretches back into history through texts and artifacts. In one of the novel's beautiful moments of astonishment, Larry imagines the life and journey of a flower in his hand: "Larry thinks how the alstroemeria head he cups in his hand has no memory and no gratitude toward those who delivered it to this moment. *It toils not, neither does it spin.* It's sprouted, grown, bloomed, that's all" (76). In the italicized echo of Christ's Sermon on the Mount is heard the both blessed and cursed difference between humans and other living creatures—the knowledge of toiling in time. In this vein, the narrator shares that "[s]ometimes Larry sees his future laid out with terrifying clarity. An endless struggle to remember what he already knows" (88). The task of remembering becomes, for Larry, the work of living.

Beyond this memory work, the narrative characterizes personal history, and perhaps all history, as driven by mistakes, both fortunate and catastrophic. Indeed, the novel grew out of a short story titled "By Mistake" published in *Prairie Fire*. That story constitutes an early version of the novel's first chapter, "Fifteen Minutes in the Life of Larry Weller, 1977." Others have commented insightfully on how the concept of mistakes is foregrounded in this chapter and establishes a theme for Larry's life, as well as for the lives of others (Cariou; Goertz). Beyond the idea that "[a] mistake can work both ways" (9–10), let me simply foreground the broader implications for time and history. Toward the end of the chapter, we read, italicized, "*Wait a minute, it's all a mistake.*" The narrator then continues, "A mistake that led to another mistake that led to another. People made mistakes all the time, so many mistakes that they aren't mistakes anymore, they're just positive and negative charges shooting back and forth and moving you along. Like good luck and bad luck. Like a tunnel you're walking through, with all your pores wide open. When it turns, you turn too" (12). The emphasis on it all being a mistake, on chains of mistakes made by people, and on the pronoun *you* universalizes the experience of mistakes, characterizes human history in these terms. In a memorable moment, Larry discards the jacket he took mistakenly, not caring if stuffing the jacket into a garbage can was itself a mistake. What is striking is his sense of doing so with an audience. "There were plenty of eyes on him," explains the narrator, "he could feel them boring through to his skin. In about two minutes some guy was going to pull that Harris tweed jacket out of the garbage and put it on. But by that time Larry would be around the corner, walking straight toward the next thing that was going to happen to him" (13). This passage gestures in a number of directions: Larry's self-consciousness in the face of witnesses, the potential for another man to take the discarded jacket and make it part of his history, and Larry's disappearing around a corner, reappearing in a new space. This initiating episode thus presses readers to meditate on the laws that govern lives in time, that govern historical patterns and movements.

In this opening chapter, readers may catch the reference to the tunnel in the passage about mistakes. Perhaps that tunnel reference is being echoed in the description of the Winnipeg wind tunnel in which the jacketless Larry is alternately puffed up Superman size and pressed down puny (13). In the chapter's earlier account of how Larry ended up enrolled in a Floral Arts rather than a Furnace Repair program, we are told, "Well, someone must have been sleeping at the switch" (8). These references to tunnels and switches are part of an architectural and mechanical motif meant to characterize time and human participation in time; the motif alludes to one shape of history. Recall, for example, Larry's visit to his co-worker Viv Bondurant's home, where Larry meets her husband Hector, who repairs clocks in his basement workshop. At that moment, Larry experiences a "stab of irrational jealousy" (67). In this same chapter, "Larry's Work," such work is what "turns the gears of life," and the narrator, forecasting trouble ahead, shares that when Larry's life was going badly, he "came to see work as the only consolation for persisting in the world" (68), that being "a cog in the great turning wheel of desire and intention" becomes "all that stands between himself and the bankruptcy of his soul" (77). In the chapter on "Larry's Words," Larry defines labyrinth as "a complex path" (81), giving examples such as an overpass, a golf course, an airport, and a subway system. The narrator reflects, "It seems those who live in the twentieth century have a liking for putting ourselves on a predetermined conveyor track and letting it carry us along" (81). In her interview with Eleanor Wachtel, Shields herself admits, "I think we're moving along a kind of tunnel of time or through a maze of time, and there's no going back" (79). Strikingly, Larry describes mazes as machines, with people as the moving parts, an idea that he has picked up in his reading, though he cannot remember the source (218). While Beth is resistant to this metaphor, Larry finds comfort in it, in being part of a larger whole, even if the whole cannot be fully seen or understood— that whole unfolding of historical time.

Such comfort in and confusion about the workings of life in time is enacted in the very narrative methods and structures of the novel. On the one hand is the appearance of life in time's orderly unfolding: the twenty years spanned by the chapters, a round score of years in Larry's life, the measure of a generation; the sense of life as a series of chapters; the real aging of Larry from twenty-six to forty-six, with milestones of marriage, fatherhood, and career; even the division of the final chapter, "Larry's Party," into sections of before, during, and after. Adding to this sense of narrative order are the chapter titles, which establish a thematic order of Larry's life history. Larry, himself, looks for a mystical roundness when he thinks of his life: born in 1950, he hopes to live until 2050 (138). And, in the end, the novel does give the sense of culmination, of arrival, fulfilling what Shields describes as the goal of "an individual finding his or her true home" (Wachtel 77). Nevertheless, the narrative method is infinitely more complex than this clean temporal arc suggests. As Nina van Gessel argues, "The novel's many instances of narrative reversal severely undermine the neatness of the chronologically dated chapter titles" (165).[4] Each chapter spills out of its temporal container, recounting earlier events and forecasting events yet to come. Already narrated events are revisited, deepened, fleshed out, recast from different perspectives. Chapters recount narrative markers established in earlier chapters, making individual chapters read almost as self-contained narrative essays. As Shields herself has explained, the chapters function as images from a CAT scan, as compartmentalized elements of Larry's life (Wachtel 80–81); or as individual mazes through which narrator, reader, and Larry travel (84–85). In the chapter "Larry's Living Tissues," Larry himself characterizes his life as "not so much a story as a sequence of soundings—real soundings, bouncing in his inner ear" (267). In the telling of "his story," Larry's history, Shields holds its meaning in suspense; she holds it up in the interrogative mode.

This interrogative narrative mode is partly what creates bewilderment in and about Larry, conveyed through a narrative voice, female inflected, that freely moves in and out of Larry's consciousness, making the novel's discourse double-voiced. Bewilderment of all varieties is indeed the response of Larry to his life in time. As Howells puts it, "Far from taking control of his life, Larry's most characteristic state is a mixture of bewilderment and anticipation" (*Contemporary Canadian* 92).[5] Nina van Gessel argues of Larry, "[b]ewildered and mistake-prone, the protagonist of this fictive biography lacks the qualities identified with hegemonic masculinity" (154). Taken together, these critical comments align bewilderment with a nontraditional masculinity, with the momentous changes in gender identity felt especially in Western cultures since the 1960s. Larry's bewilderment, however, goes beyond gender into other territories. It is the confusion he feels when his father asks whether he loves Dorrie (10). It is "the sensation of being unplugged from the world or the heightened state of panicked awareness" that he experiences that first time in the Hampton Court maze (35), a sensation that makes him feel "the fourteen days of his marriage collapsing backward and becoming an invented artifact" (36). It is Larry at his thirtieth birthday learning about the world through "sideways comments" so that "his baffled self stands back and says: so this is how it works" (58). It is the absence and uncertainty he feels in the collapse of his two marriages, but also the dreams that tell him to "[b]e careful of chaos, of silence, of words, of other people, of myself, that stranger Larry Weller"; moreover, it is the struggle to learn how to manage "the daily calendar, a new red number every day, pushing you into the tunnel of an ever-receding future" (112). It is turning forty, with a crisis right on schedule, "a sad man but without the sad history to back it up" (164), complete with the abrupt narrative intrusion in italics, "*Who is this guy? Give me a break*" (166). It is "[h]is own good luck, his dangerous history" (201), his comfortable success in tension with expectations of "exposure and ruin" (207–08), the "great day of awakening" from his coma but also the desire to return to the "maze without an exit" (272–73). This bewilderment perhaps culminates at Larry's party in the spot of time that Larry and Dorrie experience, where they are (re)united as husband and wife: "They are, in this alternate version of reality, partners in a long marriage, survivors of old quarrels long since mended. The journey they appear to have taken separately has really been made together. After all, after all" (328). In the repetition of "after all" echoes their personal, familial, and familiar history, which it seems can be redeemed.

Larry's bewilderment is deeply tied with who he is as Larry, which rhymes, the narrative tells us more than once, with ordinary. In the end, ordinary Larry is an Everyman; as his friend Larry Fine says, maybe all men are named Larry (260). But what's in that name, Larry Weller? The narrative discourages readers and Larry's wife Beth from making much of his first name. After all, he is named after no one, not even St. Laurence, though Beth seems to wish it were so (252). Larry cares more for his last name, whose historical origins might mean "boiler of salt" or "one who dwells by a stream or spring, a sort of professional water overseer" (253). Larry, of course, prefers the second meaning, making him "a water man, a well man, a custodian of all that is clear, pure, sustaining, and everlastingly present" (253). As readers, we may choose to consider Larry Weller as part of the salt of the Earth, or we may link him with those ever flowing waters, this image of flux and vitality. In the end, Larry Weller becomes an emblem of what it might be to be a man at the end of the twentieth century, the product of its history, indeed of a millennium of history:

> [W]hat is it like to be part of the company of men at the end of our millennium? What do they want once their names are inscribed in the book of life? Wait a minute—there isn't any book of life.
>
> Men. These curious upholstered assemblages of bones, the fearful mortality that attends them, the clutter of good luck and bad, the foolish choices, the seeds of the boys they'd been—and those seeds sprouting inappropriately even as their hair thins and their muscles

slacken. Fighting for a little space in the world. Needing a little human attention. Getting it up, getting it off. When does it stop? Does it ever stop? (330–31)

The narrator offers these curious ponderings in a moment of reflection during the conversation at Larry's party. From the play of *our* and *they* to the emphasis on aging bodies that were once boys' to men's needs for both space and contact to questions about continuity in time—the narrative voice (again female inflected) probes to the heart of life's meaning for all ordinary Larrys, for the Everyman.

The reference above to the "seeds of the boys they'd been" reminds us of the novel's emphasis on the seeds of Larry, the family history that has made him, all the forms of inheritance that are in his very flesh. That physical reality is referenced already in the title-page photograph of a bewildered baby Larry outdoors in his high chair, a photo that invites us to study this child but also to imagine the photographer and to ask what lies outside the frame. The narrative comes back to this photograph repeatedly, asking us to consider the origin and fate of this child, the child in the high chair who "started all this" (260), as the narrator puts it at one point. In a real sense, however, it was Larry's parents who started all this, giving Larry not only their "genetic tissue" but also their "perpetual confusion" (280). Their histories lie at the roots of Larry's history. In 1949, Larry is in his mother's womb in England when she fed tainted beans to her mother-in-law. In the wake of the resulting death, Stu and Dot Weller fled the wrath of Stu's father, immigrating to Winnipeg, where Larry was then born in 1950. For years, Dot pays for her mistake, and her real work becomes "sorrowing, remembering" (45–47). This is the story into which Larry is born; he grows up "with a bad chapter of someone else's life, in the toxic glow of someone else's guilt, a guilt that became rooted in sorrow" (52). This is the "full level of bruising knowledge" that the narrator sees in that photograph of Larry (48).[6] And a similar bruising knowledge accompanies Larry on his honeymoon with Dorrie, when each morning he meets his father's "solid, ruddy presence" in the mirror (21–22). It is, once again, only in the reconciliation between Larry and Dorrie that this family history is redeemed. As Howells argues of this moment in the novel, "[w]hat is evoked is intimate familial space, with the story of parents and children rooted in a long historical process, imaging the reconstitution of a shattered family unit" ("Larry's A/Mazing Spaces" 130).[7]

What lies in the background of this reconciliation, this second chance, is the maze of Larry's first marriage, that maze damaged but then preserved by Dorrie, described as "the most unexamined mystery of [Larry's] life, a circling, exquisite puzzle of pain, and pain's consolation" (156). Obviously, mazes loom large in the narrative, and have been insightfully analyzed by several critics (Cariou; Goertz; Howells, *Contemporary Canadian*; Howells, "Larry's A/Mazing Spaces"; Paillot; van Gessel). Quite rightly, these readings have emphasized the prominently spatial and visual nature of the maze, the source of its symbolic power and resonance in the novel. Here, I will simply add some comments that stress the temporal and historical nature of the maze imagery. After all, it is Larry who describes mazes as "designed to deceive the travelers who seek a promised goal" (81). His emphasis on travellers and goals, like his description of people as the moving parts of the maze machine, highlights the temporal dimension, life in motion. The mazes Larry loves are organic, green living things cultivated through time by their human creators. They are emblematic of life in time itself, as the novel's epigraph suggests, with its likening of the earth to "a wild maze the moment of our birth" (vii). Competing interpretations make of the maze either the tracing of a sexual desire or "a holy pilgrimage in microcosm, a place where a pilgrim might wend his way to the maze's secret heart and therein find sanctuary and salvation" (138–39). Given the echoes of John Donne in the novel, it is not farfetched to claim that both desires, and perhaps others, are reflected in the maze. Certainly for Larry it is a site of "spiritual excitement" that "ignites [his] sense of equilibrium and sends him soaring" (171–72). During their Guggenheim tour of Europe's mazes, Larry and Beth debate the spiritual significance of mazes. At the Hollywood stone maze, they sense that the practical and the spiritual lie side by side, with the maze on the stone warning of a difficult road to the Celtic sanctuary while also pointing to "the difficulty of life and life's tortuous spiritual journey" (215). When Beth resists Larry's machine metaphor for the maze, asking what kind of God wants his creatures in confusion, Larry responds, "Isn't that what we've always had? Chaos from the first day of creation? But mazes are refuges from confusion, really. An orderly path for the persevering. Procession without congestion" (219). The idea that mazes are refuges from confusion is something Larry discovered, of course, in his first marriage, in his experience in the Hampton Court maze and in the building of the maze around his marital home.

More than this, however, Larry's maze craze, along with love for the people in his life, represents his participation in history, his embracing and making of history. This history is indeed an alternative to that Maps and Chaps history. As his first business card suggests, it was "a/mazing" that Larry found himself in maze making, an amazing grace in his life.

"In getting into formal gardening," we are told, "he has caught, entirely by accident, one of the generational updrafts: the realization that there is time at the end of this long, mean, skeptical century for leisure, time for the soul's adornment" (145–46). The narrator then explains that "[m]aze aficionados tend to possess an off-key imagination, a sense of history (be it warped or precise), a love for teasing mysteries or else a desperate drive toward the ultimate of conspicuous affectation" (146). Larry's calling matches, by pure good fortune, the historical moment; moreover, he finds himself in an odd corner of history, and he makes it his own. And this curious corner of history is populated by a whole range of playful phenomena that exist alongside all the painful verities of history:

> What a wonder, he thinks, that the long, bitter, heart-wrenching history of the planet should allow curious breathing spaces for the likes of mere toys and riddles; he sees them everywhere. Games, glyphs, symbols, allegories, puns and anagrams, masquerades, the magician's sleight-of-hand, the clown's wink, the comic shrug, the somersault, the cryptogram in all its forms, and especially, at least to Laurence J. Weller's mind, the teasing elegance and circularity of the labyrinthine structure, a snail, a scribble, a doodle on the earth's skin with no other directed purpose but to wind its sinuous way around itself. (152)

The maze, like these other playful phenomena, escapes historical utility but is necessary to history, offering a counter-narrative to discourses of power, certain myths of progress, and possible memories of horror. In his making of mazes, Larry links himself to this playful history and contributes to it with his own curious breathing spaces; in this work, Larry's bewilderment becomes a gift to his community, his own history's gift to the present and the future.

Larry's Party thus calls for nothing less than a rethinking of history in light of personal whims, curiosities, and loves. More narrowly, it aims to recalibrate maleness in relation to history, to replace Maps and Chaps with mazes and men working their way through bewilderment—in all its forms—to find a good and true goal. Larry's particular journey begins with a photograph of a pensive child in a high chair, carrying already the burden of his family's history, their flight from England to Winnipeg. That journey continues through all the productive and painful mistakes, accidents, and surprises of Larry's life, including his surprising participation in mazes. The journey finds its goal in unlooked-for reconciliation that mends a history. What is left for Larry, of course, beyond the novel's ending, is his journey toward the exit, that exit we all one day find. As Shields explains in "The Arc of a Life," she is concerned with the "arc of aging: growing older and then, of course, the shadowy end of life, illness and eventual death" (Wachtel 76). But for Shields as author and for us as readers, that final part of Larry's story, the wake, can wait. We can enjoy the party a while longer. In her interview with Wachtel, Shields explains her affection for Larry in these terms: "He lets his life happen to him in a sense. He's carried along in the stream of things. I suppose I can only say that my own life has been something like that. I think most lives are" (73). Maybe all of us, male and female, in our personal histories and in our relation to larger histories, are a little bit Larry.

NOTES

1. Shields's comment about Daisy Goodwill also echoes Daisy's own description of her mother experiencing the beginning of childbirth, making a sound that is "formless, loose, a wavy line of bewilderment." Daisy as narrator confides parenthetically, "Later, these words, more than any others, will attach themselves to my image of my mother: looseness, bewilderment" (*The Stone Diaries* 4).

2. I am using the term "history" in a traditional, somewhat naive fashion. The idea of history here is informed by Paul Ricoeur's thinking. "The grammar of the past is a twofold grammar," he writes, "It is no longer, and yet it *has been*. In a sense we are summoned by what was, beyond the loss of what is no longer, to be faithful to what happened. Here we confront the problems of historical representation and reference to the past, but we must never eliminate the truth claim of what has been. This is so for ethical as well as epistemological reasons" ("On Narrative Imagination" 49).

3. The presence of this concern in Shields's fiction is worthy of further attention. In *Happenstance*, a double novel originally published separately as *Happenstance* and *A Fairly Conventional Woman*, Shields tells the stories of Jack and Brenda Bowman, conveying their competing notions of history, embedded in their understandings and misunderstandings of each other. Consider, as well, the mystery of *Swann*, in which biographer Morton Jimroy begins to "lose faith in his old belief that the past is retrievable" (135) and where publisher Frederic Cruzzi finds himself "confused by tears" (289) when he discovers that not only his remaining copies of *Swann's Songs* but also his file on Mary Swann has been stolen. Similarly, Cuyler Goodwill in *The Stone Diaries* represents this conjunction, not only with his speeches about time and chance working to produce destiny (82), but more concretely with his stone tower, "a museum of writhing forms, some of which he has discovered in the *Canadian Farmer's Almanac* or the Eaton's catalogue or in his illustrated Bible" (64).

4. Van Gessel describes this narrative process as "accretion and repetition," concluding that "the novel's layering technique images the methodology by

which Larry himself constructs his life narrative(s) in his ongoing, ultimately fruitless quest for (self-)comprehension" (167). While this description is helpful, I would argue with the conclusion that this quest is fruitless, given the measure of wisdom maze-making brings Larry and the insights brought about by his party.

5. While I have suggested that the narrative voice is "female inflected," there is some ambiguity on this point. In *Contemporary Canadian Women's Fiction*, Howells argues that "[t]here is no intrusion of the female biographer here, just an anonymous recording voice that is elided into Larry's indirect interior monologue" (92). Elsewhere, however, Howells admits that "one has the impression that the biographer is female, based mainly on the kinds of experience that are selected as significant in Larry's life story" ("Larry's A/Mazing Spaces" 118). See also Lorna Irvine's "A Knowable Country: Embodied Omniscience in Carol Shields's *The Republic of Love* and *Larry's Party.*"

6. This locating of Larry's origins in maternal sadness functions as the mirror image of Tom Avery's embrace by twenty-seven mothers in *The Republic of Love*: "Such love, such love—ah, God, he'd never know love like that again" (3). I am indebted to Aritha van Herk for suggesting this connection.

7. As van Gessel suggests, this family history is also overlaid with "shifting class identity," complicating Larry's story with issues of upward mobility (162–63).

WORKS CITED

Anderson, Marjorie. Interview of Carol Shields. In *Carol Shields: The Arts of a Writing Life*, ed. Neil K. Besner. Winnipeg: Prairie Fire, 2003: 57–71. Print.

Cariou, Warren. "*Larry's Party*: Man in the Maze." In *Carol Shields: The Arts of a Writing Life*, ed. Neil K. Besner. Winnipeg: Prairie Fire, 2003: 87–96. Print.

Goertz, Dee. "Treading the Maze of *Larry's Party*." In *Carol Shields, Narrative Hunger, and the Possibilities of Fiction*, ed. Edward Eden and Dee Goertz. Toronto: University of Toronto Press, 2003: 230–54. Print.

Hollenberg, Donna Krolik. Interview with Carol Shields. *Contemporary Literature* 39.3 (1998): 339–55. Print.

Howells, Coral Ann. *Contemporary Canadian Women's Fiction: Refiguring Identities*. New York: Palgrave Macmillan, 2003. Print.

———. "Larry's A/Mazing Spaces." In *Carol Shields and the Extra-Ordinary*, ed. Marta Dvořák and Manina Jones. Montreal and Kingston: McGill-Queen's University Press, 2007: 115–35. Print.

Irvine, Lorna. "A Knowable Country: Embodied Omniscience in Carol Shields's *The Republic of Love* and *Larry's Party.*" In *Carol Shields and the*

Extra-Ordinary, ed. Marta Dvořák and Manina Jones. Montreal and Kingston: McGill-Queen's University Press, 2007: 139–56. Print.

Paillot, Patricia-Léa. "Pioneering Interlaced Spaces: Shifting Perspectives and Self-Representation in *Larry's Party.*" In *Carol Shields and the Extra-Ordinary,* ed. Marta Dvořák and Manina Jones. Montreal and Kingston: McGill-Queen's University Press, 2007: 157–71. Print.

Ricoeur, Paul. "On Narrative Imagination." In *Debates in Continental Philosophy: Conversations with Contemporary Thinkers,* ed. Richard Kearney. New York: Fordham University Press, 2004: 33–52. Print.

Shields, Carol. "About Writing." In *Carol Shields: The Arts of a Writing Life,* ed. Neil K. Besner. Winnipeg: Prairie Fire, 2003: 261–62. Print.

———. Afterword. *Dropped Threads: What We Aren't Told,* ed. Carol Shields and Marjorie Anderson. Toronto: Vintage Canada, 2001: 343–47. Print.

———. "By Mistake." *Prairie Fire* 16.1 (Spring 1995): 13–21. Print.

———. *Happenstance.* 1980 and 1982. Toronto: Vintage Canada, 1997. Print.

———. *Jane Austen: A Life.* New York: Penguin, 2001. Print.

———. *Larry's Party.* New York: Viking Penguin, 1997. Print.

———. "Narrative Hunger and the Overflowing Cupboard." In *Carol Shields, Narrative Hunger, and the Possibilities of Fiction,* ed. Edward Eden and Dee Goertz. Toronto: University of Toronto Press, 2003: 19–36.

———. *The Stone Diaries.* New York: Penguin, 1995. Print.

———. "A View from the Edge of the Edge." In *Carol Shields and the Extra-Ordinary,* ed. Marta Dvořák and Manina Jones. Montreal and Kingston: McGill-Queen's University Press, 2007: 17–29. Print.

van Gessel, Nina. "'A Man's Journey': Masculinity, Maze, and Biography in Carol Shields's *Larry's Party.*" *Studies in Canadian Literature* 32.1 (2007): 154–72. Print.

Wachtel, Eleanor. "'The Arc of a Life': *Larry's Party.*" Interview of Carol Shields. In *Random Illuminations: Conversations with Carol Shields.* Fredericton: Goose Lane, 2007: 69–88. Print.

Departures, Arrivals:
Canada/United States Migrations and the Trope of Travel in the Fiction of Carol Shields

ALEX RAMON

> Contemporary literature is populated by . . . those beings who are, to use
> Georg Lukács's term, deprived of a transcendental shelter or abode.
> Or they are in transit, in a state of what George Steiner calls
> in-betweenness, and further confused by disappearing
> landmarks or by the absence of shared events or ceremonies.
>
> —Carol Shields "Narrative Hunger" (29)

The reductive classification of Carol Shields as a "domestic" novelist continues to obscure the extent to which travel is a central and recurrent aspect of her fiction. Although several critics—most notably Stephen Henighan in his contentious chapter "'They Can't Be about Things Here': The Reshaping of the Canadian Novel" in *When Words Deny the World* (2002) and Gillian Roberts in her incisive article "Sameness and Difference: Border Crossings in *The Stone Diaries* and *Larry's Party*" (2006)—have explored Shields's fiction in relation to issues of Canada/ US border crossing and cultural exchange, Shields's work still tends to be associated with domesticity and "the home-front." This essay seeks to extend the analyses offered by Henighan and Roberts by arguing for a reassessment of Shields as a writer of travel, one whose work is concerned with challenging national stereotypes and with the effects that "the 20th century condition of migrancy" (Boehmer 233) might have upon identity, in North American contexts and beyond. My title alludes, of course, to Shields's first play, *Departures and Arrivals*, in which an airport functions as a performative space of multiple narrative possibilities inhabited by transient characters who, like so many of Shields's protagonists, are situated in "a state of in-betweenness."

The continued association of Shields's work with the domestic sphere is surprising, since all of her novels and much of her short fiction involve her protagonists in physical journeys of some kind, whether between cities, states, provinces, countries, or continents. In Shields's early work, these trips may be as extended as the Gill family's year spent in England in *Small Ceremonies,* or they may be as brief as Charleen's return to the family home for her mother's remarriage in *The Box Garden*, a train journey between Vancouver and Toronto, which is economically but evocatively described in the text. In the *Happenstance* novels, Brenda Bowman travels from Chicago to Philadelphia for a five-day craft convention, the texts establishing the academic conference as one of the key Shieldsian locales for exploring the multiple opportunities for strangeness, temptation, and renewal that travel offers. Indeed, despite their relative brevity, journeys such as those undertaken by Charleen and Brenda assume a singular importance in these novels and are evidence of the reluctance of Shields's fiction to present any kind of journey as insignificant. Liberated, albeit momentarily, from the strictures of everyday routine, Shields's early traveller characters glimpse new possibilities of identity and experience during their short voyages from their daily circumstances, as they are alerted to the realization that—in Brenda's at once disturbed and excited formulation—"[a]nything could happen" (Shields, *Happenstance* 74).

In Shields's more experimental short fiction, shifts between locations are increasingly radically rendered. In a mere six pages, the title story in *Various Miracles* moves rapidly between a range of places and spaces, locating its synchronicities and coincidences in settings as diverse as Cincinnati, a Moroccan village, Exeter, and Toronto. A similar fluidity is central to the structure of "Home," which opens in an aeroplane in flight over the Atlantic, detours to Greenland and to New York, and climaxes at Acapulco airport with the image of 109 passengers disembarking from the plane "all of them—without exception—wearing blue jeans" (Shields, *Collected Stories* 186). Such fluid crossings between countries and continents allow Shields's stories to demonstrate, formally, the perspective of one of the ensemble characters in "Home," the unnamed high-school teacher on her way to visit Dove Cottage, who recognizes that "the world . . . was accessible; oceans and continents and centuries could be spryly overleapt" (Shields, *Collected Stories* 181).

Whether journeying for leisure and pleasure, study or work, Shields's traveller characters often experience such moments of epiphanic vision as they are brought into contact with unexpected others and undergo experiences beyond their daily frames of reference. Accordingly, reluctance to travel often connotes rigidity and inflexibility on the part of characters in Shields's fiction, such as Malcolm's wife in "Collision," a woman who, the narrator informs us, "hated to travel, to pack and unpack, to plug her hairdryer into complicated converters and risk danger" (Shields, *Collected Stories* 326). Furthermore, with their ethnically diverse ensemble casts and their collage design, the *Various Miracles* stories also constitute Shields's most direct and sustained response to the challenge of constructing the Canadian mosaic in her fiction—an endeavour that, inevitably, moves the texts far beyond the Canadian border. The cumulative effect of these stories, indeed, is to construct a world of unfixed national boundaries and constant border crossing, one that reflects what Christopher O'Reilly has termed "the 20th century's loss of easy demarcation" (15). What Shields's stories forge, however, is a particular vision of what I would term transient transnational community, in which the differences of language and culture which separate the protagonists are mitigated by the collisions and coincidences which momentarily unite them, and which gesture towards shared human experiences.

Refusing to present its traveller characters as *irredeemably* alienated, or as *perpetually* "confused by disappearing landmarks or by the absence of shared events or ceremonies," Shields's fiction is drawn, repeatedly, to the narrative of the chance travelling encounter, a moment in which the barriers between strangers dissolve, however fleetingly. Martä and Malcolm's symbiotic walk in the rain under Malcolm's umbrella in "Collision" remains the most emblematic of such encounters; others include the impromptu embrace between Frances and the stranger seated next to her as their aeroplane makes an emergency landing in a barley field in "Scenes": "Later, he gave her his business card" (Shields, *Collected Stories* 100). Such moments of sympathetic connection—often presented as more fulfilling and sustaining for the protagonist than their relationships with their friends or family members—are figured, in "Home," as "the million invisible filaments of connection, trivial or profound, which bind them one to the other, and to the small green planet they call home" (186).

In this way, a postcolonial sense of the twentieth century as "the century of movement" in which "individuals and groups . . . were . . .

thrown more widely across the planet than ever before" (Iyer 10) pervades Shields's fiction. Her work combines the "various discourses of intimacy, home, and neighbourhood . . . with others of global distance and multi-national community" which Frank Davey in *Post-National Arguments* views as central to contemporary Canadian literature (Davey 285). While scenes at checkpoints or borders feature relatively infrequently in Shields's texts, the kinds of transitional spaces identified by Davey—airports, "air flights and international hotels" (Davey 259)—are, as much as kitchens or living rooms, the habitual locations of Shields's restless, mobile, and border-crossing works.

Shields's engagement with issues of travel and migration predates her fiction writing however. It is evident, initially, in her master's study on Susanna Moodie, later published as *Susanna Moodie: Voice and Vision*, which explored Moodie's position as witness to and participant in "the great democratic experiment of Canada" and challenged the critical conception of her as "the mythic figure of the anguished immigrant who embodied the alienation and neurosis of the whole nation" (1). This classification of Moodie as "a bridging figure" (74) is, moreover, one that might be applied to the author of the text herself. For it is difficult not to read Shields's concern with travel and migration as being connected to her own position as an immigrant, a writer who was born in the Chicago suburb of Oak Park and who moved to Canada upon her marriage in 1957. In an interview with Donna Krolik Hollenberg, Shields addressed the question of her dual nationality:

> I see myself as a Canadian because I live here, and have for forty years, and I know more or less how things work in this country. But I also had an American childhood, and an American education. Today I carry two passports . . . I have to say that I feel fortunate to have a foot on each side of the border. (Hollenberg 352)

With its Bhabhaian resonances, Shields's affirmative figuring of her own liminality here accounts for the distinctive doubleness which, as I have argued elsewhere, characterizes much of her fiction: a perspective which is at once that of an outsider and an insider to Canadian culture (Ramon 2008). As Peter Dickinson reminds us, "border consciousness, and particularly, consciousness of the U.S. border, has a long history in Canada" (Dickinson 84), but in this particular quotation Shields is clearly figuring her own "border consciousness" in positive terms and suggesting that "having a foot on each side" of the American/Canadian border is a privileged and comfortable position. In post-2000 interviews, however, Shields expresses a sense of alienation from the United States, stating that she "couldn't imagine writing a novel set in the States; I don't understand how it works now or how American society thinks" (Shields, qtd. in Neville 33). Shields's sense of disconnection from the country of her birth was further explored in her last poetry collection, *Coming to Canada*, in which the American speaker of the title poem finally identifies Canada as her home: "the place she came to," she asserts, has now become "the place she was from" (27). The speaker admits that her sense of belonging in Canada "took years to happen," suggesting that her relocation there was far from an easy transition. In fact, the majority of the *Coming to Canada* poems focus upon the speaker's childhood and adolescence in the United States, an intimation that Shields's rejection of the country of her birth may not have been as all-encompassing as she came to claim. Indeed, "Segue"—the text that Shields was composing at the time of her death—returns her work to a Chicago setting, and an exploration of post-9/11 anxieties. In this way, Shields's attitudes to Canada, the United States, and her own sense of national affiliation are revealed, through her interview statements, as appropriately "unsettled."

Elsewhere, Shields discussed the other migrations which marked her life, speaking of the challenge of "having to make my home—permanent and temporary—in such places as Toronto, Manchester, Ottawa, Brittany, Paris, Vancouver, and now Winnipeg" (Hollenberg 353). Here, again, she (de)constructs the notion of home (domestic or national) in postcolonial terms, presenting it not as a stable, permanent entity, or as something simply bestowed upon the individual, but rather as a more transitory space which is constantly in the process of being renegotiated and reconstructed by the peripatetic subject. In interviews, however, it is Winnipeg that Shields talks about with most affection. The city, she told Hollenberg, "provided the most complete sense of community that I had known since growing up in the American Midwest" (353). Unsurprisingly, then, it is Winnipeg in Canada and Chicago in the United States that are the locations to which Shields's fiction most frequently returns.

Of Shields's novels, *The Stone Diaries* and *Larry's Party* reflect most directly an ambivalence about North American migration experiences. These are, famously, texts marked by crossings between Canada and the United States, in short by a sequence of departures and arrivals. In *The Stone Diaries*, Daisy Goodwill is born in rural Manitoba in 1905 and ends her life in Florida in the 1990s, after a series of moves between Ottawa and Bloomington, Indiana. In addition, the text is supplemented by several other interrelated migration narratives, notably the story of the

Jewish Albanian Abram Skutari and the return of Daisy's father-in-law Magnus Flett to his birthplace in the Orkney Islands.

Like Daisy's, the experience of Larry Weller in *Larry's Party* is also one of Canadian-American migration: Larry grows up in Winnipeg, moves to Chicago for work, and returns to Canada in the penultimate chapter of the text. Shields has described this kind of crossing between Canada and the United States as "a reality for many of us" (Hollenberg 353), and Daisy and Larry's oscillations between the two nations allow these novels to develop complementary enquiries into the difficulties of belonging, as their protagonists' identities are, to paraphrase Rosemary Marangoly George, "linked only hypothetically . . . to a specific geographical place on the map" (200). The effect of such journeying upon individual identity—the way "people sometimes take on a different persona when they travel" (Shields, *Collected Stories* 187)—is explored most directly in Daisy's construction of the "several metamorphoses" undertaken by her father Cuyler who "travelled in his long life from one incarnation to the next" (Shields, *Stone* 91). A shy man in Manitoba, a silver-tongued orator in the United States, Cuyler finds his voice, significantly, while "in transit," opening up to Daisy as the pair travel the "thirteen hundred mile distance" between Winnipeg and Bloomington (Shields, *Stone* 86).

In this way, Shields's traveller characters develop what Pico Iyer has termed "a porous sense of self that change[s] with [their] location" (18). But while Cuyler may not spend "one minute grieving for his lost country" (Shields, *Stone* 93), the Canada-America border crossing he and other characters undertake does permit a considerable amount of satire at the expense of American attitudes towards Canada. Cuyler, for example, finds that "there are educated Bloomingtonians who have never heard of the province of Manitoba, or if they have, [are] unable to spell it correctly or locate it on a map. . . . It's as though a huge eraser has come down from the heavens and wiped out the top of the continent (Shields, *Stone* 93). This same sense of Canada's invisibility to its southern neighbour is explored in *Larry's Party*, in which Larry finds that Winnipeg is conceptualized by his Chicago friends as "somewhere *up there*, somewhere northerly, a representative piece of that polite, white, silent kingdom" (Shields, *Larry* 206). As Roberts astutely argues, "[t]he narrative voice fluctuates between aligning itself with these generalized images and puncturing them" (88). For Roberts, indeed, both *The Stone Diaries* and *Larry's Party* "interrogat[e] the circulation of cultural power across the Canada-America border, addressing relations of sameness and difference and hospitality and hostility . . . [to] demonstrate the discrepancy in cultural and economic power between these two nation-states" (86). I agree with Roberts's contention that Shields's work offers a more nuanced analysis of Canada–United States relations than has been acknowledged but would suggest that her essay at times tends to undervalue the comic, satirical tone of Shields's explorations of Canada's presence—or, rather, absence—in the American imaginary, the perspective expressed by Tom Avery's American one-night-stand in *The Republic of Love* who "thought that 'Winnipeg' sounded like the name of a board game" (Shields, *Republic* 237). (That *Newsweek* magazine, in its review of *Larry's Party*, described Larry as a resident of "Winnipeg, Ontario," attests to the accuracy of such judgments [1997].)

Shields's texts express impatience with the American perception of Canada as "a country where nothing seems ever to happen," a nation with a melting pot set to a curiously "low temperature" (Shields, *Stone* 93). While her characters could seldom be termed Canadian nationalists, such sly elements of critique, usually treated with humour, frequently feature in her work. The protagonists of "Accidents" express anger at the way in which Canadian news is "condensed and buried on a back page" or else entirely absent from the European *Herald Tribune* (Shields, *Collected Stories* 44).

At the same time, Shields's fiction refuses a cosy sentimentalizing of Canada itself. It is made clear, for example, that Daisy's view of the country of her birth as "a cool clean place . . . [a] healing kingdom" is an entirely idealized one borne of loneliness and longing, a view which in fact fails to correspond with her childhood memories (Shields, *Stone* 133). Again, this ambivalence would seem to reflect the ability of Shields's fiction to view both Canada and the United States with what Salman Rushdie has termed the migrant's "double vision" (Rushdie, qtd. in Bhabha 5). It demonstrates, furthermore, a subtle resistance to the consoling national myths which sustain both Canada and the United States in different ways. "I was told recently that [in contrast with Canadians] Americans 'know who they are,'" Shields said in 1998, "but I wonder if this is true" (Hollenberg 353). As such, Shields's work attempts to deconstruct the notion of essential United States/Canada difference and to stress the complexity and unresolvablity of questions of national or personal identity. Ultimately, then, the presentation of migration experiences in Shields's fiction moves beyond the specifically national to the existential. If contemporary literature is "populated by . . . those beings who are . . . deprived of a transcendental shelter or abode," then Daisy's impossible quest for "refuge, for a door marked with her own name" is emblematic of the human quest for a place to belong (Shields, *Stone* 305). And the trope of travel in Shields's work—the "departures and arrivals" that characterise her fiction—can be understood to relate not only to specific migrations but also to the human cycle of birth and death, regeneration and replacement. These crucial formulations remain in danger of being overlooked by commentators who emphasize only the domestic aspects of Shields's writing.

Shields's presentation of United States–Canada migrations receives analysis of a more critical kind in Stephen Henighan's 2002 study *When Words Deny the World: The Reshaping of Canadian Writing*, which deems *The Stone Diaries* to be the flagship text of "Free Trade Fiction." Henighan's argument revolves around a rather nostalgic figuring of the development of Canadian literature in the twentieth century. The "best" Canadian fiction, Henighan contends, was produced between 1965 and 1975, the years between what he figures as Canada's two colonizations: the first by Britain, the second by the United States following the implementation of NAFTA in 1994. Henighan claims that "nothing memorable" has been written by Canadian authors throughout the 1990s because "no sooner had the Free Trade Agreement gone through than Canadian novelists lost the thread of contemporary Canadian experience" (Henighan 180). Asserting that "[t]he pungency of the best writing of the 1960s—with its Canadian settings, its evocation of people, place and language . . . disappeared in the 1990s" (180), he is disturbed by the tendency of contemporary Canadian novelists to set their work outside of Canada, a trend which has resulted in "the drastic disappearance of Canadian reality from our fiction" (198). In the case of Shields's work, he perceives a lack of attention to Canadian contexts in her writing, and argues that her fiction ignores "the cavernous psychological and historical differences," the "discrepancies of history, culture, outlook, landscape, climate, language and institutions," which separate Canada from the United States (14). Most significantly, he suggests that the acquiescent presentation of migration experiences in *The Stone Diaries* means that the text is little more than the archetypal NAFTA novel:

> *The Stone Diaries* . . . is the flagship novel of Free Trade Fiction. At the beginning of the novel the Goodwill-Flett family is Canadian; by the novel's close they are American, with only great-niece Victoria Louise still resident in Canada. . . . Other writers . . . have written fiction about characters who move between Canada and the United States. But all these writers have defined their characters' moves as a transit between different histories and cultures: as an ordeal of disorientation. . . . Shields is unique in preaching an untroubled, ahistorical North

Americanism in which Canadians placidly assimilate into continental (i.e., U.S.) norms. It can hardly be a coincidence that this book was one of the most popular works of fiction in both Canada and the U.S., particularly among wealthy professionals, during the months in which NAFTA was implemented. (Henighan 184)

This assessment seems problematic and selective. On the one hand, Henighan claims that Shields is "*unique* in preaching an untroubled, ahistorical North Americanism" (emphasis added); on the other, he suggests that *The Stone Diaries* is part of a *wider* 1990s movement in which *many* Canadian novelists began to divest their work of Canadian elements and to defer instead to American cultural values in order to ensure commercial success. It is true that several of *The Stone Diaries*' Canadian characters do end up in the United States and that the text does not present these migrations in the hyperbolic terms outlined by Clark Blaise: "[e]ach Canadian emigrant must come to America prepared to die a subtle, psychic death" (4). It is unfair to suggest, however, that Shields's fiction does not present such migrations as "ordeals of disorientation" for the characters. When Daisy deletes a reference to Canada as "home" from her diary, or when Larry, in Chicago, recognizes that "Winnipeg was still his here and now, the black sphere that enclosed the pellet of his self" (Shields, *Stone* 132; *Larry* 154), the texts are clearly demonstrating how problematized the notion of belonging has become for these protagonists, and how difficult sustaining a home "between borders" might be in practice. Indeed, Larry and Daisy's shared feelings of inauthenticity, of alienation and estrangement, may all be interpreted in the context of their status as migrant characters in "a state of in-betweenness." If Daisy has "placidly assimilated" into the United States, why is she, at age 70, still figuring herself to be "a wanderer, longing for refuge" (Shields, *Stone* 305)? In this way, Henighan's suggestion that Shields's characters are "untroubled" by their moves into or out of the United States seems misguided.

An analysis of Shields's attention to such issues can be supplemented by reference to *Swann*, a novel also concerned with Canada–United States border crossing. Here, the observations of the Manitoban Jimroy during his time in Palo Alto constitute Shields's most direct engagement with Canadian and American difference. As Jimroy observes contrasts of climate, dress, humour, accent, spelling, and social mores, as he encounters "Californians . . . mired in their own crises, their mudslides and earthquakes and major art robberies" (Shields, *Swann* 94), the text presents a Canadian protagonist experiencing the United States precisely as a foreign country: "a puzzle" (Shields, *Swann* 94). In addition, Jimroy's experiences in Palo Alto are complemented by those of *Swann*'s most inveterate border crosser, the French-Moroccan editor Frederic Cruzzi. Prior to settling in Kingston, Ontario, Cruzzi has been resident in France and England, Turkey, India, and Japan, countries in which he has "test[ed] the shock of strangeness" (Shields, *Swann* 182). The phrase "the shock of strangeness" seems an especially apt one to describe the sense of displacement and disorientation which may be experienced by the migrant and serves to challenge accusations that Shields's presentation of cross-cultural encounters and experiences tends towards the sentimental. Indeed, Cruzzi's ethnic hybridity has resulted in unpleasant— though comically muddled—racist labelling: "[t]he word foreigner was invoked: Frenchy, Limey, Wog—there was understandable confusion here" (Shields, *Swann* 201). Clearly, then, Shields's traveller characters do not simply experience joyous epiphanies as they move across borders. "Travelling is hard work," Shields writes in "Travelwarp," her piece for *Writing Away: The PEN Canada Travel Anthology*, the text identifying "the travel demons" as "fatigue, despair, aching bones, primal angst, simple homesickness"—and proposing immersion in a book "that reads against the journey" as a defence strategy to help combat such threats and terrors (Shields, "Travelwarp" 279).

Notably, though, Henighan restricts his analysis to *The Stone Diaries* and makes no mention at all of *Swann*, or indeed of *Larry's Party*, in which the trajectory of *The Stone Diaries* is reversed and the protagonist returns to Canada at the end of the novel in order to be near "family— and the familiar" (Hollenberg 353). As Roberts suggests, "[i]f nation occurs to Larry as an afterthought, Canada is nevertheless a base he actively chooses to rejoin" (100). Nor does Henighan allude to the many other migration narratives *The Stone Diaries* itself contains. The experiences of characters such as Magnus and Abram Skutari (whose history is written and published by his Canadian grandson in the 1960s) are presented in counterpoint with those of the Goodwill-Flett family and allow the text to broaden out into a range of perspectives.

Since Henighan claims that he is "not arguing that it is evil, or a betrayal of one's heritage, to set one's fiction outside of Canada" and that "[i]t is natural for Rohinton Mistry to write about India, where he lived until the age of twenty-two" (171), one may question why it is not equally "natural" for Shields to write about the United States, where she also lived until the age of twenty-two. But Henighan's analysis carefully elides reference to Shields's American background, preferring to present her approach as a calculating attempt to appeal to American publishing markets. Clearly, his principal objection is to the *way* in which the United States is presented in Shields's fiction; his analysis suggests that there is not enough resistance or critique of American dominance in these portrayals. But Shields's willingness to identify and interrogate American perceptions of Canada is evident even in her earliest work, and her commitment to Canadian-specific settings and contexts in her own writing is clear in such elements as the minutely detailed evocation of small-town Ontario in the "Rose Hindmarch" and "Frederic Cruzzi" sections of *Swann*. Shields's double position—"a foot on each side of the border"—may account for her reluctance to see Americans and Canadians in terms of essentialist difference; indeed, she rejected Hollenberg's attempt to classify Larry as a "genial" Canadian "type" (Hollenberg 349). Rather, Shields's fiction indicates that appraising the differences between the two countries may result in nothing more than glib generalizations about alleged national "characteristics"—of the kind evinced by McGraw-Hill, who told her that the characters in a short story she submitted failed to "typify" an American family because they were "far too gentle" (Shields, qtd. in Wachtel 34).

Indeed, the strict categories of "Canadianness" and "Americanness" which Henighan's text appears to advocate were satirized by Shields as early as *Small Ceremonies*, in which Furlong Eberhardt—a writer whose rural novels have been received as "definitively Canadian" and the "embodi[ment] of the national ethos"—is "outed" (though not publicly) as an American-born draft dodger (Shields, *Small* 138, 4, 154). As Faye Hammill shows, Furlong's successful "passing" for Canadian may be read with characteristic doubleness: as both a critique of American infiltration of Canadian culture and a satire on the notion of any distinctly or definitively Canadian "voice" (Hammill 87–100). Composed during a period in which discussion of what constitutes a Canadian literary text was at its height, *Small Ceremonies* is Shields's first critique of such endeavours, "a sceptical analysis," as Hammill phrases it, "of those critical categories which posit the existence of the *essentially* Canadian in experience, culture or writing" (91). Moreover, Furlong's situation may constitute Shields's ironic comment on her own ambiguous position as a United States–born Canadian writer. (In Shields's fiction, issues of national identity are often explored through the prism of literary culture. In *Swann*, Kurt Wiesmann, the first poet published by Cruzzi and Hildë's Peregrine Press, has had his work rejected for the following reasons: "Publishers in Canada found Wiesmann's poems 'too European'; American publishers thought them 'too Canadian'; and a British publisher sensed 'an American influence that might be troubling' to his readers" [Shields, *Swann* 202].) In any case, *Small Ceremonies'* insistence that literary Canadianness may constitute a set of tropes that can be successfully "faked" reveals the irony, ambivalence, and quiet subversiveness of the exploration of American and Canadian cultural exchange which is undertaken in Shields's fiction, aspects which are overlooked in *When Words Deny the World*.

Notwithstanding its rather hostile tone, Henighan's text does raise some pertinent questions about the past, present, and future of Canadian fiction, and its engagement with the experience of migration. Is the "trend for foreign settings" in Canadian fiction a disturbing or a positive trend? What challenges *does* the implementation of NAFTA pose for contemporary Canadian novelists? Can a novel set entirely or partially outside of Canada be classified as Canadian? Such questions remain beyond the scope of the present analysis to address in detail. But I would argue that the literature of a nation of immigrants would naturally reflect the disparate backgrounds and ethnicities of its writers and that this need not be equated with an avoidance of "Canadian" reality. Moreover, any novel about United States–Canada migrations must involve an intelligent acknowledgement of what these nations share as well as what differentiates them, an exploration of their "sameness and difference," to borrow Roberts's phrase. It is to be hoped, then, that Carol Shields's work will continue to form part of any such discussion.

WORKS CITED

Bhabha, Homi K., *The Location of Culture*. London: Routledge, 1994. Print.

Blaise, Clark. "The Border as Fiction." *Borderlands Monograph Series # 4*. Orono, ME: Borderlands Project, 1990: 1–12. Print.

Boehmer, Elleke. *Colonial and Postcolonial Literature*. Oxford: Oxford University Press, 1995. Print.

Davey, Frank. *Post-National Arguments: The Politics of the Anglophone Canadian Novel since 1967*. Toronto: University of Toronto Press, 1993. Print.

Dickinson, Peter. *Here Is Queer: Nationalisms, Sexualities and the Literatures of Canada*. Toronto: University of Toronto Press, 1999. Print.

Eden, Edward, and Dee Goertz, eds. *Carol Shields, Narrative Hunger, and the Possibilities of Fiction*. Toronto: University of Toronto Press, 2003: 19–36. Print.

George, Rosemary Marangoly. *The Politics of Home: Postcolonial Relocations and Twentieth-Century Fiction*. Berkeley: University of California Press, 1999. Print.

Hammill, Faye. "Carol Shields's 'Native Genre' and the Figure of the Canadian Author." *Journal of Commonwealth Literature* 31.2 (1996): 87–100. Print.

Henighan, Stephen. *When Words Deny the World: The Reshaping of Canadian Writing*. Erin, ON: Porcupine's Quill, 2002. Print.

Hollenberg, Donna Krolik. Interview with Carol Shields. *Contemporary Literature* 39.3 (1998): 339–55. Print.

Iyer, Pico. *The Global Soul*. London: Bloomsbury, 2001. Print.

Neville, William. "Carol Shields and Winnipeg: Finding Home." In *Carol Shields: The Arts of a Writing Life*, ed. Neil K. Besner. Winnipeg: Prairie Fire Press, 2003: 27–37. Print.

O'Reilly, Christopher. *Postcolonial Literature*. Cambridge: Cambridge University Press, 2001. Print.

Ramon, Alex. *Liminal Spaces: The Double Art of Carol Shields*. Newcastle: Cambridge Scholars, 2008. Print.

Roberts, Gillian. "Sameness and Difference: Border Crossings in *The Stone Diaries* and *Larry's Party*." *Canadian Literature* 191 (2006): 86–102. Print.

Shapiro, Laura, "*Larry's Party*," *Newsweek* 6 October 1997. Web. 10 Dec. 2005. www.highbeam.com/doc/1G1-19803249.html.

Shields, Carol. *The Box Garden*. 1977. London: Fourth Estate, 1995. Print.

———. *Collected Stories*. London: Harper Perennial, 2004. Print.

———. *Coming to Canada*, ed. Christopher Levenson. Ottawa: Carleton University Press, 1992. Print.

———. *Happenstance*. 1980. London: Fourth Estate, 1991. Print.

———. *Larry's Party*. London: Fourth Estate, 1997. Print.

———. *The Republic of Love*. London: Fourth Estate, 1992. Print.

———. *Small Ceremonies*. 1976. London: Fourth Estate, 1995. Print.

———. *The Stone Diaries*. London: Fourth Estate, 1993. Print.

———. *Susanna Moodie: Voice and Vision*. Ottawa: Borealis Press, 1977. Print.

———. *Swann*. 1987. London: Fourth Estate, 2000. Print.

———. "Travelwarp." In *Writing Away: The PEN Canada Travel Anthology*, ed. Constance Rooke. Toronto: McClelland & Stewart, 1994: 276–80. Print.

———. *Various Miracles*. 1985. London: Fourth Estate, 1994. Print.

Wachtel, Eleanor. "An Interview with Carol Shields." *Room of One's Own* 13.1/2 (1989): 5–45. Print.

"To Be Faithful to the Idea of Being Good": The Expansion to Goodness in Carol Shields's *Unless*

MARGARET STEFFLER

In her final novel, *Unless*, and in a number of interviews toward the end of her life, Carol Shields drew attention to the concept of goodness. She told Eleanor Wachtel at the beginning of 2002 that goodness was "the main preoccupation of [*Unless*]" and that she had been "interested in the idea of goodness for a number of years" (Wachtel 153). An earlier comment on a more contained version of goodness focused on Shields's fondness as a child for the world and characters of "Dick and Jane readers" and the way in which "everyone was terribly good to everyone else." She claimed that "this sort of extraordinary goodness is very appealing to children" (Wachtel 32–33) and admired L. M. Montgomery's Anne Shirley as "a female model of . . . goodness" (Shields, "A View from the Edge" 21), who "transformed her society to a vision of goodness" (Levin 133). Shields's sustained interest in goodness is shared by her character Reta Winters, who remembers her seven-year-old self questioning the "goodness" of her "exceptionally docile and obedient" childhood friend, Charlotte, whose fate, according to an older friend and accepted by Reta, was to be among "the good [who] die young (*Unless* 151)."[1] As an adult, Reta claims that "the problem of goodness—what is it? where does it come from?—occupies me still" (152). She comments, for example, on the Anglican Church's Promise Hostel in Toronto, wondering "where did the goodness begin, the germ of goodness, the primal thought to offer food and shelter to strangers?" (191). Although Reta asks the question, she does not expect or want an answer, preferring to view the source and substance of goodness as mysterious and unknowable. The "germ of goodness, the primal thought" to which she refers can easily be located in the classical concept of hospitality and in the Aristotelian virtue of generosity (Aristotle 60), but it is the unfathomable persistence of such generous hospitality into a twenty-first-century secular society that renders it so incomprehensible and thus so powerful.[2] In Reta's mind, attempts to explain the motivation for performing acts of goodness, such as "following Christ's example" and "social responsibility," do not come close to accounting for the "powerful tide of virtue flowing from the veins of men and women who will not be much rewarded or even recognized for their efforts" (191–92).

Although Shields believed in "a flow of goodness in the world" and said that she knew it when she saw it, she, like Reta, could not define "what it [was]" and did not "know why people [were] good" (Wachtel 153–54). In response to a comment that this "is going to be the century where we discover the meaning of consciousness," she expressed a hope that "along with the answer to the question of what consciousness is will come the answer to the question of the nature of goodness" (163). Despite her inability, and perhaps her unwillingness, to articulate the cause of goodness, Shields did venture to identify its motivation and effect, which she located in happiness: "I think people are happier when they perform acts of goodness. That's all I can say" (154). Reta, writing as Xeta d'Orange, says much the same: "It just seems that our species is happier when we are good" (248). This may be true, but also deliberately superficial and unsatisfying. The goodness explored in *Unless* is much more complex and expansive than this narrow speculation allows, originating in generosity and hospitality, virtues that have an impact on community and reach far beyond the individual happiness of those performing the acts. Happiness may be one of the motivators and effects of goodness, but there is much more to say—and Shields says it in her final novel.

Similarly to the way in which Shields objected to fiction's lack of happy marriages and families in its emphasis on broken and dysfunctional ones (Shields, "Narrative Hunger" 33), so she voiced her dissatisfaction with literature that bypasses goodness in favour of evil. According to Maria Russo, "it was just as [Shields] was finishing *Unless* in September [2001] that talk of evil began to seem inescapable, but she was, she says, undeterred in her conviction that goodness is the more interesting, more important story" and that evil "is ultimately 'a kind of minor corruption of this major force [of goodness]'" (Russo F35). In her conversation with Ann Dowsett Johnston, Shields worded it slightly differently, seeing evil as "the breakdown of goodness, a very occasional rupture" (Johnston 51). She made it clear that her private life as a breast cancer patient undergoing treatment brought with it a sense of "the mysterious fact that people are, more often than not, good" (Russo F35). Although Shields provided a warning—"I am always concerned when people mistake my novels for my autobiography because they're not" (Wachtel 114)—she does, through a degree of disclosure in a number of interviews, invite readers to connect the "real" goodness with which she was treated by others during her illness with the elusive goodness at the heart of *Unless*. Prompted by the metafiction of this final novel, readers are acutely attuned to the presence of the writer behind the text. With a mixture of playful and profound enticements, Shields trusts readers to make connections without resorting to reductive autobiographical readings.[3]

Shields wrote *Unless* after she had been "throttled by astonishment" at her diagnosis of breast cancer, had subsequently experienced the initial feelings of "sorrow," and then registered "surprise" at discovering "how good people were to [her]"; it was written during the period when she had accepted the necessity of "giving over," which resulted in a "loss of self sovereignty" (Wachtel 108–09). She made it very clear that she wrote this novel out of her experience as a recipient of goodness and, in the process, wrote herself into a desire to bestow goodness: "When I finished this book . . . I felt like I wanted to go out into the street and give people money and do their mending for them or whatever" (173).

Although Shields was clear that she was not writing an autobiographical novel about breast cancer (Russo F34), *Unless*, written in the aftermath of diagnosis and with an awareness of mortality, contains some of life writing's impulses to challenge the linearity and exclusion of life and death.[4] A self-reflexive exploration of such impulses is of course at the heart of *The Stone Diaries*, which Marie-Louise Wasmeier refers to as a fictional (auto)biography and has studied in terms of its "complex relationship between life, death and text" (439), arguing that the novel "soften[s] the delimitations" and "break[s] down the seeming opposition between life and death" (439). *Unless*'s emphasis on goodness reflects Shields's longstanding interest in this Aristotelian virtue, specifically in relationship to death and in the context of the life well lived in the face of mortality. In her final novel Shields directly addresses the way in which goodness, although perhaps prompted by the promise and habit of happiness, is more powerfully called into action by brushes with mortality, specifically those experienced by Norah and Reta.

THE LIMITATIONS OF THE GOOD

In the writing of *Unless*, when Shields was feeling brave and capable of "blurting" like Reta (*Unless* 270),[5] she took advantage of the novel form, which she viewed as "roomier than [she'd] ever thought" (Wachtel 55), to expand the short and restrictive adjective "good" into the generous noun and concept of "goodness." The word is enlarged even further through context and contrast in its position with respect to the "little chips of grammar" (313) featured in *Unless*. In a letter to Wachtel in July 1994, Shields responded to a page from *Middlemarch* by saying, "The optimism of the Victorians!—who would dare to speak today of the 'growing good of the world'" (66). Several years later, with the extension of good into goodness, Shields dared to entertain the possibility of a growing good.

In her earlier fiction and in her readings of Susanna Moodie and Jane Austen, Shields explored the much more limited concept and construction of the "good" woman. In particular, *Small Ceremonies* (1976), *Susanna Moodie: Voice and Vision* (1977), *The Stone Diaries* (1993), and *Jane Austen: A Penguin Life* (2001) introduce the "good" woman in her many roles—the good girl, wife, mother, daughter, writer, elder. In *Small Ceremonies* Judith Gill, who is writing a biography of Susanna Moodie, comments that Moodie "had abandoned the sharp divisions between good and evil which had troubled her as a young woman," the "two qualities becoming bridged with a fibrous rib of irony" (123). This comment is echoed in Shields's 2002 statement that she had rejected what she termed the "very old-fashioned paradigm" that "good and evil are the opposites of each other" (Johnston 51). Dogmatic certainty and exclusionary oppositions are thus dismissed by both Moodie (according to Gill) and by Shields. In terms of Moodie as a good woman, Gill concentrates on the mother, explaining that Moodie's core or essence is buried beneath the pose and behaviour of the "good Christian mother," which makes up merely one of her many "layers and layers of affectation." Gill explains that the "real" Susanna, the "personality," is "lost under all the gauze" (173). The image is one of a minute kernel of authenticity swathed in filmy layers of tulle, which double as protective bandages.

In her own study of Moodie, *Susanna Moodie: Voice and Vision*, Shields notes that Moodie believed that women possess "a natural predilection for good" (37) and argues that in Moodie's work "there is a significant absence of men who combine both strength and goodness," and that "heroism as it is traditionally understood, a combination of daring and determination, nobility and virtue, is never demonstrated by the male characters," but "is the property of wives, mothers, daughters" (50). Female characters "have the appearance of genteel ladies, but a strength and resourcefulness that is generally associated with male behaviour" (7). Women serve as "the initiators of action, the guardians of morality, and the saviours in times of distress" (7). According to Shields, Moodie, who positions herself as the "generous, humourous, resourceful deliverer" (31), establishes her fictional women as "advisor[s] and reformer[s] of the male," and is fond of "the tableau of the upright female nursing the prone male" (44).[6] Despite Shields's detection of strength in Moodie's female characters, which involves removing the layers of affectation and gauze that hindered Judith Gill, Moodie herself remains a "docile" if somewhat "grudging" wife (49). Imposed standards of morals and manners continue to clothe and disguise inner strength and good acts, which must be applied in a way that do not draw attention to themselves or to the woman as heroic, but serve instead as sources of salvation to others. The disguise worn by the woman is balanced by her ability to penetrate the exterior of others, as suggested by Shields in her comment that Moodie demonstrates that "part of female strength," as opposed to male strength, that "springs from a more subtle understanding of human nature" (46). It is such subtle understanding that gives her the ability and desire to perform the good.

In *The Stone Diaries* the concept of goodness exposes the limitations of the good, but Daisy, like Moodie, remains trapped in the good. The narrator of *The Stone Diaries* asks "what exactly does being good mean in the context of the Flett family?" (158). The answers are superficial: good children make their beds, eat meals, go down for naps, help with housework, avoid whining, use good manners, and keep quarrelling to a minimum. Daisy, "deeply, fervently, sincerely desiring to be a good wife and mother," reads *Good Housekeeping, McCall's,* and *The Canadian Home Companion* (185). In Daisy's period of depression, however, "goodness cannot cope with badness" because it is "too stupidly good" (229); it fails to realize that it does not exist in isolation but is part of a continuum. Daisy's daughter, Alice, comments that people feel obligated "to be good, to be faithful to the idea of being good. A good daughter. A good mother. Endlessly, heroically patient." She maintains that "these enlargements of the self can be terrifying" (326). And so they can be, particularly for her mother, Daisy Goodwill Flett, who feels that she is missing the "kernel of authenticity" (75) and is perceived by her family as being "afraid to look inside herself. In case there was nothing there" (356). It is safer to stick with the limited good than look into the terrifying enlargements of the much larger concept of goodness. The emphasis in

The Stone Diaries is confined to the fulfilled life, attained by being good; the imagery focuses on filling the empty vessel of life and body with meaning—on the often futile attempt to transform the inner vacuum into substance.

The women in Moodie's work, including Moodie herself, engage in conventionally formulaic behaviour, such as "pious asides," compared by Shields in *Jane Austen: A Penguin Life* to Austen's pauses "for a moment of reverence" (5). But Shields's identification of Austen's "politics of the glance" is a much different matter. Unlike compromising asides and pauses, the glance employs techniques of powerful subversion, while simultaneously conforming to expectations of manners and courtesy. According to Coral Ann Howells, Shields's voice in *Jane Austen: A Penguin Life* is "unmistakably the same" as the voice in *Unless,* as are the "author's preoccupations" (107); in particular Howells points out that anger is regulated by the "politics of the glance" and the "politics of feminine goodness" (107). Shields argues that in *Mansfield Park* Austen "must be serious . . . mute her natural irony and deal with the subject of goodness and virtue" (*Jane Austen* 152). Shields describes Fanny's actions as those of the "helpless coming to the rescue of the even more tragically helpless" (156), and interprets the novel as a narrative "about belonging and not belonging, about love between siblings, about fine gradations of morality, and, ultimately, about human noise and silence, action and stillness" (158). The same could be said of *Unless*.

EXPANDING THE GOOD INTO GOODNESS

Reta Winters is ironically aware of the superficiality of domestic goodness practised by characters such as Daisy Goodwill Flett and herself, which involves the attempt to fill vacancy and nurture hunger so that there is no space left for longing or pain: "I've got two chickens roasting in the oven right now, enough for leftovers tomorrow; a potato casserole that just needs heating up, and the makings of a salad. My, my such a good woman, so organized, too" (47). Like Daisy, Reta Winters regrets feeling "absent from [her]self" (12) and notes vacancies caused by a desertion of "essence" and "bodily evaporation" (56) in other women, such as Mrs. McGinn, who inhabited her house before her. But Reta also longs for a positive version of emptiness—a space of promise and possibility—even as she condemns as a deliberate "project of self-extinction" the actions caused by similar longings in her daughter, Norah (165). The familiar movement in *The Stone Diaries* to fill the hollowness is reversed in *Unless* to a risky and experimental desire to hollow out the full. The fear of emptiness or the void is replaced by the panic of having too much—too much information, too much emotion, too much thought. Reta, for example, describes her head as a "ringing vessel of pain" (67) and longs for "a lobotomy, a clean job, the top of my head neatly sawn off and designated contents removed" (261). To be nothing is no longer the danger; the danger lies in a fullness that is pushed down inside and repressed. Neither stuffing full the empty nor scooping out the full is a viable solution for asserting identity. A third possibility exists and is clearly demonstrated in *Unless*. Rather than filling space or releasing content, a more promising and less intrusive movement is expansion—allowing whatever is within to grow without containment, naturally and organically.

It is in *Unless* that Shields uses the novel genre, "enormously expansive, capacious," a form that "will hold everything" (Wachtel 167), to enlarge the dutiful, flat, and limited idea of "the good," to challenge the simplistic, competitive separation between good and bad, and to expand out of, rather than simply fill, the vessels of female life and body. In doing so, she confronts the terrifying in the form of the enlargement of the self and the sublimity of goodness, which encompass rather than compete with masculine greatness. This vaster version of goodness can accommodate and nurture an expanded female self rather than simply fill the existing container. The subjects of vast goodness and expanded self both stretch and are stretched by the novel form, which is "elastic," "a big, baggy thing" (118): "you can put anything in [the novel], you can stretch it in any direction you like, and more or less get away with it" (55). For Shields, the novel is "a way of enlarging [her] own experience" (109). By stretching, overflowing, and breaking through the vessel instead of conforming to its conventionally imposed shape and size, goodness takes on a new shape without edges, suggesting limitless potential. Repeated attempts of the past to fill the vessel so that the good woman can become the fulfilled woman have failed, resulting in excess and painful bloating or deficiencies and hollow emptiness. *Unless* urges more extreme and radical action, instigated by the decision of Reta's daughter, Norah, to sit on a Toronto corner with a begging bowl and a sign proclaiming "GOODNESS." The situation, seen by Reta's mentor, Danielle Westerman, as the result of patriarchal oppression, promotes feminist responses in Reta, calling forth righteous anger.

Danielle Westerman is closely modelled on Simone de Beauvoir (*Unless* 170; Wachtel 160), a relationship which Bethany Guenther works with in her essay "Carol Shields and Simone de Beauvoir: Immanence,

Transcendence and Women's Work in *A Fairly Conventional Woman*, *The Stone Diaries* and *Unless*." Immanence, defined as "indwelling, inherent; actually present or abiding *in*; remaining within" (*OED* def.1), is explained by de Beauvoir's editor and translator, H. M. Parshley, as referring in *The Second Sex* to "confinement or restriction to a narrow round of uncreative and repetitive duties; it is in contrast to the freedom to engage in projects of ever widening scope that marks the untrammeled existence" (de Beauvoir 63). Guenther equates "miniaturism" and goodness with immanence, and greatness with transcendence, arguing that in Shields's fiction it is woman's work that provides the transcendental and thus the escape from the confinement of immanence. De Beauvoir speaks of women "wallow[ing] in immanence" (211) and "doomed to immanence" (248), with the woman shut "up within the circle of herself" (448). And indeed *Unless* is pervaded by what Reta sees as the heaviness of "too much inwardness" (6–7) and the "dull . . . circularity and lack of air" (107) caused by "introversion" and "the examined life" (107).[7] As Guenther notes, Reta's description of "uncoded otherness" is a description of immanence: "The power to assert ourselves and claim our lives has been displaced by a compulsion to shut down our bodies and seal our mouths and be as nothing against the fireworks and streaking stars and blinding light of the Big Bang" (*Unless* 270). Reta buys into de Beauvoir and Westerman's fight against immanence, literally allowing Westerman's "hypothesis" about Norah to "move into" her own vacant body and occupy "more and more space" (218). Westerman's hypothesis is that Norah is reacting to her realization of her lack of power and is claiming her existence by ceasing to exist. Out of Westerman's hypothesis and from her own feminist stance, Reta rails against the veneer of goodness, specifically female goodness, singling out "charm" as the most unrewarding of the social virtues, which, when compared with "real goodness," is "nothing but a crumpled tissue paper, soiled from previous use" (29). She also rejects sincerity, politeness and courtesy as shallow by-products of good behaviour, devalued by society and thus inviting invisibility by those who practise them, namely women.

The rejection of these superficial acts and attributes of the good and thus devalued woman leaves Reta with no alternative. Although she pursues an understanding of a higher level of goodness and discusses it with her friends, such a quality does not seem viable in Reta's world of Orangetown. What she and her friends come up with is soft—not rigorous or demanding enough, as it becomes simply "a matter of what we wanted to do all along. Whatever is convenient." It "has no force; none" (257). Attempts to define "real goodness" are unsuccessful; the best

Reta and her friends can come up with is "an abstraction," "an imaginative construct," and "a luxury for the fortunate" (115). Dr. McClure claims that Norah is "embracing the ineffable" (214), supposedly a vague form of the goodness represented by the much more concrete version proclaimed on her sign. The vagueness contrasts with the specific examples provided by Aristotle in his study of "the good" as "that at which everything [every skill and every inquiry, and similarly every action and rational choice] aims" (Aristotle 3). The virtue of generosity, for example, is clearly explained in *Nichomachean Ethics*:

> So, since generosity is a mean concerned with the giving and spending of money, the generous person will give and spend the right amounts, on the right objects, in both small and large matters alike, and he will do it with pleasure. He will also take the right amount from the right sources; because the virtue is a mean concerning both, he will do both as he ought. For taking in the right way implies giving in the right way, while the wrong sort of taking conflicts with it; and so the giving and taking that imply one another are found at the same time in the same person, while those that conflict clearly are not. (62)

Norah's behaviour appears to be at odds with any logical explanation, but a close look at this Aristotelian definition of the virtue of generosity describes her actions of taking and giving—"Nine-tenths of what she gathers she distributes at the end of the day to other street people" (11–12)—as concrete and grounded, as opposed to the vague theories floating around in society and the novel.

Associated with what Reta sees as the outmoded and powerless goodness practised by women, including Norah, is their inclination to be "too easily satisfied," too humble, and too "undemanding" (89). She also identifies a "lack of knowing" as a major reason for women remaining limited in immanence, claiming that "we are too kind, too willing— too unwilling too—reaching out blindly with a grasping hand but not knowing how to grasp for what we don't even know we want" (98). Rather than exchanging feminine goodness for masculine greatness, Shields suggests that self-knowledge and self-esteem attached to goodness could allow it to grow beyond the "not knowing" and immanence in which it has been confined. The centrality of such self-esteem and self-knowledge is based in the Aristotelian virtue of magnanimity or greatsouledness and in what Descartes in *The Passions of the Soul* refers to as the supreme virtue of *generosité*. According to Aristotle, "a person is thought to be great-souled if he thinks himself worthy of great things—and is indeed worthy of them" (68):

> Greatness of soul, then, seems to be a sort of crown of the virtues, because it
> makes them greater and does not exist in isolation from them. This is why it is
> hard to be truly great-souled, since it is not possible without a noble and good
> character. (69)

The argument asserts that "the truly great-souled person must be good" (69). The attainment of greatsouledness and by association, goodness, depends on self-knowledge; according to Aristotle, the small-souled person "seems not to know himself" and vain people are "ignorant of themselves" (72). Similar to Aristotle, Descartes claims that true generosity "brings it about that a person's self-esteem is as great as it legitimately can be" (43). He argues that "the most generous people are usually also the humblest," explaining that "for someone to be abject, or unvirtuously humble, . . . is directly opposed to generosity, and it often happens that the most abject people are the most arrogant and haughty, just as the most generous are the most modest and humble" (44–45). Further, "generosity serves as a remedy for all the disorders of the passions," providing "complete command" over "desires, jealousy and envy, . . . hatred of other people, . . . fear, . . . [and] anger" (44). The source of weakness is not goodness itself or introspection or even immanence but the lack of self-knowledge that prevents accurate assessments of self-worth and wants. Reta chooses to redraft her novel, so that her character, Alicia, "will expand in her self-understanding, and the pages will expand" (173). Rather than stuffing or filling Alicia from the outside, Reta facilitates expansion from within, each layer pushing itself out into the next. Eventually, Alicia is "intelligent and inventive and capable of moral resolution, the same qualities we presume, without demonstration, in a male hero" (320).

In *The Second Sex* de Beauvoir argues that "women have never set up female values in opposition to male values," that "men have presumed to create a female domain—the kingdom of life, of immanence—only in order to lock women therein" (65). The oppressive and exclusive patriarchal literary world against which Reta rails is an obvious example of a "female domain" created "in order to lock women therein." Self-absorbed Colin Glass provides a more intimate example of the thoughtlessness that creates and perpetuates such a domain. Reta's brave attempt to articulate the nature and texture of goodness—"isn't it possible . . . to think that goodness . . . could be a wave or particle of energy?"—is ridiculed and abruptly dismissed by Colin's "No, it is not possible" (22).

Reta's sudden exhaustion at this point accentuates the immanence into which she has been pushed by Colin's aggressive response. Norah, before moving to actively pursue goodness, also tries to articulate large concepts, including her love of the world and existence (128). Expressing a desire to move from the internal to the external, she speaks vaguely of wanting to pursue everything she loves—"whole continents, India . . . millions of town squares" (129)—in an attempt to break out of confine-ment, in de Beauvoir's words, to "transcend [her]self, to engage in freely chosen projects" (xxxv). Norah's aimless desire to simply exchange immanence for transcendence overwhelms her, however, and cannot be simply transferred into action. De Beauvoir talks of the woman's body as "a thing sunk deeply in its own immanence; it is not for such a body to have reference to the rest of the world" (157). It is through Norah's touching of "a Muslim woman" (118) that she takes herself out of her own body into another space and is thus afforded reference to at least a small portion of the rest of the world. This is no grand transcendence, but a meeting of two spheres of immanence. This meeting is reminiscent of Shield's description of the coming together of the reader and the novel in which she sees the novel as "a sphere that we open" and says "I like this thought very much—that it allows us access to any place" (Wachtel 170). Her belief in "numinous moments" that come from "the accidental collision of certain events" (47) certainly describes the coming together of the spheres of immanence of Norah and the other woman, resulting in the traumatic opening and expansion of Norah's own immanence.

The "ennui" (de Beauvoir 572) Norah is feeling in her Toronto life is dealt with in a different way than imagined—by one local touch rather than by mystical wandering throughout the trails and squares of the world. Reta speculates that Norah "wants to belong to the whole world or at least to have, just for a moment, the taste of the whole world in her mouth" (*Unless* 166). The desire to belong, which demands a connection outward and a grand transcendence, is mentioned and then exchanged for the merest transitory taste, which asks for only the slightest intake of the outer into the inner, for it is more than enough. There is no expectation or attempt to take in or ingest the outer world or the other in total, but simply an acknowledgement that a brief intersection, in this case traumatic, is enough to touch, through inward expansion, the heavy insularity of immanence, lifting and lightning it as it grows out of and beyond itself.

Norah's actions and Reta's relationship with her fictional character, Alicia, suggest that immanence is not dependent on an external force to initiate a grand transcendence, but can open up and expand from the inside out when moved to do so. Shields speaks of "rare transcendent moments when you suddenly feel everything makes sense and you perceive the pattern of the universe" (Wachtel 45) as moments she wants to "hold still in a net of words" (83). The impulse is internal. These moments, orgasmic in nature, originate in an inner core, well up from inside, and expand beyond the container of the individual in order to be captured by external words. Immanence and an accompanying goodness, functioning as the woman's inner life, can expand into immensity, extending beyond the bounds of themselves and their original space. It is not a matter of immanence and transcendence, goodness and greatness, being competitive opposites or exclusions. Indwelling is not necessarily stagnant and reductionist if immanence is accompanied by self-knowledge, which allows it to swell and rise upon and beyond itself but retain itself in the process.

When writing *Unless*, with "a chair in every chapter," Shields said that she "had this notion of a seated woman, a kind of woman in repose who is taking in the world from that position—not a fighting position, not a standing position, not a sleeping position, but seated and composed" (Wachtel 171–72). Reta's publisher, Arthur Springer, describes the seated Alicia as displaying "generosity," "tolerance," and "goodness" (*Unless* 212) but does not quite comprehend the power of the seated position. This wakeful alertness, concentrated on connecting immanence with the external world, does not depend on and wait for the external but swells and expands from within. Reta writes her letters against the exclusion of women as a seated woman. In the letter in which she signs her real name and address as opposed to playful versions, she admits that although she is still "sorting out the details" of goodness, she is "trying to be one of the faithful" (311). She describes goodness as elevated— "Goodness is respect that has been rarified and taken to a higher level"— as well as cleared and purified: "It has emptied itself of vengeance, which has no voice at all" (310). Its ability to empty itself of what is undesirable in order to intensify and concentrate its essence speaks to its agency and dependence on nothing but itself.

The seated and alert woman, curious, inquisitive, and aware of the world, nurtures the self-knowledge that allows the internal lifting and transformation of immanence. In the reclamation of charm (319) and in the concept of "inversion" Shields provides the clues that support the possibilities of a swelling of both immanence and goodness. Reta parts ways with Westerman and re-embraces charm, a concept "[she] thought

[she] had given up on" (319). She claims "that charm can be a gesture toward the authentic when it allows itself to be caught in the wings of an updraft and when it pushes its way into a different kind of cultural weather" (319). Like the politics of the glance, charm can be co-opted and used in ways to subvert the very limitations of the immanence to which it is relegated, rising on itself to enter and surround the culture of greatness traditionally denied to it, and not waiting for an invitation or permission to make reference to the wider world. The word "inversion" is much more complex than Arthur Springer's "turn around," a perverse call to Reta to change her novel by placing Roman rather than Alicia at the centre. Reta quotes Danielle Westerman's view of inversion: "'Subversion of society is possible for a mere few; *inversion* is more commonly the tactic for the powerless, a retreat from society that borders on the catatonic'" (218). Westerman speaks of Norah's act as a "clever inversion." Reta, or perhaps Shields, when dealing with the goodness and immanence that have puzzled her in their paradoxical limitations and potential, applies a more complicated definition of inversion than Westerman's retreat or turning inward. According to the *OED*, to invert is to turn the opposite way, to "turn things outside in, or inside out," (*OED* 9); either action brings the inner to the outer and the outer to the inner. Immanence then, when inverted or "turned inside out," is, to use several *OED* definitions, "turned in an opposite direction" (*OED* 2a), "emptied" (*OED* 9b), "transformed" (*OED* 10). Immanence is not obligated to strive for transcendence, and goodness does not need to reach for greatness; instead they invert themselves, turn on themselves, transform themselves as they literally turn inside out. In her attempt to focus her "thoughts on the immensity rather than the particular" (*Unless* 231) and to promote an inversion that works on its own, Reta approaches the Deleuzian concept that "absolute immanence is in itself; it is not in something *to* something; it does not depend on an object or belong to a subject" (Deleuze 26).

I turn now to Iris Murdoch's essay, "The Sovereignty of Good Over Other Concepts," as an essay that is particularly relevant to *Unless* and resonates with the novel in a powerful way. Reta refers to Murdoch, along with Woolf and Westerman, when objecting to "old What's-his-crust's" (99) thoughtless exclusion of women writers as literary influences. Woolf, de Beauvoir, and Murdoch are central among the women writers remembered and honoured by Reta and Shields in *Unless*. Alex Ramon, in his recent critical work on Shields, notes her reading of Murdoch (*Liminal Spaces* 34), and argues for the influence of Murdoch on Shields, claiming rather extravagantly that Shields "can only be properly contextualized [as contributing to world literature] by reference to her engagement with the fiction of Iris Murdoch" ("Literary Foremother" 146).[8] Although I am uneasy about such a claim of influence, I am comfortable with Ramon's discussion of intertextuality and am also led to link the work of the two writers. "The Sovereignty of Good Over Other Concepts" converses easily and effectively in tone and content with the cruxes raised in Shields's final novel. Murdoch's essay argues that goodness and consciousness combine "not to escape the world but to join it" (90).[9] The essay also explores the relationship between goodness and humility. *Unless* is similarly concerned with the dilemma of whether enacting goodness involves joining or withdrawing from the world and the degree to which the ego and humility are engaged by acts of goodness. Through Norah's acts, Reta's responses, and Shields's authorial presence, *Unless* advocates turning immanence and goodness outward into practical action without destroying the value of introspection, and encouraging empowerment through transforming feelings of worthlessness into worthiness, based on the Aristotelian mean in which the individual "reckons his [or her] own worth in accordance with his [or her] real merit" (Aristotle 68). This mean allows for the emergence of true humility rather than vanity caused by excessive feelings of self-worth, or self-deprecation resulting from a deficiency in the measure of self-worth. Murdoch stresses that "humility is not a peculiar habit of self-effacement, rather like having an inaudible voice, it is selfless respect for reality and one of the most difficult and central of all virtues" (95). The movement against self-effacement and an inaudible voice is repeatedly taken up by Reta in her feminist letters. Murdoch urges the "relation between virtue and reality," which depends on "a *task* to come to see the world as it is" (91). This is what I argue Norah is attempting to do by placing herself on the street instead of wandering vaguely throughout the world (Steffler 236). According to Murdoch, the statement "'Good is a transcendent reality' means that virtue is the attempt to pierce the veil of selfish consciousness and join the world as it really is" (93), which again seems to be what Norah is attempting to do with her begging bowl and sign of goodness. Although "it is an empirical fact about human nature that this attempt cannot be entirely successful" (Murdoch 93), just as the concept of "the good" "refers us to a perfection which is perhaps never exemplified in the world we know" (93), the pursuit and attempt are still highly desirable.

Murdoch suggests that "the indefinability of the good should be conceived of rather differently" (97) and instead of seeing vagueness as a problem, she celebrates the assurance that "a genuine mysteriousness attaches to the idea of goodness and the Good" (99). Although Reta in a sense wants goodness to remain mysterious, she still feels compelled to nail it down. Using the sun as a metaphor, Murdoch argues that "It is *difficult* to look at the sun: it is not like looking at other things. . . . There is a magnetic centre. But it is easier to look at the converging edges than to look at the centre itself. We do not and probably cannot know, conceptualize, what it is like in the centre" (100). She argues, however, that we should nevertheless try to look, which is exactly what Reta and Shields are doing. Consolation for the vagueness is found in the realization that "the world is aimless, chancy, and huge, and we are blinded by self" (100). Like Shields and Reta, Murdoch also believes that "there is a place both inside and outside religion for a sort of contemplation of the Good, not just by dedicated experts but by ordinary people" (101). Murdoch advises "a turning of attention away from the particular" (101), again a shift followed by Reta, who tries "to focus [her] thoughts on the immensity rather than the particular" (*Unless* 230–31), as does Shields.

Murdoch's final point is one that I see as being implicit in Shields's *Unless*:

> Goodness is connected with the acceptance of real death and real chance and real transience and only against the background of this acceptance, which is psychologically so difficult, can we understand the full extent of what virtue is like. The acceptance of death is an acceptance of our own nothingness which is an automatic spur to our concern with what is not ourselves. (103)

Norah's confrontation with death in her contact with the burning woman shocks her into a sense of nothingness, interpreted negatively by Danielle Westerman and others, but it is not necessarily a worthless nothingness, as such views assume. It partakes of the humility put forward by Murdoch, which results in the clarity of moral vision that comes from cleared space: "because he [the good man] sees himself as nothing, [he] can see other things as they are" and can also see "the pointlessness of virtue and its unique value and the endless extent of its demand" (103–04). The connection of humility with goodness provides a better direction of thought, in Murdoch's view, than "that suggested by more popular concepts such as freedom and courage" (103), the traditional masculine virtues. Despite accusations against goodness as vague and immanence as weak, Shields remains faithful and Reta tries to be "one of the faithful" (311) to the idea of being good, seeing in goodness and immanence the rich depth of untapped potential that is not offered by the hardened term and public concept of virtue, by the masculine quality of greatness, or by a transcendence that leaves immanence behind, shedding that valuable inner life. Shields's inversions turn the inside out, make the private public, and bravely expose the hidden inner life or immanence to the rest of the world. Shields's sense of her own nothingness, like Norah's (and as briefly felt by a resistant Reta at the very edge of such a realization), is the essence of humility and provides the condition that invites the expansive goodness that goes far beyond the single and measurable acts of the good woman. A temperament disposed to humility makes Shields's own expansion into goodness easy and breathtaking. We expect it and are grateful for all that it offers us.

Notes

1. Later in the novel, readers learn that Charlotte actually did die young. Lois, Reta's mother-in-law, in reference to Norah Charlotte, says, "The Charlotte was after a friend of Reta's who died very young in a car accident" (297).

2. For recent discussions of hospitality, the foreigner, and the stranger, see Derrida as well as Kearney and Semonovitch.

3. Never an advocate of erasing the author, Shields argued that "New Criticism failed because there's always a presence behind a novel, and you can never forget that presence," and further claimed that "we need to know the connection between the words and the person who makes them up" (Bolick). She admitted to Wachtel that she was "always curious about the person behind the voice, behind the writing hand" (Wachtel 143). It comes as a "surprise" to Judith Gill in *Small Ceremonies* that "anyone would deliberately set out to purify prose by obliterating the personality that shaped it" (*Small Ceremonies* 138–39). In her final interview with Wachtel, Shields said that "people, or novelists, have an easier time of it if they assign their particular feelings to one of their characters rather than carry these themselves" and with specific reference to the feeling of unhappiness, she advised changing "the quality or the cause of the unhappiness from one thing to another so that you're not forever writing your own autobiography" (Wachtel 151). Perhaps Shields was unusually generous in her interviews because she believed that "the more we know about a writer, the more we understand how the novel was put together and why and what it means" (143), and she reluctantly agreed with the comment that "the best writers reveal something about themselves" (96) in their novels.

4. The first paragraph of Marie-Louise Wasmeier's essay, "Fictional Fossils: Life and Death Writing in Carol Shields's *The Stone Diaries*," provides a comprehensive discussion of this aspect of life writing, including references to appropriate sources.

5. For Reta, "blurting is a form of bravery" (*Unless* 270); for Shields, "we have to use the time we've got to blurt— . . . lots of blurting—blurt bravely" (Wachtel 179).

6. This tableau of upright nurse is replaced by the erect seated woman in *Unless*. The posture and poise of the seated woman will be discussed later in the essay.

7. In October 1999, before writing *Unless*, Shields experienced a similar heaviness in her worry about the dangers of "self absorption" brought about by the diagnosis of cancer, but felt that she was "getting out of this terrible introspection" (Wachtel 112).

8. I had applied Murdoch's essay to *Unless* before I read Ramon's criticism, so experienced that familiar feeling of "arriving late, as always" (*Unless* 270).

9. The emphasis on the good's relationship to consciousness brings to mind Shields's hope that the two will come together in this century (Wachtel 163).

Works Cited

Aristotle. *Nicomachean Ethics,* trans. and ed. Roger Crisp. Cambridge: Cambridge University Press, 2000. Print.

Bolick, Katie. "A Likely Story." *The Atlantic Online.* 14 Jan. 1999. Web. 30 Apr. 2011.

de Beauvoir, Simone. *The Second Sex,* ed. and trans. H. M. Parshley. New York: Vintage, 1989. Print.

Derrida, Jacques (invited by Anne Dufourmantelle to respond). *Of Hospitality.* Stanford: Stanford University Press, 2000. Print.

Descartes, René. *The Passions of the Soul.* 1649. Some Texts from Early Modern Philosophy. Website created and managed by Jonathan F. Bennett. Web. 30 Apr. 2011.

Deleuze, Gilles. "Immanence: A Life." In *Pure Immanence: Essays on a Life,* trans. Anne Boyman. New York: Urzone, 2001: 25–34. Print.

Guenther, Bethany. "Carol Shields and Simone de Beauvoir: Immanence, Transcendence and Women's Work in *A Fairly Conventional Woman, The Stone Diaries* and *Unless.*" *Studies in Canadian Literature* 35.1 (2010): 147–64. Print.

Howells, Carol Ann. "Regulated Anger." *Canadian Literature* 179 (2003): 107. Print.

Johnston, Ann Dowsett. "Her Time to Roar." *Maclean's* 15 April 2002: 49–51. Print.

Kearney, Richard, and Kascha Semonovitch. *Phenomenologies of the Stranger: Between Hostility and Hospitality.* Fordham: Fordham University Press. Print.

Levin, Martin. "Carol's Kindness." In *Carol Shields: Evocation and Echo,* ed. Aritha van Herk and Conny Steenman-Marcusse. Groningen: Barkuis, 2009: 131–33. Print.

Murdoch, Iris. "The Sovereignty of Good Over Other Concepts." In *The Sovereignty of Good*. London: Routledge and Kegan Paul, 1970: 77–104. Print.

Ramon, Alex. *Liminal Spaces: The Double Art of Carol Shields*. Newcastle-upon-Tyne, UK: Cambridge Scholars Publishing, 2008. Print.

———. "A Literary Foremother: Iris Murdoch and Carol Shields." In *Iris Murdoch: A Reassessment*, ed. Anne Rowe. Basingstoke, UK: Palgrave and Macmillan, 2007: 136–47. Print.

Russo, Maria. "Final Chapter." *The New York Times Magazine* 14 April 2002: F32–35. Print.

Shields, Carol. *Jane Austen: A Penguin Life*. Toronto: Penguin, 2001. Print.

———. "Narrative Hunger and the Overflowing Cupboard." In *Carol Shields, Narrative Hunger, and the Possibilities of Fiction*, ed. Edward Eden and Dee Goertz. Toronto: University of Toronto Press, 2003: 19–36. Print.

———. *Small Ceremonies*. 1976. Toronto: Random House, 1995. Print.

———. *The Stone Diaries*. Toronto: Random House, 1993. Print.

———. *Susanna Moodie: Voice and Vision*. Ottawa: Borealis Press, 1977. Print.

———. *Unless*. Toronto: Random House, 2002. Print.

———. "A View from the Edge of the Edge." In *Carol Shields and the Extra-Ordinary*, ed. Marta Dvořák and Manina Jones. Montreal and Kingston: McGill-Queens University Press, 2007: 17–29. Print.

Steffler, Margaret. "A Human Conversation about Goodness: Carol Shields's *Unless*." *Studies in Canadian Literature* 34.2 (2009): 223–44. Print.

Wachtel, Eleanor. *Random Illuminations: Conversations with Carol Shields*. Fredericton: Goose Lane, 2007. Print.

Wasmeier, Marie-Louise. "Fictional Fossils: Life and Death Writing in Carol Shields's *The Stone Diaries*." *Forum of Modern Language Studies* 41.4 (2005): 439–48. Print.

Narrative Pragmatism:
Goodness in Carol Shields's *Unless*

TIM HEATH

> Give me an idea that's as full of elegance and usefulness as the apple orchard
> behind my house, something from which I can take a little courage.
>
> —Carol Shields, *Unless* (228)

> Words are of two kinds, simple and double.
>
> —Aristotle, *Poetics*

Carol Shields makes *Unless* into a work that undeniably invites interpretation under the banner of postmodernism, yet to take the book
up as merely postmodern risks opening it into an unavailing exercise
that will not adequately unfold its meaning. Meaning, in particular the
meaning of goodness and of all the intuitive "little chips of grammar,"
as well as the enigmatic title of *Unless*, matters greatly because Shields
enters the realm of ethics with her inquiry into goodness, with her use
of the woman who self-immolates, and with her suggestively allegorical
feminist dialogue between Reta Winters and Danielle Westerman,
respective avatars of tempered, domestic and theoretical, continental
feminisms (313). Shields, moreover, creates Reta as mother, wife, friend,
reader, and housewife as well as poet, short story writer, translator,
editor, novelist, and narrator who says "words are my business," but this
labour involves as much play as it does work (11).

Reta's word games explain why it is tempting to read *Unless* as a
postmodern novel, one which features many of the elements Ihab Hassan
identifies as postmodern: "fragments, hybridity, relativism, play, parody,

pastiche, an ironic, sophistical stance, an ethos bordering on kitsch and camp" (4). Some such things are detectable in *Unless*. For example, the Winters' family joke that informs *My Thyme Is Up*, the metafictional structure through which Reta "deconstruct[s] Alicia's acute feminine sensibility" (111) and writes to the "unreconstructed" Dennis Ford-Helpern, author of *"The Goodness Gap"* (226), as well as the rather odd presence of Reta's "old friend Gemma Walsh, who had just been appointed to a Chair in Theology (hello there, chair!)" which secures the appearance of yet one more chair in the book, all these conspire to suggest that Shields gives *Unless* over to a postmodernism shaped by post-structuralist and structuralist semiotics bent on displaying language's diffractions, displacements, substitutions, and deferrals of meaning (313). Reta, of course, calls her own work "jokey," and this descriptor could be fairly applied to *Unless* itself if it were not for the way that Reta's yearning for an idea that is "full of elegance and usefulness" offers a heuristic that matches Winfried Fluck's description of pragmatism as "practice-oriented, situational, provisional, experimental, and processual in the sense that it is constantly emerging anew in the never-ending processes of adaptation to experience and readjustment to intersubjective encounters" (228, ix). Fluck's words signal my indebtedness to his scholar-ship and to others, such as Katrin Amian and Susanne Rohr, who seek to integrate the philosophical pragmatism of Charles Sanders Peirce, and other pragmatists, into their literary inquiry. My interests in Peir-cean thought, however, are not programmatic, in part because his work is vast, complex, neologistic, and emergent in the sense that much of it is only recently coming to press, and in part by the fact that such philo-sophical and semiotic tools offer no special insight into Shields's resourceful and suggestive literary expression when she works by means of understatement, intertext, ekphrasis, trope, and the like.

Even though Peirce was a nineteenth-century thinker, he conceived of "pragmatism as a philosophical theory about knowledge and truth, [one] evolved . . . in response to western metaphysics, [one which] attack[s] [Enlightenment] philosophy for its faith in absolutes and develop[s] a pluralist, fallibilisitic, and empiricist view of knowledge in its stead" (Amian 1). Shields shows her own pragmatist predilections when she presses against Western metaphysics aggressively in *Unless* with Reta's letter, dated 8 October 2000, to the editors of what readers might surmise is *Comment* magazine. Reta takes the publication to task for selling advertising space to a "faux institution" of some kind. The ad, hawking what surely is the equivalent of a Great Course, pitches "eighty-four (84) half-hour lecture tapes" on the "Great Minds of the Western

Intellectual World: Galileo, Kant, Hegel, Bacon, Newton, Plato, Locke, and Descartes" (135–36). Reta's letter asks the editors ("Dear Sirs") how it is possible that but one female faculty member is listed among the distinguished scholars featured on the tapes (135). The letter expresses Reta's "troubled" concern that such ads, such traditions, only display "a callous lack of curiosity about great women's minds, a complete unawareness, in fact" that communicates to any thoughtful female reader an understanding of how "casually and completely she is shut out of the universe" (136–37). The point here is not so much that Reta wants into an arena from which she has been excluded as it is that the "Great Minds of the WIW" cannot be great, or even good, if they have failed to notice "the playing field" is not level (136–37). The challenge, then, is both epistemic and ethical, for through this letter Shields displays her narrative pragmatism. This letter, and the other five that Reta writes but does not send, suggests that Shields seeks meaning, if there is "such a beast as truth," through a modulation of tone—here anger, and elsewhere through silence and understatement ("Narrative Hunger" 25).

Indeed, Shields pointedly upholds and mobilizes her heuristic through litotes. That is, by means of simple understatement Shields calls things less in order to make them more significant and thus achieves the laudatory aim of this trope. The very title of the novel serves as Shields's hint and reminder of her rhetorical stance, for *Unless* serves secondarily as a logical particle—"a little chip of grammar"—and primarily as the governing sign announcing her narrative thesis: the book, its subject matter, marriage, goodness, women, domesticity, fiction, dogs, friends, these things are not inferior (313). Rather, they are *un less*, that is, poignantly, achingly, qualitatively, essentially, and functionally not less than any other thing, subject, person, or possibility. In this sense, *Unless* is a book whose every sign demands careful attention.

When Shields changes fonts to make goodness into GOODNESS she plays with words and language in ways that signal a certain dissatisfaction with what Reta calls "too much Derrida" (4). Reta, aged forty-three, caught in her grief over her daughter's devotion to "goodness," needs to discover the meaning of this word, of all the words she uses, especially because its meaning apparently holds the key to Norah's estrangement and because as writer and translator Reta loves "the hard bite of language" at the same time she tolerates the "moments when words go swampy and vague" (2, 103). The iconic force of GOODNESS introduces what W. J. T. Mitchell calls "similitude" in "the territory of difference" (552). Mitchell's "difference" points toward the longstanding dominance of

Saussurean and Derridean semiotics in literary discourse, and at the same time underscores that the most notable alternative to such thought is that of Peirce. In Peirce's semiotics, his three classes of signs—symbols, indices, and icons—belong to his larger project of articulating a pragmatist philosophy. Thus, when Shields makes GOODNESS not merely a conventional symbol whose relationship to its object is arbitrary but rather an icon that resembles its object, she opens an opportunity to read *Unless* as a novel in pursuit of its own form of semiotic inquiry, one aimed at showing how greatly exaggerated are the claims made against the ability of language to signify availingly. That Reta's first short story is entitled "Icon" quite fortuitously supports the likelihood that Shields was aware that iconicity calls into question the dominant understandings of the relations obtaining between signs and objects (4). Indeed, given that Shields embeds both the short story's title and the typeface from Norah's sign early in the narrative makes her search to understand goodness fit with a Peircean economy where meaning is a given, an a priori, that must be discovered, while Saussurean, and therefore Derridean, thought makes meaning unstable and transient. In her "Narrative Hunger and the Overflowing Cupboard," Shields shows her Peircean inclinations, for she says, "we cannot think without words" at the same time she says language "stands beside reality" and that like a "tortoise" works constantly to overtake the immediacy of experience (23). In other words, if there is something of a gap, a delay, a différance in language, there is also something quite certain in it, and its plodding nature can be accelerated by recourse to iconicity.

Later in the novel, Shields abstains from iconicity when Reta writes "my heart is broken," for even though she says she uses "block letters" no majuscules appear in the text (66). "In a whimsical afterthought," however, Reta draws "a little heart" in the corner of the washroom cubicle's blackboard with "a jagged line through it" and, again, underscores the idea that signs and objects are linked by more than convention, even though convention operates within iconicity (66). Reta's response to her words and picture underscore another aspect of Peirce's semiotics, for she speaks of something like "jubilation" and "enchantment" as though she were "allowed to be receptor and transmitter both, not a dead thing but a live link in the storage of what would become an unendurable grief" (66–67). Reta's role in both inscribing words and drawing pictures highlights the triadic nature of Peirce's semiotics because a sign and its object depend on a third element, the interpretant, for their meaning. The interpretant is not so much a person as a sign created in the mind of someone, but, unlike thinkers such as de Saussure or Derrida who emphasize the linguistic nature of semiotics, Peirce insists that the interpretant can be non-linguistic, an understanding that makes room for Reta's response to her own signifying work: she is both "receptor and transmitter" of grief, but not merely of grief and jubilation as linguistic concepts but rather as something emotional and somatic, something which "rubs against her" (66). This passage shows the interpretant of a sign is yet another sign, for Reta makes "grief" stand for the iconic broken heart she sketches that in turn stands for the original words "my heart is broken" (66). In Peircean terms, this moment in the narrative makes thought, knowledge, and emotion form a web of "interconnected signs capable of unlimited self-generation," yet to acknowledge this possibility is not necessarily to agree with Derrida when he says in *Of Grammatology* that he values Peirce as a precursor of his own critique of the "metaphysics of presence" because "Peirce goes very far in the direction that I have called the de-construction of the transcendental signified" by postulating a dynamic of infinite semiosis that refuses "to place a reassuring end to the reference from sign to sign" (Steiner 1139; Derrida 49). It is true that Peirce's thought is patient of Derridean appropriation, but because Peirce's theory of signs is epistemological and because it drove all of his thinking on all matters, he arrived at a unique philosophical ideal-realism. Amian explains that this position holds that reality is "genuinely knowable but can be known only through signs" (32). Reality thus "exists independently of human cognition" (the realist position) but "cannot be known outside thought" as idealists argue (32). Reality and the process of its cognition are thus "interdependent from the start, allowing reality to assume the paradoxical position as both the *trigger* and the *result* of semiotic processes of reality constitution" (32). In this sense, then, Shields does not make goodness into an ever-hidden signified infinitely shifting from one sign to another when she has Reta's friend Lynn Kelly say "goodness is an abstraction" or that it is "an imaginative construct" (*Unless* 115). Rather, goodness in *Unless,* because it is a sign, like all signs, says Peirce, "stimulates our efforts to find out and know by confronting us with a never-ending series of surprising facts" and forcing us to question, probe, and correct our findings—in part by inference and in part by what Peirce called "collateral experience" (*Collected Papers* 7.218, 8.314). This last point means that although the world is constituted by signs it is not entirely reducible to them either (Amian 36). Interpreted in light of Peirce's thought, Reta's pursuit of understanding goodness, a word whose meaning she does not know, involves a kind of substitutionary semiotic where one sign evokes another such as "wearth," and this in turn summons another sign, "worth," but for Shields this process connects to the "veryness" of the world (11, 185). The apparent illogic and arbitrariness of sign substitution possesses, in Shields's hands, an uncanny logic, for "wearth" as an Old English word for "outcast" is not truly cancelled by its English "twin" "worth" (11–12). Rather, what looks like a lexical and logical non sequitur paragrammatically adumbrates the ethical logic animating *Unless*, for the novel intimates that an individual's response to the outcast is the place in which worth is manifest. This equation shows that even though Peirce conceived of inexhaustible meanings he also held the firm pragmatist belief in the progress of human knowledge and the social situatedness of the subject as the experiencing and meaning-making agent. Reta, in other words, multiplies signs and meanings, but in the very act of narrating her response to Norah's estrangement she also intervenes into the social world, forestalling the process of realizing the fuller meaning of GOODNESS while she simultaneously reveals an adequate working knowledge of its sense and the prompt for action that it betokens.

Shields routinely places signs and their objects into artful appositions aimed at collapsing the distance between word and world. For example, in the chapter entitled "Notwithstanding" in which Reta speaks about sex with her husband Tom, she seamlessly moves from citing Wordsworth's "French Revolution" ("To be young was very heaven"), a broadly accurate allusion to the more radical time of their youth, to a change of meaning wrought by polyptoton, so that "very" becomes "veryness," and this word now by apposition shows that signs beget signs but not always by means of deferring meaning (185). Rather, words can undergo a form of deposition and plant themselves. In another place, much earlier in the story, where Reta thinks through her need to clean in order to cope with Norah's estrangement, she admits that "I dust and polish this house of mine so that I'll be able to seal it from damage," yet as she works her way to this blunt statement she refuses the idea that order and cleanliness serve as some form of metaphor (61). In effect, Reta removes the standard understanding of metaphor, that it is a vehicle meant to carry meaning from one object to another, by saying that "metaphors hold their own power over us, even without their fugitive gestures. They're as real as the peony bushes we observe when we're children" (61). This kind of reasoning—an involution which makes a simile explain a metaphor—might be dismissed as a structure of Reta's grief and rationalization over Norah's waywardness, but Shields repeatedly makes words and objects abut one another rather than slip over one another. The figure within the figure, moreover, resonates with Shields's conviction that "getting inside reality rather than getting reality right is the task of narrative fiction" ("Narrative Hunger" 35).

Another example of this goal appears when Reta's misgivings about her decision to make Roman a trombonist turn to her admission that she was playing with a paperclip when assigning him his vocation: "Roman acquired his vocation in the world of brass, through an accident of association, because I the stalled writer of a first novel, happened one afternoon to be twisting *un petit trombone* in my hands and thinking about giving my male character some real work to do" (266). Reta's words stand, in effect, as a commentary on the continental tradition—through de Saussure and Derrida—of theorizing language as a differential system, one with arbitrary conjunctions between the sign and signified, but Reta makes something of a satirical carnival of sign, signified, and extralinguistic reality by translating from one language to another in ways that make the coincidence of visual and aural imagery trump dyadic semiotics insofar as the referent—the trombone and the paper clip—intrudes into the tidiness of sign-signifier relations by means of yet another manifestation of the Peircean model—the index and the interpretant. That is, by its sheer proximity to Roman's occupation the paper clip Reta handles becomes an index for trombone—the equivalent of smoke signalling fire—at the same time that her role as interpretant forms a triadic relationship between words and objects—all by means of memory and story. That Roman functions as a double entendre for *roman* only adds to the richness of this passage, for Shields here does not so much mock continental theory as revel in the ways in which even a single word tells a story. It is true that this delightful passage—its diagram in a fictional course on general linguistics comes to mind—could stand as an example of straightforward Saussurean semiotics, but the passage's context—the "real work" of fictional characters—makes clear Shields's novelistic poetics.

Shields continues her word play when she reverses traditional expectations of the *mise en abyme* by juxtaposing two different under-standings of infinite regression, and, again, a kind of intuitive allegory is at work. In her commentary on the problems novelists face with character formation, Reta says that to "create unique and substantial characters" a writer must supply a past for them (139). Shields effectively offers a poetics here, for Reta asks rhetorically "how far back does a novelist have to go in order to stabilize a character and achieve solidity?" (140). As Reta comments on Jane Austen's habit of offering at least one generation of background to create "grounding" for her characters, she notes that this scruple overcomes the "sense that the character isn't self invented or arbitrary" (140). This genealogical trajectory, with its emphasis on "grounding," "solidity," and eschewal of the "arbitrary" balances against the *mise en abyme* predicament Reta prevents by keeping Alicia in the magazine industry, not in the academy where it would be too easy to let Alicia undertake her "doctorate in, say, Chinese women's poetry in the second half of the eighteenth century" (140, 268). Reta fears that she would be a "woman writing about a woman writing about women writing" (268). This situation, of course, would lead "straight to an echo chamber of infinite regress in company with the little Dutch girl, the girl on the bathroom cleaner, the vision multiplied, but in receding perspective. No" (269).

Shields, of course, affirms what she actually denies: *Unless* and *Thyme in Bloom* present a woman writing about women writing about women, yet no abyss materializes. Indeed, regress of the genealogical type produces "solidity" and no destabilization of meaning occurs (140). Both of these passages point to Shields's rather "unreconstructed" (to use her word) sense that "the right word perfectly used" is one of life's consolations (226, 102). This understanding appears in several places where the "right word" plainly corrects the damage wrought by the wrong word. For example, Reta's childhood friend Charlotte belongs to a family whose father changes his name from "Adolph" to "Chris Christiansen" to avoid the "evil associations of that blunt, harsh Adolph" (151). The same point gets made again when Lois, Reta's mother-in-law, wins a "blue ribbon" for her "German honey cake" when it is renamed "Swiss honey cake" (298). Characteristically, Shields creates a tonal spectrum when she turns Reta to thinking about words. Where a subtle nostalgic sadness emerges in substitutions such as "German" and "Adolph" a contrasting wry and trenchant humour fills Reta's sly remark to Arthur Springer that there's "about fifteen miles" of difference between "Orangetown" and "Orangeville" (275). Words may exist in a system of difference with no positive connection to the world, yet they have an odd habit of affecting crucial relations to the object world.

One of the most significant elements of *Unless* emerges in its sincere conviction that language possesses autonomy and self-sufficiency. This order of things argues strongly against mistaking the apparently postmodern playfulness in the book as an earnest effort to forestall sincerity. Indeed, one of the central tenets of metafiction deals with the turn away from representation of the object world, yet Shields also fills *Unless* with ekphrasis, that is, the literary effort designed to embody the characteristics of the thing described. The most salient ekphrastic portion of *Unless* occurs when Reta shops the Georgetown area of Washington to discover the perfect scarf for Norah. Reta's description of the scarf quite pointedly displays the challenge of representing the visual by means of the verbal: "It was patterned from end to end with rectangles, each subtly out of alignment: blue, yellow, green, and a kind of pleasing violet. And each of these shapes was outlined by a band of black and coloured in roughly as though with an artist's brush" (90). The Horatian dictum, *ut pictura poesis*, echoes within the painterly quality and description of the scarf, but the response that Reta's friend Gwen makes—"it's just that it's so beautiful. . . . Finding it, it's almost as though you made it. You invented it, created it out of your imagination"—quite plainly shows that Shields is engaged in the formal rhetorical exercise of calling to mind that which does not exist through the power of words (96).

Gwen's presence in this passage shows another instance of why Peirce's thought helpfully suggests insight into *Unless*. Because Peirce bases his work on idealism, reality is accessible to thought, where it remains subject to continuous scrutiny and correction, and it presents itself as the result of a collective process of interpretation. "The real," Peirce says, is that which, "sooner or later, information and reasoning would finally result in" and "involves the notion of a COMMUNITY, without definite limits and capable of a definite increase in knowledge" (*Collected Papers* 5.311). In this sense, knowing is collective, familial, shared with friends, built through conversation and reflection on experience. Thus, when Gwen views the scarf Reta purchased for Norah as something practically called into being by Reta's imagination, it becomes possible to see this moment as one in which Shields dramatizes her preference for idealism over, say, the existential phenomenology of Derrida, for the writerly pact between Gwen and Reta depends on a patent connection between what can be imagined, described in words, and how "bits of the world" can be discovered by imagination and by words moved into fiction and kept in the world simultaneously (95). The scarf itself becomes an object lesson, for it is both "putty" and "half an ounce of silk, maybe less, floating free in the world, making someone happy" (97). This entire ekphrasis serves to place on view Shields's writerly sense that "both reality and literature are joined in a need for language" ("Narrative" 24).

Throughout *Unless*, Shields builds a sincere yet playful commentary on language. Reta weighs its phonological power when she says that Christine comes close to "engraving words on the air" in her defensiveness about Reta's discovery of a cigarette in her pocket, and "sooo-ooo-oo" elongates to become something that can be "sung to different tunes" (74). In a contrasting moment, Reta and Tom walk in the Orangetown cemetery, and Reta describes the monuments and words, one the depiction of "life-size kicking infant" with the inscription "Our Little Jack," and another inscription for "Mary Leland" says "She Took Good Care of Her Chickens" (174). Here, Shields lets Reta speculate that the stonemason's chisel slipped, that the inscription was meant to say "children" not "chickens," but the meaning is, of course, undecidable. That even the sound of a word can permanently inscribe an ominous and hurtful message, perform a simple conversational function, or remain cryptic and opaque underscores the overall sense that language defies neat field theories and that its practitioners know something that its philosophers and theorists do not. As Reta says of Tom's provisional investigations into the source of Norah's trauma, "a stubborn screen of common sense keeps getting in my way and cancelling the filigree of fine-spun theory" (269).

One of Shields's most disarming and innocent pieces of such resistance emerges in her use of onomatopoeia. The Winters family "blubs" in their car after discovering that Norah is in the Promise Hostel, for they are undone by the hospitality of others as much as by their heartache over Norah (193–94). Because the sound of "blubs" imitates the thing or action to which it refers it makes obvious that something as simple as onomatopoeia significantly delimits the structuralist and poststructuralist conviction that the relationship between words and signs is arbitrary. Rather, the seemingly natural connection between phonetic shape, sense, and state of the world displays how it is inadequate to think of onomatopoeic words as symbols because they are in Peirce's terminology one more instance of an icon. Shields, moreover, narrates the visit to the Promise Hostel in a way that reproduces the word brand visible on the aprons worn by the volunteers, so this entire passage actually falls under the iconic "PROMISE" (193). Because this word is emblazoned on each apron, it highlights how food and words habitually stand in apposition throughout *Unless*, something which displays Shields's pragmatic—in both a popular and philosophical sense—conviction that the abiding hunger for sense, meaning, and narrative must be fed. I allude, here, of course, not merely to Shields's "Narrative Hunger and the Overflowing Cupboard" but also to the way in which Reta concludes her visit to the washroom earlier in the novel. This scene concludes with Reta and Tom leaving the Frontier Bar. As they step out into the "bitingly cold" night air, Reta realizes that "for the first time in weeks I was able to take a deep breath," and then she offers one more version of the iconic message: "*My Heart Is Broken.* My mouth closed on the words, and then I swallowed" (67). Now italicized and in mixed case this simple sentence in effect becomes the title of a work that sustains Reta and hints one more time at Shields's conviction "that even the smallest narrative fragments have the power to seduce" ("Narrative" 20). The seduction, of course, lies with the statement that "my heart is broken" is the story of too many women who know the "prohibition placed on the storyteller—most often: 'Woman, hold thy tongue!'—or a simple inability to write down one's experience on paper" ("Narrative" 26). That Reta consumes her own words shows a doubleness that is characteristic of Shields: these words sustain, yet they disappear rather like the billiard ball that is woman: "we've been sent over to the side pocket of the snooker table and made to disappear" (99).

Shields shows her "stubborn screen" of common sense one more time when dealing with what Hassan calls postmodernism's "epochal crisis," that is, identity in one of Reta's autobiographical memories (5). As Reta remembers "little Reta Summers," she recalls that "my mother always spoke to me in French and my father in English" (145–46). This situation, however, is far from confusing. Instead, "two languages" afford Reta insight because "doubleness clarified the world; *la chaise*, chair; *le rideau*, curtain, *être*, to be; *le chien*, dog" (146). As Reta continues, her words advance a semiotics that differs sharply from de Saussure in that "every object, every action, had an echo, an explanation. Meaning had two feet, two dependable etymological stems" (146). This remembrance displays what Peirce calls "collateral experience" and it challenges the "fine-spun filigree of theory" insofar as de Saussure predicated meaning on the difference between signs and their referents by showing that words such as "dog" in English or "chien" in French show only the contingencies and polyvalent, indeterminate nature of interplay between signs where Reta's experience in moving from one language to another only secured meaning for her (*Collected Papers* 8.314, 269). Peirce puts it like this: "I define a sign as anything which is so determined by something else, called its Object, and so determines an effect upon a person" (*Essential Peirce* 2 478). Peirce's sign is not dyadic: rather, a sign signifies only in being interpreted. The interpreter, in fact, is central to the meaning of any sign.

This study began epigrammatically, with words by Shields about the search for an idea that is "full of elegance and usefulness" in order to foreground my sense that *Unless* is a heuristic, a novel of ideas (*Unless* 228). Shields, via Reta, undeniably searches for a deeper understanding of "goodness," but because Reta mediates this investigation as a novelist, the search also becomes a kind of poetics, a set of comments about the ends of art, and, despite the fact that Reta serves notice that "unless" is a logical word, it functions chiefly in an aesthetic not propositional fashion. In this sense, the thought of Peirce aptly applies to *Unless*, for Peirce's pragmatism makes the bold claim that logic—that is all semiotic activity—is dependent on ethics and ethics is dependent on aesthetics. Peirce means here that aesthetics, that is, art, asks what is possible to admire unconditionally (*Collected Papers* 1.625, 1903). Shields addresses this question in one of her conversations with Eleanor Wachtel when she says "[e]very novel that I love and am interested in is about this, is about an individual finding his true home. It is the journey, and you can go right back to *Ulysses* to track it. I think this is what fiction is for, and what it's about" (Wachtel 77). Shields's word "love" certainly evokes unconditional admiration, and in this connection Shields joins an intrinsic and instrumental value insofar as she speaks about the end or purpose of fiction. Thus, Shields addresses an ancient philosophical and ethical question, but she does so as novelist, a point which shapes her further elaboration: "I think of this word 'home' metaphorically, but it's where you belong, where you understand the signs, the place where, in fact, you have always been destined to be" (77). Shields's diction, "the signs," undeniably links the sign that Norah wears—goodness—to "home" (77). That *Unless* ends with Norah at home certainly fulfills Shields's poetics even though by this feat Shields indulges in the "artifice of coincidence" and risks undermining the book's gravity (*Unless* 314).

At stake, of course, is not merely coincidence, but, again, the ends of art. Shields offers her reader a comedy insofar as the Winters family is reunited when Norah returns home, and the intertextual connection to Homer's *Odyssey* is made resonantly complete. Nevertheless, the book's ending also involves not merely Norah's return but also Reta's fuller realization that Norah's estrangement issues from a "coincidence" involving a "young Muslim woman" who "in the year 2000, stepped forward on the pavement, poured gasoline over her veil and gown and set herself alight," so here Shields makes her ending double by adding an element of tragedy (314). With these words—comedy and tragedy—it should be clear that Shields invests *Unless* with a classical, unruly, and abiding force insofar as she broaches the thorny question raised by Aristotle in his *Poetics*, namely whether the double or single ending best serves the construction of plot. Section thirteen of *Poetics*, of course, distinguishes between the single plot and the double by exemplifying the latter through reference to the "double thread of plot" in *The Odyssey* (55). Aristotle calls this structure one of the "second rank," which some, nonetheless, "place first"; the double plot pleases because it reaches its popular audience, yet the pleasure is not the "tragic" pleasure (55). The pleasure, rather, is proper to that of comedy (56). Shields, it seems, certainly understood this paradigm, for when she brings *Thyme in Bloom* to its "whimsical conclusion" she knows she conforms to the conventions of "comic fiction" (314). By the same token, as Reta projects the next book, *Autumn Thyme*, she vows to make it a more singular story, a sadder one with "stillness and power, sadness and resignation, contradictions and irrationality. Almost, you might say, the materials of a serious book" (320). In its note of diminishment, this nearly final piece of understatement connects tonally and intertextually to *Middlemarch*, from which Shields selects her epigraph for *Unless*. Shields's affection for George Eliot's great novel—"I love *Middlemarch*"—and her focus on goodness in *Unless* make possible a closing speculation, one consonant with Reta's last words: "It is after midnight, late in the month of March" (Wachtel 176, 320). Because these words stand last they evoke closure by way of recalling the epigraph from *Middlemarch*, and this framing energy gains additional power by its evocative association of sounds— "*mid*night . . . March"—in Eliot's title (emphasis added 320). In light of the fact that Shields says "I always read the epigraphs because I can feel the novelist telling me, This is the way I want to go, so I read them with this idea in mind," some warrant exists for considering the direction Eliot sets with her own Prelude and epigraph to Chapter One (176). Eliot, unsurprisingly, opens *Middlemarch* by deliberating on goodness:

> Here and there is born a Saint Theresa, foundress of nothing, whose loving heart-beats and sobs after an unattained goodness tremble off and are dispersed among hindrances, instead of centring in some long-recognizable deed. (26)

Eliot's characteristic note of diminution, of unrealized effort, recalls the "big female secret of wanting and not getting," but, ironically, the secret of *Unless* is quite an open one, for Norah's efforts to extinguish the flames of the woman who "set herself alight" are unavailing (97, 314). Moreover, this tragedy serves to remind her readers of the grievous and disastrous ethical failure that makes "half the world's population" "routinely overlooked" (220). Insofar as the temporal reference— "midnight . . . March"—that evokes the spatial—Eliot's *Middlemarch*— brings together time and place, Reta's thoughts about "this problem of women" come to mind, and the bromide "*But we've come so far*" eventuates in her emphatic remark: "Well, no, we've arrived at the new millennium and we haven't 'arrived' at all" (99). Read in light of Shields's habitual understatement, Eliot's emblematic words—"If we had a keen vision and feeling of all ordinary human life . . . we should die of that roar which lies on the other side of silence"—become a road sign pointing toward Shields's qualified giving of voice to "goodness, that biddable creature" which cannot "be depended on, not yet" (Eliot 226, 310). Reta, however, "is trying to be one of the faithful," trying to attend to and to articulate "the tiny piping voice of goodness" that Norah "took up" (310). Yet, even in this clearest of statements about the nature of goodness Shields has Reta say, "I'm afraid I don't put that very clearly," and thus she emphasizes that something unutterable lies "on the other side of silence" (310). What Shields will not let Reta say suggests what Eliot will not say in her epigraph to Chapter One of *Middlemarch*. That is, Eliot takes her epigraph from Francis Beaumont and John Fletcher, the seventeenth-century dramatists who wrote *The Maid's Tragedy*. Evadne speaks the lines that Eliot quotes: "Since I can do no good because a woman / Reach constantly at something that is near it" (29). Evadne's next words, "I will redeem one minute of my age," remain silent by not appearing in the epigraph, but suggestively they accord with Reta's habitual understatement and remind that such work, even if as fleeting as "one minute," is work that is truly the stuff "almost, you might say, the materials of a serious book" (320). Evadne's words nicely evoke Reta's words that by virtue of their autobiographical freight break the diegetic frame to speak for Shields, to speak of a "life spent affixing small words to large, empty pages. . . . This matters, the remaking of an untenable world through the nib of a pen; it matters so much I can't stop doing it" (208). Unless such work continues, the world surely will remain untenable.

WORKS CITED

Amian, Katrin. *Rethinking Postmodernism(s): Charles S. Peirce and the Pragmatist Negotiations of Thomas Pynchon, Toni Morrison, and Jonathan Safran Foer.* Postmodern Studies 41. Amsterdam/New York: Rodopi, 2008. Print.

Aristotle. "Poetics." In *Critical Theory Since Plato*, ed. Hazard Adams. San Diego: Harcourt Brace Jovanovich, 1971: 48–66. Print.

Derrida, Jacques. *Of Grammatology: Corrected Edition*, trans. Gayatri Chakravorty Spivak. Baltimore and London: The Johns Hopkins University Press, 1997. Print.

Eliot, George. *Middlemarch.* 1874. London: Penguin, 1985. Print.

Fluck, Winfried. "Pragmatism and Aesthetic Experience." *REAL: Yearbook of Research in English and American Literature* 15 (1999): 227–42. Print.

Hassan, Ihab. "Beyond Postmodernism: Toward an Aesthetic of Trust." *Angelaki: Journal of the Theoretical Humanities* 8.1 (April 2003): 3–11. Print.

Mitchell, W. J. T. "Iconicity." In *The New Princeton Encyclopedia of Poetry and Poetics*, ed. Alex Preminger and T. V. F. Brogan. Princeton: Princeton University Press, 1993: 552. Print.

Peirce, Charles Sanders. *The Collected Papers of Charles Sanders Peirce*, ed. Charles Hartshorne, Paul Weiss, and Arthur W. Burks. 8 vols. Cambridge: Harvard University Press, 1931–58. Print.

———. *The Essential Peirce: Selected Philosophical Writings, Volume 2 (1893–1913)*, ed. The Peirce Edition Project. 2 vols. Bloomington, Indiana University Press, 1998.

Shields, Carol. "Narrative Hunger and the Overflowing Cupboard." In *Carol Shields, Narrative Hunger, and the Possibilities of Fiction,* ed. Edward Eden and Dee Goertz. Toronto: University of Toronto Press, 2003: 19–36. Print.

———. *Unless: A Novel.* Toronto: Vintage, 2002. Print.

Steiner, Peter. "Semiotics, Poetic." In *The New Princeton Encyclopedia of Poetry and Poetics*, ed. Alex Preminger and T. V. F. Brogan. Princeton: Princeton University Press, 1993: 1138–43. Print.

Wachtel, Eleanor. *Random Illuminations: Conversations with Carol Shields.* Fredericton: Goose Lane Editions, 2007. Print.

Shields's Guerrilla Gardeners:
Sowing Seeds of Defiance and Care

SHELLEY BOYD

In an interview Carol Shields once stated, "I would never write a war story, I mean *the* war story, as it were, is entirely a male-modelled genre. . . . violence has not been a part of my experience and I am far too fond of my characters to want to do them violence" (Anderson 143–44). Although Shields rejected war narratives as unfamiliar and unappealing, she was drawn to an alternative form of battle taken up entirely by her female characters—guerrilla gardening. Among the many homeowners who tend their yards in Shields's fictional worlds is a peculiar cast of characters who cultivate property without permission: the blisterlily women from "Today is the Day," Miss Anderson from *Happenstance*, and Norah Winters from *Unless*. These women pursue what Richard Reynolds describes in his study *On Guerrilla Gardening* as this "little war" (5).[1] The term "guerrilla" reflects the individual or small-scale nature of guerrilla gardening: its covert attacks that alter the physical and social landscape. The movement's combatants—who arm themselves with plants, bulbs, and the ever-infamous seed bombs—are activists who trespass and cultivate terrain that does not belong to them. Despite the abundant use of war rhetoric, one must keep in mind, as David Tracey writes in *Guerrilla Gardening: A Manualfesto*, that "non-violence" is the standard approach (6). This peaceful aspect undoubtedly attracted Shields to this form of social activism as a method of resistance and change for her female characters. Undertaking missions marked by a politicized impulse to nurture, these cultivating women exert their visibility and influence within larger landscapes from which they have faced delimited access or been denied entry altogether. Shields's guerrilla gardeners operate, therefore, as unexpected, embodied forms of socio-political commentary: questioning an assumed separation of the private and the public, and thereby extending the role and value of *domestic care* (work traditionally attributed to women in the home) to the community at large.

A MISSION OF CARE: CULTIVATING THE DOMESTIC IN PUBLIC

Unfortunately, the notorious descriptor "suburban miniaturist" has often led to characterizations of Shields's work as limited in scope: she is "said to do domestic ordinariness wonderfully (but not wider social issues)" (Morrison). In a 1999 interview with *The Atlantic*, Shields explicitly addressed this phrase as a "subtle put-down" and noted the double standard since it was rarely if ever applied to male writers (Knowles, "A Likely Story").[2] Refuting such minimizations, Shields's supporters contend that her narratives illuminate domestic complexity, detailing women's fraught desires for more than "the quiet immanence of home" (Guenther 157). Shields also redefines the purview of the domestic itself; she challenges assumptions of its private containment, its irrelevance to the public domain, and its apolitical nature. Indeed, Shields's questioning of old conceptual models that separate "private" from "public" is observed by Marjorie Anderson when she comments that "the world of the two sexes" is represented as "parallel lines rather than spheres" (147), a statement with which Shields agrees. A critical shift in perspective is needed, therefore, in order to see beyond notions of smallness—that "limiting circle of familial duties" (Guenther 156)— and to appreciate how the so-called "public" domain potentially serves as another kind of domestic space in Shields's fiction.

Shields's writing of the domestic (in the more private sense of the word) almost always involves a metaphoric pairing of indoor and outdoor maintenance. As one of her characters openly declares, "lawns mean middle class" (*Small Ceremonies* 81). In *Happenstance: The Wife's Story*, Brenda Bowman tends her backyard just as she "tells herself she could get busy and *weed out* a few" of the housekeeping items on her "to do" list posted in her kitchen (1, emphasis added). Gardening is *the* form of domestic care in the sense of to "take care of," "look after," "deal with and provide for" as well as "to charg[e] the mind with anything" (*OED Online*).[3] In *Unless*, Reta Winters acknowledges, "A house requires care" (60), a term she comprehends as both home and garden maintenance, as well as her worry over "whatever presents threat or disorder" (61), which is mainly her daughter's homelessness. While Shields's middle-class homeowners fastidiously tend the worlds that exist within the boundaries of their properties, there are a number of gardeners who break this pattern by making the public domain another kind of home-space. Such boundary crossing reveals that for Shields the domestic is not a singular site or topic, but a mode of writing through which stories are told and through which, some argue, her very sentences are crafted.[4] Her artistic vision extends to the spatial characterization of her guerrilla gardeners whose domestic-styled activism adjusts the range and definition of "home," as they assume responsibility for their communities' surroundings and well-being. Attending to property that is not their own, these female characters prompt others to reconsider how they inhabit a spectrum of spaces. In other words, Shields's activists reveal that varied conceptualizations and treatments of space necessarily influence human relationships, identities, and the valuations of different forms of work and experience.

Shields's rebellious cultivators are in keeping with actual guerrilla gardeners who foster confluence between private and public spaces in order to challenge the constructed nature of land ownership, its authority of control and exclusion, and its ways of determining how individuals relate to their environments (whether they assume the responsibility of care or not). According to Reynolds, guerrilla gardeners typically select a location that is close to home for both practical and ideological reasons. Proximity allows for "regular maintenance" of the chosen terrain, for easy access to one's supply route and home base, and for "strengthen[ing] one's role" in the community (Reynolds 123). This last point is cogent as the fact that guerrilla gardening takes place at all in Shields's fiction suggests that aspects of her communities—the terrain and the residents—have been either neglected or neglectful. When guerrilla gardeners cultivate land that is not their own (whether publicly or privately owned), they use it as a means of influence, extending the community's awareness of, and responsibility for, a sense of "domain" that exists beyond private dwellings. They rework the community's identity and values as made manifest through the material environment. Scarcity of arable land and lack of community pride are just a couple of the motivating factors behind these "little wars." Growing out of such pre-existing conditions means, then, that guerrilla gardening is an "organic movement" (Reynolds 9) that challenges a community's habitual modes of existence and perception. While food cultivation is most often emphasized by present-day guerrilla gardeners, the movement's central principle (no matter the type of mission) is about critical expression: communicating through plants by reconfiguring the landscape. This work prompts nearby residents into perceiving their environment anew, thereby changing their relationships with it and each other. As Reynolds states, "[gardening] in public, on land that is not yours, sends an even stronger message. . . . Society needs this kind of creativity" (33).

With a desire for social reform, Shields's guerrilla gardeners treat public space askance, altering its arrangement and meaning through critical forms of care. Their questioning of the present order aligns them with what Alex Ramon identifies as Shields's liminal or double vision. Situating "Shields's texts on a series of borders: between self and other, realism and postmodernism, auto/biography and fiction, male and female narratorial perspectives, randomness and pattern," Ramon contends that a "trope of doubleness" is central to Shields's artistic career and that critical investigations should be cautious of describing her writing as an "unequivocal celebration" (17). In the context of Shields's landscapes, her guerrilla gardeners literally and figuratively tend "liminal spaces" that either fall outside the private-domestic, or do not constitute a valued part of the community. Bestowing profuse attention onto negligible terrain, these gardeners traverse the physical and conceptual boundaries of private and public, self and other, and, most importantly, their communities' present circumstances and future potential. As such, these rebellious gardeners—many of whom are property owners themselves—serve as middle-class "ex-centrics": individuals who, according to Linda Hutcheon's theory of the postmodern, possess "the power to change the perspective of the centre" by enacting creative, critical forms of expression (103).

Shields's guerrilla gardeners embody liminality or "ex-centricity" in numerous ways. Some are secondary figures, not central yet important to the stories. Most have odd physical appearances and behaviours that set them apart. All are women who, in challenging estimations of the landscape's barrenness, share a gendered mandate to make visible the fecundity of their presence and their knowledge of care. Although it is tempting to read Shields's Brother Adam from *The Box Garden* as the exception, since this male gardener spreads his back-to-nature message by mailing grass seeds to his ex-wife Charleen (surreptitiously creating a box garden in her apartment), he clearly fails as an "ex-centric." A narcissist focused on his solitary paradise, Brother Adam does little for the betterment of others and never gets his hands dirty.[5] In contrast, the nurturing work and productive marginality of Shields's women activists are pivotal to their wider influence. Indeed, Shields evokes women's historical and cultural associations with plants as a means of empowerment, a strategy she has used elsewhere, most notably in *The Stone Diaries,* where "female art forms . . . —the folk arts of cooking and gardening, " according to Lisa Johnson, "reiterate the alchemy of women's imaginations on everyday materials" (206).[6] As instigators of social change, then, Shields's guerrilla gardeners promote the public domain as shared domestic space, a neglected site of daily habitation and social connection. They mobilize their desire to cultivate and in doing so intimate that if women want to be revolutionary, they need to change the world around them and their positions within it, revising how the domestic—as a changeable space, outlook, and mode of action—is both perceived and valued.

THE BLISTERLILY CAMPAIGN

Shields's most remarkable guerrilla gardeners appear in the short story "Today Is the Day" (from *The Orange Fish*) in the manner of what Reynolds would describe as a "spectacular horticultural campaig[n] by [an] organized . . . cell" (5). In the story, all the women of the village, regardless of age or background, gather annually to plant flower bulbs on public land. Their unnamed village is situated near a major highway, and the encroaching infrastructure and external population alter the rural residents' ways of relating to each other and to the physical environment. Neighbours are no longer as hospitable as they once were. The church is now locked when not in use. The village has long since "paved over" the old well, turning it into a "tot lot and basketball court" (271). Sadly, the blisterlily, a native plant whose root system is sensitive to water loss, has become scarce. Numerous theories abound pertaining to this flower's disappearance, but one explanation resonates: there is "only so much root room available at the earth's surface" (272). It appears "larger, more aggressive species" of plants have crowded out the blisterlily, which is noted for being, in a typically feminine manner, "soft-fleshed," "acquiescent," and "far too obliging for its own good" (272). While the locals mostly give way to urbanizing forces, the women of the village safeguard their community and preserve the displaced flower, planting bulbs along the verges and medians of the stretch of highway. The location of their campaign is in keeping with actual guerrilla gardeners' manifestos that list roadways as a "strategic priority" as they are "likely to be neglected, lost between the boundaries of responsibility," yet "can be appreciated by thousands every day" (Reynolds 123, 124). Rather than succumbing to a nondescript landscape of suburban sprawl and a loss of community cohesion, the women extend the range of this flower, and by association, their village's heritage or "roots." In other words, they transform a public space used merely as a traffic thoroughfare into a site connected with local origins and residential care.

Infusing their activist work with specialized knowledge, these guerrilla gardeners are vital for the village and its surrounding landscape, as Shields uses folklore and magic realism (as she has in other works) to render the women's power of care both tangible and transformative. The blisterlily is sensitive to water loss, and fortunately the women revert to an old secret language on this ritual day of planting, communicating "in a murmuring way" that sounds "like cold water continuously falling, as if a faucet were left running into a large and heavy washtub" (271). Even Sally Bakey, the troll-like spinster who is the defiant leader of the campaign, is credited with the discovery of "a new preserve of virgin blisterlilies in a meadow on the other side of the shiny westward-lying lake" (272). Working against external, homogenizing forces, the women pledge absolute allegiance to their gardening collective, as even its married members remove their wedding rings and string them together to form a golden "necklace, or wreath or garland" (274) that is hung in a nearby beech tree. Floral lexicons decipher the beech tree as "wedded love" (Waterman 40), and the golden circle of multiple rings symbolizes the women's public commitment to each other and to their work in sustaining their community. Just as the blistlerlily is "nothing spectacular" on its own (271), but "compelling" when viewed as "several million" (272), the women "fa[n] out along the highway" (273). They use what Reynolds calls "the impact strategy" when guerrilla gardeners plant "large blocks of colour [that] are visible from a distance" (89). The women's silver silhouettes "scatter the light," and "pin the dark ground to the lowering sky, the way table-cloths and sheets are pinned to a slackly hung clothes-line" (273). Ronald Nelson reads this scene as a "homely marriage of heaven and earth" (24), but there is also a marriage of the domestic and the public. The women combine both their near-magical gardening work (and its associations with washing and laundry) with their social activism: maintaining the appearance and identity of the village, as they plant both the bulbs and their working bodies along the horizon.

Because the women are at once the guerrilla gardeners and the figurative plants responsible for their village's resilience, it is significant that the blisterlily appears to be a fictional botanical of Shields's own making. In a footnote, Nelson mentions his failure to locate a picture of the flower and opts to decipher it according to the symbolism of the lily: purity, royalty, fertility, and femininity (27). Pushing back against the lily's regal qualities, the narrator uses humble descriptors, comparing the plant to a crocus: "unprepossessing" and growing "close to the ground" ("Today" 271). According to floral lexicons, springtime crocuses "are messengers of hope and symbols of a return to gentler times" (Dumas 14). This symbolism speaks to the women's restorative presence: nurturing the landscape for the future (by planting bulbs in the fall) and renewing the community's historical but dwindling "roots." The *blister* identification further enhances the gardeners' ambiguous characterization. A soft-fleshed, feminine flower, the blisterlily suffers from a tendency to chafe and erupt when crowded out by other plants, losing vital water when under "minimal pressure" (272). But blistering also entails a protective expansion, which the blisterlily women enact. Their "upright" bodies transform the appearance of the village, which is situated under a "punishing" horizon, in much the same way as the blisterlily alters the winter landscape with the "first small faintly colored shoot, surprised by its upright shadow" (276). Perhaps this mysterious, unclassifiable botanical is Shields's mischievous way of highlighting both the rarity of women's collective agency and the perceived paradox of domestic work (typically viewed as limited, private, and dreary) when it comes up against an imposed threshold and pushes outward, magically revitalizing the public domain into a shared site of habitation and belonging.

CACTUS CUNT AND THE "SEEDING" OF FERTILITY

If "Today Is the Day" imagines an extraordinary collective campaign, Shields's novel *Happenstance* features the curtailed agency of an isolated guerrilla gardener whose solo mission is to sow diversity within a well-tended but exclusionary social landscape.[7] In Elm Park, one of "the oldest, most established suburbs" of Chicago (*Happenstance: The Wife's Story* 14), heterosexual couples and their growing families dutifully care for their yards and, one would hope, for their community, but Shields provides a subtle critique of the residents' narrow views regarding women's identities as solely tied to youth and procreation. She has faced criticism for the seeming homogeneity of her middle-class housewife characters, those "quiet, unappreciated . . . artistic women who have lost themselves (albeit quite willingly) in their attention to their families" (Groening 14). In *Happenstance: The Wife's Story,* however, Miss Anderson, the Bowmans' elderly neighbour, stands alternatively as a woman who faces delimited social status precisely because of the fact that she has no family to tend. Denigrated by neighbours, she is reduced to the caricature of an old crone. The men bestow upon her the nickname "Old Cactus

Cunt" (126), the children identify her as the local "witch" (125), and others refer to her as "The Coat Lady" (126) when they forget her name after her death. These negative assessments derive principally from Miss Anderson's spinster status, sickly health, low income as a pensioner, and unusual mode of dress despite the change in seasons (she always wears a long black coat). Even the open-minded Brenda Bowman concedes that Miss Anderson's "age had made her seem, to a younger Brenda, not worth bothering about" (126). Most troubling, though, is how "quickly" and "thoroughly" (125) Miss Anderson's presence is eradicated from the neighbourhood following her death: her house is sold to Larry and Janey Carpenter, who gut the property, dig up the garden, and erect a large wooden deck. Despite being deemed fashionable and innovative, the Carpenters' renovations "obliterat[e]" part of the neighbourhood's social fabric, culminating in missed potential as "no mythology [grows] up around" this deceased resident (126). Shields uses the neighbours' negligence to underscore the diverse reasons for women's exclusion from, or limited representation within, historical and literary traditions, but she also posits the possibility of resisting such erasures through Miss Anderson's rebellious domestic care of her community.

In contrast to the suburbanites' destructive treatment of others and their property, Miss Anderson sows a message of life-affirming diversity that challenges the status quo. She gardens illicitly in the terrain perceived as "small waste spaces": those areas of "packed earth" and weeds located "between neighbourhood garages and board fences and garbage cans" (125). During her "annual spring mission" (125), Miss Anderson "stalk[s] up and down the back alleys," scattering hollyhock seeds in a "willful, arrogant, almost random sowing of them" (125). A tall, multi-bloomed flower, hollyhocks symbolize "fruitfulness" (Waterman 100) and in the Elm Park suburb, "a surprising number of these seeds [take] root" (125). Miss Anderson's guerrilla strategy is what Reynolds would identify as "incongruous" planting (90): among the neglected property margins of single-family dwellings, the unexpected hollyhocks beautify those spaces that initially reflected the elderly woman's own diminishment. Through her rebellious cultivation, she becomes, paradoxically, a figure of fertility, persisting "remarkably" in the public record of the larger landscape (125) and undermining Jack Bowman's claim that domestic work (such as meal preparation) lacks full artistic status because it is ephemeral. Despite the neighbours' callousness, the "long fuzzed stalks and delicate, frilled blooms" (125) of Miss Anderson's decidedly feminine flowers regenerate long after her death and in direct contrast to her supposedly prickly nature.

Although Miss Anderson's border crossing may have limited impact in comparison to the extraordinary blisterlily campaign, she nonetheless influences Brenda Bowman, who identifies with this bold recontextualization of domestic work when she attends an out-of-town quilting conference in Philadelphia. This large gathering and its disruption of routine, as Wendy Roy attests, are pivotal to Brenda's artistic development and politicization: Brenda now recognizes domestic work and crafts as "impetuses for social change" ("Brenda Bowman" 128). While the conference is the main event, Miss Anderson previously "seeded" a sense of domestic agency in Brenda's mind. Brenda recalls this guerrilla gardener during a key moment of inspiration and awakening when she opts to wear one of her own quilts through the downtown streets of Philadelphia: "Miss Anderson and her vigorous, purposeful back-alley striding spoke to that part of Brenda she kept unexamined. Shouldn't she have tried to get to know her a little better when she was alive?" (126). Identifying with the elderly gardener's posture and attitude, Brenda is absolutely transformed when she wears her quilt as a "cape" (124), garnering effuse admiration from passersby and bringing to mind a series of interrelated memories: her viewing of the Winged Victory of Samothrace at the Louvre in Paris (123); her young son Rob dressed in a Superman costume, bounding over the fence into Miss Anderson's yard (124); and her eccentric neighbour scattering seeds while dressed in the infamous black coat, "absurd, flowing, out of style, and made of shiny, elegant material like taffeta" (125). These varied semblances of wings and cape-like garments have to do with "with rising above the earth, and with the ability to glide effortlessly from one place to another" (Atwood 32). Tracing the origins of superheroes' attire, Margaret Atwood claims that such outfits propel the self into alternative, generous roles (26), as even paleolithic shamans donned costumes along with "their magic alter egos in order to serve the community" (27). In the case of Shields's novel, the "caped" domestic crusaders of Brenda Bowman and Miss Anderson confidently traverse perceived boundaries, pursuing modes of work beyond their usual contexts and for the benefit of a wider public.

While Shields is known for depicting the encroachment of the outside world and especially the media into women's house-bound lives, generating a kind of "enforced domesticity," as Roy refers to it ("Brenda Bowman" 124), she also imagines inverse scenarios: where domestic-minded work and visions reshape the social realm, providing critical commentaries. Miss Anderson challenges the conformist yards and attitudes of many Elm Park residents. Her ingenuity alters the social landscape and taps into neglected terrains: the spaces between properties that facilitate connection and fertile exchange. Roaming the neighbourhood, this elderly woman transforms the "thin dirt" of back alleys (125), reflecting Brenda's own propensities for the "meander stitch" (*Happenstance: The Husband's Story* 192) and for "irregular borders" sewn beyond the quilting frame that challenge rigid patterns and meaning (*Happenstance: The Wife's Story* 15, 45). Miss Anderson's recurrence in both Jack's and Brenda's portions of *Happenstance* is not insignificant, then, as this guerrilla gardener manages to traverse not only properties, but different narrative contexts, breaking free of limited definitions of her subjectivity and pushing others to perceive her anew. In this regard, Jack, who always "loathed" this elderly woman, finds himself narrating her in surprisingly varied ways: he tells "a tawdry fiction, a melodrama about this marvellous old crone, this real-life stoic and neighbourhood character, this heroine, in fact—the old darling herself, bless her" (72).

A SIDEWALK GARDEN: NORAH'S PROTEST FOR GOODNESS

Through the witch-like Miss Anderson and the troll-like Sally Bakey, Shields plays with the figure of the old crone as an essential part of the life cycle. Both women occupy ex-centric roles, driving cultural renewal for their communities. But if Miss Anderson and Sally Bakey represent an older generation's boundary-crossing activism, then the young Norah Winters of *Unless* carries this expanding vision of domestic care into the future. With respect to the ex-centricity of Shields's guerrilla gardeners and their publicly directed missions, it is significant that Hutcheon's term has appeared in scholarship focused on Norah's ambiguous characterization. Christiane Struth's and Margaret Steffler's re-evaluations of Norah's liminal agency question earlier criticism that has emphasized the young woman's silence and disempowerment.[8] Describing her as "marginal or 'ex-centric,'" Struth posits Norah as "the container of collective and/or cultural memories" through her commemoration of the Muslim woman's self-immolation on the Toronto street (209). Likewise, Steffler asserts that Norah's direct engagement with the "other" results in her growing sense of social responsibility despite the "complacency" that surrounds her (234–35). In keeping with this focus on Norah's ex-centricity, her role as the final guerrilla gardener in the trajectory of Shields's rebellious cultivators seems likely, even though Norah neither sows nor plants in a literal sense. Indeed, of the three guerrilla-gardening missions, Norah's is the most difficult and unsettling because of its prohibitive conditions and non-generative presentation.

Several details situate Norah as both a revolutionary and a gardener. Reta repeatedly refers to her daughter as her "brave little soldier" (90, 98), and readers are told that in the months leading up to her disappearance, Norah "was thinking about goodness and evil, about harm to the earth" (202). When first discovered on a downtown sidewalk, this homeless woman was wearing a pair of gardening gloves, an item she was never without, as she even "slept in those gloves" at the hostel, the staff assuming the behaviour was just one of her "eccentricities" (303). Her out-of-place attire is reminiscent of Miss Anderson's black coat, especially since Norah wears her gloves for the duration of the "boiling hot" summer months (302). Even though Norah's continued absence throughout the winter carries mythological weight from the point of view of Reta, who mourns for her missing daughter as Demeter does for Persephone (Stovel 58), the fact that Norah first claims a piece of sidewalk in the early spring implies she is not entirely a lost figure, but rather one of quiet action and hope, rebelliously "gardening" in public in the optimal season.

Norah's role as a guerrilla gardener is further substantiated by the imagery of seeds, bulbs, and gardening work that inform the novel as mother and daughter pursue divergent modes of domestic care. The explosive potential of seeds is a central component of any guerrilla gardener's arsenal since "scattering seeds is the easiest way" to do the work: "It is gardening in an instant, free from tools" (Reynolds 103). In terms of political expression, Reynolds further reflects, "Putting a message out there really is like planting a seed: you cannot be sure whether it will flourish or wither" (150). As with the planting of blisterlily bulbs and the scattering of hollyhock seeds, the "seeding" process in *Unless* takes place through the women's varied domestic-minded vocations. Reta introduces the figurative notion of sowing ideas (albeit not in guerrilla gardening's political sense of the term) in the opening chapter when she mentions that her first novel *My Thyme is Up* began as "a seed, and nothing more" (13), just as the unwritten sequel "popped out of the ground like the rounded snout of a crocus on a cold lawn" (16). This spring-time generation of literary ideas promotes a contained domestic world, "the island" of Alicia and Roman's relationship in Reta's first novel (13). Like her protagonist, Reta imagines her own life as a personal paradise: "the seventies said home, . . . create a home of your own, dress yourself in warm earth colours, get back to the earth, dig yourself into your life" (186). With her daughter residing inexplicably on the streets, Reta looks to isolate and protect her family even further: "I dust and polish this house of mine so that I'll be able to seal it from damage. If I commit myself to its meticulous care, I will claim back my daughter Norah" (62).

Scholars often align Reta with Shields, but a distinction must be maintained not only to ascertain Reta's "naivety," as Rosenthal asserts (184), but also to appreciate the more public acts of care, as opposed to Reta's "sealed" vision. Whereas Reta longs to withdraw, the world instead confronts her with alternative domestic models: "Those Buddhist monks I saw not long ago on a TV documentary devote two hours to morning meditation, followed by one hour of serious cleaning. . . . they actually go out into the world each day with buckets and rags, and they clean things, anything that needs cleaning, a wall or an old fence, whatever presents threat or disorder" (61). The monks' proactive, guerrilla-style cleaning contrasts both with Reta's private retreat and with people's typically careless treatment of urban space.[9] Unfortunately, what Reta fails to appreciate, at this point, is that like the dedicated monks, her daughter has assumed the care of the public domain—first, by coming to the aid of an unknown dying Muslim woman, and second, by continuing to tend the same sidewalk where the event took place.

Rejecting her mother's insular vision, Norah challenges the assumption that domesticity is always too limited in its outlook and social relevance. To this end, she expands her nurturing work into a revised context and with a newly adopted, if not fully articulated, political mandate. Just as Reta tends her suburban yard and the grandmother loved her "patch of garden" (148), Norah carries this tradition forward and outward by attending to her "patch of sidewalk" (159) as a form of social protest. Norah sows her revolutionary ideas regarding the lack or marginalization of "GOODNESS" within contemporary Canadian society—a message that holds great relevance not only for Toronto's waning reputation for benevolence, but also for the profound and even small acts of kindness that appear throughout the novel.[10] Wearing her gardening gloves, Norah promotes change in the heart of the city (the site of the Muslim woman's tragic death) by clearing space for the presence and message of "GOODNESS." Her embodied form of protest, her physical planting of herself on the street, is reminiscent of the blisterlily women who transform the landscape. Noting Norah's agency, Steffler contends that while Reta believes "Norah in her role as a street person . . . 'embodies invisibility,'" Norah in fact "is anything but invisible; she functions more as an affront than an absence to those who walk by and cannot make her vanish" (232). Norah is certainly visible, but there is also something about her presence, attitude, and message that *appeals* to the public, as opposed to affronting them, as one of her sisters reflects, "'She just keeps smiling and people keep giving her money. . . . She gets more money than anyone else on that corner, and there are about four other guys. People just seem to like her, people going by'" (161). Just as Norah prods a root of kindness in others, her message of "GOODNESS" occupies visible space within the pages of the novel through its incongruous, handwritten lettering. Steffler comments that the word "is reproduced in Reta's mind and on the page of the novel as it appears on the sign, thus stressing its material physicality and the word's need for a relationship with small words, such as 'unless' and the 'little chips of grammar' . . . that hold together narratives and lives" (224–25). As with Miss Anderson's out-of-place hollyhocks, Norah's message demands that others (her parents, passersby, and even Shields's readers) take notice and connect with its meaning.

If guerrilla gardeners are about spreading a message and changing how people relate to their communities, then Norah attains small victories precisely because she sparks discussion. Stovel contends that "*Unless* is a novel of interpretation—how to interpret Norah's defection from life" (53), and while this analytical process is key to understanding "GOODNESS," Norah has not entirely withdrawn from the world. Rather, she has placed herself conspicuously at its centre, challenging Torontonians in the city's core. Through the lens of the Persephone myth, Stovel suggests that in Reta's mind, Norah is disempowered, having "swallowed, like the fatal pomegranate seed, the Old English word wearth meaning not 'worth' but 'outcast'" (56), becoming an entrapped figure of silence and passivity. Another possible reading, but from Norah's point of view, is that this young gardener has not *swallowed* a seed but *sows* one. Norah's activism is not often assessed as such (by other characters or by critics) precisely because she does not use familiar or extreme forms of protest, such as targeting the government, writing letters, picketing and shouting demands, or setting oneself on fire, as in the tragic case of the Muslim woman. In his manifesto, Reynolds states that the guerrilla gardener is a unique kind of activist who "directly confronts the problem through the landscape rather than the person—a strategy that more often than not helps to avoid conflict" (39–40). If the "two main enemies" of guerrilla gardeners are "*scarcity* and *neglect*, problems that come from how we all use the land" (Reynolds 39), then Norah expresses these concerns through her figurative understanding of them: as "goodness and evil," as "harm to the earth" (202), and through her own feeling that she "love[s] the world more" than any one person (128). Her abiding concern is for society at large and its neglected "home ground," or human terrain, in which all people share but mostly shirk their responsibilities. Addressing the problem directly, Norah protests in a peaceful manner, occupying public space and bringing about a revised relationship with others through her modelling of care.[11]

Because Norah can only garden in a figurative sense on impervious pavement, the lack of literal growth is not without its implications. One is forced to contemplate the curtailed impact of Norah's message, just as others read this young woman as a figure of silence. A number of critics grapple with the novel's urban setting, which is especially ripe with the challenges that attract guerrilla gardeners. Driving to the city centre from the suburbs, Reta sees Toronto glow "monumental and lonely," its "outskirts . . . ragged, though its numbered exits pretend at a kind of order" (25). This (dis)orderly sprawl brings denser, more impersonal populations and growing infrastructure, processes that in "Today Is the Day" threaten the village's identity and cohesion. During one of many commutes, Reta observes that the city is "endless, repetitive, the colour of cement" (179), a decided contrast with her own garden. Reading *Unless* as a work of urban fiction that exposes the "marginalization of women" within Canadian culture and the literary tradition, Rosenthal believes Shields radically reworks the periphery (183). Reta must confront her life as enmeshed with urban realities, as *Unless* "dissolves the hierarchies and binary oppositions, those of domestic versus public, female versus male, small town versus metropolis" (Rosenthal 185). The reference to the "endless" city that is "the colour of cement" (*Unless* 179) not only evokes a lifeless, uniform landscape in need of care but also challenges the public world's supposed non-domestic status and outlook as it is shared and inhabited by all. Arguing for the value of connection in *Unless*, Steffler quotes a passage from Shields's speech "Narrative Hunger and the Overflowing Cupboard" in which the author claims that realist fiction "passed too quickly through the territory of the quotidian," emphasizing that which divides, rather than that "rich, potent, *endlessly replenished cement* that binds us together" (Shields, emphasis added 34). Shields's phrasing resonates with her description of Toronto in *Unless*, as the metaphor of humanity's daily cohesion—its "cement" of quotidian experience—is made literal in the physical landscape and especially in Norah's sidewalk garden.

With the urban environment becoming a shared "home ground" in *Unless*, places in which people find comfort and belonging are in dire need of care. Norah sets the example by working for the betterment of her community. Her small patch of sidewalk is, as Struth reads it, a site of vigil for the deceased Muslim woman others overlook or forget (214). Norah's "act of commemoration" (Struth 214) touches on the kind of guerrilla gardening that works to memorialize, as Reynolds describes such instances: "A garden's colour and cheerfulness transform the spirit of a landscape that has become associated with tragedy" (35). Sadly for

Norah, there is no alteration of the street corner, except through her body and her sign of "GOODNESS."[12] The fact that this urban environment remains unchanged accentuates Shields's critique of the unsustainable, callous state of a society that has lost, or rather closed itself off from, the value of care. Reynolds acknowledges that some "battlegrounds are quite hostile to nature" and are "chronically short of the essential ingredients for plant life" (91). In Norah's case, these "ingredients" are nonexistent in a near-barren city, yet she gardens nonetheless: a sign of tenuous renewal in landscape where other "goodish places," as Reta terms them (37), are disappearing. Not coincidently, at the same time that Norah tends the sidewalk, the Orangetown Library—built out of stone "the colour of the earth beneath that good rich agricultural land so wisely set aside for the public good" (39)—is at risk of being closed because of budget cuts and underuse. Two female librarians dutifully share "dominion" over its upkeep (39), and Reta, who frequents the library as a "good citizen" (38), enjoys the space for the familiarity and imaginative shelter it fosters: people are "at one with each other in [their] need for retreat and for the printed word" (45). The threatened library suggests that the value of public "good" is literally losing ground. Tossed coins and mailed cheques are the most common forms of support readers witness in *Unless*, but these detached gestures fall short of the direct, personal engagement that is required. Ultimately, the fact that Norah never gardens in a literal sense serves as a sad reproach of her society, which despite living in increasing proximity, fails to appreciate the relevance of the domestic to the socio-cultural life of the public domain. Unlike the blisterlily women who pin heaven to the earth, or Miss Anderson who brings waste-spaces to life, one of the final images of Norah is of a young woman soldiering on in an overwhelming landscape: "In the obscuring distance, melting into sunsets and handsome limestone buildings and asphalt streets and traffic lights, the tiny piping voice of goodness goes almost unheard" (310).

The conditions in which Norah gardens are prohibitive to the extreme, and this is precisely why she is there and why she is needed. If the world is "split in two" (270), as Reta believes it is when contemplating the encoded "seeds" of men's and women's DNA, then the denial of one half of the population and the domestic work and values traditionally associated with the feminine leads inexorably to an unnatural state. Women's "generative responsibility" which, to Reta's mind, formerly meant "bearing ... children" and "gathering ... edible grasses and bulbs" (100), must be more broadly defined and embraced as a central component to any society's well-being and culture. Without it, a devastating state of "homelessness" will result through the erosion of community and lost opportunities for renewal. The elderly guerrilla gardeners demonstrate this very principle through their future-oriented practices. Although Norah carries this mission of care forward as an activist of the next generation, the situation appears to have worsened. The unreceptive ground that Norah confronts is indicative not only of Shields's frustrations with the continued minimization of the domestic, but also of her boldness as a novelist tending to the future: "She was braver about expressing her feminist beliefs in *Unless* because she did not think she would be alive to read the reviews" (Stovel 51). Regardless of their relative degrees of success, all of Shields's guerrilla gardeners extend outward from private domains and realize an illicit desire to cultivate their communities by challenging the status quo. While it may be easy to summarize Shields's characters as being "upper-middle class contemplative types living in stable environments and politically uninvolved" (Glaser 367), the presence of guerrilla gardeners signals that her settings are not entirely "stable" and that elements of social activism are quietly at work. This recurring form of cultivation suggests a need to reassess the purview of Shields's writing and of the domestic itself, as she variously constructs it. Guerrilla gardening often enlists domestic gardeners who have gone rogue by venturing into terrain not designated or understood as theirs—what an apt metaphor and model for the rebellious literary work and boundary crossing undertaken by Shields herself.

Notes

1. Reynolds notes that the word "*guerrilleros*" was first used to "describe the military response to Napolean Bonaparte's invasion of Spain in 1808. For six years, irregular bands of Spanish fighters attacked the . . . imperial French army with little ambushes and civilian agitation" (5). The term was first adopted by the Green Guerrillas of New York in the 1970s to "describe their illegal gardening on abandoned lots in the East Village. . . . Six years before their dig, in 1967, the most famous guerrilla [Che Guevara] had been executed, and became a martyr and a poster-prophet in the fight for a more equal society" (7).

2. When men write "so-called domestic novels," Shields reflects, "they are not called that at all; they are called sensitive, contemporary reflections of modern life" (Anderson 141). In contrast, Shields has been pegged irrelevant by Stephen Henighan, who describes her writing as "life-affirming" in that it supports, rather than criticizes, "the social status quo" (181), and anti-feminist by Laura Groening, who assesses her fiction and characters as "still in the kitchen" (14).

3. The *OED* also highlights "mental suffering, sorrow, and grief" as part of the definition of "care." This denotation holds particular relevance for Reta who mourns the loss of her daughter.

4. One way Shields creates stories of human relationships is through subtle grammatical acts of "guerrilla domesticity," as Aritha van Herk termed them during her presentation at the 2012 Shields Symposium.

5. Brother Adam's rooming-house Eden of grass, mirrors, and lights benefits only himself. His shirking of parental responsibility and rejection of (sub) urban society lead to his eventual dismissal by others. See my book *Garden Plots: Canadian Women Writers and Their Literary Gardens* for further discussion of Brother Adam and Shields's recontextualization of national myths out of the solitary wilderness and into suburbia.

6. See also Nora Foster Stovel's tracing of Shields's use of "the most female of myths" (52), the ancient Greek myth of Demeter and her daughter Persephone, in *Unless* to construct a feminist re-visioning of mother-daughter relationships and women's divine connection with the seasons (55).

7. Miss Anderson appears in both *Happenstance* and *A Fairly Conventional Woman,* which were first published separately in 1980 and 1982, respectively. Quotations and references in my article are from *Happenstance,* the single, retitled volume with both novels published end to end. This combined version appeared in the United Kingdom in 1991, and in Canada in 1994.

8. Several critics interpret Norah's silence. Wendy Roy reads *Unless* as a "satisfying conclusion" to Shields's career-long "concerns about women's silencing" through traditional life plots ("*Unless* the World" 132). Stovel similarly suggests that Norah "goes under ground figuratively" (56) through her silence and passivity, as she "personifies the woman dropped into a black hole in the masculine game of pool, female power undermined in patriarchal culture" (64). Hilde Staels emphasizes not only Norah's silence as representative of "the homelessness of women in language" (120), but also her isolation and inability to communicate with others after suffering post-traumatic stress (128).

9. Reta notes that civic authorities usually have to prevent the soiling of public space: "(It is illegal to shake a dust mop out of a window in New York, and probably even in Toronto; I read that somewhere)" (61).

10. Rosenthal traces the famous adage "Toronto, the Good" by noting the city's British roots and "high density of Anglican churches and charity," features that contrast with "many American cities . . . ruled by municipal law and civic order" (176–77). Despite Toronto's challenges, Reta now and then detects a "germ of goodness" within the city, such as the charity of the Promise Hostel for the homeless, where Norah takes shelter (191) and to which Reta mails a donation.

11. Other critics have similarly noted Norah's re-visioning of the public domain in terms of the familial. Steffler argues that when Norah "withdraws from one lifestyle, she enters another to the extent of sharing her earnings with the street community" (232). Steffler adds, "Exchanging filial bonds for the looser bonds of affiliation, Norah is exploring her place not only in a different family but also in a less rigid system of familial denotation" especially when she tries to help the Muslim woman and is burned in the process (237). See also Linda Knowles's article on Shields's depictions of Canadian cities in which she argues that the street corner in *Unless* is Norah's "room": "her sisters, spending their Saturdays with her, think of themselves as her guests" (105).

12. See Steffler's and Struth's fine analyses of Norah's burnt hands, which are marked by the tragedy of the Muslim woman's self-immolation. As Struth acknowledges, because "the place is devoid of any traces" of the event, Norah's "body becomes its very site of inscription" with the untended scars on her hands "signif[ying] a lack of public interest" (214).

Works Cited

Anderson, Marjorie. "Interview with Carol Shields." *Prairie Fire* 16.1 (1995): 139–50. Print.

Atwood, Margaret. "Flying Rabbits: Denizens of Distant Spaces." In *In Other Worlds: SF and the Human Imagination*. Toronto: McClelland and Stewart, 2011: 15–37. Print.

Boyd, Shelley. *Garden Plots: Canadian Women Writers and Their Literary Gardens*. Montreal and Kingston: McGill-Queen's University Press, 2013.

Dumas, Anne. *Book of Plants and Symbols*. London: Hachette Illustrated, 2004. Print.

Glaser, Brigitte. "Digressing in Inner Worlds: Carol Shields, 'Our Men and Women.'" In *The Canadian Short Story: Interpretations*, ed. Reingard M. Nischik. Rochester: Camden House, 2007: 365–73. Print.

Groening, Laura. "Still in the Kitchen: The Art of Carol Shields." *Canadian Forum* (Jan.–Feb. 1991): 14–17. Print.

Guenther, Bethany. "Carol Shields and Simone de Beauvoir: Immanence, Transcendence, Women's Work in *A Fairly Conventional Woman, The Stone Diaries*, and *Unless*." *Studies in Canadian Literature* 35.1 (2010): 147–64.

Henighan, Stephen. *When Words Deny the World: The Reshaping of Canadian Writing*. Erin, ON: Porcupine's Quill, 2002.

Hutcheon, Linda. *The Canadian Postmodern: A Study of Contemporary English-Canadian Fiction*. Toronto: Oxford University Press, 1988. Print.

Johnson, Lisa. "'She Enlarges on the Available Materials': A Postmodernism of Resistance in *The Stone Diaries*." In *Carol Shields, Narrative Hunger, and the Possibilities of Fiction*, ed. Edward Eden and Dee Goertz. Toronto: University of Toronto Press, 2003: 201–29. Print.

Knowles, Linda. "'Kronk City': Canadian Cities in the Novels of Carol Shields." *London Journal of Canadian Studies* 22 (2006/2007): 85–114. Web. www.londoncanadianstudies.org/Journal/22/22-5.pdf.

"A Likely Story." *The Atlantic Online* 14 Jan. 1999. Web. www.theatlantic.com/past/docs/unbound/factfict/ff9901.htm.

Morrison, Blake. "Hell Hath No Fury." *Guardian* 27 Apr. 2002. Guardian News and Media Limited. 2009. Web.

Nelson, Ronald J. "Inconclusive Closure in Carol Shields' *The Orange Fish*." *Postscript: Publication of the Philological Association of the Carolinas* 22 (2005): 21–28. Print.

Ramon, Alex. *Liminal Spaces: The Double Art of Carol Shields*. Newcastle-upon-Tyne: Cambridge Scholars, 2008. Print.

Reynolds, Richard. *On Guerrilla Gardening*. London: Bloomsbury, 2008. Print.

Rosenthal, Caroline. "Textual and Urban Spaces in Carol Shields's *Unless*." In *Reading(s) from a Distance: European Perspectives on Canadian Women's Writing*, ed. Charlotte Sturgess and Martin Kuester. *Studies in Anglophone Literatures and Cultures*. Vol. 2. Augsburg: Wissner, 2008: 175–86. Print.

Roy, Wendy. "Brenda Bowman at Dinner with Judy Chicago: Feminism and Needlework in Carol Shields's *A Fairly Conventional Woman*." *Atlantis* 33.1 (2008): 120–30. Print.

———. "*Unless* the World Changes: Carol Shields on Women's Silencing in Contemporary Culture." In *Carol Shields: The Arts of a Writing Life*, ed. Neil K. Besner. Winnipeg: Prairie Fire, 2003: 125–32. Print.

Shields, Carol. *The Box Garden*. Toronto: McGraw, 1977. Print.

———. *Happenstance: Two Novels in One about a Marriage in Transition*. Toronto: Random House, 1997. Print.

———. "Narrative Hunger and the Overflowing Cupboard." In *Carol Shields, Narrative Hunger, and the Possibilities of Fiction*, ed. Edward Eden and Dee Goertz. Toronto: University of Toronto Press, 2003: 19–36. Print.

———. *Small Ceremonies: A Novel*. Toronto: McGraw, 1976. Print.

———. "Today Is the Day." 1989. *Carol Shields: The Collected Stories*. Toronto: Random House, 2004: 271–76. Print.

———. *Unless*. Toronto: Random House, 2002. Print.

Staels, Hilde. "Verbalisations of Loss in Carols Shields' *The Stone Diaries* and *Unless*." *Zeitschrift für Kanada-Studien* 24.2 (2004): 118–31. Print.

Steffler, Margaret. "A Human Conversation about Goodness: Carol Shields' *Unless*." *Studies in Canadian Literature* 34.2 (2009): 223–44. Print.

Stovel, Nora Foster. "'Because She's a Woman': Myth and Metafiction in Carol Shields's *Unless*." *English Studies in Canada* 32.4 (2006): 51–73. Print.

Struth, Christiane. "Speaking from the Margins: Abandoned Women and Magic(al) Realism in Carol Shields's *Various Miracles* and *Unless*." *Ahornblätter: Marburger Beiträge zur Kanada-Forschung* 19 (2007): 207–31. Print.

Tracey, David. *Guerrilla Gardening: A Manualfesto*. Gabriola Island, BC: New Society, 2007. Print.

van Herk, Aritha. "Prepositional Domesticity." The Worlds of Carol Shields. Canadian Literature Symposium. University of Ottawa, Ottawa. 28 Apr. 2012. Address.

Waterman, Catharine H. *Flora's Lexicon: The Language of Flowers*. 1860. Ottawa: Algrove, 2001. Print.

Cool Empathy in the Short Fiction of Carol Shields

MARILYN ROSE

> Imagining what it is like to be someone other than yourself is at
> the core of our humanity. It is the essence of compassion,
> and it is the beginning of morality.
>
> —Ian McEwan, "Love, Empathy and 9/11"

In reviewing Carol Shields's short story collection *Various Miracles* (1985), *New York Times* book reviewer Josh Rubins refers to her "serious whimsy," a "fragile amalgam that . . . is sometimes surprisingly powerful as well as highly engaging. (11)" He notes the way that some of Shields's "tiny fictions" have "sizable impact" and observes that her stories are somehow "disarming," and pull "the reader inside her reckless imagination before the usual resistances can take shape." He concedes that not all of her stories are equally successful: some are merely droll or seem to strain for effect. The best, however, exhibit a kind of "minimalism" that manages to be "ambiguous" and "slippery" in a "dainty" but "full-hearted" sort of way.

Rubins is onto something here, although I would use a term that he does not. It seems to me that Carol Shields's most remarkable stories are those that masterfully evoke *empathy* in her readers, and that it is the key mechanism by which we are drawn into so many of her stories "before . . . resistances can take shape." Her handling of empathy, moreover, is particularly deft in that it does not require forfeiture of the "slipperiness" and "ambiguity" that are hallmarks of Shields's style and vision, as Rubins suggests.

That much of Carol Shields's short fiction should be characterized by empathy is not surprising. She has often been celebrated for her commitment to the need for understanding and other kinds of love in human relationships. In *Random Illuminations: Conversations with Carol Shields*, for example, Eleanor Wachtel repeatedly characterizes Carol Shields as a writer of extraordinary "compassion" (10), "humanity (15), and "gener[osity]" (16). In conversation with Wachtel, Shields states that living fully is not a matter of "standing by" (155) but of sympathetic engagement with one another, of "love" in other words (87). She speaks of the mutability of human beings (18), the way that we must constantly change and evolve in response to the "random accidents" that shape our lives (73). Life is a "maze," she says: we are never sure of our direction and always making wrong turns (78). But she is moved by what she sees as our "longing for belonging," for "home," which she defines broadly as a "place where we are enabled, where we can be at ease . . . where we're free to be creative, where we're at peace with other people . . . " (117).

I am interested in the way that Shields's short fiction explores human relationships and particularly our apparently intrinsic drive to find ways of being at one with others—despite the competing drives, needs, contrarieties, and general prickliness of the egocentric inner self in its ongoing struggle for self-realization and control, which also governs thought and human behaviour. While Shields's characters are seldom entirely loveable, I see her as managing to trigger compassion for them—or what might be called empathetic engagement with them—through fictional mechanisms that generate empathy in interestingly indirect ways.

Such indirection is part of Shields's self-identified aesthetic. In quoting Emily Dickinson in the epigraph to her first collection of short stories, *Various Miracles* (1985)—"tell all the truth but tell it slant"—Shields runs up the flag, so to speak. She, like Dickinson, will prefer the circuitous and the oblique to the overt. And nowhere is this more evident than in her generation of what I call *cool empathy* in so many of her short stories. By this term I refer to her employment of literary strategies that generate identification or fellow feeling in her readers while avoiding levels of emotion that might dismissed as sentimental or even mawkish by contemporary readers and critics, who tend to see overt sentimentality as more properly appropriate to genre fiction than to serious art.

"Fiction" encompasses many kinds of writing, and it is true that some kinds of fiction invite intellectual more than emotional investment on the part of readers. Stories that focus on puzzles of one kind or another or on metafictional play are cases in point, and such narratives have abounded during the postmodern period of the late twentieth and early twenty-first centuries. The fiction most avidly consumed by readers of all kinds, however, remains stubbornly realistic, and the work of Carol Shields in which I am interested belongs to this category. Such fiction rests for its success upon the evocation of emotion, on the reader's losing himself or herself in the alternative world that the narrative represents through identification with the characters in the story as it unfolds. Indeed some would argue, as does Keith Oatley, that realistic "fiction is all about . . . emotions" and that we read realistic fiction primarily because "we want to be moved" by it (*Passionate Muse* 15–16), which is to say that we seek to empathize, to feel with the fictional other in ways that will allow us to incorporate the imagined, vicarious experience into our own ways of being.[1]

But what does it mean to be "moved" by fiction? And why should we yearn for this experience? Notions of empathy and its importance in fiction have been bolstered by new scientific discoveries and paradigms in the fields of cognitive and social neuroscience[2] that support the idea that art, especially narrative art, *inevitably* evokes emotion, *can* stimulate empathy, and can do this to good social effect.[3] A brief overview of that complex scientific landscape may be helpful in understanding the relationship between emotion and narrative as currently construed—and hence the ways through which emotion may be generated in storytelling.

Emotion is seen by contemporary neuroscience not as amounting to "bursts of irrationality" (Hogan, *On Being Moved* 240) but as measurable physiological/somatic responses to sensory "triggers" in our environment that (and this is the cognitive side) engage with our stored memories (Hogan, *Cognitive Science* 162) and "move" us into feeling and potentially into action. More to the point for literary scholars, relatively new brain imaging techniques, such as fMRI imaging (Keen 61),[4] demonstrate that " . . . our brains respond in roughly the same manner when we imagine something," such as the suffering of others, as when we experience it directly ourselves (Hogan, *On Being Moved* 243).[5] Of even more significance is the evocation of "motor mimicry" during such "pre-empathic or emphatic arousals" (Snow 72)—that is, the fact that during vicarious experiences to which we fully attend, our bodies themselves register and experience motor changes that parallel the movements of embodied figures as they move within the narratives we read, hear, or (in the case of film or television) watch.

We seek such experiences, it would seem, because of their utility as a tool for the construction and reconstruction of our social selves. Novelists have understood this for a very long time. As Sheila Heti observes in "On First Looking into *Pride and Prejudice*," the work of Jane Austen—a writer whom Shields admires and aligns with in interesting ways[6]—is all about "what other people are like." Heti says of Austen, "She knew that life is not about who we are alone, but who we are in relation to others." Contemporary neuroscience supports what Austen and others, including Shields, have understood intuitively. Human beings are by far the most social of primates: Oatley goes so far as to argue that being social is in effect our "ecological niche" (*Such Stuff* 39). In this regard, fictional narrative represents a kind of laboratory in which we can develop what Raymond Mar has called "a repertoire of social emotions" (qtd. in Oatley "Entertainment") through engagement with imagined others. Cognitive evolutionists affirm that humans spend much of their time throughout their lives attempting to understand what others are thinking or feeling as a strategy for interacting with them and learning thereby how to navigate social situations.

The principal technique for doing so appears to be attempting to "read one another's minds"[7] in order to make sense of the behaviour of others and to ascribe meaning to our own lives.[8] In speaking of "mind-reading" in this sense (alternatively called "theory of mind" or "perspective taking"), such advocates point to the universality of narrative as an instrument for accessing the minds of others and processing their feelings,[9] and to our seemingly innate yearning for stories.[10] Ellen Spolsky, for example, speaks of "narrative as nourishment" (37), and goes so far as to argue for the existence of an evolved *representational hunger* in human beings (38),[11] an idea echoed by Shields in her essay, "Narrative Hunger and the Overflowing Cupboard," in which she examines our profound "need" for narrative (19).[12]

The main mechanism for the generation of empathy in representational art is thought to be the "sympathetic identification" of the reader or viewer with the character or characters central to the fictional world that is being experienced[13]—through the reader's or viewer's participatory immersion in the "concrete detail" located in the fictional experience (Feagin 59). Critics like Oatley argue that the process of identification involves the generation of "fresh emotion" (*Such Stuff* 115) that moves us through the "observation or imagination" of another's emotions (113).[14] It is a matter of engagement, and when so engaged, we bring our own experiences and "schema" (or patterns of thinking) to texts (60).

We try on, or "simulate," the emotions of those with whom we identify—but at an aesthetic distance that permits us to assess or think about implications as we vicariously experience the intuited feelings of others (43–44).

Cognitive space, or room for the processing of vicarious experience within narratives, is essential to notions of empathy, as can be seen in the distinctions made between empathy and the related concept of sympathy. Generally "empathy" is assumed to involve *feeling along with* or *in line with* a fictional other, whereas "sympathy" is thought to constitute *feeling for* another and is closer to *pity* (Barnes and Thagard). In the words of social psychologist Lauren Wispé:

> In empathy one substitutes oneself for the other person; in sympathy one substitutes others for oneself. . . . *The object of empathy is understanding.* The object of sympathy is the other person's well-being. In sum, *empathy is a way of knowing*; sympathy is a way of relating. (qtd. in Barnes and Thagard)

The emphasis on empathetic understanding—on knowing, thinking, and applying what we are experiencing vicariously to our own lives—helps to explain the assumption that persists into our own time that there are higher and lower orders of narrative.[15] Narrative marked by blatant sentimentality is typically seen as lower in the hierarchy, which is to say suitable for "popular" or "genre" fiction but not for high art, whose subtlety is assumed to be predicated on openness and greater room for varieties of feeling and interpretation than is typical of genre fiction.[16] Oatley contends that while genre fiction leaves little room for unexpected feelings and complex judgments, works of art invite exploratory "conversation" (*Such Stuff* 180) and are by nature "surrounded by orbits of discussion" (178). Along similar lines, David Miall suggests what he calls "sub-literary genres" (such as romances and thrillers) lack the "[i]ndeterminacy" that engenders "more fresh emotions." Higher order narratives elicit novel rather than familiar feelings; their delicacy and ambiguity invite, through cognitive processing, the "retuning" or "recalibrating" of the reader's feelings, which in turn enable self-modification ("Emotions" 334–35). A key assumption among such critics is that sophisticated art will avoid overt evocations of feeling that solicit sympathy or pity, or what might be called, I suppose, "hot empathy," such as might be found in narratives designed simply for entertainment or to recruit readers to particular political causes.[17]

And so the trick for serious writers of fiction in our own time—this wintry age of irony, in Frygean terms—is to attempt instead to generate "cool empathy" in ways that skirt easy sympathy and engage intellect as well as emotion, which is to say in ways that invite engagement and require thought and processing, rather than obviously assigning feeling to readers in hot-button fashion.

What can be taken from what we currently know of the human brain in relation to narrative, then, is that empathetic fiction will deploy tactics that play into the ways in which the body and brain collaborate in processing emotional triggers. This includes the adroit handling of point of view, so as to assure what Suzanne Keen calls "interior representations" of a character's or characters' consciousness (69), along with an abundance of sensual detail so as, in Elaine Scarry's words, to "skillfully [recruit] the same processing mechanisms that the mind relies upon in live perception," and thereby "tacitly instruct the reader in re-creating" the experience as he or she absorbs a text (qtd. in Waugh 551).[18] It will include physical cues, such that a character's positioning or movement will trigger mirroring physical responses in the body of the reader or viewer.[19] It will also employ the judicious use of descriptive detail in order to create an immersive social world in which focal characters reside, which some refer to as attentiveness to the subject's "status life"—everyday manners, customs, habits, gestures, furniture, clothing, and styles, and related domestic detail as they pertain to focal characters (Oatley and Gholamain, 273; Oatley, *Such Stuff* 136–37).

But all of these must be enhanced by cognitive prompts—invitations to think and process that allow "the brain and the body to ruminate over particularly difficult social puzzles in good time" (Spolsky 50). Miall speaks of defamiliarization ("Emotions" 334) and Oatley of unexpected juxtapositions (*Such Stuff* 30–31), both of which require readers to navigate unusual connections. Miall notes the presence of a "degree of uncertainty, challenging the reader to locate a meaning for themselves" through the feelings evoked (Miall, "Emotions" 333). Keen makes reference to "aspects of the discourse that slow the reader's pace" and "invite more active reading that opens the way for empathy" (73). And both Keen and Oatley note the importance of authorial manipulations at the "discourse level," which is to say ways in which the author inserts "direct and indirect speech acts" into a story—acts "intended to influence the reader" (Oatley and Gholamain, 272) and that amount to metafictional commentary that moves readers towards desired emotional states (Keen 69).

Carol Shields published three short story collections in her lifetime, *Various Miracles* (1985), *The Orange Fish* (1989), and *Dressing Up for the Carnival* (2000). Her *Collected Stories* (2004), published posthumously, includes the stories found in all three collections, along with one new story, "Segue." To read them together is to be impressed by Shields's cleverness and the variety of kinds of stories attempted, from the realistic to the fantastic. But more impressive is the variety of their approaches to readerly engagement and questions of empathy. One of her stories, in fact, serves as a kind of negative tutorial, an example of the "*un*empathetic," a depiction of what empathy is *not*.

"Poaching" (*Various Miracles* 1985) is narrated in the first person by a supercilious woman whose circle of disdain apparently includes not only those with whom she crosses paths, such as tiresome innkeepers, but also her husband Dobey—who insists, for example, upon using the downscale word "serviettes" for "napkins" and is sometimes too soft, she feels, on hitchhikers, such as "those poor bloody Aussies" they had picked up that day (75). Hitchhikers are their prey, in effect, and she is proud of their tactics in prying stories from these hapless passengers: they keep the back seat of their car clear of luggage in order to inspire trust in those they pick up, and wring stories from some by affecting silence and from others by "prim[ing] the pump" (75). She notes, and apparently agrees with him, that Dobey knows that the poaching of personal narratives is a crime, a form of "stealing," though no one has thought to outlaw it (75). Their victims are for the most part awkward and unfortunate individuals whom they can easily look down upon. In listening to them, the husband and wife are criminally unsympathetic. An Australian mother and daughter are portrayed as brash and tiresome colonials: everything the mother says seems "electrically amplified by her bright, forthcoming Australia-lacquered voice" (76). A lisping doctoral student from Canada is ruthlessly mocked for his speech impediment and dismissed as a simplistic Anglophile fixated on "Oxthford" (77). They have their individual preferences: Dobey favours strangers who are already distraught who "unwind" more easily, although she tends towards the more diffident or composed—harder nuts to crack, perhaps (77–78).

In the mobile laboratory that is their automobile the couple collects stories from people they despise while deliberately concealing their own. They dismiss their passengers as self-involved. The narrator agrees with her husband that "people care only about themselves" and "the machinery of their own adventuring" (77), and the fact that she secretly longs to "float my own story on the air" (79) ironically confirms their assumptions about the ubiquity of solipsism. There is no immediate use for the stories they collect. He thinks in terms of a long-term project, claiming that the stories will link up in some way at some point, allowing their curators to descend into a "deep cave" where there may be something significant to see (79). She, however, has grown tired of the sameness of it all. Are the stories not becoming thinner? Is it not possible that there will be nothing to see in the end?

Here Shields appears to be playing with the conventions that surround empathy. While the story's point of view is first person, conventionally the most intimate of narrative positions, the woman reveals little of herself and nothing of the inner lives of those to whom she listens. She and her husband are depicted as moving through space not as flesh and blood creatures, whose embodied selves we can "feel" through the motor mimicry mechanisms identified by cognitivists, but rather as ruthless, near-mechanical inhabitants of the metallic carapace that is the moving automobile that surrounds them. Their own "status life" is invisible and their bodily movements constrained: he drives stiffly, eyes on the road; she sits with her "brain screwed up in a squint from looking sideways" (77) constantly looking "aslant" (78). They are spectators—as we all are in listening to the stories of others, in whatever medium—but entirely non-empathetic practitioners of the art of listening who have ruled out feeling for, making "personal judgments" about, or identifying in any way with their passengers. In a word, they are parasites: their stated goal is to "dwindle, grow deliberately thin, almost invisible, and live like aerial plants off the packed fragments and fictions" of those whom they pick up (76–77).

In contrast, Shields provides a humane touchstone in this story, a foil who clearly embodies values that are beyond the ken of her main characters. A "remarkable Venezuelan" passenger appears to resist their efforts at containment and exploitation (78). She is open to natural beauty and loves to hitch rides and "commune with the air" through open car windows. She grows "fat" on the sight of mountains and clouds. Sensual details—the open car windows, the glorious ingestion of open air, and the sense of growing "fat" with sensation as she drinks in the scenery—invite identification with her. In addition, we are told that that in abandoning her profession as a doctor, a scientist, she has opened herself instead to a love of language, with its capacity for imprecision, for every word to be "picked up and spun like a coin on the table top" (78).

Within this story, this figure serves as a kind of discursive instrument," in Oatley's and Miall's sense—a presence whose insertion into the narrative temporarily interrupts its flow and invites reflection. The reader is not recruited to feel for the Venezuelan in any discernible way; she is not in crisis, for example, as the narrator is. Rather she serves only to throw her non-empathetic short-term captors into relief. The cool and barren scientists who drive the story, and champion objectivity and detachment above all, are quietly trumped by this passenger's warmth and scope—the very things that they have disciplined their eyes not to see, as is clearly their loss.

Stories that do generate empathy abound in Shields's short fiction and some are quietly traditional. In "Fragility" (*Various Miracles*) for example, the grief experienced by a couple whose handicapped son has recently died is recounted as they search for a new home in Vancouver that will allow them to begin over—hopefully in a house not marked by grief and loss. That quest at first seems likely to be fruitless, since the houses they are most drawn to seem to be marked by barrenness or tragedy. There are a "divorce house," "bankruptcy houses," and a house that is a shrine to a grown son who has deserted his ageing mother in his own quest for fame and fortune—all of which the wife finds "depressing" (96). It is not until their cheery real estate representative tells them that she has lived in a "divorce house" for the past year, her own, and that "sometimes it's darned cheerful" (102), that the bereft couple begins to reconcile themselves to choosing a suitable home despite any sense of loss that might linger within its walls.

The story's narrator, Ivy's husband, is tender as he regards his wife, whom he describes as a "*crack* accountant" and a senior partner in an accounting firm, whose willingness to leave her job, and their small but obviously beloved home in one city for another, thousands of miles away, seems meant to signal the depths of her sorrow (97). Yet he tells us little about her that is moving. He characterizes her as "a positive, good-natured woman" (97) with a "rhythmic voice" (93), but his descriptions of her are generally spare and unevocative. Graceful and composed, she is said to turn pages of her book "in the same way she handles every object, with a peculiar respectful gentleness," an "abstracted grace" that is, her husband says, "a gift some people have" (92). She has a charming "patrician" way of pronouncing "stupid" as "*stewpid*" (95). At one point she reaches for his hand with a "cool, light, lazy touch" (93) and he kisses her fingertips in what he calls an "attack of poignancy" (94). At another, her eyes are said to "fill with tears" (95).

There is, however, little emotion attached to this portrait. Nor is his own sorrow made much evident until the end of the story. Rather he is given to analytical statements about grief and about life: the way that we do not really want to go back in time, despite our sorrows, preferring instead the "healthy resignation" that comes with age (93); the way that the couple's own homelessness is underscored by those happily ensconced in domesticity, as glimpsed through lighted windows in the evenings (10), and the way that he has come to understand that life itself is fragile, with "miniature accidents of chromosomes" able to "spread unstoppable circles of grief" (103).

Instead, the most emotional point in the story comes at the end, when attention is directed towards their young son's room in their Toronto home. The father recalls the way that he and Ivy re-wallpapered Christopher's room over the years in their continuous attempts to create an evolving "marvellous green cave" for a boy with little muscular control, almost no sight or hearing, and no real consciousness "as that word is normally perceived" (104). The father pays tribute to the boy's "valour" and it is easy for readers at this point to ascribe valour to his parents who have obviously cared for him to the best of their ability. The ending is somewhat sentimental, as may be thought to suit a story whose first publication was in a popular magazine, *Saturday Night*. But, from a narrative point of view, it is worth noting that the emotion generated by the description of the boy's room is carefully deflected, in keeping with the perspective of the father-narrator: we are shown nothing of the relationship between these stoic parents and their son, that "tough kid" who lived "a good five years longer" than expected (95). Their grief is entirely projected onto and viewed indirectly through the room he inhabited.

The careful management of narrative perspective is evident in virtually all of Shields's stories. In fact, I would go so far as to say that her success in her more complicated stories depends heavily upon strategies of indirection that are achieved through careful management of points of view—in combination with a willingness to work with characters that are often flawed and rather unsympathetic. In "Hazel" (*The Orange Fish*), for example, Hazel herself is not a winning character. After the death of her philandering husband, she determines to change her life by seeking work outside her home, not as a route to self-realization so much as a way of obliterating time, "burning it away so cleanly she hardly noticed it" (48).

Shields chooses to narrate the story in the third person but limit herself to Hazel's perspective—a point of view that can lend itself to intimacy and readerly affiliation with a principal character. As if to avoid any potential for sentimentality, however, the narrator opens the story with an uncomplimentary portrait of its central figure. Hazel is immediately positioned as having accepted "compensatory gifts" from her husband in exchange for accepting his infidelities (34), even though he has conducted affairs with her friends, which she finds humiliating (46). She is recorded as noting dispassionately, and somewhat disparagingly, that it took him ten days to die after his heart attack, long enough for the minor wounds testifying to his clumsiness to have healed (35). Her inner life, such as it is, is neither attractive nor compelling. Hazel admits that she is a fifty-year-old woman who has managed thus far "to avoid most of the arguments and issues of the world" (36), and there is no indication that this will not continue to be the case. Her night time reading consists of "trashy, fast-moving New York" novels "about alienated wives" (35), and although she sheds a "few miserable tears" the first night after her husband's death and writes "I am alone and suffering unbearably" on the flyleaf of one such book, that statement is immediately undercut by the fact that having written it she pays less attention to the words themselves than to the fact that her handwriting in doing so was not at its best (36).

Once she decides to look for work, Hazel's career trajectory is rapid but unimpressive. Although she rises quickly in the Kitchen Kult organization, her success is clearly fuelled by cold calculation and rank opportunism. She learns all she can from a pathetic predecessor then neatly and serenely replaces him, and after a workplace injury accepts a somewhat dodgy offer from her employer that she knows is intended to ensure that she will not seek an insurance settlement. What matters to Hazel at this point is her belief that one can progress in this world so long as one keeps in mind the "bargains" that must be made (59). She positions herself as a self-made woman from Porcupine Falls who has catapulted herself into management despite all odds. She can now wear her "opal-toned silk suit with its scarf of muted pink, pearl and lemon" ("so much better than a bloody smock") with pride (55). She is living testimony to her "power" to shape her own life.

At the same time, it is difficult not to feel some degree of empathy with Hazel, particularly when the third person narrator provides details about her body and its suspension in or movement through the space she inhabits. We are told of her early days on the job, when she awakens feeling flattened, as if a "steamroller of sorrow" has passed over her, leaving her "squashed limbs . . . emptied of blood [and] her breath . . . thin and cool and quiet as ether." She mouths unanswerable questions ("What was she to do? How was she to live her life?") against the blanket binding, "rubbing her lips frantically back and forth across the stitching"

(39). Her valiance in getting into her car, peering at maps, and reading tiny print, in preparation for accessing her "revolving cycle of twelve stores" is oddly touching (39). Here Shields includes corporeal detail of the kind that is likely to initiate the "motor mimicry" process in readers that Snow and others see as fundamental to empathetic arousal, the kind of sensual description that Alan Richardson sees as implicitly instructing readers about how to feel as they immerse themselves in texts and identify with characters (551).

Later in "Hazel" other physical details invite further such engagement: Hazel is described as "loving" her "small tasks"—whitening her shoes, rinsing out her smock, setting her alarm, and otherwise fulfilling rituals of competency that signal the diligence of her attempt to winch herself out of a previous existence wherein she had been "unimaginably mute," like a woman who had swallowed her tongue and "couldn't make a sound" (51). When, within a single paragraph, Shields sets small domestic gestures and motions against the monumental size of the larger task Hazel is undertaking—that of engineering her escape from a past in which, metaphorically speaking, her own tongue was jammed down her throat (51)—she is presenting an unsettling juxtaposition of the kind that Oatley identifies as a potent empathetic trigger in fictional texts.

The story ends, moreover, in the kind of ambiguity that invites thought and further "conversation," in keeping with the argument of Oatley and others that significant fiction generates not just feeling but rumination. When Hazel visits her mother-in-law, now helpless and unresponsive in a nursing home, does she do so from a sense of pride in having risen above and beyond the old woman's earlier disapproval? The infusion of physical details of caretaking—the fact that Hazel holds the old woman's hand, wets her lips with a damp towel, and applies Vaseline to keep her skin from cracking, although the old woman cannot know she is offering such succour (60)—invites empathy for a protagonist who has been consistently portrayed as shallow and unfeeling. Yet all of this is set against a moment of rather trite self-realization on Hazel's part, the idea that accidents of fate rather than personal power decide destinies, thereby signalling once again Hazel's limitations in a way that averts potential slippage in the direction of easy sentiment.

Shields's portrayal of domesticity—and particularly the strange and variegated forms of intimacy that characterize every long marriage—is perhaps her most familiar theme,[20] and a number of her stories involve the privileging of a husband's point of view, which is permitted to dominate, without however entirely obliterating the obliquely observed entity that is his wife. "The Orange Fish" (from the collection of that title) and "Mirrors" (*Dressing Up for the Carnival*) fall into this category, as does "Accidents" (*Various Miracles*). In all three, a husband observes and describes a wife whom he neither fully understands nor appreciates. The challenge for the author in each case is to generate readerly feeling for the scrutinized but marginalized wife, the more silent partner, to whom attention must be paid and whose small movements and actions therefore must speak volumes.

In "Accidents," a husband recounts the way that three accidents have impinged upon his life during a vacation to "the French coast" (19). The second accident occurs when his wife's earring slashes his face as he tries puts his arm around her after a first accident involving the spontaneous explosion of a glass on the balcony of their villa. His injury leads to their entanglement in the aftermath of a third accident—when the husband is required to share a hospital room with a young man who has suffered a serious motorcycle accident. The narrator comes across as callous and self-centred. Even before his accident, he observes his wife rather coldly, pointing out at the story's start her immodesty when in France as she bears her breasts while sunbathing, and comparing those bared breasts to the Zubaran painting in which St. Agatha cheerfully proffers her severed breasts, as "ordinary and bloodless as jam pastries," on a royal platter (19). His pique increases after his injury. He records that his wife at first wept over her accidental slashing of his face (which may leave a scar, he frequently emphasizes), but by the next day had stopped crying, gone shopping and treated herself to a new outfit (22–23). He goes on to diminish her careful appearance, noting that despite the new cardigan, "so fresh and springlike" (22), she has aged noticeably in the last year and he feels "grieved" that he cannot help her "fight against the puckering of her mouth and the withering away of the skin on her upper arms" (23). Is he simply jealous of her attentions to the frightened and bewildered young man in the next bed? In any case, his need for control is evident in his decision at story's end to conceal the young man's death from his wife by means of judiciously disingenuous language. He has already admitted that he is an "abridger" of texts by trade and that abridging requires a "kind of inverse creativity" that sometimes requires him to "interfere with the truth"—which he does not consider to be dishonest but simply a matter of "clarity and balance" (26). He is simply applying his talents to the situation at hand.

"Accidents" is a sad story of a controlling husband and a depleted marriage, it would seem, but if readers are to feel for the wife, emotion must be imbedded in the story. The young man's suffering is tangible, of course, and clearly he is to be pitied. He coughs, sighs and moans, and expresses his fears of death as he lies alone in a hospital in a foreign country far home. It is the wife, however, in whom Shields invites us to invest, and it is the depiction of her feelings and actions that arouses contemplative empathy. She is a person of feeling: she weeps at the damage she has accidently inflicted upon her husband and refrains from wearing earrings thereafter as if in atonement. She buys a *Herald Tribune* and brings it to the hospital, "something she normally refuses to do" (22), and takes pains to read him whatever stories from Canada she can find. She outlines plans for their customary visit to Aigues Mortes once he is released, as if to cheer him up (22). Her gestures embody feeling. When she leans over and speaks comforting words into the injured boy's ear, reassuring him that the word "morte" in their previous discussion did not refer to him or indicate that he is dying, when she wipes his tears and offers to contact his "people" in England, and when she places her hand on his forehead until he sleeps (22–25), her tenderness can be felt and her generosity of spirit recognized.

At the same time, however, we are left with questions that keep us from sentimental attachment to her. Why does she stay in this marriage when she is clearly a professional woman of means, one who wears suits, takes the subway and rushes off to work without stopping for breakfast each day (19)? Why has she chosen to remain constrained by marriage to such a small-minded man? She is "still a beautiful woman," her husband says—do her attentions to an injured young man indicate a desire to make him jealous? Here is again is the ambiguity, the invitation to discussion, that Miall and Oatley see as markers of sophisticated fiction and that I see as contributing to cool empathy in aesthetic works—empathy that assiduously avoids easy sentiment and requires instead thoughtful processing.

Shields's most remarkable achievement may be those stories in which she uses more complex narrative perspectives and strategies to illuminate focal characters who are "felt" and engaged with to a certain extent, but who remain elusive in the end. The delicacy of "Chemistry" (*The Orange Fish*), for instance, originates in its retrospective narrative perspective. The story is told by someone who directs it to an unnamed "you," as he recollects with considerable nostalgia an advanced recorder class that they both attended in Montreal many years ago. The story is framed by hypothesis and retroactive desire: "If you were to write me a letter out of the blue," the story begins (11), and it ends, "We could take possession of each other once again, conjure our old undisturbed, unquestioning chemistry" (33). As he recollects the past, the narrator signals his unreliability, warning readers of the slipperiness of his narrative. He is unsure whether these events happened in the winter of 1972 or that of 1973 (11). He admits that he exaggerates and can be reproached for romanticizing (25). He is driven to write, however, about the experience—about the individuals who came together at that time, and the ephemerality of this amazing little group that existed for only one season and then dissolved, never to meet again. He is fascinated by the strange chemistry that characterized their attempts to make ethereal music together under the direction of their inscrutable teacher, Madame Bessant.

In his attempts to make a remembered world come alive, the narrator fills his account with details of the social world the students and their instructor jointly inhabited. He describes the room in which the music class met, with its "clumsy old-fashioned wooden folding chairs" drawn tightly together, and "[d]usty slats . . . pinned loosely with metal dowels" (12). Their environment, a "linoleum-floored basement room," could scarcely be less conducive to ethereality, with its dirty pink ceiling, its spotted ceiling globes, and the pervasive "secretive decaying scent" of human skin (14). Yet in their music the students aspire to "Alpine reaches," pursue "God marching in his ziggurat heaven," and revel in intoxicating "[o]xygen mists that shiver the scalp" (12). They don't just play the music, but "*find* it" and pull out "the notes just as they came, unclothed out of another century" (15). The students are for the most part a rag-tag lot, who see themselves as "accidental survivors crowded to the shores of a cynical economy" (17), and their "status life" is signalled by such details as their sharing of news about urban bargains. Their elders are little better off: Mr. Mooney, older than the rest, appears to possess modest means but strikes them as loud and uncouth. And then there is Madame Bessant, respectable if not quite genteel in her poverty and the ostensible focal point of the narrative.

She is a figure who invites compassion. Her students are motley at best, and she herself is far from charming. Though only about forty, she is old in the eyes of her pupils, and "[n]ot a beauty, not at all." She smiles little and wears the same earrings each week, along with plastic-lensed glasses, "dragging skirts," and "unbecoming blouses." She fails to button her coats properly in her haste to leave to leave class on time each week in order to get home to her three children (15–16). Her "blunt womanly elbows" are said to "rise out sideways like a pair of duck wings" (12). She exhibits little personality and speaks rarely—the odd "*pas mal*" at best (12).

And yet, the narrator indicates, she is intriguing. She pulls music from her class in some magical way, while beating energetically with a wand that looks like—and may be—a knitting needle (14). At times she seems spare and spindly: her gestures are birdlike in the way she greets them with a dipping of her shoulders as she arranges sheets of music with little throat-clearing "chirps" (11–12). At other times she is seen as "sumptuous," with the stem of her neck and the backs of her "busy rhythmically rotating hands," which are "pink with health" (15). Her very reticence inspires strategies of detection in her students and they carefully piece together—through hearsay—a melodramatic narrative (which may or may not be true) of her supposedly difficult life: her tragic widowhood and subsequent economic constraints, which may explain her quickness in donning their gift of new earrings and her eagerness to take home a "shopping bag loaded with leftover food" (31) after their end-of-term recital. And yet Mme Bessant is hard to read: she arouses easy sympathy, but we know too little about her to engage deeply in her emotional life. We are all too conscious of the flimsiness of our knowledge of her, given both the unreliability of the narrator and the vagueness of third-party evidence.

And, to complicate things further, there is another figure in whom readers may also feel invited to invest. Who is the mysterious "you" to whom the story is dedicated, and can she be read as a counterpoint to or an amplification of Mme Bessant, the more obvious target of the narrator's excavated memory? "You" emerges slowly and remains a shadowy figure. The narrator records "the bony intimacy" of her instep as she keeps time with the music she is playing (12), the contraction of her throat which forms "a lovely knot of deliberation" (13), the way she shakes cough drops "musically, out of a little blue tin" (14), and the way she finds a Kleenex for another student, Rhonda, in her "big woven bag" and covers for her by commenting on the way that "March wind" brings tears to the eyes (21). At one point he notes that as the group plays, the "folds of your skirt aligned with my thigh," though "you" appeared not to notice (25). In the end the students depart without exchanging addresses, and yet to this day he still thinks of "you" as "my darling, with your black tights and cough drops" (32) and recalls her "foot with its circling journey, around and around, keeping order" (29).

There is something vaguely predatory about the treatment of "you" in this story. In the end the narrator expresses his hope that she will feel an "urge" to write him a note "for the sake of nostalgia" (32). His language is somewhat troubling. He speaks of the way the past has a way of "putting *tentacles* around the present" (32) and says that perhaps they "could take *possession* of one another once again," although she has never indicated attachment to him according to his own recollections (35; italics mine). Even the word "nostalgia" is telling: it has become something of a commonplace to see nostalgia as a kind or yearning for and fetishizing of lost objects. Is the narrator really only a harmless "romantic," as he himself suggests (25), or is he someone whose reconstructions of the past are controlling and exploitative—and cause us to feel for the unfortunate objects of his voracious retrospective gaze? Shields, of course, guarantees nothing: we must think what we think. The cool empathy generated, sometimes indirectly, in regard to the figures of Mme Bessant and the even more elusive "you" is a product of the interleaving of emotion and thought in the rich cognitive space that is this short story.

It seems fitting to close with Shields's most anthologized—and arguably most sparkling—short story, "Mrs. Turner Cutting the Grass" (*Various Miracles*). The title suggests portraiture, something static and fixed wherein a single perspective is offered, that of an outsider looking in. At the same time, the gerund in the title suggests motion, continuing action, which is to say resistance to immobility or fixation, which is presented in the story as a good thing.

Here too, as in so many of Shields's stories, the protagonist is presented as less than appealing at first glance: Mrs. Turner is said to be a "sight" as she mounts her riding lawnmower in ancient shorts, crepe-soled sandals, and a halter top, with her "red-grey frizz" topped by her dead husband's golf cap (7). She seems sublimely unaware of the consternation aroused by the visibility of "the lapped, striated flesh on her upper thighs" (8) or her failure to collect and compost her grass catchings (7). The narrator's sweeping third-person omniscient perspective is a means of sharing with readers the views of teenage girls who deplore Mrs. Turner's thoughtless exposure of "enemy" cellulite, along with the thoughts of her horrified ecologically-correct neighbours—who fervently hope for her early consignment to an "old-folks" home or, better yet, the grave (8). Later the narrator will share with readers the disgust of the poet-professor who sees Mrs. Turner as representative of the many uncouth tourists who defile the sacred sites with their "vulgarity and tastelessness" (16). Mrs. Turner is particularly contemptible in his view, a horrid "little pug of a woman," her "grapefruity buttocks" slung into a pink pantsuit that is garishly accessorized by a Mexican straw bag stuffed with hopelessly banal objects (26).

At the same time, Mrs. Turner's detractors are neatly skewered by the all-knowing narrator: Mr. Sascher for his paranoia as he imagines "quick capillary surges" of her weedkiller entering his fenced vegetable plot and stealth-bombing his green beans and lettuce (8), the self-centered high school girls as her aged body makes them "queasy" to think of their own futures (8), and the poet for his chagrin that his claim to fame, ironically, is a "crowd pleaser" of a light poem in which he mocks Mrs. Turner and her sisters—whom he can therefore never escape (14).

But it is Mrs. Turner's inner life that invites readerly engagement. On the one hand she seems rather simple at times, given the number of things she does not know, a quantity that the narrator says "would fill the Sascher's new compost pit, would sink a ship, would set off a tidal wave, would [or should?] make her want to kill herself" (8). At the same time, however, we learn of the "secrets she keeps locked away inside her mottled thighs or in the curled pinkness of her genital flesh" (12) and a more complex picture emerges. Clearly she has had to struggle to be herself and to do the best that she can "under the circumstances" (12) all her life. Given what appear to be her inborn and dangerous tendencies towards non-conformity, it is not surprising that she "got herself in hot water" (9) as a young woman and ended up pregnant and then having to give her mixed-race baby away. Her eventual move back to her home town and marriage to the placid Gord appears to have been a satisfactory solution for a time, especially since that gentle and taciturn husband of hers is said to have liked to take her into the woods and remove her dress and underthings and kiss "every part of her body" (13).

Mrs. Turner is at heart a free spirit. Her unabashed sexuality is apparently tied to her sense of adventure, her desire for open air and the open road. When, as "Girlie Fergus," she first runs away from home, taking the bus from Boissevain, Manitoba, to Winnipeg, Minneapolis, Chicago, and New York, she is "full of happiness" at the wonder of it all (10). Once there she is constantly in motion. She moves—and we with her—as she shows patrons to their seats by sending streams of light from her little flashlight into the "furry darkness" of the movie theatre (10), as she carries her baby "all the way to Brooklyn Heights" and deposits him in a pretty wicker baby carriage on a lovely wide porch with a curved railing (11) and then walks back home "swinging her legs" (11). She reports that her life has "never known such ease" as since her husband's death, after which she begins to travel, if only once a year given her tight budget (13). She knows nothing of "history or dates" and remembers little of her travels but gets on tour buses and just "goes and goes, and that's all there is to it" (16). She has a "grand time," and even though her reduction of the world to "sameness" (17)—to seeing the similarity of little lives lived everywhere—may strike us as simplistic, there is energy and appeal in her joyful conviction that in just living one's life to the fullest, which is her *credo*, one can "understand so much" (18). Life is there for the plucking, as accessible "as bars of music floating out of a radio" (17). In a nutshell, Mrs. Turner personifies *jouissance;* she knows how to live in the moment, and without the burden of knowing or caring what others think.

In a sense "Mrs. Turner" is not a complicated story and some might see it as simply escapist or verging on the sentimental. Its crafting, however, is impeccable. In employing an Olympian narrator, who knows all but tells it in ways that enable the insertion of certain kinds of bias into the text, Shields has created a complex ecosystem.[21] Mrs. Turner and her perceivers are all treated as a spectacle.[22] Her detractors are seen as from above, their foibles evident in their actions: Roy Sascher plucks dandelion leaves in deadly earnest and with fussy precision (8), the shallow schoolgirls are caught in a moment of callow revulsion at the sight of an aged woman's flesh, and the poet-professor is pictured superciliously jotting notes "almost continuously into a little pocket scribbler" wherever he goes (14). In turn Mrs. Turner herself is "spectated" and laid bare, though the amount and the delicacy of the attention paid to her by the narrator in and of itself tips the empathy scales in her favour.

What is unusual in this story, and gives it the edge that saves it from sentimentality, is the degree to which the third-person perspective, that of the Olympian narrator, is discursive: his or her "speech acts" frequently stand between the reader and the story proper and serve to instruct the reader in charming but overweening ways. "Oh, Mrs. Turner is a sight in cutting the grass on a hot afternoon in June!" cries the narrator, in opening the story, and that rhetorical apostrophe and emphatic exclamation mark ensure that the story begins in wry judgment (6). The interruptions continue: "Oh, the things she doesn't know!" we are reminded, mid-story (9); and when Mrs. Turner boards a tour bus, and does not know whether she is going east, west, north, or south, "What does it matter?" we are asked in a rhetorical question that invites concurrence with the narrator's stance that in the larger scheme of things it does not really matter at all where Mrs. Turner goes or what she does (17). At times, Mrs. Turner's lack of moral compass is highlighted, ironically, by the jauntiness of the narrator's language, as when we are told that she casually deposits her baby (with his innocent sleeping face "round and calm as the moon") on a stranger's porch and runs away, even though, as she herself thinks later, he might have been bitten by a rabid cat before being found in the morning (11–12). Then, again at story's end, there is another rhetorical gesture, a repetition of the opening exclamation, though with a slight embellishment: Oh, what a sight is Mrs. Turner . . . and how like an ornament, she shines!" (18).

The effect of such narrative intrusion is decidedly bilateral. On the one side, the narrator clearly cherishes this odd duck and tolerates her eccentricities and urges us to plunge into partaking of her *joie de vivre*. On the other hand, however, what are we to make of those rhetorical flourishes signalling Mrs. Turner's outlandishness and vacuity—or that final word "ornament"? Is it complimentary, gently ironical, dismissive? It is unsettling and at the very least "cools" empathy at story's end, opening up the processing space that cognitive critics identify as crucial to the generation of empathy in the arts.

Carol Shields revelled in making art, as she indicates in her conversations with Wachtel (97). Her commitment to experimentation in style and form is evident in her comment to Wachtel that in her short stories she wanted to "do all the narrations," try all of the narrative forms that she could, telling stories from "close up or from far back," and letting each "story find its own way" (47). Her success in the management of cool empathy, a substantial technical challenge in contemporary writing, is testimony to Shields inventiveness and suggests one of the ways through which her "tiny fictions" manage to achieve the great impact that critics have celebrated in her best work.

Notes

1. In literary studies, where interpretive theory has dominated critical discourse for the last near-century, David Miall, quoting Meir Sternberg, observes that there has been a tendency to place "cognition against (at least above) emotion." However a reversal is underway at the present time owing to "neuropyschological evidence . . . that emotion is at the basis of, and shapes the purpose of, all cognitive activity" ("Emotions" 324). Elsewhere he refers to a shift from an emphasis on interpretation to an emphasis on "the experience of literature," on "the text and its effects in itself, not in relation to some external reference to political, historical, or other issues (interesting though these may be)" ("Literariness").

2. Singer and Lamm, for example, refer to the field of "social neuroscience" as having enabled "substantial insight into the neural underpinnings of empathy in the past few years," while noting that "we are just starting to

understand the neuronal and behavioral foundations of this complex psychological phenomenon" (92).

3. There is growing evidence—for example in the work of Oatley's research group at the University of Toronto—that virtually engendered empathy can actually change hearts and minds, if only incrementally and over time, and can lead to positive behavioural changes. See, for example, Oatley, "Why Fiction is Good for You" and *The Passionate Muse* (123–25), as well as Allison Flood, "Reading Fiction 'Improves Empathy.'"

4. Keen refers to the way that "[s]imply hearing a description of an absent other's actions lights up mirror neuron areas during fMRI imaging of the human brain" and that those who score high on empathy tests appear to have "especially busy mirror neuron systems" that activate in response to such vicarious experience (61).

5. According to Hogan, humans are entirely capable of experiencing the indirectly rendered experience of real or fictional others as fully as they do their own "real" experience in what we think of as "real life": "Our emotional response is a matter of trigger perception, concrete imagination and emotional memory. The issue of fictionality just does not enter [into the equation]" (Hogan, *Cognitive Science* 185).

6. In her biography of Austen, *Jane Austen* (2001), for example, Shields emphasizes the search for a home of one's own as a core issue in Austen's fiction. She argues that "the true subject of serious fiction is not 'current events,' ongoing wars or political issues but the search of an individual for his or her true home," and that for Austen's characters, home, "both in its true and metaphorical sense, becomes a desired but denied destination" (13).

7. As Lisa Zunshine notes, this adaptation is rooted in a shared conviction among cognitivists that humans are an intensely social species and spend much of their time attempting to "read each other's minds"—at least "since the 'massive neurocognitive evolution' that took place during the Pleistocene (1.8 million to 10,000 years ago)," when our ancestors were facing a "staggeringly complex challenge," in that "they needed to make sense of the behavior of other people in their group, which could [by then] include up to two hundred individuals" (Zunshine, *Why We Read Fiction* 7).

8. This argument depends upon the contention that humans, as evolved, are very essentially meaning-making entities and that the arts, including narrative arts, have always comprised a way of making sense of human experience—one's own and that of others (see Dissanayake xvii–xix).

9. Evolutionary cultural cognitivists argue that the human species has an evolved ability "to 'leave' the ['real'] world and to construct whole realms of abstract thought or fanciful imaginative alternatives . . . " on the basis of arousal—which is to say the stimulation of bodily senses, "what we see, hear and touch, in particular" (Dissanayake 149).

10. Our desire for and attraction to fictional narratives may be connected to our need to practise our perspective-taking skills in environments that are both safe (because they are virtual rather than real) and provide vicarious experience that is far more far-ranging than any individual can possibly access in real life. Oatley and Gholamain argue that in engaging with fiction, we create "simulations" in our own minds, "models" of the world that "run on [our minds] as a computer simulation runs on a computer," in order to test and expand our understanding of the world beyond our own direct experience of it (265–66).

11. Spolsky's contention dovetails with current research on theory of mind and its literary applications, such as the work of Zunshine, who also argues that we are "greedy for" stories (Zunshine, "What to Expect" 116).

12. Shields goes on to say: "Everyone recognizes that narrative hunger is part of the human personality. Why else are our newspapers filled with advice columns? It's not, I think, for the solutions that we devour this daily stream of print, but for the glimpses of the human dilemma, the inaccessible stories of others" (20).

13. Snow sees empathy as "an emotion that is similar to the emotion that another feels *because the other feels it*" (italics mine; 67), and Singer and Lamm note that "empathy crucially depends upon self-awareness and self-other distinction," which is to say on our "ability to distinguish between whether the source of our affective experience lies within ourselves or was triggered by the other" (83).

14. Miall indicates a sense of the priority of emotional response when reading in providing evidence that readers will typically experience "significant emotional processing as soon as they begin to read, around 25 msecs after a word is first seen, or possibly earlier" ("Emotions" 327). Indeed the "processing of emotional aspects of language does not occur at a prelexical stage, but is a part of semantic processing" (328).

15. Some argue that a hierarchy of genres, which is ancient, still persists, a tendency to "rank'" texts, with melodrama and polemicism at the bottom, light romantic comedies next lowest, then serious romances (like Jane Austen), and at the top tragedies. The more sophisticated the reader the less the tolerance for overt sentimentality (Hogan, *Cognitive Science* 172–73). Hogan observes that the fact that many wept openly at the film *Titanic* ensures that it will not be taken seriously by most critics.

16. Hogan speaks of the "Emotional Low Road in Film and Music"—where creators rely on "direct emotive stimulation" involving "subcortical emotive arousal"—in contrast to "the High Road" wherein "Appraisal, Memory and Imagination" create a richer and potentially more ruminative empathetic experience (*Cognitive Science* 176–79).

17. An example of serious polemical fiction is Joy Kogawa's *Obasan*, which one reader has characterized as being "Between a Scream and a Sigh" (Izubachi),

which documented the internment of Japanese-Canadians in Canada during World War II, and which was designed to support the case for restitution—which it succeeded in doing.

18. Dissanayake notes that as early as 1939, in the early days of German thinking about empathy and its relation to emotion, Victor Lowenfeld stressed "the importance of *kinesthesis*, the awareness of tensions inside the body made possible by neural receptors in muscles, tendons, and joints, and *tactility*, the exploration by touch of the shape of physical bodies, in appreciating art. He called both of these processes *haptic perception* . . . " (146). Starr mentions the importance of multisensory imagery in creating such experience in fiction.

19. Research undertaken in the area of mirror neurons is extensive. See Keen (61) and Oatley (*Such Stuff* 21), for example.

20. Shields herself has said that "a long relationship—the union of two souls, the merging of contraries forever—can be as complex, as potentially dynamic, and as open to catharsis as the most shattering divorce"—though this is often thought to be "narratively unpromising" ("Narrative Hunger" 33).

21. Simone Vauthier refers to Shields's stories as involving a "complex microcircuitry" (117).

22. Clara Thomas has said that "to read [Shields'] stories is to have a privileged view of people who are quite unconscious of eyes on them," and that is one of the great pleasures of her text.

Works Cited

Barnes, Allison, and Paul Thagard. "Empathy and Analogy." Philosophy Department, University of Waterloo, 1997. Web. 13 May 2013.

Dissanayake, Ellen. *Homo Aestheticus: Where Art Comes From and Why*. New York: Macmillan, 1992. Print.

Feagin, Susan L. "Imagining Emotions and Appreciating Fiction." In *Emotion and the Arts*, ed. Mette Hjort and Sue Laver. New York: Oxford University Press, 1977: 50–62. Print.

Flood, Allison. "Reading Fiction 'Improves Empathy', Study Finds." *Guardian* 7 Sept. 2011. Print.

Heti, Sheila. "On First Looking into *Pride and Prejudice*." *Globe and Mail* 26 Jan. 2013: R15. Print.

Hogan, Patrick Colm. *Cognitive Science, Literature and the Arts: A Guide for Humanists*. New York and London: 2003. Print.

———. "On Being Moved: Cognition and Emotion in Literature and Film." In *Introduction to Cognitive Cultural Studies*, ed. Lisa Zunshine. Baltimore: Johns Hopkins University Press, 2010: 237–56. Print.

Izubachi. "Between a Scream and a Sigh: Conflicting Duties in Joy Kogawa's *Obasan*." 26 Jan 2006. Web. 13 May 2013.

Keen, Suzanne. "Narrative Empathy." In *Toward a Cognitive Theory of Narrative Acts*, ed. Frederick Luis Aldama. Austin: University of Texas Press, 2010: 61–93. Print.

McEwan, Ian. "Love, Empathy and 9/11." *Guardian* 15 Sept 2001. Print.

Miall, David S. "Emotions and the Structuring of Narrative Responses." *Poetics Today* 32.2 (Summer 2011): 323–48. Print.

———. "Literariness." *On Fiction: The Online Magazine on the Psychology of Fiction* 15 October 2008. Web. 13 May 2013.

Oatley, Keith. "Entertainment as Play." *On Fiction: The Online Magazine on the Psychology of Fiction.* 21 October 2008. Web. 13 May 2013.

———. *The Passionate Muse: Exploring Emotion in Stories.* Oxford and New York: Oxford University Press, 2012. Print.

———. *Such Stuff as Dreams: The Psychology of Fiction.* Chichester, UK: Wiley-Blackwell, 2011. Print.

———. "Why Fiction Is Good for You." *Literary Review of Canada* (July/August 2011): 7–9. Print.

Oatley, Keith, and Mitra Gholamain. "Emotions and Identification: Connections between Readers and Fiction." In *Emotion and the Arts*, ed. Mette Hjort and Sue Laver. New York: Oxford University Press, 1977: 263–81. Print.

Richardson, Alan. "Cognitive Literary Criticism." In *Literary Theory and Criticism*, ed. Patricia Waugh. Oxford University Press, 2006: 544–56. Print.

Rubins, Josh. "They All Want a Piece of the Legend." Rev. of *Various Miracles* and *Swann* by Carol Shields. New York Times. 6 August 1989: 11. Print.

Shields, Carol. *The Collected Stories.* Toronto: Random House, 2004. Print.

———. *Dressing Up for the Carnival.* 2000. Toronto: Vintage, 2001. Print.

———. *Jane Austen.* Toronto: Penguin, 2001. Print.

———. "Narrative Hunger and the Overflowing Cupboard." In *Carol Shields, Narrative Hunger, and the Possibilities of Fiction*, ed. Edward Eden and Dee Goertz. Toronto, Buffalo, London: University of Toronto Press, 2003: 19–36. Print.

———. *The Orange Fish.* 1991. Toronto: Vintage, 1990. Print.

———. *Various Miracles.* 1985. Toronto: Vintage, 1995. Print.

Singer, Tania, and Claus Lamm. "The Social Neuroscience of Empathy." *The Year in Cognitive Neuroscience 2009: Annals of the New York Academy of Sciences* 1156 (2009): 81–96. Print.

Snow, Nancy E. "Empathy." *American Philosophical Quarterly* 37.1 (January 2000): 65–78. Print.

Spolsky, Ellen. "Narrative as Nourishment." In *Toward a Cognitive Theory of Narrative Acts*, ed. Frederick Luis Aldama. Austin: University of Texas Press, 2010: 37–60. Print.

Starr, C. Gabrielle. "Multisensory Imagery." In *Introduction to Cognitive Cultural Studies*, ed. Lisa Zunshine. Baltimore: Johns Hopkins University Press, 2010: 275–91. Print.

Thomas, Clara. "Everyday Comforts." Rev. of *The Collected Stories of Carol Shields*. *Books in Canada* 33.8 (2004): 5–6. Print.

Vauthier, Simone. "Closure in Carol Shields's *Various Miracles*." In *Reverberations: Explorations in the Canadian Short Story*, ed. Simone Vauthier. Concord, ON: House of Anansi Press, 1993. Print.

Wachtel, Eleanor. *Random Illuminations: Conversations with Carol Shields*. Fredericton, NB: Goose Lane Editions, 2007. Print.

Waugh, Patricia. *Literary Theory and Criticism: An Oxford Guide*. Oxford and New York: Oxford University Press, 2006. Print.

Zunshine, Lisa. "What to Expect When You Pick Up a Graphic Novel." *SubStance* 24.1 (2011): 114–34. Print.

———. *Why We Read Fiction: Theory of Mind and the Novel*. Columbus OH: Ohio State University Press, 2006. Print.

The "Perfect Gift" and the "True Gift": Empathetic Dialogue in Carol Shields's "A Scarf" and Joyce Carol Oates's "The Scarf"

Elizabeth Reimer

> Giving and receiving gifts permits individuals to lose their autonomy to a ritual or activity that nobody can entirely control"
> —Mark Osteen (26)

Mothers, daughters, and gift giving: in two mirroring stories written by Carol Shields and Joyce Carol Oates we are invited to penetrate some of the mysteries of these expressive transactions. The titles themselves suggest a dialogue between the two writers: Oates's "The Scarf" was published in 2001, one year after Carol Shields's "A Scarf" appeared in *Dressing Up for the Carnival*. Oates reviewed Shields's collection of stories but it is not known whether her story responds directly to Shields's or whether the stories germinated independently. Nevertheless, they form a dialogue with each other even as they highlight the importance of gift giving as a form of dialogue, an ongoing conversation between giver and recipient.

At the University of Ottawa Symposium on Carol Shields in April 2012, many speakers paid tribute both to Carol Shields's exceptional conversational "gifts" and to her well-renowned generosity. Eleanor Wachtel ended her tribute to Shields with the statement that her "friendship with Carol was a gift." During the closing panel discussions, Jane Urquhart acknowledged Shields's "enormous generosity of spirit" and

Martin Levin described an act of Shields's that represented "as kind an act of human generosity" as he had ever witnessed. Yet Shields's story about gift giving contains her familiar satiric lens that is used to subtly uncover the ways that our impulses towards generosity as well as our failures of generosity may be connected to our imperfect perceptions of the "other." In "A Scarf," which later formed a chapter of Shields's final novel *Unless*, Reta attempts to find "the perfect scarf" (16) as a birthday gift for her college-aged daughter, Norah, to provide emotional, symbolic sustenance for her "bravely undemanding" (17) daughter's journey to adulthood. While Reta is filled with "intoxicating power" (18) when she finds a scarf that seems to transmit this message, the perfect gift never reaches its intended recipient. Reta's friend Gwen, to whom Reta recounts the heroic details of her shopping feats, disrupts the trajectory of Norah's gift, claiming it for herself in an act of misrecognition, appropriation, or, perhaps, perception, an act that expands Reta's ideas about the gift. Through the capricious workings of her "empathetic dialogue" with Gwen, Reta is left to ponder larger, unanswered questions about the gap between a potentially trivial gift and the force of unrecognized female desire contained within it.

The gift in Oates's story "The Scarf" follows a similar trajectory; in this story it is the daughter, eleven years old, on the cusp of puberty, who searches for, and finds, the "perfect gift," "not a mere store-bought item, but a love-offering" (153), for her mother, hoping the right scarf might cast a "spell against hurt, fear, aloneness; sorrow, illness, age and death and oblivion" (153). Like Reta, the girl is "triumphant," purchasing, with her eight dollars, a scarf that is a "work[] of art" (155) for her beautiful mother. However, the twists in this story multiply as the mother, fifty years later, at the age of eighty-three, has lost much of her memory; she forgets who has given her the scarf and whether she ever wore it. A second misrecognition involving the gift is highlighted when the narrator, as an adult, becomes aware that she has failed to recognize the generosity of the gruff, condescending store clerk who had "practically given away an expensive scarf" to the girl, likely "making up the difference out of her own pocket" (157). This mysterious other woman, like Gwen in "A Scarf," interrupts and expands the mother-daughter dyad, challenging the narrator's expectations about the gift. Both narrators are forced to look away from the "perfect" object and onto the more risky prospect of creating a "true gift," the term Lee Anne Fennell uses to define the "empathetic dialogue" surrounding gift giving that "can create or solidify a relationship of mutual identification and empathy" (99).

THE "PERFECT GIFT"

The first half of each story ends on a note of triumph as each shopper believes she has found the "perfect gift" (Oates 153). Various theorists of the gift have attempted to categorize such an entity; of these perhaps Russell W. Belk's "ideal" (76) most clearly helps to delineate each narrator's quest. Belk defines a "perfect gift" (76) as a "luxury" item attained through "extraordinary sacrifice" by the giver whose motive should be "solely to please the recipient" who, in turn, is "surprised" and "delighted" by the desired and "appropriate" (61) gift; Belk admits such a gift is "the rare exception rather than the rule" (69). The relationship between giver and recipient is crucial as the gift is "only a symbolic vehicle" (68): "intangible thoughts and feelings" take precedence "over the tangible object" (61), possibly consolidating mutual feelings of "agapic love" stemming from motives that are "unselfish, nonpossessive, and sacrificial" (60).

In Oates's story, the girl's "extraordinary sacrifice" "propel[s]" (153) her to hostile foreign territory, the "'better' womens' stores" (152), that she remembers, even fifty years later with a sense of "recoil" (153) and "a kind of instinctive physical chagrin" (153). Her diction suggests her sense of the risk and potential heroism involved as in her primal "fevered . . . eagerness" for the hunt she locates the holy grail in the "glittery glass display cases and racks" which contain objects she envisions as the "slain carcasses of animals" (153). Her adversary reveals herself in the form of a clerk whose "scratchy steel-wool bun," "smacking-red downturned mouth," and "cold, doubtful voice" (153) hint that she is a modern Medusa; in her "gaze" the girl stands "paralyzed" (154). At this moment, sensing that she is perceived as "an intruder, a trespasser," the girl confronts her "deepest wish" which "until that moment" remained "unknown" to her: to "steal" (154) the treasure. Instead, the girl "surrender[s]" all her "secretly hoarded money" in order "to make the transaction sacred" (153). The luxurious beauty of the scarves' "exquisite fabrics and designs" (155), indicate the success of the girl's sacrifice; they are as non-utilitarian as "those dreams of surpassing sweetness that, as we wake and yearn to draw them after us, break and disintegrate like strands of cobweb" (155). Indeed, it is the unexpected extravagance of the gift that succeeds in surprising the girl's mother who becomes "speechless . . . [a]s if words failed her" (157). While the extraordinary expense signalled by the "luxurious wrappings" accounts, in part, for the mother's "alarmed" (157) response as she is "rendered speechless" (Belk 68), this is also the "perfect" (Belk 68) reaction to signal her "surprise" and "delight" (Belk 61).

For Reta, in the excitement of her "mission" (Shields, "A Scarf" 16), the scarf transcends its commodity status and becomes "an idea" (17). Warming to her task, she fleshes out the particular form of perfection this "idea" should take: something "brilliant and subdued at the same time, finely made, but with a secure sense of its own shape" (17). But unlike the girl in Oates's story, Reta ironically undercuts her own hero narrative, noting with satiric understanding the illusory nature of such a quest: she writes: it "seemed to me that my daughter Norah's future happiness now balanced not on acceptance at Smith or the acquisition of a handsome new boyfriend, but on the simple ownership of a particular article of apparel, which only I could supply" (18). Reta is also more aware than the girl in Oates's story of the artful illusions created in the exclusive boutiques to whet shoppers' appetites for the "spare merchandise" that the "squadron" of saleswomen caress "in such a loving way" (16). And yet, simultaneously, Reta holds on to the hope that she "could provide something temporary and necessary: this dream of transformation" (18) and when she finally finds "it," she is moved by its extravagant beauty, "its shimmer dazzling and its touch icy and sensuous" (18). The transformation from mere commodity to perfect gift is signalled by Reta's own reaction to the disproportion between her pleasure and the "price" of the scarf: "Sixty dollars. Was that all?" (18). While the search may involve less "sacrifice" for Reta than it does for the girl, their goals are similar: to nurture and possibly to re-define their relationships through the "symbolic vehicle" of such "extraordinary" and "desired" gifts.

THE GIFT

There is no doubt that each shopper attains feelings of pleasure that seem personally transformative: the girl in Oates's story believes that her purchase transports her into a world of "enchantment" (155) and Reta feels, briefly, like a magician who can "procure" (17) a "dream of transformation" (18). Such feelings of transformation and enchantment suggest that it is the givers themselves who accrue the rewards and power from giving. Indeed, numerous theorists of the gift express suspicion about the existence of a pure, disinterested generosity. As Mark Osteen states in his extensive summary of gift theorists, many have tended towards the "conclusion that giving gifts involves bad faith, that we lie to ourselves by choosing to ignore or forget our calculation of self-interest" and that "the pleasure we gain in giving gifts is just self-gratification" (16). Marcel Mauss, in his hugely influential 1950 text *The Gift: The Form and Reason for Exchange in Archaic Societies*, writes that the "generously given" gift is a "polite fiction" since it is only "apparently free and disinterested," being, in fact, "constrained and self-interested" since it must be "obligatorily reciprocated" (4). Not surprisingly, when the gift is viewed as part of such a closed trajectory, the obligatory social bonds impose a loss of personal freedom that Ralph Waldo Emerson's early, oft-quoted essay "Gifts" emphasizes as a threat of "inva[sion]" to the "self-sustained" existence that leaves "degrading dependence" in its wake; for this, Emerson writes, "[w]e do not quite forgive a giver" (26). Pierre Bourdieu's discussions of the "social," "symbolic," and "cultural capital" attained through giving detail how one "possesses by giving," since

> there are only two ways of getting and keeping a lasting hold over someone: debts and gifts, the overtly economic obligations imposed by the usurer, or the moral obligations and emotional attachments created and maintained by the generous gift, in short, overt violence or symbolic violence, censored, euphemized, that is, misrecognizable, recognized violence" ("Selections" 217).

Not surprisingly for Bourdieu and many other theorists, the "major characteristic of the experience of the gift is, without doubt, its ambiguity" ("Marginalia" 231).

There are hints of ambiguity in the "magic" and power each shopper feels upon procuring the "perfect gift." Reta admits that her discovery of the stark pleasure of "pleas[ing] someone fully," includes pleasing "even one's self" (18), suggesting the "self-gratification" (Osteen 16) involved. Also, in Reta's "idea" that the scarf must embody a feminine presence that communicates "[s]olidity . . . but in sinuous, ephemeral form" (17), we might see a remedy to her own concerns about female invisibility, ones that are more fully explicated in the novel *Unless*; this might signal that her gift involves a projection her own desires onto her daughter, a subtle form of control or a possible misreading. And finally, the sense of power she feels when she "procure[s]" (17) the scarf, might be designed to revive her fading maternal influence as her daughter leaves the nest. In Oates's story there are hints of narcissism in the girl's romantic heroism as she fantasizes about bringing a holy grail to her "pretty" (153) mother whom she imagines as a damsel in (future) distress. Other suggestions that undermine notions of simple altruism stem from each shopper's awareness that she is already entangled in a circle of gift exchange. Each is conscious of giving back. The girl gives back to the woman to whom, even at the age of eleven, "in weak moments [she'd] hear [her] voice cry Mommy" (152). Reta believes that a perfect scarf "was what Norah at seventeen, almost eighteen, was owed" (Shields, "The Scarf" 17; my emphasis) in exchange for her "bravely undemanding" (17) childhood: this was a gift to her parents to spare them from her childhood fears, as their "brave little soldier daughter, shap[ed] her soldierly life" (17).

And yet, despite Shields's use of the word "owed," there is little sense that it is either obligation or self-interest, principally, that motivates each giver. In these stories the pleasure of giving seems more clearly tied to a desire to nurture the recipient and the relationship. Both stories depict mother-daughter relationships in transition, the gifts marking two rites of passage: the eleven-year-old narrator on the cusp of puberty and greater independence, Norah leaving home and going to college. Against conventional models of separate, autonomous subjects, the narrators are attempting to form bridges to renewed forms of intimacy within an evolving emotional interdependence. To each giver the gift seems to promise not power over the other, but, potentially, mutual empowerment. The beautiful scarf that signals "[s]olidity . . . but in sinuous, ephemeral form" (17) to Reta is associated with a subjectivity that Reta wants Norah to inhabit; in *Unless* she explicitly desires such feminine potency for her other female intimates, as well as for herself. Similarly, the emotional weight Oates's girl attaches to her quest suggests a desire for greater equality with her mother, one that might lead to a sense of complicity between them: her pleasure stems from the anticipation of her mother's "warm whispery voice, as if this were a secret between" them saying, "'Oh honey, what have you done ---!'" (153). In *The Gift: Imagination and the Erotic Life of Property*, Lewis Hyde questions the notion that "ties of affection" must be experienced as "bondage": "[w]hen gift exchange achieves a convivial communion of spirits, there is no call for liberty; it is only when our attachments become moribund that we long to break them" (70). In each story, the transition into greater independence is balanced by a desire to remake, not to shatter, the parent-child bond, at least on the part of each giver.

Admittedly, arguments about mutuality are problematic in both stories since we receive only the givers' perspectives; thus discussion of the gift as a form of conversation must remain inconclusive. But it is, nevertheless, important to account for each giver's orientation towards the other; in these two stories this orientation calls for a theory, and thus a terminology, that moves beyond determinations of "self-interest" *versus* "self-sacrifice," or "self-transcenden[ce]," a term used by Belk to suggest how "the other's well-being" becomes "*more* important" (64; my emphasis) than the giver's. As Antonio Callari argues, "selfishness and generosity are . . . but two sides of the same coin" since "self-interest is about getting the goods for oneself, altruism is about the goods of another, but the construction remains entirely about the goods" (254). Rather than a "calculable generosity," Callari argues for a "more general, more open, alterity" (254). Such openness comes about, these stories suggest, when the rational, stable, autonomous self is deconstructed through gift giving that forms a rather precarious dialogue, one that "permits individuals to lose their autonomy to a ritual or activity that nobody can entirely control" (Osteen 26).

One important deconstruction of the autonomous subject of Mauss and Emerson is found in the "open, extravagant subjectivity" (164) posited by Hélène Cixous in her essay "Sorties." "Sorties" describes an "economy of femininity" (164) that forms the liberating "escape" from the masculine economy of "loss" and "expropriation" (152): it is the "masculine" interpretation of the gift that, according to Cixous, "always turns the gift into a gift-that-takes" (158). Though Cixous includes male participation in her "economy of femininity," she simultaneously argues that it is "a woman's instinctual economy" (154) that tends to be free of the masculine economy of "loss" since, "[i]f there is a self proper to woman, paradoxically it is her capacity to depropriate herself without self-interest" (159). Against dominant models of reciprocity and exchange, Cixous posits giving as an abundant, renewable sources of power, a "feminine energy" (163) that does not "calculate its influence" (164), its power or hold *over* another. Thus, for Cixous, the "extravagant subject" does not "take" in giving to the recipient, but, rather, endangers the kind of autonomous self that would find any debt to or dependence upon the other to be, as Emerson suggests it is, "degrading" (26).

More recently, theorists such as David Cheal and Aafke E. Komter have focused a sociological lens on personal gift giving in contemporary Western societies; without reference to Cixous's "economy of femininity," they explore a specifically female economy, since, as Cheal states, much evidence exists that "women are more active in all forms of [private] gift giving than are men" (*Gift Economy* 6). Komter and others are less sanguine than Cixous about the empowerment attained through female giving. In contrast to Cixous's affirmation of the "extravagant" female subject, Komter argues in "Women, Gifts and Power" that "women's supposedly greater altruism is an improbable explanation" (121), as well as an overly "simple and superficial" (120) one, for women's tendency to give more gifts than men. Komter sees a "paradoxical tension" in the "fact that women in western society are the greatest givers," a point which cannot be disentangled from, on the one hand, their more vulnerable societal and economic position compared with men and, on the other, from the power they are invested with by being society's prime intermediaries in creating and recreating social relationships by means of gift giving. (129)

She concludes that the central problem with gendered "asymmetries" in "[i]nformal gift exchange," though such an economy "may certainly be an important supplement to formal market exchange by men," is that it is "not equal" to the formal economy in terms of the "type and amount of power" (128) it bestows. To Komter, then, the significance of private exchange remains marginal other than in the "pleasure" (129) it gives to its participants. Significantly, Komter fears that women's belief that they are "actually obliged" to give is a sacrificial view equated with a loss of self: she writes, "giving in extreme amounts and with extreme intensity is . . . not psychologically healthy because of the risk of losing one's self" (129). Thus, she expresses the reverse side of Emerson's anxiety about the "degrading dependence" visited upon the recipient of the gift; for Komter it is women, who, "as a consequence of giving abundantly . . . fac[e] the threat of undermining their own autonomy," unlike men whose "greater societal and economic power . . . protects them from losing their own autonomy through giving gifts to other people" (131).

Unlike Komter, for Cixous the reward of giving lies not in acquiring "greater societal and economic power" (Komter 131), but in what she considers to be the significant rather than marginal rewards of "pleasure, happiness" and "enhanced self-image" (Cixous 159) that accompany giving; and though she is not concerned with "altruism," she does acknowledge that "[r]eally, there is no 'free' gift" since everyone "gives *for*" (159). Legal scholar Lee Anne Fennell's nuanced and useful essay, "Unpacking the Gift: Illiquid Goods and Empathetic Dialogue" shares some of Cixous's beliefs about the "return" attained through giving, including in her "broad definition of what counts as a return" such things as "appreciation, gratitude, affection, loyalty, love, respect, power, status, understanding or simply the knowledge that she has pleased another person" (87). Referring neither to the "economy of femininity" nor to the "female economy," Fennell suggests that with personal gifts between intimates, the "real exchange is taking place in the realm of the emotions" (89). Fennell's primary concern is not with "altruism," or the ways that gift transactions support a "moral economy" and the "maintenance of balanced relationships" (Cheal, *Gift Economy* 15), or on the question of whose "well-being is truly more important" (Belk 64); rather she focuses on the precise ways these transactions are "recognized," dialogically.

Her theory of the "empathetic dialogue," formed through giving that is responsive to the other, is Fennell's valuable contribution to gift scholarship and forms part of a "new vocabulary" (85) that moves away from a recurrent focus on reciprocal obligations, or the binary of altruism and self-interest, areas that she feels have already been given "tremendous scholarly emphasis" (85). The notion of "empathetic dialogue," she writes, "taps into certain desires that are rarely discussed by scholars: the desire to identify with another; the desire to have one's true preferences divined by another . . . ; the desire to surprise and to be surprised (86). The latter is not trivial, since "the desire to surprise and to be surprised arises out of this deeper desire to know and to be known by another" (94). A "good gift," then, functions "like an act of recognition, in which the donor makes her knowledge of the recipient known to the recipient, who in turn may come to recognize something new about herself, or the donor, or the relationship" (94). In "the idealized gift situation" (86), an "empathetic mutual identification" (94) "add[s] richness and depth" (90) to both giver's and receiver's knowledge of self and other and their dialogically "evolving identit[ies]" (94). She rejects comparisons with models of market exchange since it does not make "sense to think of people 'trading' emotions with each other in a market-oriented manner" (89); for Fennell gift giving takes two participants committed to "cumbersome and wasteful exchange transaction[s]" (85) whose value lies not in their market worth, or even their social or symbolic capital, but in the "specialized form of communication" (86) they engender.

The word "recognition" requires glossing. Fennell's use of the term to suggest a responsive *reading* of another person's desires diverges from several interpretations of the word that Megan Watkins helpfully summarizes in her essay "Desiring Recognition, Accumulating Affect." Watkins cites Bourdieu's belief that "recognition" is "a form of 'symbolic dependence,' 'an egoistic quest' for the approval of others" that "'enables forms of domination which imply dependence on those who can be dominated by it'" (272). Bourdieu's understanding of "recognition" as "acclaim" (*OERD*, 2nd ed.), then, is tied to public achievement, (what Reta refers to as "greatness" in *Unless*). Watkins as well as Fennell, in contrast, view recognition as a "steady . . . gift[] of acknowledgement" (Shields, *Unless* 44), acknowledgement that "requires considerable insight into the dynamics of the [other's] evolving identity" (Fennell 94). Focusing on "interpersonal relations" rather than "social reproduction" (275), Watkins notes a beneficial "mutuality" (273), not necessarily "an equal one," within "recognition[s] of worth by both parties with this intersubjective acknowledgment being integral to their sense of self" (273). It is interesting in this regard that in *Unless* Reta Winters repeats to herself the phrase "'[w]e are real only in our moments of recognition'" (127), suggesting, as does Fennell, that an "evolving identity" (Fennell 94) is moulded and remoulded through a dialogical process with intimates, rather than through "forms of domination" by the powerful, as Bourdieu suggests (Watkins 273). Indeed, Watkins affirms that the "affects" of recognition "accumulate over time," potentially creating "an affective force" (273) which in the mother-child relationship constitutes a "dialogic play" or, as Jessica Benjamin describes it, "'a dance of interaction'" in which "the desire for recognition is not one-sided; it is mutual" (Watkins 277).

Watkins's investigations into recognitions within the parent-child bond are germane to both "scarf" stories and contribute to alternative models of gift theory. Several theorists define the gift through models of parent-child bonds rather than commodity exchange: Cixous validates mothering through the "metaphor of bringing into the world" the "not-me within me" (162). Cheal uses the evidence of the "generosity of most parents," male and female, to demonstrate the "importance of empathy," as a way of resisting the ubiquitous image of autonomous consumers in the exchange economy; the latter represents, to Cheal, "a male bias towards competitive interaction" that assumes that "individuals are fundamentally separate and purely concerned with their own interests" (*Gift Economy* 8). Genevieve Vaughan has argued that in twentieth-century theories of the gift "its connection with mothering has rarely been made" (7); Vaughan notes that "the fear of essentialism has thrown the mother out with the bathwater for many feminists" and argues that we "need to consider mothering/gift giving as basic economic logic and process, not an essence, for all humans" (8), male and female, parents and non-parents alike. This wider social lens on gift giving, and "recognition" of the other, like Fennell's theory, perceives that "the logic of gift giving is also the logic of communication" (Vaughan 20).

While Fennell does not pose gift giving as an alternative to "basic economic logic and process," she does account for the potential challenges to the stable, autonomous "self" within this "specialized form of communication" (86), never suggesting that personal gift giving is a limited or "marginal" alternative to the "real" market economy. But, unlike Cixous, Fennell offers no assurance that such gifts necessarily bring social empowerment, "pleasure, happiness" or "enhanced self-image" (Cixous 159), or even an affirmation of one's desires. In fact, Fennell details some trenchant examples of gifts that fail because of "lack of empathetic imagination" or "imaginative exercises inappropriate to the relationship" (86). And while at times she suggests empathetic dialogue may help the formation of "stable relationships" (99), her emphasis stays on the "unwritten" nature and often unanticipated effects of "rules" (85) that are based on one person's capricious, conjectural reading of another's intimate signals. This notion of risk, and the possibility of failure, speaks to the heart of giving in both scarf stories.

A "TRUE GIFT"

By destabilizing the trajectory of the gift itself within each narrative, the stories prefigure the potentially destabilizing nature of giving and receiving on the identities of the mothers and daughters. Each giver initially intends to give a "true gift," one that "engages both giver and receiver in empathetic mutual identification" (Fennell 94), but learns that this undertaking is more fraught, more complex, and more open to chance than she predicts. Despite a momentary sense of triumph, the giver's fantasy of the "perfect gift" exposes her own vulnerabilities. Thus, while attempting to shore up the vulnerabilities of her loved one with "feats of shopping perfection" (Shields, "A Scarf" 18), the shoppers, paradoxically, experience feelings of unworthiness and shame. The girl in Oates's story feels like an imposter while shopping in the "'better' women's stores" (152). She believes the salesclerks are suspicious that she has come to steal and she introjects their view of her; in this shifted internalized perspective, she suddenly sees that her "dark hair was suspiciously curly-kinky like moist wires" and she, "a poor girl, an ungainly girl, a shy girl," might suddenly "therefore" appear to be "a dishonest girl, a sneaky little shoplifter," and, indeed, in her imagination she suddenly becomes one of a "sprawling family" of "gypsies" with her "soiled skin, shifty eyes, and run-down rubber boots" (154). While it is really age and economics that marginalize her in these stores, her imagination can only conjure images of a racial "other." Certainly, the effects of this unexpected view of herself include physical and psychological symptoms, as her "face pounded with blood as if [she]'d been turned upside-down" (153-54); in this vulnerable position she identifies her feelings of "hurt and resentment" and "shame" (154).

In Shields's story Reta's shame can be discerned through her recurring anxieties about ill-proportion in the story that are associated with both her gift and her writing; it is interesting to note the preponderance of diction used to measure value in terms of "weight" or relative amount. Just as she comes to lament that the scarf, "half an ounce of silk, maybe less, floating free in the world," doesn't "amount" (24) to much in the end, so is Reta upset, and yet in some agreement, with critics of her "slim novel" who accuse it of lacking "weight" (9): she admits "that there was something just a little bit *darling*" (10) about her book. Reta's fear about her own triviality extends to the huge writer's suite that seems out of proportion to her writerly ego and reinforces the imposter syndrome she experiences at her book signing where she feels the "impulse . . . to apologize" for being "*overly* ebullient with the book buyers, *too* chatty" (14; my emphasis), and for being too old, insufficiently dressed, and possibly malodorous. She feels, in short, "ashamed" (14) and thus unable to comfortably extend her intended generosity towards her readers. The idea that she buys an extravagant gift to compensate for her own lack, or against her underlying anxieties, distances her from Cixous's "extravagant subjectivity" (164) as the spectre of shame haunts her fears and dreams. And yet in both stories the contradictions contained in the shoppers' impulses towards honouring and nurturing their loved ones and their own feelings of lack do not simply cancel each other out, even though they are intimately connected. Instead, the initial attempt to purchase a perfect "talisman" must be relinquished or mediated through the presence of an unforeseeable, seemingly capricious encounter with another woman that helps to uncover the complexities of the "empathetic mutual identification" contained in a "true gift" (Fennell 94).

Significantly, both Oates and Shields pose an intermediary as a "destabilizing tremor" (Callari 250) that expands the mother-daughter dyad; this is exactly the way gifts must circulate, according to Hyde, since an exchange between two people "soon goes stale" (17) and a gift circle "needs at least three points" (16). The responsiveness or "recognitions" of the "other" woman help each narrator to see, as Osteen argues, that "gift practices do not follow rules; they seep outside of our categories . . . like games, or a form of social theater in which shifting relationship are dramatized, created, dissolved" (25). In Oates's story it is a stranger, the salesclerk, who causes the narrator to more fully "comprehend[]the nature of the gift" (157) by performing an "utterly mysterious transaction, one of those unfathomable and incalculable events that mark at rare intervals the inner curve of our lives" (155). We don't find out why this unlikely fairy godmother, with her "thin, graying brown [hair] caught in an angry-looking bun, her face . . . heavily made up yet not pretty, her bright lipstick-mouth downturned" (156), becomes silently complicit with the girl, helping her purchase the scarf; as an adult, the narrator muses that the clerk may have been moved by "simple pity" or the possibility that "she felt in the air the tremor and heat of my blood" (155). The latter suggests that the clerk's sensitivity to the girl's desire may have sparked an unspoken "empathetic dialogue" between them. Evidence in the story supports the idea that, beneath her gruff, contemptuous façade, the clerk becomes attuned to the girl as her "weak voice" (154) and the "heat of [her] blood" form visceral signs that prompt the clerk "to consider" the girl "as if for the first time" (155). By considering these signs she manages to deduce the importance of the scarf to the girl and responds empathetically. The clerk's responsiveness instantly overturns the girl's earlier reactions. As the clerk is transformed in the girl's mind from outsider to insider, the "ill luck" (154) she feels at the clerk's "fiercely concentrate[d] . . . attention" when she enters the shop becomes her good luck; in her imagination she transforms from an "intruder" (154) to an unacknowledged "child-relative" (156) of the clerk. The clerk masks her gift, frowning and speaking "with an edge of adult annoyance" (155), yet she gives what many critics would consider to be the "perfect," that is a free, spontaneous, and unconstraining, gift. The "grace" of this act implies that, in some ways, the clerk is, indeed, "the proper authority, to render the [gift] transaction valid" (153).

The clerk's unexpected generosity seems to have a ripple effect, but only many years afterward, when the grown narrator is able to appreciate her "gratuitous" (155) generosity. Fifty years later the girl's "talisman against harm" (153) has failed in its "mission" (153); rather than being worn protectively around the mother's neck, it sits at "the bottom of a drawer" (156). The mother suffers sad losses, of her husband and her memory, her "life grown mysterious to her as a dream that continues ceaselessly without defining itself" (156). Forgetting the origin of the gift, believing that this "favorite scarf," "too pretty to wear, and too thin" (157), had been a present from her late husband, the mother "re-gifts" the scarf to her daughter. To the narrator, as the title of Oates's short story collection suggests, her mother seems "faithless" to the spirit of her gift. Seemingly the scarf no longer "stands as a place marker for the empathetic dialogue that accompanied it" (Fennell 95) despite the daughter's continued attachment to her gift: seeing it again, fifty years later, she "can't speak" and goes "entirely numb" (157). If the job of the gift in empathetic dialogue is to "facilitat[e] and document[] each party's imaginative participation in the life of the other" (Fennell 93) we can see how poignant the loss of the mother's memory is for her daughter. In mourning the loss of her mother's recognition of her love token, the adult daughter indicates her ongoing investment in their emotional interdependence. And Fennell's view that the "work of the gift may be accomplished only years or decades later" even, possibly "after all opportunity to continue a dialogue with the original giver [or recipient] has been lost" (96), seems to be perilously close to the mark in this story. Significantly, it is directly after the mother re-gifts the scarf to her daughter, with an offer "[s]omewhere between a plea and a command" (157), that the daughter recalls the gift of the salesclerk; as an adult she rebukes herself because as "a reputedly clever girl of eleven," she "hadn't comprehended the nature of the gift" (157). She simultaneously recalls her mother's "subtle sense of tact" in not "rude[ly]" (157) asking her daughter how she, a young girl, could afford such an extravagant gift. Only at this moment, then, does the narrator understand both women's complicity with and responsiveness to her desires; at this point she becomes fully initiated into the language of the gift as empathetic dialogue.

This belated, destabilizing understanding of the gift prompts her to quietly become complicit with her mother's complex needs expressed through her gift of the scarf. She discerns that her mother "has come to an age when she knows exactly what she wants and what she doesn't want, what she needs and doesn't need" (158) and she divines her mother's method for keeping panic about her encroaching dementia at bay by avoiding the "rude interruption of lucidity" (156). Ironically, or appropriately, by accepting her mother's gift of the scarf, the narrator returns a "true gift" to her mother. Her action suggests that their empathetic dialogue is not irremediably broken by the mother's memory loss; the conversation adapts to the "evolving identity" (Fennell 94) of each woman as it "deepen[s] and sustain[s]" (Fennell 86) their relationship. The narrator divines the "secret meaning," the impenetrable nature of her mother's "gift-giving" (156) as this second (or third) manifestation of the gift becomes more truly empathetic on the girl's part, less about her need and more a response to her mother's desires. By accepting her mother's lack of "lucidity," the narrator, like the salesclerk, divines the unspoken, and accepts the mysterious, incalculable "nature of the gift."

Conversely, the mother's gift of the scarf could be seen as a "gift-that-takes," one that selfishly foists the "encumbrances of life" (158) onto the unwilling daughter. To some extent the mother's need does seem to erase some equality within their "imaginative participation" in each other's lives, just as the young girl's needs did earlier in the story. Nevertheless, the context of the ending suggests another reading of the mother's actions, one that hints at her continued investment in their empathetic dialogue. By passing the scarf back to the daughter, ironically, the mother does save it from falling into the "bottomless ravine" into which so much has been "lost" (156); she converts it into what Annette Weiner would label an "inalienable possession," a family heirloom, or "transcendent treasure[] to be guarded against all the exigencies that might force [its] loss" (Weiner 33). The story ends with a mirror image of the daughter's original vision of the protective and enhancing role of the talismanic scarf, with the mother "lightly tying . . . then untying" the ends of the scarf on the daughter in front of the mirror, admiring how "beautiful" (158) the scarf looks on her daughter. The "nature of the gift" here, again, is complex and elusive; it is as if by divesting herself of her treasures, the mother invests in her daughter's "beauty," or worth, while also affirming the "sacred" (153) nature of the daughter's original gift given to celebrate their bond; she does so even as she prepares them both for her death, their final separation.

Though this mother-daughter dialogue remains somewhat ambiguous, even less evidence of a mother-daughter dialogue appears at the end of Shields's story. Norah does not appear and Reta seems to lose faith in the promise of "transformation," bitterly reflecting that the women in her life were not "going to get what [they] wanted" (24); "[w]e are," she thinks, "reaching out blindly with a grasping hand but not knowing how to ask for what we don't even know we want" (25). One wonders if Shields had indeed been reading Cixous, who writes in "Sorties," "[i]t is precisely because there is so little room for [women's] desire in society that, because of not knowing what to do with it, she ends up not knowing where to put it or if she even has it" (154). But, while "A Scarf" and much of *Unless* seem to share Cixous's concerns about the fate of female desire in masculine culture, Shields's reserved, ironic writing stands in opposition to Cixous's polemic, and her conclusions resist Cixous's confidence about the connection between power and female generosity.

In "A Scarf," Gwen's more radical feminist positions are set out in contrast to Reta's budding feminist consciousness. Gwen, a "writer-in-residence for a small women's college" ("A Scarf" 20) is working on a novel-in-progress that contains a "feminist structure" (20); her style is "off-centre and steers a random course" (22), a possible nod to Cixous's "écriture féminine," and a clear contrast to the popular, tidy-plotted "beginning, middle, and an ending" (11) that has won Reta her Offenden Prize. Gwen's writing is connected to her "feminine" clothing style; at lunch, Reta takes in Gwen's extravagant "salmon" pink "folds of unstitched, unstructured cloth, skirts and overskirts and capes and shawls" (21). But Gwen is a most unlikely Cixousian heroine, unable or unwilling to give freely and powerfully as an "open, extravagant" subject. Urgently trying to reclaim the lost feminine identity she gave away too freely in her marriage, she takes back her unmarried name and is "looking into a navel reconstruction" (21) to re-expose her "erased . . . primal mark" which she had surgically "closed" when "her husband complained that it smelled 'off,'" one of the many "sacrifices" (20) she made in the marriage. And while she may have given up *too much* of herself in trying to "satisfy . . . every demand" (20) of her ex-husband, Gwen seems quite adept at taking, inappropriately, from Reta. We learn that she had "used" the neophyte writer Reta's "whalebone" (20) image in a published short story without acknowledging this debt. Gwen had been the "informal but acknowledged leader" (19) in a group of fledgling writers who "offer[ed]" gifts of "tentative suggestions" as they "kindly encouraged each other" (19) and thus Reta feels "flattered" (20) by the compliment implied in Gwen's theft. But despite having surpassed Gwen in worldly recognition for her writing by the time they meet in this story, Reta continues to long for Gwen's approval; suddenly, at lunch with Gwen, Reta's desire for recognition from Gwen suddenly becomes "as strong as the need to urinate or swallow" (22). But she doesn't get it. Having earlier damned Reta's novel with faint praise, saying "it sounds like a hoot" (21), Gwen continues to be stingy, refusing to give Reta the praise she longs for.

Significantly, the intermediary in Shields's story, Gwen, is in some ways the reverse of the unaccountably generous salesclerk figure in Oates's story. While Gwen's refusal might indicate that she has moved beyond or is defying the "constellation of psychological tendencies to be self-sacrificing" (129) that Komter suggests restricts women's autonomy, what her refusal to satisfy Reta's desire primarily highlights in the story is their broken or non-existent empathetic dialogue. Indeed, the manoeuvres in their conversation resemble a well-established game, or standoff. Reta, for her part, is sometimes emotionally grudging about Gwen: she resists empathy and notes, with sadness, pity, or possibly contempt, Gwen's clothing and her "lumpy plastic bag" (21) purse. She also considers the ambiguous nature of Gwen's "gift" of navel surgery, performed, she imagines, either "to please or punish" (20) her husband. The two women's guardedness depicts a "system[] of reciprocities that [is] uncertain in form—appearing either as generosity or hostility, or an undecidable combination thereof" as Callari defines such an "economy," one that is "incompatible" (254) with the "hau" or spirit of the gift.

But something prompts Reta to move their exchange beyond this "system[] of reciprocities" when she decides to "offer" (23) a gift to Gwen, not the scarf itself, but a compelling narrative about it. This move may be motivated by simple generosity, but there are also hints of pity (she sees that Gwen "looked sad"; 23), of a need for affirmation (Reta "could tell [Gwen] was disappointed in [her] for some reason"; 23), and of a complicity that possibly originates in her identification with Gwen's affect of shame. Whatever the impulse, Reta moves past the feeling that Gwen owes her recognition and demonstrates "the gift's eroding effects on the very notion of borders" (Callari 256). Gwen's responsiveness to Reta's story, signalled by her "gratitude" (23) and her tears, punctuates her recognition of Reta's previously unarticulated insight into the art of giving, and despite her greater ironic detachment, Reta "almost crie[s]" herself when Gwen puts into words what the experience has meant to her, that "[f]inding it, it's almost like you made it. You invented it, created it out of your imagination" (24). Gwen's understanding of the significance of the potentially trivial, both the shopping "mission" and the beauty of the scarf itself, becomes her gift to Reta as she affirms Reta's desire as well as her creative artistry. Their shared understanding is the whisper of a "true gift," one that documents each woman's "imaginative participation in the life of the other" (Fennell 93): a gift can be art and so can conversation be both art and gift.

When Gwen subsequently pockets the scarf itself it is uncertain whether her act signals her continued sense of entitlement to Reta's creative acts or an oddly fitting acknowledgement of the "true" gift that passed between them. When Gwen says "[y]ou don't know what you've given me today" (24), Reta thinks to herself "[b]ut I did, I did" (24); Reta's words seem to indicate resignation and an expanded understanding of the costs of such "gifts." She remains silent on her decision to allow Gwen to keep Norah's "perfect" scarf, but something in the passage of the gift from her intended to an unintended recipient causes Reta to lose faith in its "talismanic" properties. Despite the fact that this tiny "half an ounce of silk" does make her friend perfectly happy, and that Reta is affirmed by Gwen's understanding of the gravitas of the potentially weightless, Reta receives their interaction as evidence that women are "so transparently in need of shoring up" (24), that "[n]ot one of us was going to get what we wanted" (24).

THE "GOOD GIFT" IN *UNLESS*

The momentary empathetic connection with Gwen, rather than empowering Reta, then, seems almost to unhinge Reta's sense of self and, in the novel that this story inspired, increase Reta's despair about the exclusions of women from the cultural and political centre. More hopefully than the short story, the novel ends with two small victories as Reta moves the question of female desire, its "uncoded otherness" (270), a little further from the margins. She prevails against the bullying editor of her novel-in-progress by allowing, against his advice, the heroine, not the hero, to "triumph" "in her own slightly capricious way" (317), and to remain the central figure of narrative desire; thus the question, "what does *she* want?" is allowed to predominate. Reta also resolves to write her own feminist novel, one that contains "stillness and power, sadness and resignation, contradictions and irrationality" (320). This sounds like the "nonclosure" Cixous advocates, an openness that cannot be identified as "passivity" or "submission," but rather as "confidence and comprehension . . . not an opportunity for destruction but for wonderful expansion" (158). Reta thus gives the gift of new narratives to her readers, making public her private dialogues and internal monologues.

These hard-won gifts are complicated by their somewhat uneasy relationship to Norah's unspoken assertions about the place and practice of "goodness," a relationship that bears some investigation within the context of the gift in empathetic dialogue. While both Reta and Norah desire to give to others, there is an apparent gulf between the "perfect," but commodified, scarf Reta had wished to place around her daughter's neck and the homemade sign Norah chooses to hang around her own. In the novel, Norah has decided, inexplicably to Reta, to sit "cross-legged with a begging bowl in her lap" wearing a sign printed with the word "GOODNESS" (11) on the street corner in Toronto where she attempted to save a stranger, a "Muslim woman" from an apparent act of "[s]elf-immolation" (117). Her "goodness" in reaching out to a stranger is sustained by her continued circulation of the gifts of money she receives each day as she donates "[n]ine-tenths" of them to "other street people" (11). Hyde refers to the "begging bowl of the Buddha" (23) that acknowledges "'the interdependence of all beings" and becomes "the vehicle of that fluidity which is abundance"; thus the "gift gathers there, and the mendicant gives it away again when he meets someone who is empty" (24). In Reta's growing feminist awareness, it is women who are "empty" and who need, as Wendy Roy states it, the world to "understand the self-blame and undeserved guilt that women such as Lois, Danielle, Reta, and Norah carry with them" (129). If, on various levels, *Unless* honors both the spirituality and the politics of Norah's generosity, "the condemning, grieving mother" (12) does not find it easy to affirm Norah's "malaise" (220), her word choice implying her confusion and alarm at Norah's actions.

It is tempting to conclude that Reta needs to learn from her daughter's broader understanding of the gift. Margaret Steffler, in her perceptive essay "A Human Conversation about Goodness: Carol Shields's *Unless*," seems to think that this is the case. She convincingly warns that Reta makes judgments about Norah's "submissive or despairing" acts" "from the 'norm' of the centre" (232), from which, despite her "puzzled concern about the isolation imposed on women," she fails to "consider her own acts of exclusion" (232). Thus, Reta's attempts to close the gap between herself and Norah amount only to attempts to "save" Norah through "a process that exploits, stereotypes, and erases the 'young Muslim woman'" (227). Alex Ramon, summarizing Rana Dasgupta's arguments, also concedes that what happens to Norah in *Unless* "may indeed be interpreted as a destructive encounter with an anonymous ethnic 'Other' who remains entirely objectified by the text" (172); Ramon, though, later argues that Dasgupta's reading "falters" by looking at the Muslim woman's "suicide in isolation" (172) and he notes the way the novel "mocks the notion of narrative 'closure,' undermining the neatness of the conclusion which the text itself has ostensibly provided" (173). Indeed, the lack of closure in Reta's arc of perception is important to her role as an "unreliable, because ignorant narrator" (Staels 127). And if we see her character as "dynamic," not only in the conventional sense of the term, but in her ability to simultaneously hold contrary views, then we must pay attention to the "labors" she devotes to understanding her daughter's transformation, suggesting that "we cannot receive the gift until we . . . submit ourselves to the labor of becoming like the gift" (Hyde 51). Norah's "gifts," her gentle, "undemanding" childhood, and her mysterious, embodied "goodness," seem to elicit perplexing feelings of obligation, inadequacy, impotence, and sometimes gratitude from Reta. Clearly, through most of the novel, Reta is uncertain about the meaning of Norah's gifts. Thus, as Nora Foster Stovel states, if she hopes "to discover her daughter she must follow her along the path to goodness," Reta "realizes she must work at it" (62).

The "groundwork" of Reta's "period of travail" (Hyde 50) consists primarily of reflecting on past events. She seems particularly haunted by her last real conversation with Norah when she panics and jumps to hasty certainties, failing to recognize Norah's needs and desires, a failure she repeats in some of her interpretations of Norah's later actions. But Reta belatedly realizes that during this pivotal conversation she "projected [her] own fears and panics onto Norah" (133) when, frightened by the change she noticed in her daughter and feeling "out of control," she finds herself "shouting into [Norah's] face," pushing her to submit to an authority, her father or "[s]omeone in the counseling area" (131). Allowing her own fears to dominate Norah's words, she destroys any chance of empathetic dialogue. After this, Norah "close[s] her eye against the light and against [Reta]" (127) and leaves "without saying goodbye" (133). Having failed in this opportunity for "recognition," Reta becomes a "dance anthropologist" (263), an apt metaphor as Reta must examine the traces of her now silent, motionless partner who speaks to her only once after this on the street corner, "in her own voice, but emptied of connection" (12). When Reta reconstructs their pivotal conversation she recalls Norah's non-verbal movements, the way Norah "made a grab for [Reta's] waistline . . . and hung on" (128). Despite Reta's failure to recognize Norah's form of communication, she does recall, with heartache, that her "thumb fit . . . perfectly" (128) on Norah's back and that her own "heartbeat" spoke loudly during these moments, "drilling straight through [her] calm speculations" (132). Not surprisingly Reta wishes for the one thing she can't have: "that moment back" (128), presumably to do over, more responsively to Norah's conversational offerings.

If responsive dialogue can be a gift, then blocking Norah's expression possibly precipitates the separation that Norah maintains; she tells Reta she "could not 'be' with" (12) her family. To the extent that Norah may be trying to break free of familial bonds, her "refusal of gifts" from her family indicates her "desire to cut off an unacceptable . . . empathetic dialogue" (Fennell 95). And, though she sits still, clearly Norah is in transition. But images of stagnation, of being "frozen," abound in the novel, illustrating, as Stovel outlines in her insightful analysis of Demeter-Persephone elements in *Unless*, that Reta "enters the winter of her discontent when her daughter goes underground" (58), Norah's disappearance "plunging" Reta's "world into winter" (57). In the novel it is the loss of conversation, a lifeline of their emotional interdependence, that is "killing" (13) the family. Reta feels as if they have "become actors in Norah's shadow play . . . turned wary, guarded, angered . . . each of [them] frozen to the bone and consigned to a place where nothing ever changes" (234). Reta's mother-in-law also becomes "silent" (234) and Reta becomes divided from herself, finding it "harder and harder to pronounce" (197) the pronoun "I." Interestingly, Steffler believes Norah exhibits a "fluidity of . . . identity," one that "initiates more liquid family dynamics that separate all of the family members from the complacency they had taken for granted" (238). While ultimately Norah's acts seem to encourage such fluidity, the destabilization she causes is first experienced by the family as immobility. Reta also sees this in Norah's "desperate" (132) embrace; she notices something "hard, fixed, chitinous" (127) in Norah's face that begins the "guessing game" (263) Reta plays since she can find no easy way to melt away the distance between herself and her daughter.

Reta's "game" of sifting and editing accessible narrative clues remains open-ended. In one instance, however, she seems to find confirmation that the changes in Norah stem from an indignation about women's "uncoded otherness" (270) that Reta shares; Norah's literature professor informs Reta that Norah had "one or two altercations" on the subject of Flaubert's act of "reduc[ing]" Madam Bovary "to a puff of romanticism" as she is "forced to surrender her place as the moral centre of the novel" (217). This information, however, does not fully resolve questions about the shared concerns of mother and daughter; it is up to readers to interpret such clues as well as gaps in the text. Stovel believes that Reta's reflection on women's "uncoded otherness" is so "vivid" because it "reflects the violence of her recognition of issues of gender and power inspired by Norah's loss" (64) and the women are joined through "the mother's quest for her daughter [that] leads to Reta's own discovery of the disempowerment of women under patriarchy" (70). Bethany Guenther also sees strong suggestions of an active dialogue transpiring through this "feminist connection between mother and daughter" (159); Guenther believes that Reta's subsequent rewriting of her own novel comes in "light of Norah's marginalization" and thus "it is all the more urgent that Reta keep Alicia as the centre of the her novel, if not to save Norah, then at least to begin to understand, and even combat, the powers that have forced her into self-exile" (160).

Not all critics agree that Reta connects with her silent daughter. Yet even Steffler, who believes Reta fails in her "attempt to understand, diagnose, and categorize Norah" (232), affirms one link between Reta's and Norah's quests; Steffler notes that, although the quality of goodness in some ways "proves its resilience" in the novel, it "is forced to manifest itself perversely in attitudes of self-sacrifice embodied by female characters," suggesting that "the goodness taken up by Norah . . . will continue to be disregarded because society valorizes measurable, tougher, and more masculine greatness" (240). Indeed, this mirrors Komter's concerns that unacknowledged, private female generosity will remain marginalized beside mainstream economic power, forming a "pre-scripted plot" according to Roy, that insists on women's "goodness, quietness, and above all sacrifice to others" (131). It is possible to see how Reta's newfound vigilance about feminine "goodness" to a certain extent complements and supports Norah's non-competitive, non-exclusionary "goodness." And yet, as Ramon suggests, "Reta's attempt to construct a feminist metanarrative to 'explain' Norah's withdrawal is not entirely supported by the text," since Reta herself "continually undermine[s]" her own "assertions" (171).

Yet, by "laboring" to resist closure, Reta remains open, at times, to re-connecting with Norah. As Hilde Staels argues, "Reta gradually realizes" that "[p]eople's isolation . . . is the result of a lack of proper communication, and, therefore, understanding of others" (128). The novel asks: what constitutes "proper communication"? How can Reta reach greater understanding of her daughter since "[w]ithout spoken words from Norah, nothing can be assumed" (Steffler 233)? "Proper communication" in *Unless*, I suggest, is linked to the "imaginative effort" expended in "discern[ing]" "the dynamics of the [other's] evolving identity" (Fennell 94). Conjecture is needed at times: while "assumptions" can be linked to the "arrogance" of "the act of . . . accepting without proof," "conjecture" can be defined as "a proposed reading" (*OERD*, 2nd ed.). In the end, Reta validates the "uncertainty principle" (318), not only in her new novel, but in all the diverse "readings" of Norah, including her own, accepting that her feminist interpretations do not offer a "total solution for Norah's actions" (Ramon 167). In her final summing up of the varied conjecture about Norah, all of which Reta believes may be "partly right and partly wrong" (310), she rests with the conclusion that "[w]e'll never know why" Norah chose to "register her existence," and her "tiny piping voice of goodness" (310), in the way she did. Significantly, she admits again here that "it is . . . probable that [she] was weighing [Norah] down with [her] own fears, [her] own growing perplexity concerning the world and its arrangements" (310). Reta thus arrives at a similar conclusion to the one Shields suggests in her insightful article "Women: Others," where she states that the way forward in the enterprise of knowing the other is through "gently probing," and "risking ourselves and our small truths . . . hoping to get it right at least part of the time" (T4). Reta's reward for risking her "truths" comes at the end as Norah begins "planning her way on a *conjectural* map" (320; my emphasis), a "map" that does not "assume" Norah can be located at any fixed point.

Staels suggests that Reta "creates and 'edits' a narrative about Norah" that "endows her own daughter with a narrative identity and misinterprets her behaviour" (127). While this is true at certain points in the novel, it is highly significant that Reta's continued "editing" remains responsive and open to revising a "narrative identity" that she admits may be "partly right and partly wrong" (*Unless* 310). Reta tries to become responsive to Norah by watching her daughter carefully, without, her as friends advise, attempting to "[u]se a little force," (213; though she does try this once), or "[a]rrang[ing] to have [Norah] kidnapped," and then "professionally deprogrammed" (213), or to write off Norah's actions as merely a stage she is going through. The psychiatrist Reta consults recommends "non-interference" (214) in Norah's process, something Reta has already, at least partly, come to understand from her failed attempt to rescue Norah during their last conversation. There are some suggestions that Reta learns to listen more perceptively to Norah; indeed responsive listening becomes a repeated motif at the end of the novel. Reta is amazed as Arthur Springer, her boorish, interrupting, sometimes comic, editor brings her mother-in-law out of her long silence simply by listening to her life story. Reta realizes that, in her own way, she needs to listen to Norah; to do so she must relinquish the heroic role she adopts when purchasing the scarf, imagining she is "procuring" *for* Norah a "dream of transformation." She needs to edit that script and adopt a position from which, despite the novel's warning epigraph, she can hear the "the roar which lies on the other side of" her daughter's "silence." Significantly, while sitting beside Norah's bedside, imagining her as Sleeping Beauty, Reta conflates two fairy tales and adopts the role, not of the rescuing prince, but of a domestic companion, one of several "curious dwarves" (301). The title of the final chapter, "Not Yet," indicates Reta's state of waiting and hoping for the full "'reunion of mother and daughter'" that Stovel cites as the "essential motif" (56) of the Demeter story. And although Norah does not speak but only makes "the shape of [the] word: 'Yes'" to her mother, Norah's body language, as she smiles and "cover[s]" Reta's "wrist with her roughened hand" (305), implies a desire for some degree of reconnection.

There is another important image of a "seated woman" purposefully watching and listening, the protagonist of Reta's new novel. Carol Shields has admitted that Reta's vision of her new protagonist as a figure from a "painting titled: *Seated Woman. Woman at Rest*" (319–20) could be interpreted as a "passive" image, but Shields argues that "it can also be very alert and engaged, and that's how [she] saw it: a woman seated but aware and listening (Wachtel 172). Reta's growing self-awareness and her desire to sit and listen suggest she may be ready to honour Norah's "otherness," an act that may bring them back into a renewed kind of "dialogic play" (Watkins 277). Like the narrator in Oates's story, Reta searches for "that moment of grace or surprise" (*Unless* 44) associated with the gifts given through empathetic dialogue. The psychiatrist suggests that Norah may be giving herself the "gift of freedom" (214). If this is true, Reta's eldest daughter offers the same kind of "gift" that the aging mother extends to her daughter at the end of Oates's story, one that is threatening to the recipient but necessary to nurture the evolution of their bond. In both scarf stories and in *Unless* each woman seems to recognize her debt to the other, a debt that produces not a "degrading dependence" (Emerson 26) but the possibility of a more vulnerable, destabilized "self" becoming open to the possibility of the dialogic nature of a "true" or a "good" gift.

Awareness of one's necessarily incomplete self-knowledge seems to be both a precondition for entering empathetic dialogue and a gift that flows from it. The narrators in both stories end up with expanded "recognitions" of self and other, unexpectedly, and at the expense of the heroic self that purchased the gift. They are not necessarily happier as the result of their new perceptions, but are, nonetheless, enriched through the empathetic dialogues with their "uncoded others" that emerge from such profound emotional transactions.

WORKS CITED

Belk, Russell W. "The Perfect Gift." In *Gift Giving: A Research Anthology,* ed. Cele Otnes and Richard F. Beltramini. Bowling Green, Ohio: Bowling Green State University Popular Press, 1996: 59–84. Print.

Bourdieu, Pierre. "Marginalia—Some Additional Notes on the Gift." In *The Logic of the Gift,* ed. Alan D. Schrift. New York: Routledge, 1997: 231–41. Print.

———. "Selections from *The Logic of Practice.*" In *The Logic of the Gift,* ed. Alan D. Schrift. New York: Routledge, 1997: 190–230. Print.

Callari, Antonio. "The Ghost of the Gift: The Unlikelihood of Economics." In *The Question of the Gift: Essays Across Disciplines,* ed. Mark Osteen. Routledge: London, 2002: 248–65. Print.

Cheal, David. *The Gift Economy.* London: Routledge, 1988. Print.

Cixous, Hélène. "Sorties: Out and Out: Attacks/Ways Out/Forays." In *The Logic of the Gift,* ed. Alan D. Schrift. New York: Routledge, 1997: 148–73. Print.

Emerson, Ralph Waldo. "Gifts." In *The Logic of the Gift,* ed. Alan D. Schrift. New York: Routledge, 1997: 25–27. Print.

Fennell, Lee Anne. "Unpacking the Gift: Illiquid Goods and Empathetic Dialogue." In *The Question of the Gift: Essays Across Disciplines,* ed. Mark Osteen. Routledge: London, 2002: 85–101. Print.

Guenther, Bethany. "Carol Shields and Simone de Beauvoir: Immanence, Transcendence, and Women's Work in *A Fairly Conventional Woman, The Stone Diaries,* and *Unless.*" *Studies in Canadian Literature* 35.1 (2010): 147–64. Print.

Hyde, Lewis. *The Gift: Imagination and the Erotic Life of Property.* New York: Vintage, 1979. Print.

Komter, Aafke E. "Women, Gifts and Power." In *The Gift: An Interdisciplinary Perspective,* ed. Aafke E. Komter. Amsterdam: Amsterdam University Press, 1996: 119–31. Print.

Mauss, Marcel. *The Gift: The Form and Reason for Exchange in Archaic Societies,* trans. W. D. Halls. 1990. London: Routledge, 2001. NetLibrary. Web. 29 Aug. 2012.

Oates, Joyce Carol. "The Scarf." In *Faithless: Tales of Transgression.* New York: Harper Collins, 2001: 152–57. Print.

Osteen, Mark. "Introduction: Questions of the Gift." In *The Question of the Gift: Essays Across Disciplines,* ed. Mark Osteen. Routledge: London, 2002: 1–41. Print.

Ramon, Alex. *Liminal Spaces: The Double Art of Carol Shields.* Newcastle upon Tyne: Cambridge Scholars, 2008. Print.

Roy, Wendy. "*Unless* the World Changes: Carol Shields on Women's Silencing in Contemporary Culture." In *Carol Shields: The Arts of a Writing Life,* ed. Neil K. Besner. Winnipeg: Prairie Fire Press, 2003: 125–32. Print.

Shields, Carol. "A Scarf." In *Dressing Up for the Carnival.* Toronto: Random House, 2000: 9–25. Print.

——. *Unless.* London: Fourth Estate, 2002. Print.

——. "Women: Others." In Women: Summer Madness Series. *The Guardian* 25 August 1997: G2, T4. Print.

Staels, Hilde. "Verbalisation of Loss in Carol Shields' *The Stone Diaries* and *Unless.*" *Zeitschrift für Kanada-Studien* 24.2 (2004): 118–31. Print.

Steffler, Margaret. "A Human Conversation about Goodness: Carol Shields's *Unless.*" *Studies in Canadian Literature* 34.2 (2009): 223–44. Print.

Stovel, Nora Foster. "'Because She's a Woman': Myth and Metafiction in Carol Shields's *Unless.*" *English Studies in Canada* 32.4 (2006): 51–73. Print.

Vaughan, Genevieve. "Introduction: A Radically Different Worldview Is Possible." In *Women and the Gift Economy: A Radically Different Worldview Is Possible,* ed. Genevieve Vaughan. Toronto: Inanna, 2007: 1–37. Print.

Wachtel, Eleanor. *Random Illuminations: Conversations With Carol Shields.* Fredericton, New Brunswick: Goose Lane, 2007. Print.

Watkins, Megan. "Desiring Recognition, Accumulating Affect." In *The Affect Theory Reader,* ed. Melissa Gregg and Gregory J. Seigworth. Durham: Duke University Press, 2010: 269–85. Print.

Weiner, Annette B. *Inalienable Possessions: The Paradox of Keeping-While-Giving.* Berkeley: University of California Press, 1992. Print.

Prepositional Domesticity

Aritha van Herk

Carol Shields claimed once, in my hearing, that she wasn't a very good cook. I registered the comment's wry self-deprecation, and immediately knew that she had performed one of those marvellously ironic sleights of hand that made her very talent both inconspicuous and adroit. She was not about to broadcast her abilities with *boeuf en daube,* how she had perfected exactly the dish that Mrs. Ramsey presides over in Virginia Woolf's *To the Lighthouse:* the "beef, the bay leaf, and the wine" (Woolf 80) combining into the "exquisite scent of olives and oil and juice" (Woolf 100) rising from the great brown pot that celebrates those gathered around the Ramsey table. No, that would have been too close to boasting, and so Carol Shields contended the opposite, a congruent position that would enable her to segue attention to the talent of someone other than herself. It was as if, like Jane Sexton, of the story "Segue," she was quietly admonishing herself to "Be plain. Be clear" (Shields, *Collected Stories* 1), even though her "despairing good cheer" (3) concealed, like Mrs. Ramsey, an inner sadness ineluctable as time.

Like their author, Carol Shields's fictions are deceptively transparent, performing transformational morphology with a touch so subtle that it eludes capture or description and is thus shelved as "quietly domestic" (an oxymoron of tremendous imprecision). Shields's narratives effect a deft alteration from what appears an unruffled surface to frequently disturbing consequence. That the writing achieves such sequelae almost invisibly is an indication of Shields's stylistic mastery, but also a measurement of linguistic dexterity so elegant as to be indiscernible. This brilliant execution is articulated by a prepositional disposition carved as intricately as silken petroglyphs. Unfastening some of those relational aesthetics and their particular character within the work of this Austenian successor—who nevertheless enunciated an entirely unique art—requires attention to the detail of temporal, spatial, and emotional linkage.

Carol Shields would not have laughed out loud at my deliberate calibration of her domestic skill with her literary prowess; she was too polite for dismissive response and never in my experience cruel, but she would have composed a properly grave and attentive face, silently warning me not to allow myself to get tangled up in the fishing nets of the esoteric or the academic. Even if she were bent double inside, "in stitches," she might say, at the pomposity of the comparison. From which might result a discussion of the word "sequelae" (a condition that is the consequence of a previous disease or injury as in *the long-term sequelae of infection)*, that antiseptic and distressingly clinical thread distracting the whole arrangement with its pathological insistence, its complicated complications. Leading to an exploration of examples: how neck pain is a common sequela of whiplash, and whether kidney disease is a sequela of diabetes, and that some medical conditions are diagnosed retrospectively, from their sequelae (the plural sounds even graver than the singular), like, for example, pleurisy. "The Pleurisy," Carol would repeat reflectively, "the way illnesses were announced with articles," and then she'd be off on one of those curious digressions that made spending even five minutes with her such pleasure—about Aunt Betts who had once been told she had pleurisy and ever after would avoid visits from her hated sisters by going to bed and claiming that "the pleurisy" had flared up, and she couldn't possibly be expected to offer them tea. And I would rejoinder with the story of how my mother had pleurisy, which went undiagnosed for too long and really did send her to bed, resulting in a strange winter when my sister and I were in charge of the house. "In charge of the house," Carol would echo, that line of duty and responsibility far less grand than it sounds and which in my doubtless fictionalized memory had mostly to do with washing sink after sink of dishes, or perhaps one long continuous sinkful of dishes that were never done and so seemed to last months. "But she recovered?" Yes, she recovered, and hated her pleurisy with a vocalized passion, and claimed for her recuperation a trip by transcontinental train, down east to visit her brother and his family because she hadn't seen him for fifteen years.

"She hadn't seen him for fifteen years. Were they estranged?"

"No, just far apart, one in Ontario and one in Alberta, and at that time without the means to undertake such a trip."

And so the conversation would develop—a real conversation, without barking questions or snide interventions, but an exchange, where two people who love language and its tantalizing digressions puzzle through the narrative lurking behind the frontage of information. A segue rather than an exposition or a colloquium, quite different from the situation of unsteady Fay in *The Republic of Love,* offering her investigations on mermaids to her colleagues at the National Centre for Folklore Studies. That scene, with its lectern and shifting audience, the way those who promulgate ideas balance on a version of gangplank, which becomes itself a preposition, springs to mind. Fay, "to give herself courage . . . jams her hands in the pockets of her new grey pleated skirt" (Shields, *Republic of Love* 288). Which would necessarily detour into the garmented arena of clothing: a grey pleated skirt with pockets? What fashion was that, capacious enough for both pleats and pockets now that we live in an era with barely room for the snuggest of snug knickers beneath either skirts or trousers? Carol would know, would be able to identify precisely the season and the year, because she was as aware of accessories as she was of recipes, while I can only grope vaguely, suggesting 1992 for pleated skirts; they recur as an item of clothing with Danielle Westerman in *Unless,* whom Reta visits once a week in her Rosedale apartment. "Her pleated grey skirt and cardigan are part of her daily uniform, as they have been for years. Where does she find such terrible cardigans?" wonders Reta (Shields *Unless* 181). Women who wear cardigans are either starchy and upright or craned into hunching, both postures gestures of anxiety. During her lecture on mermaids, Fay tries to remember to "hold [her] head straight and not to let it go into a weak sideways tilt" (Shields, *Republic* 288), as she has been advised by her friend Iris Jaffe. I can attest that women with glasses, without advice from anyone, become acutely aware of slumping, the demarcation of those who hover too long above a keyboard. As Fay might declare, "Ve-ry pro-found" (289). But Carol would not laugh at my observation that posture is a matter of flexion and so both prepositional and domestic.

Such rhizomes spread their inquiring and adventitious roots through any conversation with or reading of the work of Carol Shields. I confess that as a writer and a critic, I am besotted with, even consumed by, Carol Shields's extraordinary application of prepositions. Notice how this innocent-sounding sentence is replete with its own examples: "with" and "by" and "of." One might be tempted to think of prepositions as technical tools, part of the "adposition" family, grammatically distinct in their class. Or dismissively, to assume their innocence, as if they were bystanders to the work of narrative: the characters, the time, the unfolding tension of action and surprise. Prepositions serve as the delicate balance beams of meaning, pacing the space of relations, complementary but tricky for their idiomatic legerdemain. These are the words that get new speakers of English in trouble, that test and trap them. (Why do we hang pictures on a wall, while German speakers hang pictures at a wall?) In Shields's writing, prepositions are often camouflaged but beautifully stationed, admonitions to the intimacy shaping their insight. If one part of speech could be considered as belonging to Carol Shields particularly, it would be the preposition, its relational imperative, its sturdy utility, its steadfast linkage and connective tissue. Prepositions are the words tucked between the covers of Carol Shields's meticulous sentences, hospitable yet directive, but gently so, a guiding hand under an elbow rather than a rude shove in the direction of meaning and outcome. In the rub of relationship, the snag of affection and its fortuitous junctures, the surprising disruptions and *volte-face* that stalk those not expecting be sideswiped, the possibilities suggested by prepositions unfurl.

These governance relationals are most obviously foregrounded in Shields's final novel, determined to declare contingency with its title, *Unless*. There are those who will argue for "unless" as a conjunction, but it reads more powerfully as a preposition of late Middle Ages provenance, appearing somewhere around the early sixteenth century, full of doubt and anxiety, somewhat courtly, with its "except under the circumstances" or "except on the condition that" disclaimer, rather like an umbrella. Umbrellas too offer linkage in Shields's stories, most notably in "Collision," where two strangers from two entirely different worlds and without a shared language partake of a brief walk together under one umbrella, through pouring rain that erases "the futility of language" (Shields, *Collected* 330). "Dazed by a distortion of time and light," the two unite in their understanding of "how this round black umbrella gives an unasked-for refuge" (332) and connection. Carol and I discussed umbrellas, their role as accessories and sanctums, how they declare both style and security. I tell her about the one I lost two years ago and still hunt for in closets and corners of my house, certain it will turn up somewhere, an umbrella with the stained glass rose window of Chartres a perfect nylon membrane between me and the rain, but like all umbrellas, contingencies in case of inclement wetting, accompaniments to walking and errands. They can be fiercely incisive, standing in for rapiers and swords. Or temptations: I lost a few good, wooden-handled umbrellas at UBC's Faculty Club, because I trusted enough to slot my umbrella into the umbrella stand and expected to find it there when I was ready to leave again. Never suspecting that any large-bellied and unscrupulous professor would be capable of rummaging through that umbrella stand in search of the best, the sturdiest, and the most expensive portable roof to march off with, ready to declare surprise at his innocent mistake if an intrepid owner pursued him and accused him of stealing an umbrella not his own. Such mistakes are easy to make. There were either many umbrella thieves or one repeat offender, for I lost at least five expensive umbrellas at that faculty club perched on the cliffs above the long waters of English Bay. Until I wised up and, having come to the rather rude conclusion that academics are both parsimonious and thieves, began to buy cheap, disposable umbrellas. I am willing to wager that Malcolm Brownstone, he of the bald head and bearing the unwieldy title of "Recreation and Resort Consultant" (323) in "Collision," has not stolen his "folding umbrella, a marvel of hinged ribs and compacted nylon" (329) but has purchased it properly, with a platinum credit card, in a specialty shop that understood his need for a travel umbrella compact but not remotely flimsy. That is why he is allowed the serendipitous kilometer of rain-protected stroll between Hotel Turista and the People's Square with Marta Gjata. He has earned that refuge and memorable connection. Yes, umbrellas are prepositions, unless they insist on being parasols. Unless.

In *Unless*, Reta Winters measures the work of "unless" precisely. "*Unless* is the worry word of the English language. It flies like a moth around the ear, you hardly hear it, and yet everything depends on its breathy presences. Unless—that's the little subjunctive mineral you carry along in your pocket crease. It's always there, or else not there" (Shields, *Unless* 224). And then, as if to prove the very magic that prepositions possess, Reta adds one of those inimitable detours as a signal to herself, to the novel, and to the reader, that there is always more to be discovered in the interstices of suggestion. "(If you add a capital *s* to *unless,* you get *Sunless,* or *Sans Soleil,* a very odd Chris Marker film)" (224). French of course, the film from 1983 is considered "a meditation on the nature of human memory" which opens with a quote by Jean Racine: "L'Éloignement des pays répare en quelque sorte la trop grande proximité des temps" (The distance between countries compensates somewhat for the excessive closeness of time). In the English version of the film Marker replaced Racine with some lines from T. S. Eliot's *Ash Wednesday*:

> Because I know that time is always time
> And place is always and only place
> And what is actual is actual only for one time
> And only for one place (Eliot)

Shields does not introduce this reference innocently, occurring as it does in the very heart of Reta's argument with her preposition, which proceeds in its inimitably worried course.

> Unless you're lucky, unless you're healthy, fertile, unless you're loved and fed, unless you're clear about your sexual direction, unless you're offered what others are offered, you go down in the darkness, down to despair. *Unless* provides you with a trapdoor, a tunnel into the light, the reverse side of not enough. *Unless* keeps you from drowning in the presiding arrangements. (224–25)

First an exception, the opposite of hopeful, and then a life raft, a suggestion of transformation, a change in angle. Except for, shifted from gentle irregularity, away from deviation to lonely isolate. Which is further tracked to the distance between not countries, but languages. Reta thinks,

> Ironically, *unless,* the lever that finally shifts reality into a new perspective, cannot be expressed in French. *A moins que* doesn't have quite the heft; *sauf* is crude [and is closer, I would say to "except"]. *Unless* is a miracle of language and perception, Danielle Westerman says in her most recent essay, "The Shadow on the Mind." It makes us anxious, makes us cunning. Cunning like the wolves that crop up in the most thrilling fairy tales. But it gives us hope." (225)

This passage, reflective, troubled, piercing in its apprehension of loss and optimism, reflects Shields's brilliant capacity for ambivalence. One preposition and the entire eponymous novel is pivoted in a new direction, moved forward but sideways, with oblique delicacy, as if a tray had suddenly appeared under a silver pot or a hand conjured, with one gesture, an upside down and unknown world. Here is performed the prepositional disposition so integral to multiple and resplendent epiphanies that Carol Shields's writing sparks, those sudden showers of coruscation that can transpierce every dull expectation or simply froth with beauty, like wands of sparklers on a birthday cake.

And yet, impossible the task of pinning down Carol Shields's particular prepositions and their vocations, their guerrilla domesticity. Yes, these are the domestic parts of speech, doing the housework, arranging the furniture, dusting under the unmade beds. Building blocks and timetables, daily necessaries. I drive downtown in my car, but I fly to Ottawa on a plane. Why? Why, I want to ask, why do we do this? Deliberately place every object and human and yet make real connection between real people intransigent and heated or by contrast so cold and undemonstrative? Because we can, Danielle Westerman might say.

Westerman is the poet translated by Reta; it is she who declares translation a prepositional art: "Writing and translating are convivial, she said, not oppositional, and not at all hierarchical" (3). That is certainly one of the tasks of the preposition, to translate and decipher, to adapt the nouns and the pronouns and the phrases within a sentence to one another, to make them coordinate. They render a relationship entire.

Although Carol Shields's work repeatedly addresses the untranslatability of pivotal ineffabilities, coincidence and accident, mischance and serendipity, her use of translation as a key aspect of Reta's life in *Unless* is pointed, precise as scalpels. When she modestly lists her literary *oeuvre*, Reta tells us that her translation of the first volume of Danielle Westerman's *Pour Vivre*, which Reta interprets as *Alive*, "was slammed in the *Toronto Star* ('clumsy') by one Stanley Herald Howard, but Danielle Westerman said never mind, the man was *un maquereau*, which translates, crudely, as something between a pimp and a prick" (6), presumably the object of the preposition himself. Danielle's calm dismissal prepares the novel, if not Reta herself, for the wonderfully acerbic interview crouching toad-like in the chapter entitled "Once." Reta's summary of the conditional world that surrounds writing—reviewers and interviewers and book tours and book stores and "that nice Sheila person who does publicity" (29)—addresses the entire publishing world as preposition, connection necessary to sell and promote and make available the constructs that have so carefully been nourished. Reta does not come out and utter the implacable truth, but demonstrates her sense of how much the parasitic, sycophantic, and voyeuristic world of arts journalism freeloads on workers of the imagination. She is aware of the necessary exchange that "selling" a book entails: links must be made, a bargain concluded, machinery prepositioning one woman's creative work and the world that reads it.

The interview depicted in "Once," with a "young/youngish man [who] was the newly appointed books columnist at *Booktimes*" (31), is archetypal and hilarious, likely a stew of the many interviews that Carol Shields must have given over her literary life.

> He was well known for holding pious opinions about the literature of the Great North [capitalized], about his own role as advocate of a diverse new outpouring of Canadian voices, the post-colonial cry of blaming anguish. The stream of current fiction about middle-class people living in cities was diluting the authentic national voice that rose from the landscape itself and—
>
> Oh, shut up, shut up." (31–32)

Thinks Reta, and "up" is transformed into a preposition interruptive as well as directional. The interviewer asks her a series of careless and inappropriate questions as if he has forgotten that he is supposed to be interviewing Reta about Danielle Westerman's new book, instead slyly digging for personal information about Reta's astray daughter, and disclosing that he is of course working on a novel himself (the underbelly ambition of all interviewers is that they are desperate to be known as authors of books).

The utter lack of connection between Reta and her interlocutor is echoed in the text by the very few prepositions used in Reta's deposition of his voice.

> He had two young children at home, he said. Christ, what a responsibility, although he loved the little bastards. One of them was quite, quite gifted; well, they both were in their separate ways. But the work of raising kids! Never enough time to read the books he had to review, books all over the house with little markers in them, books he would never finish. So much was expected, and of course, like all journalists, he was underpaid.
>
> Oh, shut up. (33)

Clearly, Reta does not say this out loud. But within a novel that explores an economy of prepositions, Reta encounters one who should provide linkage but who does not care about his responsibility, which is to connect readers and writers. His printed summary of her is shabby by virtue of its innate belittlement, and deeply hurtful to Reta.

> And when I read in the paper tomorrow that "Mrs. Winters looked all of her forty-three years" and that "Mrs. Winters with her familiar overbite was reluctant to talk about her work schedule," I will want to phone the editor and complain bitterly. This from the pen of a small, unattractive man, almost entirely lipless beneath a bony, domineering nose, sweating with minor ambition, head tilted like something carved out of yellow wax. (30–31)

Reta has been subjected to the recreational cruelty of a preposition that wants to be a proper noun. But he is smaller than cruel; Reta is enraged because this terrier-like creature has no intention of writing a piece that will express relation, has not configured the work of explication and elucidation as being part of his job. He belongs to the school of disaffection and disgruntlement parading under a banner of ill-judged honesty rather than courtesy, his self-importance inflated, "pathetically in need of human attention, thinking his superior thoughts" (31), and determined to outreach his subjects by disparaging them.

Prepositionally tempted by this minor character, I find it impossible as a writer not to step into this situation, impossible to resist embellishing this customer, giving him a name, and then tracking his insignificant fame. I am delighted if not surprised to find that he is writing reviews of self-published books about credit card fraud and how to recycle plastic bottle caps, and that no novel under his name has appeared, which leads to speculation about whether he actually managed to write one, despite being able to blame book reviewing for swallowing up (ah, that lovely "up" again) his time. And I cannot resist going farther, furnishing him with a pair of difficult parents, a noted but not-very-famous poet father and a vaguely lunatic mother, in and out of lenient institutions—and no wonder, given the father's penchant for trivial sexual misdemeanours, the worst of which became his reputation for creeping his fingers up the thighs of women unluckily seated next to him at dinner parties. Young women, old women, middle-aged women, but not so far as was known men, or at least, no man confessed to having been the object of his strange and repast-located courting.

The father that I invent for this fictitious interviewer receives, for some reason, invitations to a good many dinner parties; he must be endowed with a facility for dazzling conversation, or else why would he be invited to dinner? Most women, politely horrified, and not wanting to upset the composure of a formal table or to offend their hosts, simply freeze and hope that he will stop his digital assault before he reaches their crotch area, although shifting and crossing their legs does not seem to deter him in the least, until one woman—a character for Carol Shields, oh yes, bold and unrepentant, with a lacrosse-player's strength and a bull-rider's determination—seizes the wrist of that cavilling hand and in a thrice, without giving the poet a chance to pull away, wrenches the same hand from under the crisply ironed linen cloth, jerks it captive past the edge of the table, and holds it triumphantly aloft, the poet squirming, his horn-rimmed glasses askew on his domineering nose (his son having inherited this feature honestly), while she announces, loudly and clearly, yet without excessive drama, "Look what I found!" That will be the end of that dinner party, the hostess dissolving in tears, the host grown red with puffy umbrage—it is not clear at whom—and insisting that everyone "have a scotch and calm down." The main course (a succulent *boeuf en daube*—for the hostess is a devotee of Virginia Woolf) goes unfinished, and dessert (pear flan after a recipe of medieval vintage) is never served, although the guests agree to coffee and brandy, as if needing some denouement to the excitement. It is thus no wonder that the interviewer conducts himself so shoddily, his constricted childhood marked by

Oedipal nervousness, the extraction of the self from prescribed lineage, a prepositional parent inescapable as breath. Although it is not clear whether this fictional arts journalist is aware of his father's fictional immoderations, and it is entirely unsporting of me to lumber him with such a parentage. But that is the effect of Carol Shields's prepositions. They invite expansion, conjecture, speculation, and most of all connection, that luxuriant gift.

Which is merely to demonstrate that all of Shields's work dances with alliance, unexpected and predictable, surprising and convincing. Carpers who grumble that these implausible synergies lack realism deny the potential of confrontational cause and effect, miss entirely Carol Shields's achievement, how her language does not merely describe but performs the very fibre that is its subject. Isolated events attach and hitchhike and adhere, nudge one another, bump noses and elbows in a manner that provokes unexpected juxtaposition, far more satisfying than forcing characters to perform specific roles in a preconditioned master narrative. This play of surprise is a facet of fiction that only the best of writers notice and utilize, and it performs as one of the novel's material threads, for Alicia and Roman, the characters in the novel that Reta herself is writing (a brilliant recursive strategy within *Unless*), surprise their author. Rather than forcing them to march to her diagram, Reta pays attention, becomes creative preposition for their unfolding— although she is well aware of the extent to which art cannot emulate life and life yearns to emulate art. She says, of *Thyme in Bloom*, "Everything is neatly wrapped up at the end. . . . I have bundled up each of the loose narrative strands, but what does such fastidiousness mean? It doesn't mean that all will be well for ever and ever, amen; it means that for five minutes a balance has been achieved at the margin of the novel's thin textual plane" (318). Reta believes that she has achieved such balance, a prepositional tripod between language and life, only for "the millionth part of a nanosecond" (318). "The uncertainty principle" (318) is always present, for Reta muses, a few pages earlier,

> A life is full of isolated events, but these events, if they are to form a coherent narrative, require odd pieces of language to cement them together, little chips of grammar (mostly adverbs or prepositions) that are hard to define, since they are abstractions of location or relative position, words like *therefore, else, other, also, thereof, theretofore, instead, otherwise, despite, already,* and *not yet.* (313)

Here is engaged the preposition "of": life full *of* events, odd pieces *of* language, chips *of* grammar, abstractions *of* location. "Of" serves the terrible duty of carrying Norah's protest. It is "of" that Reta assigns to watch over her daughter, who is "gone to goodness" (62). Instead of using what a flat-footed writer would, as for example, "Norah wanted to be good," or "Norah is being good," the verb "to be" too ubiquitous, Shields writes in Reta's voice, "My oldest daughter has gone off to live a life of virtue" (42), *"a life of goodness"* (42). The compact two-letter word "of" signals Reta's enormous pain and bewilderment; that modest "of" is the dangerous gap between one chasm and another, the fragile little rope bridge that connects life with its value. In trying to put out the woman on fire, Norah burns herself with a plastic dish rack, "its purchase evolved from some fleeting scrap of domestic encouragement" (315). "Of" becomes the disconnection that is neither safe nor domestic, the fissure that resounds with loneliness and doubt and unpredictability, for we can never be sure of where a preposition will place us as readers or where it will direct a story. There is no interpretation but to embrace this beautifully precise, carefully incised, writing. Every word is etched in such a way that it is enabled to perform brilliantly what is it meant to do. In short: its work.

Reta returns to "unless" as a writer's utensil, essential as a fork.

> The conjunction and (sometimes) adverb *unless,* with its elegiac undertones, is a term used in logic, a word breathed by the hopeful or by writers of fiction wanting to prise open the crusted world and reveal another plane of being, which is similar in its geographical particulars and peopled by those who resemble ourselves." (313–14)

Ah yes. Linkage again, between people, yearning to understand or at least make some gesture of common conviction, some gentle signal of charity and love.

Her dedicated readers surely talk to Carol Shields's ghost, tell her stories or imagine they can see the world through her eyes. They catch at unpredictable moments and repeat them, savour them like fine French macaroons. "Even the little pockets under his eyes were phlegmatic" (20), Reta writes about Colin, their friend whose wife, Marietta Glass, has left him and gone to Calgary, although she does return, doubtless because even Colin is more satisfactory than what she finds in Calgary (218). Who could ever forget the pockets under his eyes? Reta decides, when confronted with the terrible cupidity of voyeuristic journalists, that she is going to stop being polite and practise stern directness. "Rude and difficult people are more likely to be taken seriously" (30), she muses. "Curmudgeons are positively adored" (30). And yet, she cannot become someone she is not, and she is not rude. Instead, she is herself a preposition, a bridge between understanding and insight, a woman who relies on gentle lies to smooth the way and on comforting domestic rituals to furnish enlightenment. Which would be tedious were those etchings not leavened with surprising chips of information. "It is illegal to shake a dust mop out of a window in New York" (61). Was it? Is it still? And reading Reta's analysis of her cleaning—"wood and bone, plumbing and blood"—I yearn to call up Carol just to ask her if she knows it is illegal to hang laundry out of the windows above the streets in Barcelona, although it is done nevertheless, with sturdy defiance.

These are the treasures that wait to be discovered between the lines of Carol Shields's words. Reta mocks those writers who play "games for their own selfish amusement," "who put a doorway, say, or a chair in every chapter just to be baffling or obscure" (82). That is Carol's way of laughing at herself, for the chairs that she carefully placed in every chapter of one of her novels. Or the closed-off navel of Gwen, who has a plastic surgeon suture her belly-button because it smells "off" to her husband (Shields, *Collected* 414). You can suture your navel, that centre of the human body? And where did the husband get his sense of smell—how can a navel smell "off"? What smell would that be? Burnt toast, sour milk? "In France it's thought that menstruating women are incapable of making a good mayonnaise. No!" (Shields, *Unless* 120) Reta exclaims, but I want to continue the line of questioning. As opposed to bad mayonnaise, which isn't good for anyone anyway. And who makes mayonnaise? Only the French, or extreme chefs who scream at their sous-chefs. Tom's mother's list of one hundred desserts, "alphabetized in a recipe box, beginning with almond apples, moving to date pudding, on to nut brittle mousse (frozen) and ending with Zwieback pastry cheesecake" (296) syllable the novel. Where did Carol find these wistful recipes, and did she make them in a test fictional kitchen or are they invented? Or Reta's character Alicia "researching the history of women's handbags," how "it all began with the chatelaine of the medieval castle, the roving household manager needing something in which to carry her keys and her domestic accounts" (207). Now we carry saddlebags, enormous receptacles, and we are always fishing for the buzzing phone down at the bottom. How Reta holds "the phone in her left hand" and unloads the dishwasher with her right, "bashing the china about" (209), a satisfactorily punctuated disgruntlement. Reta's succinctly furious summation of how she wants women to "be allowed to be fully human" (221) in her letter to Dennis Ford-Helpern: "I think you have merely overlooked those who are routinely overlooked, that is to say half the world's population" (220). These beauty marks within Carol Shields's prose perform prepositional work, necessary and inevitable, but often overlooked. Despite their role as integral to the performance of meaning, the most revealing parts of speech diffident and even difficult in the way that language will play tricks on those who do not know it well. As well as, finally, their vermiculation, the power of their interruptive grace. Are Carol Shields's prepositions interruptions, or are they connectives? She tells the reader herself, through Reta, her recursive doppelgänger, explaining to her women friends, "'It's how the conversation goes, how it gets made, brick by brick, but with these little chipped-in bits of—'" (254) red curtains and sighs.

At least once a week, I catch myself wishing that I could dash off a note to Carol Shields, some connective aroused by a the strange texture of powdered sugar or a singular discovery that fills me with surprise. Today my note would read, "Dear Carol, In 1929 Northrop Frye went to Toronto to compete in a national typing contest sponsored by the Underwood Typewriter Company? Did you know that? He placed second! But my question is, was the competition based on speed or accuracy? Is that where the bush garden originated, on an old manual typewriter keyboard that Fryc was rattling over like an engine?"

I can hear her laughing.

And because Carol Shields has always already approached the question of the writer and her alphabet, I am reminded of the woman in the story "Absence," the woman who sits down to write and discovers that one of the letters on the keyboard is broken, "and, to make matters worse, a vowel, the very letter that attaches to the hungry self" (Shields, *Collected* 482). The writer in the story struggles to continue, but is thwarted by the missing vowel.

> Because the flabby but dependable gerund had dropped through language's trapdoor, gone. Whole parcels of grammar, for that matter, seemed all at once out of reach, and so were those bulky doorstop words that connect and announce and allow a sentence to pause for a moment and take on fresh loads of oxygen. Vocabulary, her well-loved garden, as broad and taken-for-granted as an acre of goldenrod, had shrunk to a square yard, and she was, as never before, forced to choose her words." (482–83)

She knows that she must persist, must make the connections required, and so she comes to embrace "the arabesque of the unfolded self" (485) its terrible beauty and astonishing domesticity, possessed by the preposition.

WORKS CITED

Eliot, Thomas Stearnes. *Ash Wednesday*. Web. 3 April 2013.

Racine, Jean. *Bajazet*. 1672. Print.

Sans Soleil. Dir. Chris Marker. Perf. Florence Delay, Arielle Dombasle, Riyoko Ikeda. Argos Films, 1983. Film.

Shields, Carol. *The Collected Stories*. Toronto: Vintage, 2005. Print.

———. *The Republic of Love*. Toronto: Random House, 1992. Print.

———. *Unless*. Toronto: Random House, 2002. Print.

Woolf, Virginia. *To the Lighthouse*. 1927. Orlando, FL: Houghton Mifflin Harcourt, 2001. Print.

"Grand Slam": Birthing Women and Bridging Generations in Carol Shields's Play *Thirteen Hands*

NORA FOSTER STOVEL

Carol Shields is most famous as a novelist, but she worked in many genres, including drama, producing and publishing four plays in the 1990s: *Departures and Arrivals* (1990), *Thirteen Hands* (1993), *Anniversary* (1998) with David Williamson, and *Fashion, Power, Guilt and the Charity of Families* (1995) with Catherine Shields. Her interest in theatre started early: in "I/Myself," a poem about her childhood self, she calls herself "theatrical even then" (6). Shields's interest in drama led her to view many plays: in her "Preface" to *Thirteen Hands and Other Plays* (2002),[1] she recalls: "I was an avid theatre-goer in the sixties and seventies and was greatly attracted to the experimental theatre of the time" (ix), and their influence is reflected in her own scripts.[2]

Shields began writing plays in the early eighties: *Women Waiting* won first prize in the CBC Annual Literary Competition in 1983, and *Air Talk*, a brief scene related to *Departures and Arrivals*, was published in *Instant Applause: Twenty-Six Very Short Complete Plays* in 1984. She also wrote radio plays: *The View* was published in *The CBC Manitoba Anthology* in 1982, *Face-Off* was a runner-up for the CBC 1986 Drama competition and was broadcast on the CBC in 1987, and *Sisters by Chance* was broadcast on CBC in 1999. Later, in the eighties and nineties, she viewed many plays at Winnipeg's Prairie Theatre Exchange, where her husband, Don Shields, was on the board of directors, as well as experimental plays at the University of Manitoba's Black Hole Theatre.[3]

Shields's experience in writing for the stage influenced her subsequent fiction, making her novels increasingly dramatic and honing her skills with narrative voice and dialogue. In her preface to her collected plays, she acknowledges:

> Before becoming a playwright, I was a novelist, and one who was often impatient with the requisite description of weather or scenery. . . . I was more interested in the sound of people talking to each other, reacting to each other or leaving silences for others to fall into. Always while writing I felt a quickening of interest when a patch of dialogue was about to erupt in my novels. I noticed, too, that the books I loved to read were full of human speech. (ix)

In fact, the final section her successful novel *Swann* (1987)—published just three years after the first production of her first full-length play, *Departures and Arrivals* in 1984[4]—is constructed as a screenplay. "Larry's Party," the final chapter of her penultimate novel, although not formatted as a play, is nevertheless rendered almost entirely in dialogue. The intrinsically dramatic quality of her fiction is reflected in the stage and screen adaptations of her novels: both *Swann* and *The Republic of Love* were made into feature films,[5] and *Larry's Party* was adapted for the stage by Richard Ouzounian and Marek Norman in 2001, while Carol Shields and her youngest daughter, Sara Cassidy, adapted Carol's last novel, *Unless*, for the stage in 2003, the last year of Carol's life. A frequent collaborator, Shields remarks in her preface, "The collaborative aspect of theatre has given me an almost inexpressible gift of happiness" (xii).

Shields's plays are interesting in their own right, although they have been neglected by scholars and critics thus far. Only two critics have published on them to date. In "Identity Performance in Carol Shields's Stage Plays" Glen Nichols claims Shields's dramas "are superb stage plays and deserve more critical and theatrical attention" (72).[6] Chris Johnson, in "Ordinary Pleasures (and Terrors): The Plays of Carol Shields," praises the "liberal feminist vision" of her plays, which "illuminate ordinary pleasures," such as "eaves-dropping in an airport, playing cards with old friends." But the plays, he adds, "counter-point these pleasures with ordinary doubts and terrors: departure of friends and children, loneliness, mortality. A dog howls in the distance" (161). Shields's metatheatrical drama parallels and illuminates her work in other genres, including fiction, displaying her distinctive wit, subversiveness, and feminism.

Shields's plays display the feminism that distinguishes her fiction. She remarked to me in a 2003 interview that she was "the last feminist to wake up in the world," but wake up she did.[7] Her later works address the social erasure or "abjection" of women, especially middle-aged, middle-class women. In her "Playwright's Note" to *Thirteen Hands* she says:

> For many years I've been interested in the lives of women, particularly those lives that have gone unrecorded. The last twenty or thirty years have seen, in literature and in theatre, the partial redemption of women artists and activists. But one group seems consistently overlooked, a group who, for historical reasons mainly, were caught between movements: "the blue-rinse set," "the white glove brigade," "the bridge club biddies." There were (are) thousands of these women, millions in fact. I am reluctant to believe that their lives are wasted or lost. (xi)[8]

One woman in *Thirteen Hands* remarks, "There *are* millions of us, after all. No, billions" (330). In her "Playwright's Note" Shields asserts, "*Thirteen Hands* attempts to valorize those lives" (xi). In her essay "A View from the Edge of the Edge," she affirms, "I am interested in writing away the invisibility of women's lives, looking at writing as an act of redemption" (28). In her "Playwright's Note" to *Thirteen Hands*, Shields asserts her interest in the "redemption of women artists and activists" and her desire to reclaim these women. In "Reading My Mother" her daughter, novelist Anne Giardini, confirms Shields's mission to address the "erasure" of these "lost heroines," these "invisible" women, in her writing, because such "obliteration is a tragedy" (9).

In an interview, Shields notes the command, "Woman, hold your tongue": "Women were taught to hold their tongues for the very good reason that they might scatter the seeds of unorthodoxy, thereby turning the established order upside down." In an interview with Joan Thomas, she remarks, "I think of course of my mother's generation, who are more voiceless even than we are, but I think we remain fairly voiceless and powerless" (Thomas 60). Her editions of *Dropped Threads: What We Aren't Told* and *Dropped Threads 2* (2000, 2002), which she edited with Marjorie Anderson, address the silencing of women. In her afterword to the first volume, she again quotes the command, "*Woman, hold thy tongue*" (346). She frequently cites the influence of Betty Friedan's *The Feminine Mystique*. In *Unless* (2002), Reta Winters practises Shields's habit of "bean-counting," noting the absence of women in "testicular hit list[s] of literary big cats" (164).

Thirteen Hands has been Shields's most successful play and is generally considered her most stage-worthy drama. At the Carol Shields Festival in Winnipeg in 2009 an excerpt was performed to the amusement and delight of an audience of delegates to the conference. It reminded me of a time when, teaching drama to a university class, I drew on the board the traditional architectural design of a church, with a central aisle leading to the chancel and the vestries behind, and I observed how strikingly similar it was to the traditional design of a theatre, with a central aisle leading to the stage and the dressing rooms behind. This parallel is not surprising, as drama in ancient Greece constituted a religious ritual. Observing my design, I realized that I had also drawn an approximation of the female reproductive system with the uterus as the chancel or stage and the ovaries as the vestries or changing rooms. (This, too, may not be a coincidence, since ancient Greeks were knowledgeable about anatomy.) This realization inspired my conception of the stage as a womb on which new visions could be born.

Carol Shields's *Thirteen Hands* is just such a play, for in it she gives birth to the ordinary woman as an extra-ordinary being.[9] One woman calls their world "a little planet we'd put together . . . and we'd set it whirling out there in the darkness" (415).[10] This creation is presented, appropriately, on a bare stage with no set or backdrop. At stage left is a dressing room equipped with dressing table, mirror, bench, and clothes rack (327), suggesting possible identities and allowing characters to "try on" roles on stage. Thus, the stage becomes a "changing room" both literally and metaphorically, where characters, like those in David Storey's 1972 play, *The Changing Room*, change clothes *and* identities. All the facets of theatre—set, props, costumes, sound effects—combine in Shields's metadrama to "enlarge" the lives of these "ordinary" women, making them extraordinary.[11]

Appropriate for newborns, the all-female cast is virtually naked, lacking "costumes" in the conventional sense. All are clothed, for the sake of decency, in a simple slip or shift. Over these undergarments they don accessories, much as an ancient Greek actor might don a mask, or persona. These accessories—"pearls, aprons, sweaters, hats, corsages" (326)—are symbolic of the roles—housewife, committee woman, maid—that the characters don and discard as they attempt to construct their identities. For example, stage directions dictate: "*this scene, gesturing at the commonality of women, is played with the women wearing only their slips, triple strings of pearls and large pearl earrings. Their demeanour is of women fully and formally dressed*" (388).[12] One woman's daughter recalls, "My mom used to get all dolled up, that's what she called it— these itty-bitty pincurls" (342). Initially nameless, with only generic signifiers, "WOMAN ONE, TWO, THREE, and FOUR," these no-name players are named for their accessories, such as "SCARF, STOLE, and

FLOWERY HAT." In another scene, Shields directs, "*A musical tape plays while the women in the dressing room change—one into an apron, three into rather matronly dresses*" (385). The aproned maid serves the other three women, meanwhile addressing the audience in a spirited monologue. After receiving a telephone call informing her that the woman, Doris Veal, whom they are waiting for, has died, she then removes her apron and joins them at the table, concealing the bad news. As the players perform the self, *Thirteen Hands* becomes a rehearsal for life, as the characters develop from "dolls" to women.

Shields employs cross-casting, used so effectively in Caryl Churchill's 1980 play *Top Girls*, and in innumerable subsequent plays, as her four female actors play numerous parts, including four generations of women, with the no-name generic roles of North, South, East, and West, as in Amy Tan's 1989 collection, *The Joy Luck Club* (395). Dismissed by Jimmy Porter in John Osborne's 1956 play *Look Back in Anger* as the blue-rinse brigade, such middle-aged, middle-class women have been ignored by theatre—"consistently overlooked" in Shields's words—a "lost generation" in effect. Chris Johnson concludes of *Thirteen Hands*:

> In its emphasis on matriliniarity (biological and spiritual), and its politically conscious departure from "patriarchal," Aristotelean dramatic structure, *Thirteen Hands* is . . . a liberal feminist statement valorizing not only the women portrayed but the liberal feminist women . . . who saw in the play ordinary experiences and values important to them but largely ignored by the cultural establishment." (165)

Hardly "top girls," these women have been ignored by society. A messenger, riding to centre stage on a bicycle in Act One, ringing the bell shrilly, demands of the central character, "Do you, Clara Wesley, consider yourself a marginal person?" (337). Clara replies wisely, "Wellll, I suppose it depends on where the centre is" (337). The catechism continues in bureaucratic Pinteresque staccato: "Do you, as a member of society, contribute to that society's overall stability, cultural richness and general advancement?" (338). He probes, "What, in ten words or less, is the purpose of your life?" (339). That is indeed the question. In her preface, Shields notes, "Conflict in this play is not between generations or between one woman and another, but between the differing social constructs that balance and assign the worth of a human life" (xii)—social constructs that she subverts.

These women are dismissed by SCARF as "The blue-rinse girls. The white-glove ladies. Shuffling cards. Killing time. Running away from reality" (413). When SCARF accuses Clara, "You could have been useful. . . . You could have been, you know, out fighting for political change, for the extension of women's rights. You could have bettered your conditions, enriched your lives . . . you could have made something of your selves" (412), Clara replies simply, "It was . . . not at our disposal" (412). Lacking the luxury of choice, the women list—like Brenda Bowman in Shields's *A Fairly Conventional Woman* (1982) and Daisy Goodwill Flett in *The Stone Diaries* (1993)—all the things they have *not* done: "never rode a bicycle, never went ice-skating, not once, never had a real engagement ring" (410).

Thirteen Hands becomes an existentialist inquiry, as the women ask each other, "Why we're here. What we're doing" (329). Shields's focus is primarily on the identity and value of women, as in *Unless*, because society questions "our essential value" (330), as one woman observes. They begin to wonder if they even exist: one woman says, "Sometimes—sometimes I feel invisible. It started not long after my fiftieth birthday. I could feel people looking right past me, looking for someone more attractive, looking for someone more interesting to talk to. It's like I'm not here anymore" (355). Another declares, "I want to climb up on a soapbox and scream and rage and tell the whole wide world where to gooooo" (353).

Hardly material girls, these invisible women call themselves "The Edge of Night Gang" (341), referring to the popular long-running soap opera to which they are all addicted. The group—composed of Clara Wesley, who "go[es] right back to the beginning," Doris Veal, Ruth Sprague, and Margot Heatherling—is called "the Martha Circle" (348), since they pretend to meet to do good works, like knitting socks for soldiers, because one woman's husband disapproves of cards, calling them the "devil's eyelids" (348). Gathering every Wednesday night for forty-three years—longer than most marriages— to play cards, these women turn to each other for validation of their existence. Their daughters recall, "Wednesdays were sacred," and "They got off on each other, the four of them" (343). "Caught between movements," as Shields explains in her "Playwright's Notes," these women, like Brenda Bowman, the "fairly conventional woman,"[13] have fallen into the gap between feminist waves. Nevertheless, their meetings resemble consciousness-raising sessions where they can communicate opinions they cannot voice anywhere else. In her preface, Shields comments, "It is altogether possible to believe that feminism found its early roots in just such gatherings" (xi). Shields's stage directions call for tapes of women's voices to be played throughout to convey the sense of a community of women.

Clara reflects, "it was like a kind of enchantment—well, there we were, thinking so hard about what we were doing that our tongues just went and did what they wanted to do, said things that seemed to come out of nowhere, come right up out of foreign parts of us" (415). They listen to each other's confessions and complaints, sharing their "bleeding hearts" (369) and supporting each other, promising, "we'll stand by you" (382). When Woman Two says, "I've come to . . . a decision" (374), they assume she's getting a divorce and assert, "We'll support you" (375). This supposition, erroneous, as it turns out, liberates them to fantasize about what they would do if they, too, were to divorce their husbands: "I'd probably become a vegetarian" (379); "I'd probably get myself a little puppy" (380); "I'd redo the living room" (381). Here they echo the "insurance" scene in Shields's first play, *Departures and Arrivals*, where two women, who have just seen their husbands off at the airport and then bought million-dollar insurance policies, fantasize about what they might do if "something happened" to their husbands: "I've always wanted to see Australia. And New Zealand" (17); "I'd head back to Bermuda" (17); "I thought I'd go into social work" (20). Finally Woman Two in *Thirteen Hands* announces, "I'm getting a job" (384)—an even more revolutionary decision than getting a divorce for women of their generation. This sets them off again, as they all confess their secret desires for a career of their own, and discuss "self-fulfillment" (305) and escape from "the housewifey thing" (342), as one daughter puts it.

In *Thirteen Hands* the women provide a context, making each other feel "at home. At home in the world" (415). Clara affirms, "sitting there, the four of us, we were as close together as people can get" (414), closer even than flesh and blood or husband and wife: "When people think about being close, they think of two people in bed together, a husband and wife, a man and a woman, but this was closer. At that card table we were closer, you know, than families are sitting at a dinner table, sitting with your own flesh and blood, eating a Sunday dinner" (414). Clara adds in conclusion, "At that table, I knew exactly where I was" (415). "In *Thirteen Hands*," Shields explains in her interview with Marjorie Anderson, "I wanted to show how these stereotypical, 'blue-rinsed' women are thinking individuals, worthy individuals, and how they often feel brilliantly alive in those moments when they come together with other people" (145). In her preface, Shields comments, "Something important goes on around a bridge table, a place where many women have felt not only safe but brilliantly alive" (xi).

One woman comments at the end of Act One, "I find it strange, don't you, the way a human life drains down toward one thing, just one little revealing thing" (366). That "one little revealing thing" is the game. What's the game? No *Gin Game, Thirteen Hands* is a "bridge" game where daughters replace their dead mothers, "bridging" generations in this multigenerational play. Shields explains in her "Playwright's Note," "The game of bridge is used literally and metaphorically in the play, and it is hoped that this doubleness is strengthened by the fact that the word *bridge* never appears" (xii). The play bridges birth and game playing, as one daughter claims she was conceived after her mother's first "grand slam": "I owe my life to a good spread of hearts" (345).[14] Consequently, the Edge of Night Gang nicknames her "Grand Slam" (345).

Set in Winnipeg in the period of first- and second-wave feminism, from 1920 to 1993,[15] the year the play was first produced at Winnipeg's Prairie Theatre Exchange, *Thirteen Hands* spans four generations of women, as daughters—like those around the mah-jong table in *The Joy Luck Club*—replace their dead mothers. "Thinking back through [their] mothers," as Virginia Woolf phrased it, the four women, named for the four corners of the earth—"NORTH, SOUTH, EAST, WEST," as in the game of bridge and mah-jong—recall, "We talked about our mothers" (407). Thus, *Thirteen Hands* becomes a nostalgic memory play, like Tennessee Williams' *Glass Menagerie* (1948).

The title *Thirteen Hands* has both literal and metaphorical applications: it refers to the game of bridge that is played throughout the drama—"It takes thirteen tricks to make a hand, / And thirteen hands to do the trick" (395), as the women sing—but it also refers to mothers: one player recalls, "A mother needs a dozen eyes and thirteen hands, that's what my mother used to say" (408). So bridge is a metaphor for the play's matrilinear structure.

Shields structures the play in thirteen scenes, a playwright's baker's dozen. "I liked rough theatre with episodic structures" (ix), she remarks in her preface to her collection of plays. Shields's four feminist plays are fragmentary, composed of vignettes that realize "the theatrical sense that enlarges ordinary lives," as she says in her "Playwright's Note" to *Departures and Arrivals* (2). Shields defines *Thirteen Hands* as "a musical play" (xi), and indeed the episodic vignettes are demarcated by music and singing—as in Shelagh Delaney's 1952 play *A Taste of Honey*—sometimes "*with a gospel rhythm and blues feel*" (393). Shields's "Playwright's Notes" to *Thirteen Hands* specify "[s]cenes are separated by sound, by segments of recorded music, by live music (if possible). By the impromptu and informal singing of the actors themselves, or by a tape of women's voices talking and laughing, the actual words indistinct but a mood of conviviality conveyed" (326). As the curtain rises on Act Two, the women sing a Gilbert and Sullivanesque ditty reminiscent of John Gray and Eric Peterson's 1978 play, *Billy Bishop Goes to War*, with the rebellious refrain, "Wanting to win is not a sin" (368).

Shields plays with realism and surrealism in *Thirteen Hands*, reversing time and changing modes. She notes in her preface that "the fusion between the real and the surreal, the naturalistic and the fantastic" (x) is common to all her work. In her "Production Notes" to *Thirteen Hands*, she writes, "The play's various scenes shift back and forth between the naturalistic and the abstract mode. Suitable lighting can gesture toward, and enhance, these shifts" (326). In her "Introduction" to *Departures and Arrivals*, she says, "It is also my hope that the play will realize a fusion of the real and the surreal, the naturalistic and the fantastic." Certainly, the clock striking fourteen in *Thirteen Hands* suggests another dimension or another level of reality to be explored in the next scene, indicating that the time really is out of joint (349). Reality itself is called into question as Clara claims their shared stories constitute "Real history!" (405): "Together through a major depression, a world war, . . . miraculous inventions, death, illness, birth" (389).

Shields's polyvocal play employs dialogue inventively, including simultaneous, fragmentary, and overlapping speeches—the way a group of women actually speak. It includes variations in tempo: certain speeches are indicated as "rapid-fire recitatives"—perhaps as a way of caricaturing stereotypical statements. Shields's umbilical cord of dialogue bridges inner and outer worlds. In a scene where new company wives are obliged by their husbands to play bridge together, their false politeness is revealed by the contrast between their public speech and their private asides: one woman who misses her cue says aloud, "how stupid of me," but caricatures her apology by saying to herself in a Southern accent: "Ah'm just sooo stew-pid! Pu-leese!" (35–38). Inner and outer voices unite once they begin to remember their mothers and share their mothers' stories with each other.

But "it isn't just a *game* you know" (367), Clara cautions at the end of Act One. One of the stage props is a lectern, as in Wendy Lill's 1986 play *The Occupation of Heather Rose*, from which Clara addresses the audience at the beginning and end of the play, suggesting that Shields intends to both teach and delight. Always one to challenge borders, Shields crosses the line between actor and audience, placing FUR STOLE in the front of the house to pose questions during Clara's lecture, a method of breaking down the fourth wall that was popular in theatrical "happenings" of the sixties. Clara, the central intelligence of the play, also functions as a narrator, as in Thornton Wilder's 1938 play, *Our Town*.

In her preface, Shields explains, "Two principal patterns of human behaviour play against each other: continuity and replacement. . . . Continuity is represented by the multi-generational range of the play and by the way women create and preserve history in their stories" (xi). Eventually, all the original members of the Martha Circle have been replaced, except for Clara, who is now in a wheelchair. But in the penultimate scene, there is a return to their origins. Shields conveys this time warp by including a silent film sequence in which the stage directions state, "*Clarinet music. Lights fade, then come up again in the form of flickering silent movie-lighting. Clarinet music fades to nickelodeon music*" (415). The actors carry placards, announcing, "Card Game." With her usual "sparkling subversion" (*The Stone Diaries* 337), Shields pokes a little fun at Samuel Beckett's theatre of the absurd in the sign "Waiting for Clara." Lighting is employed to highlight the epiphanic sense of community in the *tableau vivant* at the end of the drama, as in Beth Henley's 1980 play, *Crimes of the Heart*. Stage directions dictate, "*A warm, golden, steady light replaces the black and white film flicker; nickelodeon music fades to recorded music. The women freeze. Light slowly fades. Very gradual introduction of tape of women talking and laughing*" (416). Thus, *Thirteen Hands* ends as it began, with a community of women talking and laughing to convey "*a mood of conviviality*" (326), as Shields writes in her initial stage directions.

So the play comes full circle as Shields shows us just how extraordinary "ordinary" women can be, how fully they can create their own community, and how strongly their matrilinear legacy endures. She has demonstrated the truth of her faith in "the theatrical sense that enlarges ordinary lives." Shields remarked that she enjoyed writing plays because they "get her 'off the ground' because they 'have more of a surreal edge to them'" (Werlock 11). "This is a comedy with edges," Shields says in her introduction to *Departures and Arrivals*, and *Thirteen Hands* can cut, too. In *Thirteen Hands* Shields stages a feminist power play that proclaims female power right to the last trump.

Notes

1. Unless otherwise stated, all references to Shields's "preface" will be to her preface to the collection *Thirteen Hands and Other Plays*. Parts of this commentary were first published as her "Playwright's Note" (9) and "Production Note" (10) to the 1993 Blizzard edition of *Thirteen Hands*.

2. Many of Shields's protagonists view plays: Judith and Martin Gill view an early Shaw play and enjoy it in *Small Ceremonies*; Brenda and Jack Bowman view *The Duchess of Malfi* in *Happenstance* and both hate it. A caustic review of a little theatre production of *Hamlet*, which leads to a suicide attempt by the lead actor, raises questions about "the state of theatre in Chicago" (*Happenstance* 68).

3. I wish to thank Chris Johnson for giving me the list of Black Hole productions. This list mentions many plays that Shields may have seen and that may have influenced her own playwriting. I also wish to thank Cherry Karpyshin, General Manager of Winnipeg's Prairie Theatre Exchange, for providing me with a list of the plays performed by the PTE. Don Shields wrote to me on 8 October 2012, "Carol and I saw most PTE productions over the years."

4. Shields recalls, "*Departures and Arrivals* was my first attempt at a full-length play" (Preface ix). *Departures and Arrivals* premiered at the University of Manitoba's Black Hole Theatre in 1984 under the direction of Chris Johnson. *Departures and Arrivals* was produced as the opening play in the 2009–2010 season of the Black Hole Theatre.

5. *Swann* was adapted by Anna Benson Gyles in 1996 and starred Miranda Richardson, Brenda Fricker, John Neville, and Sean McCann. *The Republic of Love*, adapted for the screen by director Deepa Mehta in 2003, starred Emilia Fox and Bruce Greenwood as the central couple.

6. Nichols claims, "her plays provocatively explore the dynamics of identity formation in social space through the use of multi-faceted theatrical strategies" (51).

7. I interviewed Carol Shields in her home in Victoria in May 2003.

8. This commentary could also apply to Daisy in Shields's 1993 novel *The Stone Diaries*.

9. The concept of the stage as a womb is highlighted by the announcement that Ruth has died from "cancer of the uterus," as Clara Wesley reminds us early in the play (337).

10. All references, unless otherwise stated, will be to *Thirteen Hands* as reprinted in *Thirteen Hands and Other Plays*. *Thirteen Hands* was originally commissioned by Agassiz Theatre and workshopped by the Manitoba Association of Playwrights. The Tarragon Theatre gave it a staged public reading in 1990. The Manitoba Association of Playwrights workshopped

the play again in 1990 and provided a staged reading. The Canadian Stage Company in Toronto workshopped the play in spring, 1991.

11. Carol and Don Shields travelled to Paris in the last full year of her life, 2002, to see a production of *Thirteen Hands. Treize Mains*, adapted and directed by Rachel Salik, ran at Theatre 13 from 20 November to 30 December 2001. Arthur Motyer writes, after reading *Thirteen Hands*, "You got it all absolutely right, line after line after line, character after character, scene after scene, absolutely bang-on all the time" (145).

12. This may recall Mrs. Barker, a social worker and "chairman of [the] woman's club" (79) in Edward Albee's 1960 play *The American Dream* with her repeated response, "I don't mind if I do" (79), when invited to remove her coat, her dress, etc. Because the Prairie Theatre Exchange produced this play, it is very likely that Shields saw it.

13. Brenda Bowman is the principal character in Shields's novel *A Fairly Conventional Woman*. Shields's working title was *Broad Daylight*, but her publisher changed it. Later, it was paired with Jack Bowman's 1982 novel, *Happenstance*, as *Happenstance: The Wife's Story and The Husband's Story*. In Britain it was published as *Duet*.

14. Jack and Brenda Bowman of Shields's two-part novel *Happenstance* find "an almost laughable connection between their Sunday-night bridge games and the sharpness of their sexual love" (*Happenstance: The Wife's Story* 156).

15. These dates parallel the life of Daisy Goodwill Flett, 1905–1993, in Shields's novel *The Stone Diaries*, also published in 1993.

Works Cited

Albee, Edward. *The American Dream. Two Plays by Edward Albee: The American Dream; The Zoo Story*. New York: Signet, 1961. Print.

Anderson, Marjorie. "Interview with Carol Shields." In *Carol Shields: The Arts of a Writing Life*, ed. Neil K. Besner. Winnipeg: Prairie Fire Press, 1995: 57–72. Print.

Giardini, Anne. "Reading My Mother." *Prairie Fire* 16.1 (1995): 6–12. Print.

Johnson, Chris. "Ordinary Pleasures (and Terrors): The Plays of Carol Shields." *Prairie Fire* 16.1 (1995): 161–67. Print.

Motyer, Arthur. *The Staircase Letters: An Extraordinary Friendship at the End of Life*. Toronto: Vintage, 2007. Print.

Nichols, Glen. "Identity Performance in Carol Shields's Stage Plays." In *West-Words: Celebrating Western Canadian Theatre and Playwriting*. Regina: Canadian Plains Research Centre, 2011: 50–74. Print.

Ouzounian, Richard, and Marek Norman. *Larry's Party: A Musical Based on the Novel by Carol Shields*. Toronto: McArthur & Co., 2000. Print.

Shields, Carol. *Air Talk*. In *Instant Applause: Twenty-Six Very Short Complete Plays*. Winnipeg: Blizzard Publishing Company, 1984. Print.

———. *Departures and Arrivals*. Winnipeg: Blizzard, 1990. Rpt. in *Thirteen Hands and Other Plays*. Toronto: Vintage, 2002. Print.

———. *A Fairly Conventional Woman*. Toronto: Macmillan, 1982. Print.

———. *Happenstance: The Husband's Story* and *The Wife's Story*. 1980 and 1982. Toronto: Vintage, 1987. Print.

———. "I/Myself." In *Coming to Canada: Poems*, ed. Christopher Levinson. Ottawa: Carleton University Press, 1992: 6. Print.

———. "Playwright's Note" to *Departures and Arrivals*. In *Thirteen Hands and Other Plays*. Toronto: Vintage, 2002: 2. Print.

———. "Playwright's Note" to *Thirteen Hands*. In *Thirteen Hands and Other Plays*. Toronto: Vintage, 2002: 326. Print.

———. Preface. *Thirteen Hands and Other Plays*. Toronto: Vintage, 2002: ix–xii. Print.

———. "Production Notes." *Thirteen Hands: A Play in Two Acts*. Winnipeg: Blizzard Publishing, 1993: 10. Print.

———. *Thirteen Hands: A Play in Two Acts*. Winnipeg: Blizzard Publishing, 1993. Rpt. in *Thirteen Hands and Other Plays*. Toronto: Vintage, 2002. Print.

———. *The Stone Diaries*. 1993. New York: Viking, 1994. Print.

———. *Swann*. 1987. New York: Viking, 1989. Print.

———. *Unless*. Toronto: Random House, 2002.

———. "A View from the Edge of the Edge." In *Carol Shields and the Extra-Ordinary*, ed. Marta Dvořák and Manina Jones. Montreal: McGill-Queen's University Press, 2007: 17–29. Print.

———. *Women Waiting*. Brief radio play. 1983. Carol Shields fonds. Library and Archives Canada, Ottawa. TS.

Shields, Carol, and Marjorie Anderson, ed. *Dropped Threads: What We Aren't Told*. Toronto: Vintage, 2001. Print.

———. *Dropped Threads 2: More of What We Aren't Told*. With Catherine Shields. Toronto: Vintage, 2003. Print.

Shields, Carol, and Catherine Shields. *Fashion, Power, Guilt and the Charity of Families*. Winnipeg: Blizzard: 1995. Rpt. in *Thirteen Hands and Other Plays*. Toronto: Vintage, 2002. Print.

Shields, Carol, and David Williamson. *Anniversary*. Winnipeg: Blizzard: 1998. Rpt. in *Thirteen Hands and Other Plays*. Toronto: Vintage, 2002. Print.

Thomas, Joan. "'The Golden Book': An Interview with Carol Shields." *Prairie Fire* 14.4 (1993–94): 56–62. Print.

Werlock, Abby. *Carol Shields's* The Stone Diaries: *A Reader's Guide*. London: Continuum, 2001. Print.

Archives as Traces of Life Process and Engagement: The Late Years of the Carol Shields Fonds

CATHERINE HOBBS

For an archivist, treating the final portion of a person's archives, particularly archives one is very familiar with, is a rare privilege. I am fortunate to have been able to acquire and process the latter part of the Carol Shields fonds which traces the final phase of her story and I was able to bring to this task the knowledge I have from working with the previous instalments of her archival fonds for many years.[1] What follows are my reflections as an archivist on the latter portions of Shields's archives and what they might mean for research, both for their content and also specifically for their form. The form of Shields's archives appears contiguous with her documenting patterns and interests throughout the latter portion of her life. Her documents are not just evidence of her activities and interests but the form combined with the details found within her documents creates a rich portrait of Shields as she lived out the final phases of her career and the latter part of her life. These reflections come from my very recent contact with these archives.

At this point, I am also drawn to personal reflection on how working with the Carol Shields fonds must have affected me during my own career. I have a long history with these archives and the second accession of Shields fonds (acquired in 1998) was the first-ever archival project I worked on in the summer of 1999 when I began as an archivist. It is clear to me now that it was Shields's archives that brought me to a number of conclusions in my scholarly writing over the years. In my first article in 2001, "The Character of Personal Archives," I asked archivists to consider that the personal qualities of the creators of archives were integral to an understanding of those documents' archival value. I was grounded by the sense that the archivist's practice should do justice to the life that created the archives in ways that archival theory was not yet addressing. I think now that this was the effect of seeing Shields's own care with others and attention to the details of their lives which left traces on her archives. Her retention of these mementos of everyday personal experience within her archives is correlative to the attention to ordinary personal detail in her fiction as I have discussed before (Hobbs, "Voice and Re-vision" 48).

Working with her archives, I was also grounded in the sense that literary archivists must respond to the literary mind behind the literary fonds. This approach, in Shields's case, leads us down a hall of mirrors where her reflections on biography and literary research in her fiction and her inclusion of adjusted personal documents from real life (including her own life) into fiction belie any straightforward notion of authorial intention (Hobbs, "Voice and Re-Vision" 51–55). There is the archives without author or the author jarred out of place that Shields was so good at debunking (consider the novel *Swann*) on the one hand and on the other hand we have this genuine unknowability involved with personal archives: that "there is never enough material," as Judith Gill says in *Small Ceremonies* (Shields 54). Yet, the archivist continues despite the open-ended possibilities.

I note too that my archival activity was itself a struggle with "goodness," the theme of Shields's final novel, *Unless*. I asked in a recent article about being a literary archivist, "What is it to 'do right' by a person's archives, and to 'do right' by literary archives in the face of larger theories developed primarily to deal with the archives of government or corporate bodies and in the face of postmodernism's gestures toward archives (one of which is that centring on the acts of the writer is sometimes considered passé)?" (Hobbs, "Personal Ethics" 181–92). So my work is indebted to Shields in these obvious and oblique ways. It could well have been that a less cohesive example of a warm and caring character and one not coupled with irony about archives and writing would have allowed me to miss these cues and set me on a different path in terms of theory and practice as an archivist. The Carol Shields fonds has also allowed me to consider that the role of the archivist might involve creative or, at least, alternative interactions with the archives rather than the traditional acquisition, arrangement, and description which is at the centre of my profession. The new considerations presented here are a continuation of that effort.

The latter portion of Shields's archival fonds consists of twelve metres of textual records, photographs, and recordings from the last years of her life and career. The archives were delivered to the (then) National Library, in two accessions: one in 2000 (when the Shieldses moved to Victoria) and one in 2003 (following Shields's death). These accessions joined the other instalments previously delivered in 1994 and 1998. The material shipped in 2000 was predominantly created between 1998 and 2000; while the material shipped in 2003 dates from 1999–2003 but both shipments also contain inclusions from much earlier periods. Roughly speaking, the documents in these shipments postdate the publication of *Larry's Party* but contain much about its reception (for example, Shields's Orange Prize and the adaptation by Richard Ouzounian and Marek Norman of the novel as a musical). These archives also detail the period when Shields wrote her biography of Jane Austen (for which she won the Charles Taylor Prize); when she and Marjorie Anderson made a foray into editing *Dropped Threads* and then *Dropped Threads 2*; the editing and publication of the story collection *Dressing Up for the Carnival* and the writing and publication of her final novel *Unless*. It is also the period of the republication of all of Shields's novels in paperback and their presentation in audio book form; the adaptation of the play *Thirteen Hands* for chamber opera; the adaptation to film (directed by Deepa Mehta) of *The Republic of Love* and the filming of *Swann* (directed by Anna Benson Gyles); the editing of her collected plays and her collaboration on a screenplay about Susanna Moodie with Patrick Crowe. They also detail her appointment as a Companion of the Order of Canada, among many other honours. Of course, because they date from 1998 onward, these accessions also detail Shields's life while affected by cancer.

Time had elapsed between the acquisition (in 2006) and treatment (in 2011–2012), as is often the case in archival institutions with their resource pressures and changing priorities. These two accessions had the advantage of being almost entirely chronologically arranged. Shields had been in the habit of filling up boxes one after another, and so her archives, at least while she was alive, flowed fairly consistently from her activities including, as will be discussed below, not just composition and accumulation of incoming material but also choices about what to include. Within the original shipping boxes, then, the fonds was presented more often like a continuous swath of papers, rather than divided into files by the creator herself. The physical treatment of the fonds, therefore, involved distinguishing breaks in this swath, typically, for example, when a chunk of manuscript ended and a pile of email printouts and letters began. Titles for these files were, by-and-large, titles created by the archivist (me) based on an analysis of the content of these chunks. Determining this course of action and proceeding with it is what archivists tend to call intellectual and physical arrangement.[2]

When I had finished the treatment for these later portions of Shields's archives, I was left with one general reading of the archives as a whole. What characterizes Shields's approach as seen consistently in her archives could be couched in this way: sustained grace and generosity in the face of the ineffable. You have probably met Shields's ineffable before. She talks of the "unknow-ability" of others in an essay "Others" and she notes the role of ("shameful") curiosity for the writer even in the face of this unknowability.[3] In the speech "The Subjunctive Self" she discusses the bind of the writer to writing that reveals and yet doesn't reveal the writer's self and the contradictory relationship that archives have with the author—promising and yet not reflecting the author in a "true form."[4] Writers, fiction, biography, and documentation are bound together in possibilities of revealing something but that something is over and above the "real."

> So much in a writer's life is unwilled, capricious and inexplicable—and unrecorded, but these small papery documents that accumulate on writer's [sic] desks are often capable of pointing to steps in an imaginative process. Behind the prose of a novel or the lines in a book of poems, the personal authorial narrative gestures toward the writer's *unspoken reserves* of thought or the sad or happy sea of a diurnal existence. . . .
>
> Even so, we will never be able to reach through acid-free archival material to the *essence* of Margaret Laurence, nor of any other writer for that matter. We all recognize that when a writer picks up a pen, a second self comes out, and this applies not just to manuscripts but to letters and even personal diaries. (Shields, "The Subjunctive Self" 15, 26)

She approached her last years with the same willingness to engage through writing, despite the unbounded outside to writing: writing and documentation's irreducible remainder. At the same time she approached her own illness with tremendous generosity to friends and readers and generous gestures to fellow travellers in terms of cancer treatment. And she bore her treatment with conscious commitment in the public spotlight. This was a writer who gave her sustained attention on all these fronts despite the unknowns.

Archivists are interested in the qualities of records to provide evidence of the creator's context and this involves paying attention to how the documents were created, kept, or reused.[5] The physical and intellectual arrangement of documents and files should provide added elements of context used for deciphering the meaning of documents. Surprisingly enough, these elements of what archivists call "original order" had been very little explored concerning the archives of individuals within scholarly literature even though they are relied on in practice.

Personal archives provide evidence of choices, habits, and predilections, as the documents left in the wake of life. Archives are the accrual from a multitude of daily acts. It is impossible to separate evidence of activities from the emotional, psychological, and interpersonal implications of choices or habits: I believe this is one of the ways that personal archives are distinct from other types of archives. Looking at the Shields fonds, minute levels of physical arrangement can be determined within files or types of files as well as larger changes within her documenting practices. I am interested in the grain or texture of the Shields archives which is produced through its development in time. This type of talk can lead to simple criticism that the archivist is being unduly organicist about the fonds and its links to biography. It is clear that archives are well beyond a logical positivist formulation of naturally born evidence and/or a neutral slate for scholarship. We are informed by the postmodern bind about biography and by Shields's own work that Shields herself cannot be recouped. It concerns me, though, that we must do our best for this nest of traces, rather than dismiss outright the personal facets of the archives as tainted, if we are to allow the creator of those archives to retain agency and dignity.[6] Archives are formed through singular and repeated actions. They are formed first by creators, then custodians, then archivists and researchers, but this is not an indicator that we should ignore the first stages of this process: that is, what traces there might be of a creator in action.

We cannot get a complete picture of the life from the texture of the archives but it might still play a role in our understanding in those cases where features are clearly visible. What might constitute this texture? Choices to document in a certain way, which create the physical and intellectual elements of arrangement within the fonds, which, in turn, hint at the activities based on choices that were made during the archives' creation. This texture of archives I would take to mean old and new patterns of document making and accumulating, types of documents, chosen inclusions, and co-creation. All these features are related to documenting practices but, as I hope is clear, they are also contiguous with the creator (Shields's) ideas concerns and activities. This texture shows us, among other things, our inability to separate the form of archives from their content.

The following are some examples of the texture within Shields's archives that I noted during archival processing. There is a continuation of some facets seen within previous accessions that are also seen within these new accessions. For example, as was the case in previous accessions, copious engaged reader correspondence accompanies evidence that Shields responded personally to most of these readers with a note or a card. Many readers continue to write to Shields to point out the error she had made in using the word "prone" instead of "supine" in the early edition of *The Stone Diaries,* which was also something of a constant in the 1998 accession. Also as before, there is a remarkable reader response to Shields's adept use of photographs in her novels. In particular, the mix of family and found photographs used to illustrate *The Stone Diaries* and also the photograph of Don Shields as a baby used for the cover image of *Larry's Party* elicit strong responses. In the correspondence from the newer accessions, the relatives of the real woman in the photograph labelled "Fraidy Hoyt" in *The Stone Diaries* write to ask Shields how she came across this photograph (Hendricker). A dental hygienist, Lois Hirt, also writes to Shields about the many references to teeth which appear in her work (Hirt). In her Vancouver Institute address, Shields describes her response: "Well what could I tell her? Teeth are a part of life" (Shields, "Making Words/Finding Stories"). In her correspondence (Correspondence files 2002–2003), Shields describes how a "real" Larry Weller appeared at the launch of *Larry's Party* at Rand McNally's in New York and slapped his business card down in front of her. Also included in that accession is a photograph of this "real" Larry Weller with his mother, a golden retriever, and a lemon meringue pie. The back of this photograph says, "Larry's passion for lemon meringue pie is part of the Weller family chronicle" (Chrisman). In his accompanying letter, he writes, "My mother really does bake a lemon meringue pie every year for my birthday" (Weller). Shields seems to have found this photograph interesting or amusing enough to tack it up on a wall or a bulletin board, as the small push-pin hole at the top of the photograph would suggest.

There is the continuation from the earlier accessions of another typical pattern in her archives, that of reading and editorial commentary within the Shields family. In this portion of the archives, her daughters Anne Giardini, Sara Cassidy, and daughter-in-law Audrey all comment on the manuscript for *Unless* as evident in their annotations. Shields commented in turn on Anne's articles for *The National Post* and on poems by daughter

Sara. In the earlier accessions, Shields's daughters had commented on drafts (for example, for *The Stone Diaries*) or collaborated with her as well (see *The Stone Diaries*, TS).

There is also a new pattern in the documents made when the Shieldses move to Victoria. Email discussions with daughters and printouts from real estate sites are evidence of the work underway to find the Shieldses a house and of the family's discussion of the choices. This is followed later in the files by many strips of negatives showing visits from family and friends (Shields family, "Family negatives"). These images give us reference to the Shieldses' new home context, their beautiful Georgian house, which was described in many interviews from the period. These images show the house in one of its (most likely) intended uses: as a place to visit with children and grandchildren and particularly with the arrival of new grandchildren. The negatives help to chart this chapter fully, to say "We were here doing this."

Another change in writing and hence in the fonds itself is in Shields's adaptation to illness. She began to adapt to her new circumstances with cancer: the writing of the story "Eros" (*Dressing Up for the Carnival*) occurs very close in time to her mastectomy, for example. There are also other changes in the texture of her documentary practices which relate directly to life with this illness and decisions from this period. For example, Shields retained two assistants during parts of the latter part of her career, Ruth Partridge and Kathryn Mulders. The files that were created, kept, or annotated by either assistant show a type of mediation or co-creation of documents which was not found in her archives previously. One of the fascinating aspects of Shields's earlier archives (contained in the 1994 and 1997 accessions) is the tremendous activity of Shields herself in responding to queries of publishers, event organizers, researchers, and readers—all directly, even amidst her period of high activity as Chancellor at the University of Winnipeg and her increasingly demanding international career. In the latter period Shields's assistants annotated certain emails or attached sticky notes to correspondence and received instructions from her on how to respond. This step indicates that Shields had accepted a need for assistance on business matters. For example, we have the appearance of sticky notes in 1998 where Shields asks Ruth Partridge to explain her inability to appear due to illness (Correspondence files, 2000–04): a keen example of how the illness framed her new documenting context.[7] Ruth Partridge then kept files and forwarded mail to Shields in 1999–2000 while she was on a year abroad on a Guggenheim Fellowship.

There is further co-creation of documents when Shields is ill as well. Family members, most particularly her husband Don, stepped in to answer or direct her to particular details in emails from friends, her agent, and her publishers that needed her attention. Often Don would add his own humorous and loving commentary. There are groups of emails printed out in packages, which were likely bundled together in this way to be given to her while she was in hospital. In addition, in these accessions we also have her family members stepping in to appear in public on her behalf to receive awards in her stead (Sara at the Giller gala, Meg at Wilfrid Laurier, for example). We can know from the quality of the interactions among the members of Shields family in the correspondence that this assistance was an act of loving support which continues the thread from earlier correspondence in the archives. With her family's support to continue her affairs and the projects she was so invested in, this concerted collective effort frames the evidence of her continued high level of creative output, engagement, and interpersonal connection. This story of support is one that reframes the encouraging, loving, and active interaction that Shields had with family and friends as well as professional contacts, vivid in her fonds from its very beginnings.

Shields also continued to make very firm commitments towards friends even during her own very critical period. She decided, for example, to send one critically ill friend, Joan Hurley, a fax a day while Hurley was in hospital (Fax to Joan Hurley, Correspondence files). David Watmough's tribute to Shields recalls her sending cover quotes for his work to him while Shields was in hospital receiving treatment herself (Watmough). In line with this, Shields was consistently open about her illness in the press: this is evident in her decision to share her experiences in a publication for breast cancer survivors (*Audience*) and a publication for family doctors and to give speeches in formal settings.

There are other more anomalous changes to the texture of Shields's archives. As is sometime the case with mature fonds, the creator includes material from much earlier periods in a late accession. In the case of those inclusions present in the 2000 accession, these were clearly included by Shields herself. For example. Shields includes the invitation and order of service for her daughter Anne Giardini's 1987 wedding among her 1999 files. Of course, this act of inclusion could show her recouping and documenting bits of her past or perhaps she simply came across the bulletin in her normal activities and put it in the box: we'll never know her intentions. Sometimes, though, the inclusions that have a much earlier date are included in the normal course of events. In a letter returned to Shields after her mother's death, also included in the 2000 portion of the archives, we hear the voice of Shields writing to her mother in 1971: the writer raising young children and hoping to be published again. In this letter, Shields begins with a memory about her mother's loyalty to the Fuller Brush Company, then she recounts the details of the lives of each of her five children in turn. At the end of the letter she says, "I have had a good idea for a story for about two years and have finally figured out how to write it" (Shields, letter to her mother, Inez Warner).

Another new object/document included here gives a glimpse of Shields in her middle period: The Writers Union of Canada Directory (1991), which she had autographed by authors she met at the TWUC AGM. Lesser known writers predominate (Shields, *TWUC Directory*). In addition, there are also new documents about her career and promotion as an academic as well as her early teaching notes and humorous photographs with accompanying captions showing Shields in the classroom in the 1980s (Unknown photographer, Creative writing class photographs). These new facets may be those she had chosen to keep with her until then or those that she stumbled across again in the process of clearing up for the move to Victoria (or perhaps both).

Some of these late inclusions deepen elements of the fonds already present. Included are now notebooks and manuscript excerpts related to many earlier novels: *The Republic of Love, Swann,* and others. The fonds now holds an array of notes, postcards, and photographs for research on mermaids and the Annunciation around the creation of *The Republic of Love* (Shields, research and image files for *The Republic of Love*). Rounding out Shields's research material for *Larry's Party* is a log book from a trip to the United Kingdom, which is annotated by Shields's mother-in-law Agnes Shields and was authored by Don Shields while on a tour of the United Kingdom in 1956. This is a co-created document of a different type than Shields's collaborative writing. The log book is repositioned in Shields's fonds by Shields's reuse of the notes in writing the novel ([Shields?], Log book)[8] and the fact that she appears as a participant in the trip who leaves the "party" part way through. This trip diary included in the later accessions joins the (unannotated) red leather pocket diary from a trip made by Shields's mother found in an earlier accession of the archives (Warner).[9] Also joining this is Shields's own travel memorabilia from a trip to the United Kingdom in the 1970s, which includes an ordinance survey map of Hadrian's Wall.

These later inclusions also bring with them a few new details and potential "Aha" moments which were hitherto unknown and jar the fonds or adjust/amend our vision. Included in the 2000 accession, alongside the documents from 1999 are some early draft pages for *Swann,* a small clutch of material dating from the 1980s. These early drafts indicate that the main character for the novel was, if only briefly, a man called Samson Swann (Shields, draft material for *Swann*). A salad recipe found in a notebook for *Small Ceremonies* turns out to be a salad Larry later eats (Shields, notebook of novel draft)—indicating Shields had gone back to her previous notebooks, perhaps? An early notebook for Shields's penultimate novel sports the title *Jerry's Party* (Shields, notes for *Jerry's Party*). The inclusion of these notes in the fonds adjusts our perception of those works and their evolution, as well as couching them in Shields's intentional inclusion in her archives. This evidence of late inclusion links content to form and arrangement of documents.

Shields's later inclusions also show important examples of her reuse of her own documents. The arrangement of her files suggests that she returned to her earlier writings on Jane Austen, particularly to essays for the Jane Austen Society of North America, as a starting point for her Austen biography (Shields, "Jane Austen: Images of the Body"). There are also a large number of files which show the process of revisiting, selecting, and editing the stories that later appear in *Dressing Up for the Carnival.* Shields first used printouts, proofs for the stories as they appeared in magazines, as well as photocopies of printed versions of her stories when she reconsidered and revised her stories for this collection: these were reviewed in batches before the final typescript was brought together (Shields, drafts for *Dressing Up for the Carnival*).

Shields also continued innovating and expanding through her writing and continually revising her take on her own writing. When I watched Shields's speech to the Vancouver Institute mentioned earlier, the sudden appearance of computer printouts on golden retrievers within Shields's manuscripts began to make sense (Shields, computer printouts on the golden retriever). She mentions in the speech that she had been told that she had no pets in her novels and therefore she set about creating one for *Unless* fairly late in the novel's development (Shields, "Making Words/Finding Stories"). In a similar way, she recognized a need for expert advice on the topic of trombones to flesh out Roman's character and so she began a brief, intense email exchange on the details of the trombone with concert trombonist Carl Lenthe (Shields, email with Carl Lenthe).[10]

There is also the conundrum of the new novel notes: the suggestion that Shields was outlining a new project involving a love affair between two employees of a paper shop, a trip to Malta, love interrupted and the love story resuming (Shields, notes for a new novel [?]). It had been unclear to me while treating the archives if this was really under consideration as a new novel, although I now find confirmed in a fax to her friend in hospital that this is a request from *The Telegraph* to describe a miniseries in fifty words or less (Shields, fax to Joan Hurley). Her drafts of the novel *Segue* (which was later published as a short story) indicate Shields was always making new beginnings: in the archives these are a nod to the future anterior.

As well, there is a very keen sense of life interrupted when Carol Shields passes away that is also evident in the grain of the fonds, particularly in the arrangement inside correspondence files, the file arrangement derived from particular groupings in the swath that I mentioned above. The correspondence to Shields streamed in and her correspondence with others streamed out as long as it was possible to sustain it. The last letters Shields received are followed by the letters and cards she received after death which are followed and combined in folders with letters of condolence (Shields, correspondence files). In the arrangement of files her level of committed activity blends with how death comes in the midst of life and this is followed by the commitment of her family to respond to correspondents when she was no longer able to do so.

These, then, are fresh impressions of continuity and changes in the texture of the Shields fonds which mark changes in her activities, the adaptations of her and others in this latter part of her life, and her choices of inclusions in her fonds. The acts that went into creating these archives are retained as traces of gestures. If we are to admit to the human side of things in the face of this ineffable, they are what we go on to interpret writer-ly actions and the writing life, as Shields herself explained in the "Subjunctive Self." Yet at the same time, this doubles back to the irreducible outside of personal archives: that a person was there doing these things, that time and reorganizing documents have effaced some of the sense of these groupings, which were originally made by intention, habit, or lack of attention, and that this is what we should consider to be the double-edged quality of what is left—its irreducible remainder.

Notes

1. I realize from recent contact with the Shields estate, that there are still a number of documents outstanding that relate to Shields. These documents challenge any idea that this fonds or *a* fonds is ever finished. This being said, the third and fourth accessions described here show this period of Shields' life in fulsome detail.

2. As an arrangement note in the finding aid for the fourth accession (2003-09) also states: "Numbering of the cartons for shipping did not follow the order that Shields boxed the documents. A decision was made by the archivist to describe certain cartons (3, 4, 8, and 9) earlier in the finding aid to better reflect the chronological order (see boxing grid at the end of the finding aid). The rearrangement of the material is limited to this step." (Hobbs, Finding Aid Carol Shields fonds, 4th accession 2003-09, 2).

3. The essay "Others" appeared untitled in *22 Provocative Canadians in the Spirit of Bob Edwards*. Two drafts of this essay appear in accession 2003-09, the first written in 1997 ("Others" 13 Aug. 1997, 11 June 1999).

4. "The Subjunctive Self" is a speech that appears in many versions in Shields's fonds. The version I am referring to here is from 3 March 1998.

5. For a fuller discussion of arrangement issues and personal archives, see Hobbs "Reenvisioning the Personal: Reframing Traces of Individual Life."

6. This type of investigation of trace is a necessary triangulation of contested object/site, public forum, and expertise that is discussed with reference to the Forensic Architecture projects: where spatial analysis is used to model sites of violence within the framework of humanitarian law and human rights (Forensic Architecture). While on a different level of urgency and severity than the evidence of atrocities or cultural effacement detailed by the Forensic Architecture projects, it is clear to me that archivists, if they are to remain ethical, must attempt to address this issue of proofs of personal life in a similar way to these endeavours, or risk effacement (or even participate in the effacement) of the life and agency behind the fonds. Particularly, I think this is important with reference to life trauma which in the case of Shields' illness I show (briefly) as embedded in her documenting practices. What is ethical in the face of life process? Or trauma? Perhaps it is to engage with the notion of contested evidence, spatiality, and the manipulation of medias of recorded information to assess traces of personal and creative life.

7. Either, I should suggest, by making it the reason for the additional support or the object of discussion.

8. Carol Shields fonds R11805 (2000-04 accession) Vol. 92 f.47 contains a log of a trip to the UK made in an exercise book. The original printing in fountain pen was written by Don Shields for his parents' trip to the UK in 1956. The marginal handwriting is in Don Shields' mother's hand and is

comprised of annotations like "Warmest Spot in England" next to a reference to Newton Abbot, for example. The log also references numbers which appear to relate to films (i.e., negatives of photographs for the trip). The itinerary described here differs from the trip made by Shields' mother discussed in n. 9.

9. This is a trip diary by Inez Warner from a trip to the UK found in the second accession B. 54 f.4 which I have elsewhere described as taking on a new cast by its inclusion in Shields's archives and by its cameo appearance as the red leather diary held by Dorrie in *Larry's Party* (see Hobbs "Personal Ethics" 188).

10. Some of this correspondence is found alongside printouts on the trombonist himself.

Works Cited

Chrisman, Sally. Photograph of "the real" Larry Weller. [1999]. Vol. 89, f.5, 2000-04 accession, R11805. Carol Shields fonds. Library and Archives Canada, Ottawa, Canada.

The Enduring Enigma of Susanna Moodie. Dir. Patrick Crowe. Upper Canada Moving Picture Co., 1997. Film.

Forensic Architecture: a research project. Centre for Research Architecture, Department of Visual Cultures, Goldsmiths, University of London. 2009–13. Web. 21 June 2013.

Hendricker, David. Letters to Carol Shields. Vol. 84, f.18, and Vol. 91, f.5, 2000-04 accession, R11805. Carol Shields fonds. Library and Archives Canada, Ottawa, Canada.

Hirt, Lois. Letters. Vol. 86, f.25, and Vol. 89, f.2, 2000-04 accession; Vol. 110, f.2, and Vol. 125, f.2, 2003-09 accession; R11805. Carol Shields fonds. Library and Archives Canada, Ottawa, Canada.

Hobbs, Catherine. "The Character of Personal Archives: Reflections on the Value of the Records of Individuals." *Archivaria* 52 (Fall 2001): 126–35. Print.

———. Finding Aid, Carol Shields fonds. Former Archival Reference number: LMS-0212, Archival Reference number: R11805, 3rd accession 2000-04. Library and Archives Canada, Ottawa, 2012. TS.

———. Finding Aid, Carol Shields fonds. Former Archival Reference number: LMS-0212, Archival Reference number: R11805, 4th accession 2003-09. Library and Archives Canada, Ottawa, 2012. TS.

———. "Personal Ethics: Being an Archivist of Writers." In *Basements and Attics, Closets and Cyberspace: Explorations in Canadian Women's Archives*, ed. Linda M. Morra and Jessica Schagerl. Waterloo, ON: Wilfrid Laurier University Press, 2012: 181–92. Print.

———. "Reenvisioning the Personal: Reframing Traces of Individual Life." In *Currents of Archival Thinking*, ed. Terry Eastwood and Heather MacNeil. Santa Barbara, CA: Libraries Unlimited, 2010: 213–41. Print.

———. "Voice and Re-vision: The Carol Shields Archival Fonds." *In Carol Shields and the Extra-ordinary*, eds. Marta Dvořák and Manina Jones. Montreal and Kingston: McGill-Queen's University Press, 2007: 33–58. Print.

Shields, Carol. *Audience*. Breast cancer patient workbook, in correspondence file. Vol. 112, f.3, 2003-09 accession, R11805. Carol Shields fonds. Library and Archives Canada, Ottawa. Print.

———. Computer printouts on the golden retriever. Versos Vol. 116, f.11, 2003-09 accession, R11805. Carol Shields fonds, Library and Archives Canada, Ottawa, Canada.

———. Correspondence files. 2000–04. Vol. 82, f.23, 2000-04 accession, R11805. Carol Shields fonds. Library and Archives Canada, Ottawa, Canada.

———. Correspondence files. 2002–03. Vol. 118, f.1; Vol. 121, f.1; Vol. 122, f.4 and f.8; Vol. 138, f.1 and f.4; and Vol. 139, f.6; 2003-09 accession, R11805. Carol Shields fonds. Library and Archives Canada, Ottawa, Canada.

———. Draft material for *Swann* and other novels. [198–]. Vol. 92, f.8, 2000-04 accession, R11805. Carol Shields fonds. Library and Archives Canada, Ottawa, Canada.

———. Drafts for *Dressing Up for the Carnival*. Series VI. Short Fiction: drafts, proofs, production material; multiple files; 2000-4 accession, R11805. Carol Shields fonds. Library and Archives Canada, Ottawa, Canada.

———. *Dressing Up for the Carnival*. Toronto: Random House, 2000. Print.

———. Email correspondence with Carl Lenthe. Vol. 117, f.5 and f.7, and Vol. 131, f.2, 2003-09 accession, R11805. Carol Shields fonds. Library and Archives Canada, Ottawa, Canada.

———. Fax to Joan Hurley. 20 Mar. 2001. Vol. 134, f.3, R11805. Carol Shields fonds, Library and Archives Canada, Ottawa, Canada.

———. *Jane Austen*. New York: Viking, 2001. Print.

———. "Jane Austen: Images of the Body: No Fingers, No Toes." Computer typescript draft essay. Vol. 112, f.1, and Vol. 113, f.5–6, 2003-09 accession, R11805. Carol Shields fonds. Library and Archives Canada, Ottawa, Canada. TS.

———. *Larry's Party*. Toronto: Random House, 1997. Print.

———. Letter to her mother (Inez Warner). [1971]. Vol. 131, f.2, 2003-09 accession, R11805. Carol Shields fonds. Library and Archives Canada, Ottawa, Canada.

———. "Making Words/Finding Stories [address to Vancouver Institute]." May 1998. MISACS item #440216, R11805. Carol Shields fonds, Library and Archives Canada, Ottawa, Canada. Video.

———. Notebook of novel draft. Vol. 2, f.2, 2000-04 accession, R11805. Carol Shields fonds. Library and Archives Canada, Ottawa, Canada.

———. Notes for *Jerry's Party*. [198–199-?]. Vol. 120, f.8, 2003-09 accession, R11805. Carol Shields fonds. Library and Archives Canada, Ottawa, Canada.

———. Notes for new novel[?]. Vol. 134, f.3, 2003-09 accession, R11805. Carol Shields fonds, Library and Archives Canada, Ottawa, Canada.

———. Ordinance Survey map of Hadrian's Wall. Vol. 95, f.43, 2003-09 accession, R11805. Carol Shields fonds. Library and Archives Canada, Ottawa, Canada. Print.

———. "Others." Computer typescript draft. 13 Aug. 1997. Vol. 129, f.9, 2003-09 accession, LMS-0212/R11805. Carol Shields fonds. Library and Archives Canada, Ottawa, Canada. TS.

———. "Others." Computer typescript draft. 11 June 1999. Vol. 112, f.3, 2003-09 accession, LMS-0212/R11805. Carol Shields fonds. Library and Archives Canada, Ottawa, Canada. TS.

———. ["Others."] Untitled essay. In *22 Provocative Canadians: In the Spirit of Bob Edwards*, ed. Margaret Dickson and Kerry Longpré. Bayeux Arts: Calgary, 1999: 26–31. Print.

———. *The Republic of Love*. Toronto: Random House, 1992. Print.

———. Research and image files for *The Republic of Love*. Vol. 95, f.13, f.18, f.33, and f.37, 2000-04 accession, R11805. Carol Shields fonds. Library and Archives Canada, Ottawa, Canada.

———. *Small Ceremonies*. Toronto: Totem, 1978. Print.

———. *The Stone Diaries*. Toronto: Random House, 1993. Print.

———. *The Stone Diaries*. Copy 1. Shields's note: "Anne and Cath's comments" [daughters]. Nov. 1992. Vol. 41, f.24–27, accession 1994-13, LMS-0212. Carol Shields fonds. Library and Archives Canada, Ottawa, Canada. TS.

———. "The Subjunctive Self." Computer typescript draft. 3 March 1998. Vol. 108, f.19, 2003-09 accession, LMS-0212/R11805. Carol Shields fonds. Library and Archives Canada, Ottawa, Canada. TS.

———. *Swann*. New York: Viking, 1989. Print.

———. *Thirteen Hands and Other Plays*. Toronto: Vintage, 2002. Print.

———. *TWUC Directory 1991* with autographs. Vol. 88, f.15, 2000-04 accession, R11805. Carol Shields fonds. Library and Archives Canada, Ottawa, Canada.

———. *Unless: A Novel*. Toronto: Random House, 2002. Print.

[Shields, Carol?]. Log from trip to the UK: notebook. [195-? or 196-?], annotated [199-]. Vol. 92, f.47, 2000-04 accession, R11805. Carol Shields fonds. Library and Archives Canada, Ottawa, Canada.

Shields, Carol, and Marjorie Anderson, eds. *Dropped Threads: What We Aren't Told.* Toronto: Vintage Canada, 2001. Print.

——. *Dropped Threads 2: More of What We Aren't Told.* With the assistance of Catherine Shields. Toronto: Vintage Canada, 2003. Print.

Shields family. Files of "family negatives." 1999–[200-]. Vol. 44, multiple files, 2003-09 accession, R11805. Carol Shields fonds. Library and Archives Canada, Ottawa, Canada.

Swann. Dir. Anna Benson Gyles. Shaftesbury Films/Greenpoint Films, 1996. Film.

Unknown photographer. Creative writing class photographs. [198-]. Vol. 85, f.26, 2000-04 accession, R11805. Carol Shields fonds. Library and Archives Canada, Ottawa, Canada.

Warner, Inez. Trip diary of Inez Warner: Trip to Great Britain. May 6, 1969–June 12, 1969. B. 54, f.4, 1997-04 accession, LMS-0212/R11805. Carol Shields fonds. Library and Archives Canada, Ottawa, Canada.

Watmough, David. "Memorial Tribute to Carol Shields." Vol. 111, f.2, 2003-09 accession, R11805. Carol Shields fonds. Library and Archives Canada, Ottawa, Canada.

Weller, Larry. Letter to Carol Shields. [1999?]. Vol. 84, f.19, 2000-04 accession, R11805. Carol Shields fonds. Library and Archives Canada, Ottawa, Canada.

The Voices of Carol Shields

Joan Clark

Carol Shields and I met thirty-six years ago when we were flying to Japan where our husbands were attending a Geotechnical Engineering Conference. An hour out of Vancouver, Don Shields suggested he and I change seats, and Carol and I talked pretty well non-stop across the Pacific. We began by talking about our work: at the time Carol had published two novels, two books of poetry, and short stories; I had published two children's novels, poetry, and short stories. From there we moved onto other writers and their books, discussing those we admired, those we dismissed in the reckless way one is inclined to when surrounded by strangers. We talked about editors and agents, the world of publishing, which at the time struck us as a game of musical chairs. We talked about our families, sharing confidences about our husbands, our children, our sisters.

By the time Don reclaimed his seat, Carol and I had established a friendship based on honesty and trust that continued until her death. Although we never lived in the same city, during those years Carol and I visited one another in Ottawa, Winnipeg, Calgary, St. John's, Edinburgh, Reykjavik, London, and Victoria, and no matter the distance we exchanged manuscripts. Between visits we relied on telephone, snail-mail, and later email, none of which diminished the quality and tone of Carol's voice, which was often light-hearted and amused. At other times her voice was considered and cautionary, as was the case when she gave me Giller Award jury advice. "Bring orderly notes," she wrote, "Resist any adverse comment on any past winner, past juror or any Canadian writer; Speak in a low voice; Remember your sense of humour."

If a writer needed encouragement, Carol was always there. "Dear Distressed Novelist," she wrote me, "You aren't really distressed, not when you're flying through a new book. Why do you bite off more than you can chew? Someone said that Henry James chewed off more than he could bite—I love that."

More often than not, Carol's voice was tactful and charming, but if the occasion warranted it, she used a no-nonsense voice.

When a stranger brayed that he never read fiction, Carol said, "Don't you think you would be more intelligent if you did?"

In a letter she wrote the year after she won the Orange Prize for *Larry's Party*—and she was undergoing chemotherapy followed by radiation for breast cancer—Carol said, "I'm writing a new story and quite loving it. It's so simple, so non-post modern, so truthful, heavens!"

Months later she wrote, "I'll have the 4th treatment today. . . . I have had no real reaction so far, perhaps a little fatigue, but it's hard to separate that from overall fatigue. My hair is returning, modestly, slowly, but what a hopeful sign it is. I check it three or four times a day. Talk about watching the kettle boil. Oh my."

The last time I heard Carol's voice was May 2009 during the closing event of the Carol Shields Symposium at the University of Winnipeg. After listening to the voices of other writers, I heard Carol's taped voice, a voice that was alternately thoughtful and wise, funny and wry, brisk and matter of fact. Carol had a wide range of voices including the confident, take charge, authorial voice she used in *Various Miracles, Swann, The Republic of Love, Larry's Party*, and *The Stone Diaries,* but of all those voices, the one that rings most true is the melancholy voice of the opening paragraph of *Unless.*

> It happens that I am coming through a period of great unhappiness and loss just now. All my life I've heard people speak of finding themselves in pain, bankrupt in spirit and body, but I've never understood what they meant. To lose. To have lost. I believed these visitations of darkness lasted only a few minutes or hours and that these saddened people, in between bouts, were occupied, as we all were, with the useful monotony of happiness. But happiness is not what I thought. Happiness is the lucky pane of glass you carry in your head. It takes all your cunning just to hang on to it, and once it's smashed you have to move into a different sort of life.

The Clarity of Her Anger

Jane Urquhart

Many things could be said, and no doubt have been said, in praise of both Carol Shields and the work she created: her humanity, her ability to record and celebrate what others might see as less than dramatic lives, her skill in character development (evidenced by the veracity of dialogue, eccentricity of action, and sensitive renditions of her character's inner lives), and her ability to put together beautifully crafted sentences. I loved Carol and loved everything about her work, and, at the end of the day, what I loved more than anything was what I will call the clarity of her anger.

This was no ordinary anger, it was anger with credentials. Informed by Carol's intelligence and by what she had seen in the outer world combined with her vivid inner world of imagination and reflection, her anger with credentials becomes a force to be reckoned with. Add the wit with which she delivers the news of her anger and you have a weapon of almost nuclear ferocity.

If when encountering this anger on the page you suspect that revenge might be part of the concoction, you would be correct. But this is no ordinary revenge: this is revenge with credentials, earned revenge, revenge with a post-graduate degree. Best served cold, I agree, and so did Carol. And best served with humour of a lacerating variety. I say lacerating because one of Carol's gifts as a writer was to be able to bring together at a moment of complete surprise the humorous and the heartbreaking, laced with a compelling anger. I am thinking now of Daisy Goodwill's breakdown, and the complete lack of understanding on the part of those closest to her about what the breakdown meant. In a chapter entitled

"Sorrow" various versions of the breakdown are offered and the supposed reasons behind it scoured, examined, and reported. There is, in the sub-sections of this chapter, her daughter Alice's version (one closest to the truth: or is this just my own version clamouring to be heard?). In Alice's version we get the back story of the breakdown. This is followed by Fraidy Hoyt's Theory, Cousin Beverly's Theory, the Theory of Daisy's son Warren, her daughter Joan's Theory, Labina Anthony Dukes's Theory, Skoot Skutari's Theory, Cora-Mae Milltown's Theory, and, my favourite, Jay Dudley's Theory.

Humorous, because those of us who are woman recognize all too well the insistence of otherwise innocent men like Jay that a woman's life can only be a reaction to the lives of men, and heartbreaking, because those of us who are women recognize the man in a position of power dismissing a woman's self while assuming that her life is a reaction to the lives of men. His life in particular. And then we begin to feel the creeping anger, or is it just, once again, our own version struggling to make itself known? Could be, because Carol was a master at evoking multiple points of view including the point of view of the reader. Her writing was inclusive: everyone was invited to join in the process.

I only saw Carol, a poised and gracious woman, get really angry once. This was at the presentation of the Marian Engle Prize, an award that, at the time, was given to a woman in mid literary career, and Carol, that year, presented the award to the winner. After the award was presented, the man invited to speak at the dinner event rose to deliver a talk aimed at convincing the audience that presenting the award to women only was a violation of human rights. Carol was furious. She knew that here at home less than twenty percent of the recipients of the Governor Generals' Literary Awards were women. She also knew that internationally, in the more than one hundred years since its creation, you could count the female winners of the Nobel Prize for Literature on the fingers of one hand. The Marian Engel Prize had been founded by women to honour a woman writer who, after a life of struggle, had died of cancer in mid-career. The prize itself, possibly because of all this, did not even have a very high profile. To her mind it was both confounding and exasperating that the male author in question could begrudge the members of the opposite sex these few moments in the light. She was angry. She was disappointed. But she was not surprised.

In her final novel, *Unless*, the exclusion of women is—to my mind— the dominant theme. By the time Carol was writing this book, she had seen the feminist movement advance and withdraw, and she had seen things get much better for women and then slide back. The writer-protagonist in this book, Reta Winters, takes to writing angry letters to the editors of a publication not unlike *The New York Review of Books* or *Harpers* or the *Atlantic Monthly*, and eventually to newspapers and journals. This series of letters is also filled with an intriguing concoction of humour and anger.

Lest you think that Carol's anger or her character's anger was mean-spirited, let me assure you that it was never that. Carol had enormous generosity of spirit, evidenced in both her work and her life, and an intense curiosity about the world: her view was filled with light. And lest you think she was anti men, consider all the fully realized, complicated, and compassionate men who walk through the pages of her books, from Cuyler Goodwill, whose love of his wife Mercy caused him to create that eccentric monument, to the sometimes hapless Larry who was the protagonist of *Larry's Party* (all one has to do is think about his sock drawer to know how human he was and how fond Carol was of him). No, Carol's anger was full of clarity. It shone. It illuminated all it looked on, rather than darkening anything.

My *Seen-Sang,* Carol Shields:
A Memoir of a Master Teacher

WAYSON CHOY

In the form of a rather personal memoir, I would like to examine Carol Shields's characteristic "goodness," that is, how I now perceive her quality of "goodness," and how this quality has inspired my own writing.

It was through her teaching that "goodness" became real to me, and came to matter very deeply. If you will forgive me, I feel that I have come, at last, after thirty-eight years to understand that Carol Shields had all along been what my father in his formal Cantonese would honour as one of my *seen-sangs,* one of my "master teachers".

In 1976–77, Carol was teaching at the University of British Columbia. At that time, my mother died, and Humber College awarded me a sabbatical to study creative writing. I would be with my father, who was in his eighties living alone in Vancouver. I took three writing courses— poetry, playwriting, and short stories.

I quickly realized I had no patience for the focus required of students of poetry. By the fifth class, I completely lost interest and skipped almost half the remaining classes. I barely stayed awake for the rest. The professor earnestly, generously said to me, "If you promise never to write a single poem, I'll assign you the minimum passing grade." I didn't really care, but I kept that promise.

Meanwhile, the playwriting course taught me how to tighten up and enliven my dialogue. As for Carol, she was then to be my short story teacher, and I was lucky in every way possible. Eventually, she taught me things beyond technique and craft; more important, she directed my attention to my own personal history. "Write what you know about, Wayson," she admonished me. "We come from different worlds. You can surprise all of us with fresh details!"

If any of her students mistakenly thought she was mild-mannered, a sudden rise in her voice was warning enough to tamper any ego-cringing responses. She had a grounded way of telling you who she was, that she could sense how much more we needed to understand what "creative writing" really meant. She saw us individually and knew what we each needed to improve on. She saw our attempts in a very real way, if we actually made a worthy attempt. If you didn't, *watch out*. Her slightest frown, bracketed by an impenetrable silence, could devastate you. I imagined her five children knew the effect of that frown. I studied Carol as a character from one of her own books.

In this book Jane Urquhart has written about Carol's depiction of characters who reveal the "clarity of her [that is, Carol's authorial] anger," and here is my observation about how she would manifest her anger. The assignment for the class of twelve of us was to write a story using irony. I wrote a story about a bitchy woman who, by the ending would be revealed as an angel of sorts, the ending would surprise and delight, in the O. Henry style. Or maybe not. The story was read in class but Carol stopped the reading halfway before the end. She was angry that I had taken the easy way out and written, albeit unwittingly, a cartoon caricature, a superficial one at that, of a woman who seemed to be made the blunt end of a bad joke. Carol bit her lip. "I've had enough of this shabby stereotype," she announced, and firmly put down my effort. "Let's start on Glenda's story." Everyone put my pages away.

At once I knew it was useless for me to protest, hopeless to bleat that there was a final twist in the end that would really and truly redeem the character: Carol had found me out. Turns out, she had been told by my lifelong mentor (and family member) the late Professor Jacob Zilber that my first published story at the University of British Columbia had been—miraculously—selected for the 1962 edition of "Best American Short Stories." In fact, I submitted to Carol something definitely *way below* the high expectations everyone had set for me. I thought my second draft was sufficient for any regular workshop. But she, and the department, had rightly expected so much better of me.

By chance, she lived along my route, so after each class I gave Carol a ride to the home she and Don had rented. I wanted to discuss the story that she refused to finish, really, to apologize, but Carol did not give me a chance. She talked about other things. Family matters, for example.

How her children were adjusting. As always, she would ask about my father. In his mortal 80s, my father haunted her in some way. We were, however temporary, intimate carpool friends. It was clear we liked each other. Eventually, we even talked about her struggles with her most recent manuscript, which her agent sent back for more chapter revisions. She said, twice over, how she "*just* sometimes" wrote beneath her mark (as I had just done more than once in her class, though she didn't say this). I caught her eyes staring at me from the rear-view mirror. She gave me that endearing little smile. For some reason, we both broke into laughter. We became friends, eventually sharing two secrets that we swore we would never tell.

If Carol shunted my superficial work aside, if she did not hesitate to expose a certain snap of impatience in class about my stories, it was the justified anger of someone disappointed in me, as she, in fact, would be about her own writing if she sensed she was writing less than her best. I began to understand her point: if my writing mattered at all to me, *Why was I wasting her time?* Her anger with my brainless effort was subtle, but it hit its target. She was upset with me. I imagined she was wondering whether I really wanted success as a writer. Even allowing for my worry about my elderly father, there was still that simple but all-important question: was I a writer or not? "How's your father?" she asked. She was giving me an "out," something I could use to excuse my weak commitment and we could then discount any faith she had in my abilities. But *something* snapped in me. One writes at one's best, or one does not.

In fact, ever since I was fifteen, I had dreamed of being a writer. At fifteen, I had longed to match Françoise Sagan's brilliant success. At eighteen, she wrote the international bestseller *Bonjour Tristesse* and ended up with a Jag and a truckload of francs. At the University of British Columbia, Earle Birney, one of my first writing teachers, wanted to see me almost immediately after I handed in my first effort. Obviously, I thought, a fire-red Jag was waiting for me. Instead, the stern, gaunt man handed me back those typed pages veined with red ink. "Take it," he said, and bluntly turned me towards the door, leaving me standing outside his office, with one word blasted aloud: "*PUNCTUATE!*"

After the door closed behind me, my hands shaking, eyes burning, I poured over the X's and those red circles dotted with commas or periods. Much to my surprise, what he wrote was not at all negative. Encouraging words and phrases were scattered among the X's: "Good." "Excellent image." "Very fine." In short, he didn't say that I couldn't write; he had said, "*Punctuate!*"

I ran to buy a copy of *Punctuation Made Simple.*

Like Birney, Carol might have said, "*Create!*" Instead, she asked me, as the car slowed in front of her street, "How is your father doing?" For some reason, I answered, "Time does matter, doesn't it?"

"*Moments* matter," she answered. Do you recall this fragment from Saint-Exupéry's *The Little Prince*: "What is essential is invisible . . ."?

Sometimes a person comes along who, like Carol, embodies the invisible. Carol taught by example how kindness and empathy are often exemplified in the invisible, how "goodness" doesn't mean obedience or moral passivity: You must actively *experience* goodness. You also need courage to *choose* goodness. Looking back on her teaching, I can now see how she demonstrated her goodness; she didn't just talk about it: like her characters, I now discover that *goodness* is an invisible reality, and I have even sensed the slippery moment when I am deprived of, or lack, that quality. And I see how she had been good to me in complex ways I only understand now as I explore the time we shared together.

For example, one day when Carol decided to focus on a serious attempt of mine, a story I dumbly set in San Francisco—or was it Paris, a wistful Sagan tale of sorts—she frowned. "Wayson, why don't you ever write about what you've experienced? Why don't you tell us something about what it was like to grow up in Chinatown?" My first thought was that it wasn't Paris, but she seeded something in me to think otherwise. "Of everyone in this class, only *you* will know what that was like," she said. "Only *you* can tell us a Chinatown story."

That day, or the next class, she gave us each a slip of paper listing a colour that we were to integrate into our next story. "Be creative," she said. "Use the colour at least once if you can't make it a major part of your next story." She looked directly at me. Unfolding my slip, was hand printed: *P I N K.*

At home, I was frustrated by her challenge to create a story where the colour would be a main part of the narrative. And I was told to write from what I know: *But who would ever publish a story set in a Chinese ghetto, unless it involved an axe murder or opium?* Muttering objections, I sauntered in and out of the kitchen, reaching once again into the fridge, while my aunts were studying the jewellery my deceased mother had left behind. The two women talked about the different colours of jade. "There's a pink-coloured jade," Aunt Freda said. A moment later, Aunt Mary was describing how beautiful her garden's white peonies were, how they blushed with pink centres. Instantly, two key words came together to become the title of the story I would finally write: *The Jade Peony*. A few days later, the story was finished and ready for its first workshop reading.

In class, Carol described my narrative as "intimate and true." Everyone added his opinion. By the end of the term, she asked that at least two of our class stories—with one more rewrite—be submitted for a story contest. I hesitated to fuss over the damn thing, but there was that tempting prize of one hundred dollars. I submitted ten rewritten pages.

After its prize-winning publication, between 1977 and 1992, *The Jade Peony* was anthologized over twenty times. Finally, Douglas & McIntyre contacted me in 1992 to ask if I'd write a novel for them, one based on the short story they wanted to anthologize. They sent a contract, offered me an advance, and finally even got me an agent. *The Jade Peony*, the novel, is today in its thirtieth printing and has been translated into four languages.

In the fall of 2002, friends in Vancouver organized a roast, and they asked Carol if she would submit some words for them to read, telling about her part in seeding and inspiring that first story. Though ill with the cancer that would eventually take her life, she told them to come over to Victoria with a camera. She wanted to tell in person how I came to write *The Jade Peony*. At the banquet roast, when the large screen came down and Carol's sweet luminous face appeared, I thought not of the famous writer, but of a proud friend and colleague, someone loving and forever in her prime. When she said her last words of delight and praise, I felt suddenly as if my father, gone these many years, was commanding me to bow to the screen a traditional three times.

This was how from that first scrap of paper I randomly picked up with Carol's handwritten "PINK," all the way through her persistent encouragement to write from my own history, eventually came four bestselling books about Vancouver's Old Chinatown. Of course, they are not anything like her books on the theme of "goodness." But her mastery as my teacher had inspired me to awaken all the similar goodness I saw for the first time in my Chinatown past.

Carol's own books, her stories, are always waiting to explode in the minds of certain people, particularly those readers yet unawakened to their own potential for goodness. But no, it was not through her writing but through her teaching that she woke me up. She will ever be to me my *seen-sang*

Carol Shields

Martin Levin

The first time I met, or perhaps encountered is the better word, Carol Shields was in 1994, on assignment for the now-defunct *Canadian Imperial Oil Review*. I sense barely repressed laughter, but, despite its less than trippingly literary name and provenance, the *Review* was a well-made quarterly magazine, as interested in Canadian culture as it was in Canadian oil.

Carol, who, I was soon to learn, hid an astringent sharpness beneath an exterior of sweet agreeableness, found nothing risible in the assignment and agreed to cooperate. To begin with, she allowed me to sit in on a workshop she was giving at the Humber School for Writers at Humber College in Toronto.

And then she gave me, as well as her awestruck students, a demonstration in how to think about writing. It is essential, she told them, that we not be restrained by the traditional limits of putting words on a page (and pages were pretty much all there were at the time), that words necessarily fail in their efforts to reach the heart of matters, that, as she put it, "the labyrinth of language plods behind reality, a plodding elephant."

"The deepest truth is imageless," wrote Percy Shelley, who ought to have known. For Carol, half of all felt experience, at least half, falls away in the telling, in our largely futile efforts to contain and tame moments in time. It is a paradox all writers face, and one Carol confronted head-on.

Thus properly cowed by the enormous gulf between reach and grasp, Carol's students were given such assignments as "Write an entire story in a single sentence" (I doubt any had read the microfiction of Lydia

Davis, though some may now themselves be writing such popular "flash fiction"), or a paragraph on "Why did the surgeon sell the pink ballet slipper?" Such instruction acknowledged the necessary constraints of language in previously unexplored ways, or unexplored by these students, at any rate.

And these dozen or so students sat rapt in attention as they listened to this suddenly famous writer—she had recently won the 1995 Pulitzer Prize for *The Stone Diaries*—dissect their efforts in her gentle, fluent, and just slightly urgent manner. Make your characters more consistent, she counsels them. Do not, for instance, use simple language to express sophisticated thoughts. Privileged disciples at the feet of a literary master, they count themselves honoured to be there, ecstatic at the faintest encouragement from Shields.

The next time I met Carol: same profile, different venue. It was in her office in the charmingly named Fletcher Argue Building at the University of Manitoba. Homely, in the traditional meaning of the word, it was fitted with lamps, rugs, and art, all of which attested to the considerable trouble she had taken to make a rather cramped space seem comfortable, or comforting.

There were many editions, domestic and foreign-language, of her books. And mermaids—dolls, models, images, tiny sculptures, hangings— were everywhere: sitting on desks, pinned to the wall, even suspended from the ceiling. They were sent to her from around the world by admirers of her novel, *The Republic of Love*, whose protagonist, Fay McLeod, is a folklorist whose work centres on mermaids.

And that specificity, that Fay not only worked as a folklorist, but is shown to be working as one, is essential to understanding an aspect of Carol's idea of fiction.

She admired writers who would show, rather than simply tell, what her characters actually did with their working lives, and not simply what they were purported to do. She told me that she admired enormously Theodore Dreiser, who, in his novel *Sister Carrie*, was able to show what it was like to be a shopgirl in her hometown of Chicago at the turn of the twentieth century.

In her own *Larry's Party*, for instance, a deep and compassionate study of masculinity and its accompanying defects (so much for those who casually dismissed Carol as a woman's novelist, a novelist of domestic life), Larry Weller is a florist turned designer of mazes—and it's easy to imagine Carol's delight at coming up with this concept. When she needed to know something about working life, she researched it. If it was on a presumably manly note, such as how a car mechanic might function, she'd ask her husband, Don, dean of engineering at the University of Manitoba.

Carol needed no outside help to limn the lives of the squabbling, petty academics in *Swann* (her confessed favourite among her novels). It follows the tortured quest of feminist academic Sarah Maloney to make sense of the tragic existence of Mary Swann, an untutored but talented poet living a rustic life with a brutal husband. Inspired by the real-life murder-by-husband of British Columbia poet Pat Lowther, Carol never lost sight of a woman's personal catastrophe, while simultaneously eviscerating the preening pretenders of academe.

This was, of course, a world Carol knew from the inside, and she is savagely funny about its petty strivings. Her lithe little biography of Jane Austen also focused on the work, was a sustained act of identification with Austen as both writer and woman. The *Globe and Mail*'s review of the book was accompanied by an Anthony Jenkins drawing caricature showing the two writers together. We sent the original to Carol and she hung it on a wall in her Victoria home.

Of course, she said too that growing up in the Chicago suburb of Oak Park—also the hometown of Ernest Hemingway and the residence for several years of Yugoslav-born poet Charles Simic, giving it perhaps the highest population to Pulitzer Prize ratio of any city—she felt she had no chance of becoming a writer: "Dead males seemed to have a lock on the position there."

It was, she told me, a church-going Norman Rockwellish town. Yes, it did have high schools named for American literary giants Nathaniel Hawthorne and Ralph Waldo Emerson. "I was very impressed. They were writers; they were men; they were dead. I couldn't conceive that there'd be any room for a writer like me."

Carol did not move to Winnipeg until 1980, but we soon found that we shared an appreciation of that much-maligned and much-abandoned city. She particularly loved its connectedness, what she termed "an overlapping network of family and friends." She spoke of the feeling that, at any moment, she might encounter a friend or acquaintance anywhere—in a restaurant, window-gazing on the city's windswept main streets, at the theatre. "I love this network. It's one of the great gifts of my life," she once said.

Before interviewing Carol, I had read all her work: I was much more assiduous in those days. As a native Winnipegger, I often gasped with the shock of recognition, albeit a new kind of recognition, at the variant specificity of a city I thought I knew so well. In *The Republic of Love*, Carol turned her flat, featureless town into a Paris of the heart. Streets as familiar to me as snow in January or mosquitoes in June came to fully dimensional new life, and always with a twist—a hill where none exists, a fictive Folklore Centre. A city that is, on first acquaintance, so charmless to many is transformed through Shieldsian alchemy into love's paradise.

At once street-guide knowable and Baedeker-exotic, this was a brilliant counterfeit. And maybe not so much a counterfeit, as a dazzling investigation of the transformative power of imagination.

When a few years later, I became Books Editor of the *Globe and Mail*, I decided that I must have Carol reviewing for me as occasion allowed her. Having listened to some of her exegeses of fiction, I wanted that acute intelligence in our pages. One thing for which I am grateful is that our pages allowed her to work out her complex attitude toward Anne Shirley, the heroine of Lucy Maud Montgomery's *Anne of Green Gables* and other works. In 1998, I asked her to review Montgomery's *Journals*, a magnificent multi-volume series published by Oxford University Press. Carol showed an early and clear antipathy to Anne, followed by something completely different.

> My mother loved *Anne of Green Gables*, my daughters loved *Anne of Green Gables*, but as a girl I found myself full of resistance to this needy orphan with her romantic effusions. Anne Shirley of Prince Edward Island presumed on my affection. She rhapsodized in a manner that felt false and silly. Her breathless-ness over the wonders of nature seemed contrived for effect. I sensed, too, that she took a secret pride in her carrot-coloured hair, and not the shame she flaunted. The rhetoric rubbed in the wrong direction; the fey self-cherishing went on too long.
>
> So it was a surprise to me when I opened Volume I of Lucy Maud Montgomery's memoirs some years ago and encountered a wholly other voice. Here was the thumbprint of Anne's yearning spirit, her sense of abandonment, her longing for connection, but expressed with a contemporary freshness of tone, with intelligence and reflection, and with a piercing vulnerability that I had seldom encountered in personal journals.
>
> Montgomery's interweaving of grief and joy makes her a felt presence on the page. This is what a life is made of, one thinks. The reader reads on, often through dull or repetitive passages, knowing that these alternating moods and disproportionately weighted insights add up to

a human life in all its textural richness. Very few books in recent years have given me the depth of pleasure I've found in these first four volumes of Lucy Maud Montgomery's journals (there is one more to come). I know what the inside of another woman's head looks like. I've been privileged to travel the distance with her.

In the last exchange I ever had with Carol, just weeks before she died in the summer of 2003, she responded to my request to choose the fictional character she would most like to be, for a feature in the Saturday Books section. And what she wrote shows not only how far she'd travelled in her assessment of Anne, but indicates as well her literary flexibility: "Anne Shirley pops straight to mind, finer and more heroic in every way than Tom Sawyer. Not only did she became a 'good girl,' but she transformed her society to a vision of goodness and won the heart of Gilbert Blythe."

Carol was justly known as among the most ego-free and accommodating of writers—though she did balk when a magazine wanted to accompany a profile of her with a photo taken in an outdoor fountain.

But I do think her ego was bruised just a little in 2002. Already very ill with the cancer that killed her, she made her way to Toronto where what turned out to be her last novel, *Unless*, was shortlisted for the Giller Prize. Favoured to win, it lost, surprisingly, to Austin Clarke's ambitious but difficult *The Polished Hoe*. Carol was far too much the lady to complain, and perhaps far too ill, but she bore the disappointment with the good humour that marked her always.

Carol was many things: whip-smart, Sibyl-perceptive, Tina Fey–funny and Bono-generous. I learned a lot from her, from her books about the erasure of women from their own lives, more or less the thrust of her Pulitzer Prize–winning *The Stone Diaries*. And from her life and friendship I learned how an ardent and consistently expressed feminism need not be inconsistent with domestic happiness.

Carol had a prescient ability to engage. I always felt that she was a unique blend of the matronly and the mischievous, able to combine the sharpest eye for character with a real concern for your comfort and psychological well-being. Engage with her and you would feel simultaneously assessed and protected, as if your measure might be taken, but you would be forgiven your sins.

But I want to focus on the aspect of her character that has ultimately meant the most to me, and it is one I have both written about and spoken of on several occasions. And that is her immense kindness, her generosity of spirit—a quality widely honoured but much more rarely practised. In some ways, that was even more striking than the quality of her fiction, more impressive than her many glittering prizes, as lasting to those who knew her as her contribution to Canadian literature.

And as Carol always insisted on specificity in her students' writing, I'll offer one example.

Her unrehearsed ability to offer comfort, to solace, her talent for friendship, was never better represented to me than in the sad tale of our mutual friend Jim Keller. When I was an undergraduate English student at the University of Manitoba, Jim was my senior adviser. He was a complex man and a brilliant (no overstatement here) Shakespearean scholar.

He was also a friend. We discussed my senior paper on myth in Bernard Malamud at his apartment while he skinned rabbits he had shot, and I looked in any other direction. He showed me a boat he was building from scratch. My then wife and I, newly wed, had him to dinner and bridge several times. He brought his homemade wine, some of it very drinkable, some of it not so much.

He was, in many ways, a lonely man; he seemed . . . unaffiliated, his family distant or inconsequential, no apparent lover, his fellow professors more colleagues than friends. He was, though, always a very agreeable and entertaining companion. In fact, my bookish mother several times invited him to dinner.

Soon, though, he began to suffer severe winter depression (a condition that would later be termed seasonal affective disorder), beginning with the onset of shorter days. Not an ideal affliction in a city like Winnipeg, with its darkling winters. At first, he had to curtail his working life, teaching only when he felt the black dog taking a break. Soon, he could not work at all.

Then he developed multiple sclerosis. The university allowed him to keep an office, just down the hall from Carol's, in the Fletcher Argue Building. Jim had no family; Carol more or less gave him one. With no hint of mother-hen-ishness, nor a whisper of self-sacrifice, she made Jim (like her, American-born) part of her world, and entered his. When he spoke of his plans for a revolutionary book on *Hamlet* (which everyone was sure would be brilliant but was equally certain would never be finished), she not only listened, she advised. And she asked nothing in return. When Jim died, Carol took charge of arrangements, and she gave a deeply moving eulogy. It was as fine an act of loyalty and remembrance as I know of.

In the past few years, as Carol faced her own long dying, my communications with her were limited to email. Though these were brief, and too infrequent, they were always on her part generous, warm, and—a quality she never lost—inquisitive.

When I think of Carol these days, and I still do so rather often, I think of how she changed forever my perception of what a "woman's novel" is—or can be. Of course I do. But I also think of attentiveness, of a quality, often quiet, of being there, that both her work and her life carried.

In the words of Willy Loman's wife Linda, describing her husband's anonymously underlived life in Arthur Miller's *Death of a Salesman*, "So attention must be paid." And Carol did make me pay attention, attention to the lives of Daisy Goodwill Flett and Mary Swann. Just as she herself paid attention to the life Jim Keller. And to everyone who came into her own, whether real or imagined.

Contributors

MARGARET ATWOOD is the author of more than forty volumes of poetry, children's literature, fiction, and non-fiction. Her novels include *The Edible Woman, The Handmaid's Tale, Alias Grace,* and *The Blind Assassin,* which won the Booker Prize in 2000. Her newest novel, *MaddAddam,* is the final volume in the trilogy that includes *Oryx and Crake* and *The Year of the Flood.* Her most recent volume of poetry, *The Door,* was published in 2007. *In Other Worlds: SF and the Human Imagination,* a collection of non-fiction essays, appeared in 2011. She is a Companion of the Order of Canada.

SHELLEY BOYD is the Canadian literature specialist at Kwantlen Polytechnic University in Surrey, British Columbia. Her book, *Garden Plots: Canadian Women Writers and Their Literary Gardens,* explores the relationship between writing and gardening in texts ranging from nineteenth-century domestic manuals to contemporary fiction and poetry. Her recent publications include such topics as the literary hardiness of the potted geranium and Margaret Atwood's depictions of garden tools and composting.

WAYSON CHOY, Professor Emeritus of the Humber School for Writers, has written two novels and two memoirs. Twice a recipient of the Trillium Prize, a winner of the Edna Stabler Creative Non-Fiction Award, and a finalist for the Giller Prize, he was awarded the Queen Elizabeth Diamond Jubilee Medal and is a Member of the Order of Canada.

JOAN CLARK is the author of fifteen books for adults and children. Her work has been published in Canada, Britain, the United States,

Australia, and New Zealand and translated into eight languages. Winner of numerous awards, she is the only Canadian writer to receive both the Marian Engel Award for adult fiction and the Vicky Metcalf Award for children's fiction. She is a Member of the Order of Canada.

ANNE GIARDINI is a writer, executive, and Chancellor of Simon Fraser University. Her first novel, *The Sad Truth About Happiness*, appeared in 2005, and her second novel, *Advice for Italian Boys*, appeared in 2009. She is the eldest daughter of Carol Shields.

JOSEPH GIARDINI is a graduate student at Simon Fraser University, where his interests include English, poetry, and social movements. He is the eldest grandchild of Carol Shields.

TIM HEATH is Associate Professor and Chair of English at Ambrose University College in Calgary. His teaching and research interests lie chiefly with place and genre in Canadian fiction and poetry, particularly the Canadian long poem.

CATHERINE HOBBS is the Literary Archivist (English) and a senior archivist at Library and Archives Canada, where she is responsible for the archives of writers and other figures/organizations in Canadian literature. She chairs the Special Interest Section on Personal Archives (SISPA) within the Association of Canadian Archivists and is a board member of the Special Interest Section on Literary and Artistic Archives within the International Council on Archives.

CORAL ANN HOWELLS, Professor Emerita at the University of Reading and Senior Research Fellow, Institute of English Studies, University of London, publishes widely on Canadian literature, especially on contemporary Canadian women writers. Editor of *The Cambridge Companion to Margaret Atwood* and co-editor with Eva-Marie Kroller of *The Cambridge History of Canadian Literature*, she is a Fellow of the Royal Society of Canada.

MARTIN LEVIN was book editor of the *Globe and Mail* from 1996 to 2013. He is co-author of a play on the world's worst movie director, has run two weekly newspapers and edited another, and has contributed essays to more than half a dozen books.

PATRICIA LIFE received her PhD in English Literature in 2014 with a dissertation on "Long-Term Caring: Canadian Literary Narratives of Personal Agency and Identity in Late Life," where she focuses on texts comprising what she calls the Canadian nursing-home-narrative genre.

ALEX RAMON teaches English Literature and Film at Kingston University, London, and the University of Reading. The author of several essays on Carol Shields, he also wrote the book *Liminal Spaces: The Double Art of Carol Shields*. He also published two essays on Iris Murdoch and is working now on Rawi Hage.

MARILYN ROSE, Professor of English at Brock University, is a specialist in modern and contemporary Canadian literature. Her current research draws upon recent neurocognitive research in the field of empathy studies and focuses on what she calls the generation of "cool empathy" in contemporary Canadian short fiction.

ELIZABETH REIMER, Assistant Professor of English at Thompson Rivers University in Kamloops, British Columbia, teaches children's literature and women's literature. She has written on Carol Shields and is currently writing and researching in the area of food politics in contemporary fairy tale variants for children and adolescents.

WENDY ROY is Associate Professor of Canadian Literature at the University of Saskatchewan. She is the author of *Maps of Difference: Canada, Women, and Travel* and co-editor with Susan Gingell of *Listening Up, Writing Down, and Looking Beyond: Interfaces of the Oral, Written, and Visual*. Her current research project is on serials, sequels, and adaptations in early twentieth-century Canadian fiction.

DAVID STAINES, Professor of English at the University of Ottawa, divides his time between medieval culture and literature and Canadian culture and literature. Among the many books he has authored and/or edited are *Tennyson's Camelot: The Idylls of the King and Its Medieval Sources*, *The Complete Romances of Chrétien de Troyes*, and *The Letters of Stephen Leacock*. He is a Member of the Order of Canada.

MARGARET STEFFLER, Associate Professor of English at Trent University, is the editor of P. K. Page's *Mexican Journal*. Her current research focuses on confessions of the spiritual in Canadian women's life writing and depictions of girlhood in twenty-first-century Canadian fiction.

NORA FOSTER STOVEL, Professor Emerita at the University of Alberta, has published books and articles on Jane Austen, Margaret

Drabble, Margaret Laurence, D. H. Lawrence, and Carol Shields. Among the many books she has authored and/or edited are *Divining Margaret Laurence: A Study of Her Complete Writings* and Margaret Laurence's *Long Drums and Cannons: Nigerian Dramatists and Novelists, 1952–1966* and *Heart of a Stranger*.

CYNTHIA SUGARS, Professor of English at the University of Ottawa, is the author of *Canadian Gothic: Literature, History, and the Spectre of Self-Invention* and the editor or co-editor of numerous collections, including *Unsettled Remains: Canadian Literature and the Postcolonial Gothic* (with Gerry Turcotte) and *Canadian Literature and Cultural Memory* (with Eleanor Ty). She has co-edited with Laura Moss the anthology, *Canadian Literature in English: Texts and Contexts*.

JANE URQUHART is the author of eight internationally acclaimed novels, three volumes of poetry, and one collection of short fiction. Her first novel, *The Whirlpool,* won France's Prix du Meilleur Livre Étranger, and she has been the recipient of Canada's Governor General's Award and the Trillium Prize. She is also the editor of the most recent *Penguin Book of Short Stories.* She is an Officer of the Order of Canada.

ARITHA VAN HERK, Professor of English at the University of Calgary, is the author of five novels, four works of non-fiction, and many articles and reviews. Her most recent works, *In This Place* and *Prairie Gothic* (with George Webber), develop the idea of geographical temperament as tonal accompaniment. In 2013 she was awarded the Lieutenant Governor's Distinguished Artist Award.

JOHN VAN RYS, Professor of English at Redeemer University College in Ancaster, Ontario, teaches expository writing and Canadian literature. He has written on a range of modern Canadian writers, including Margaret Avison, Ernest Buckler, Alice Munro, and Al Purdy. His current research focuses on violence, suffering, and trauma in Canadian historical fiction as well as on the role of religion in Munro's fiction.

ELEANOR WACHTEL is the host and co-founder of CBC Radio's *Writers & Company,* which won a New York Festivals Award; she also co-founded and hosts *Wachtel on the Arts.* Her most recent books are *Original Minds* and *Random Illuminations: Conversations with Carol Shields,* which won the Independent Publisher Book Award. She is a Member of the Order of Canada.

ELIZABETH WATERSTON, Professor Emeritus at the University of Guelph, has contributed to earlier books in the University of Ottawa series, including volumes on Isabella Valancy Crawford and Charles G. D. Roberts. Her many other publications are on travel books, Scottish literature, and the writings of L. M. Montgomery. Her most recent book is *Blitzkrieg and Jitterbugs: College Life in Wartime, 1939–1943*. She is a Member of the Order of Canada.

Printed in November 2014
by Gauvin Press,
Gatineau Québec